BRITAIN, DENMARK-N
AND THE HOUSE OF S

Britain, Denmark-Norway and the House of Stuart 1603-1660 A Diplomatic and Military Analysis

Steve Murdoch

TUCKWELL PRESS

First published in Great Britain in 2000 by
Tuckwell Press
The Mill House
Phantassie
East Linton
East Lothian EH40 3DG
Scotland

ISBN 1 86232 182 5

British Library Cataloguing in Publication Data

A catalogue record for this book is available
on request from the British Library

Printed and bound in Great Britain by Bookcraft, Midsomer Norton

Contents

Table of Figures

Abbreviations

APC   England, Privy Council, *Acts of the Privy Council of England* (45 vols., London, 1890-1964).

APS   Scotland, Parliament, *The Acts of the Parliaments of Scotland* (12 vols., London, 1814-1875).

CSP   *Calendars of the State Papers Relating to Scotland* (13 vols., Edinburgh, 1898-1969).

CSPD   *Calendars of State Papers, Domestic Series*:
First Series, 1547-1625, (13 vols., London, 1856-1992).
Second Series, 1625-1649, (23 vols., London, 1858-1897).
Third Series, 1649-1660, (13 vols., London, 1875-1886).

CSPV   *Calendars of State Papers and Manuscripts relating to English affairs, existing in the archives and collections of Venice and in other libraries of Northern Italy*, (38 vols., London, 1864-1947).

DBBTI   Polisensky, J. V., et al., eds., *Documenta Bohemica Bellum Tricennale Illustrantia*, (8 vols., Prague, 1976-1981).

DBL2   Bricka, C. F., et al., eds., *Dansk Biografisk Leksikon*, (27 vols., Copenhagen, 1933-1944, 2nd edition).

DBL3   Bricka, C. F., et al., (eds.), *Dansk Biografisk Leksikon*, (16 vols., 1979-1984, 3rd edition).

DCJS   Duncan, A., ed., 'The Diplomatic Correspondence of Sir James Spence of Wormiston', unpublished manuscript E379d.

DDA   Lind, G., *Danish Data Archive* 1573: A database of officers in the Danish-Norwegian army

DNB   *Dictionary of National Biography*

DRA   Danish Rigsarkivet

HMC   Historical Manuscripts Commission

KCFB   Bricka, C. F., J. A. Fredericia, and J. Skovgaard, et al., eds., *Kong Christian den Fjerdes egenhaendige Breve* (8 vols, Copenhagen, 1878-1947).

NAS   National Archives of Scotland

RAOSB   *Rikskansleren Axel Oxenstiernas Skrifter och Brefvexling* (15 vols., Stockholm, 1888-1977).

PRO SP   Public Record Office, State Papers

RPCS   Scotland, Privy Council, *Register of the Privy Council of Scotland*, First Series, 1545 -1625 (14 vols., Edinburgh, 1877-1898).
Second Series, 1625-1660 (8 vols., Edinburgh, 1899-1908).

SAÄ   Elgenstierna, G., *Den Introducerade Svenska Adelns Ättartavlor, med tillägg och rättelser* (9 vols., Stockholm, 1925-36).

SRP   Kullberg, N.A., et. al., eds., *Svenska Riksrådets Protokoll, 1621-1658* (18 vols., Stockholm, 1878-1959).

SSNE	Murdoch, S., and Grosjean, G, *Scotland, Scandinavia and Northern Europe Database, 1580-1707.* A database of the Scottish (and English and Irish) diplomatic, military and social elite in Scandinavia. Online at <www.abdn.ac.uk/history/datasets/ssne>
SRA	Swedish Riksarkivet
TKUA	Tyske Kancellis Udenrigske Afdeling.

Stylistic Conventions

Throughout this book a variety of monetary denominations have been used. The two most common are pounds and *rigsdaler*. Unless otherwise indicated, all transactions of pounds relate to pounds sterling and not pounds Scots. After 1603 the value of these two currencies were set so that twelve Scots pounds equalled one English one.[1] The value of the *rigsdaler* is harder to assess, not least because several countries used a version of it. Indeed, it is not always clear from the sources if the currency being discussed relates to Danish-Norwegian *rigsdaler*, Swedish *rixdaler* or *Imperial thalers*, often called *dalers* or *dolouris*.[2] Of course, in most cases the currency involved is Danish-Norwegian. Martin Bellamy prefaced his thesis on Danish Naval Administration by declaring that the Danish *rigsdaler* could generally be taken as £0.25 sterling throughout the reign of Christian IV, i.e. one pound would have bought four *rigsdaler*.[3] However, the conversion rate was open to inflation and a great deal of fluctuation. Rev. G. Wishart recorded a transaction worth 24,000 *rigsdaler* between the Marquis of Montrose and Korfitz Ulfeldt in 1649. This, he observed, totalled £5,400 sterling, an exchange rate of 4.5 *rigsdaler* to the pound.[4] G. Warner noted an exchange rate of 12,500 Danish *rigsdaler* for £2,500 sterling during the 1650s, highlighting that one pound would have bought five *rigsdaler*.[5] Given these fluctuations, all monetary values have been recorded as they were presented in the sources to try to minimise confusion and errors.[6]

The dating of documents cited in the footnotes of this text can sometimes appear confusing. Various countries employed different calendars and dating practices in the seventeenth century. The Gregorian calendar was in use in the Low Countries, at a time when Scotland, England and Denmark-Norway still adhered to the Julian calendar. To compound the complication, Scotland and the Low Countries began the year on 1 January, while England, until 1752, began it on 25 March. This can cause many headaches in trying to establish

---

[1] L. B. Taylor ed., *Aberdeen Shore Work Accounts, 1596-1670* (Aberdeen, 1972), 6.

[2] The *Register of the Scottish Privy Council* contains details of 'Swaden and Zeland dolouris' being circulated at Scottish markets. See *RPCS*, IX, p.248, 13 September 1611. The Privy Council set out to prosecute the individuals responsible for importing the 'Swaden, Zeland and other dollars' impoted from Holland which they described as 'a sort of verie base and unworthy coyne of aucht deneiris fyne'. They accused the importers of trading them at '£3 [Scots] the ounce, although in weight and fineness they are not worth 45s. the ounce weight'. See *RPCS*, IX, 259-260, 13 September 1611. This case tells us that the *daler* was seen by some to be a universal currency, an early 'Euro', but that there was a degree of confusion as to its value and exchange rate even at the time it was being used.

[3] M. Bellamy, 'Danish Naval Administration and Shipbuilding in the Reign of Christian IV, 1596-1648' (unpublished PhD thesis, University of Glasgow, 1997), 8.

[4] Rev. G. Wishart, *The Memoirs of James Marquis of Montrose 1639-1650* edited by A. D. Murdoch and H. F. Morland-Simpson (London, 1893), 60.

[5] G. F. Warner ed., *The Nicholas Papers, correspondence of Sir Edward Nicholas secretary of State.* (4 vols, London, 1892-1920), III, 110-113. Korfitz Ulfeldt to Secretary Nicholas, 5 November 1655.

[6] For more on international money exchange, see J. J. McCusker, *Money and Exchange in Europe and America, 1600-1775* (London, 1978).

how a letter from 18 March 1629 would be dated. If written by a Scot or a Dane, it should be dated as above. If written by an Englishman, or someone writing to one, it might be confused with a letter dated 28 March 1630.[7] Further problems arise when diplomats and agents correspond from their host countries. It is sometimes impossible to establish if writers used the dating system of their home country, or the calendar of the state in which they were resident. For example, when James Hay, Earl of Carlisle, wrote from France on 24 February 1625 did he, as a Scotsman, mean the Scottish, English or French date? Many of the correspondents have had the foresight to place both dates on their dispatches, allowing them to be placed in a specific chronology. When the Scottish Covenanter leadership wrote to Christian IV in April 1640, they included both the Gregorian and Julian dates.[8] In some cases, the dates determined were taken as the most plausible, given the contents of the letters. Fortunately, the letters have usually already been carefully screened for dating by archivists more skilled in such matters than myself. I have, with only a few exceptions, trusted the chronology provided by them. In all cases, it is the date of the letter given on the document which has been repeated in the footnotes. If new style (ns) or old style (os) has been indicated along with a date, it is because the author him/herself has placed it there.

[7] See the letter from the Scotsman, Robert Anstruther, to the Englishman, Sir Thomas Roe (from Hamburg to Poland) dated 18/28 March 1629/30. PRO SP 88/7, 2, f.241.
[8] DRA, TKUA Skotland A II 4. Scottish nobles to Christian IV, 24/14 April 1640.

Acknowlegements

The writing of this book would not have been possible without a great deal of help from a variety of people and organisations. Firstly I would like to thank Professor Paul Dukes and Professor Allan Macinnes who have provided wise guidance and friendship throughout the course of my studies. In addition to good will, I have also been fortunate to receive funding for this project from a variety of sources including scholarships from The Carnegie Trust, The Catherine MacCaig Trust, The Robert Nicol Trust and The Sutherland Page Trust. I also received a special award from The Scottish International Education Trust to study the Danish language at Aarhus University during the summer of 1996. The University of Aberdeen also provided me with a Faculty Award for the duration of my post-graduate studies and a generous travel allowance. I thank all the bodies mentioned for making my research both possible and enjoyable. Dr Gunner Lind of Copenhagen University showed great kindness to me in Denmark on my first visit and provided much valuable information. Rune Blix Hagen of the University Library in Tromsø has also been extremely helpful in tracking down numerous sources in Norway that would otherwise have been missed.

It would be unfair of me not to acknowledge the many people who helped me make sense of the variety of languages used in this thesis. I must thank Sophia Larsen and Blanche Dalberg for taking time off their studies in Aberdeen to give me weekly Scandinavian language lessons. In writing this book I often used sources written in languages for which I claim no great knowledge. My express gratitude goes to Mike Turner, Ardis Dreisbach, Alena Kolkavova and Alexia Grosjean who have all helped me decipher the contents of documents in German, French, Czech, Dutch, Italian and Latin. Without this help, my work would have been much more limited in both outlook and conclusions. In the production phase of this book, Gillian Brown from the Department of History, University of Aberdeen, was extremely patient and calm! I must also thank my good friends Jette Esbjørn and Emil Hess for their endless hospitality in Denmark. Finally I must again thank my wife, Alexia, who inspired me to begin this study and has encouraged me all the way through, discussing the most diverse problems at all hours of day and night until they were (usually) resolved. To all the people mentioned above, my most heartfelt thanks.

INTRODUCTION

For the first half of the seventeenth century 'Great Britain' and Denmark-Norway were bound together through a series of military and mercantile alliances. This book sets out to examine the relations between the royal houses, political institutions and military élites of these two North Sea allies in the period following the union of the British Crowns in 1603. This cannot be done without a glance back to the older alliance between Scotland and Denmark-Norway which resulted from the marriage of James VI of Scotland to Princess Anna in 1589, sister of Christian IV of Denmark-Norway.[1] In addressing the process by which that association evolved to encompass England and Ireland after 1603, arguments have been raised which challenge the assumption that the only important historical axis for the British Isles thereafter formed itself in a line linking England, France and Spain.[2] Scotland's economic and historical links lay in a different direction to those of England, towards the North Sea and Baltic countries. Once James VI assumed the English throne in 1603, a new era for dawned in the foreign policy of the British Isles which centred on his existing Scottish alliance with Denmark-Norway.

An appraisal of the relations between 'Great Britain' and Denmark-Norway would not be complete without considering the complexities the multiple monarchy brought to the three Stuart kingdoms and the 'British state' which the House of Stuart tried to create. From the outset of his reign, Christian IV of Denmark-Norway ruled over a multiple monarchy that included the two main kingdoms, the duchies of Schleswig and Holstein and a variety of Atlantic possessions. The Copenhagen led monarchy had not faced any significant challenges since Sweden broke free of the Kalmar Union between 1521-1523. Christian IV ruled over a relatively stable polity seldom threatened from within. The situation in the British Isles was not so straightforward. The fledgling Stuart-British

---

[1]   L. Laursen, and C. S. Christiansen eds, *Danmark-Norges Traktater 1523-1750, med dertil hørende aktstykker* (11 vols., Copenhagen, 1907-1949), IV, 14. 'Ægteskabstraktat mellem kong Jacob VI af Skottland og kong Frederik II's datter princesse Anna, 20 August 1589'.

[2]   This argument builds on previous works such as J. H. Burton, *The Scot Abroad* (2 vols, Edinburgh and London, 1864); T. A. Fischer, *The Scots in Germany* (Edinburgh, 1902); T. A. Fischer, *The Scots in Eastern and Western Prussia* (Edinburgh, 1903); T. A. Fischer, *The Scots in Sweden* (Edinburgh, 1907); A. F. Steuart, *Scottish Influences in Russian History, from the end of the 16th to the beginning of the 19th century* (Glasgow, 1913); P. Dukes, *A history of Europe 1648-1948: the Arrival, the Rise, the Fall* (London, 1985); T. Munck, *Seventeenth Century Europe: State, Conflict and the Social Order in Europe, 1598-1700* (London, 1990).

entity received various degrees of support from different sections of the communities within Scotland, England and Ireland. Understanding how the British polity was perceived at home and abroad is crucial for the simple reason that, after 1604, no treaty or alliance was made between the House of Oldenburg and Scotland, England or Ireland before the mid-1640s. All international treaties were made with Great Britain and Ireland through the agents of the House of Stuart.[3] What makes this situation more complex is that after 1603 there was no specific treaty made between the King James and Christian IV to deal with the new Stuart kingdoms of England and Ireland. An updated alliance was not made until 1621, and then it was between the kings of Great Britain and Denmark-Norway rather than between the countries.[4] In the interim period, business proceeded between the two monarchs based on the existing Scottish alliance of 1589. English and Irish relations with Denmark-Norway were simply subsumed under a treaty pertaining to the Scottish royal house.

The Scottish-Danish Royal Family in England

A major problem in the study of British relations with Denmark-Norway after 1603 occurs through a failure to recognise the significance of Scotland and Scotsmen within the overall British administration and agenda of James VI & I.[5] When James moved to England, many Scottish nobles also travelled to London with him, and many received prominent positions in the new Stuart kingdom. An example of Scots dominating the Stuart Court in England is revealed in the unsuccessful experiment to integrate some Englishmen into James's Bedchamber in 1603 which lasted only a year. After that the Bedchamber remained an exclusively Scottish enclave until 1615, when George Villiers was admitted. Such a strong Scottish presence prompted Sir John Holes in 1610 to write that the Scots stood 'like mountains between the beams of his grace and us', and indeed some 158 Scots found places in his government and household during his English reign.[6]

---

[3] For an early example see Anon., *Articles concluded at Paris the XXIIIJ of February 1605 stylo Angliæ* (London, 1606).

[4] *Danmark-Norges Traktater*, III, 380-411. 'Alliance og Handelstraktat mellem Danmark-Norge og Storbritannien, 29 April 1621'

[5] The issues discussed in this section were first published in S. Murdoch, 'The House of Stuart and the Scottish Professional Soldier 1618-1640: A Conflict of Nationality and Identities', in B. Taithe and T. Thornton eds, *War: Identities in Conflict 1300-2000* (Gloucestershire, 1998), 38-43.

[6] Quoted in Wormald, 'James VI, James I and the Identity of Britain', in B. Bradshaw and J. Morrill eds, *The British Problem, c.1534-1707; State Formation in the Atlantic Archipelago*

Conrad Russell has recently commented on another significant Scottish influence in James's post-1603 government. He noted that the proverbial 'stroke of the pen' only worked because the Scottish Privy Council and the Scottish members of the Bedchamber had carefully prepared the piece of paper on which the said mark was to be placed.[7] In reviewing his reign, Jenny Wormald claims that James ensured that Scotland essentially remained Scottish, but 'England – or, more specifically, the English capital and the English Court as well as, to an extent, the English government – had been made Anglo-Scottish'.[8] Scottish influences on James's administration remained strong after 1603, and not just for Scotland, but also in his political relationship with England which in turn had an impact on British relations with Denmark-Norway. But the strongest link for the House of Stuart's relations with Christian IV remained the marriage of Anna to James in 1589.

Queen Anna added a Danish element and compounded the Scottish influence at the Stuart Court, even after it moved to England. When she arrived in Scotland in 1589, Anna quickly became Scotticised and learned the court language, Scots.[9] She also added a direct link to the continental mainland and her presence facilitated much cross-fertilisation of cultural and political ideas. Thomas Riis has argued that the heyday of contact between Scottish and Danish men of learning followed in the years immediately after she became the Scottish queen.[10] Anna brought her Scottish and Danish companions with her to England in 1604. The Dane, Anna Kroas, remained the queen's personal attendant between 1589 and 1619, and other Danish attendants such as her doctor, her chaplain and the official Danish resident remained in her household throughout her life.[11] Her Scottish companions included Lady Jean Drummond – Anna's First Lady between 1603 and 1617, and the Countess of Nottingham, Lady Margaret Stuart, daughter of the second Earl of Moray and lady of the Drawing Chamber. The Scots at Anna's court were not confined to her Court ladies. Her chief maid was one Barbara Abercrombie; her chief

---

(London, 1996), 158. For references to the Bedchamber see 157 and 164.

[7]   C. Russell, 'Composite monarchies in early modern Europe: the British and Irish example', in A. Grant and K. J. Stringer eds, *Uniting the Kingdom? The Making of British History* (London, 1995), 138-140.

[8]   Wormald, 'James VI, James I and the Identity of Britain', 165.

[9]   DRA, TKUA Skotland A II 4; 25 May, 1595. Johannes Seringius to the Rigsråd; 'nunc tam scotici loquitur, quam aliqua princeps faemina in hoc regno nata'.

[10] T. Riis, *Should Auld Acquaintance Be Forgot ... Scottish-Danish Relations c.1450-1707* (2 vols., Odense, 1988), I, 125.

[11] *DNB*, I, 440. Wilhelm Below, Danish agent in Britain 1606-1626.

gentleman usher was John Stewart; her 'master cook' was John Ferris while one of her favourite employees was Malcolm Groat, her 'musician for Scotch music'.[12] Anna never gave up her Scottish attendants or lost the love for Scotland that she had developed in her early years. She even told the Venetian ambassador, Antonio Foscarini, that Scotland 'seemed to her like her native land'.[13]

The Scottish-Danish dimension of the House of Stuart in England was also strong and maintained by the royal children. Historians have proffered many contrasting views over the personal identity of Charles I which are wide-ranging, simplistic and usually unsatisfactory. Charles is most often regarded simply as an Englishman, Kevin Sharpe advancing the claim that he was 'the first adult Englishman to succeed to the throne since Henry VIII'.[14] John Morrill suggests that to the Scots Charles was 'an authoritarian, unfeeling, foreign king'.[15] The Scottish view is usually that Charles was either 'thoroughly anglicised'[16] or 'wholly English'.[17] Keith Brown is one of the few to challenge that view and directly call Charles I a Scot.[18] Perhaps a more interesting evaluation is given by Sir Charles Petrie who argued that Charles was 'half Englishman and half Scot, [and] it was an irony of fate that made the king an Englishman at Holyrood, and a Scot at Westminster'.[19] Gerald Howat adds another hybrid dimension during his discussion of the marriage of the Elector Frederick of the Palatinate to Elizabeth Stuart, Charles's sister. He footnotes her description as an 'English addition to European Calvinism' with the incidental comment that 'in fact, Elizabeth was half-Scottish and

---

[12] Anna's attendants at her death are noted in *CSPD*, 1619-23, 30. See also L. Barroll, 'The Court of the First Stuart Queen', in L. L. Peck ed, *The Mental World of the Jacobean Court.* (Cambridge, 1991), 199; *CSPV*, XV, 1613-1616, 5-6; M. Lee Jr, 'James VI's Government of Scotland after 1603', in *Scottish Historical Review*, LV, I, no.159, April (1976), 47.

[13] *CSPV*, XIII, 1613-1616, 36-7. Antonio Foscarini, 2 September 1613. This seems to be in direct conflict with the claim made by David Stevenson that once out of Scotland, Anna never wished to think of the country again; however, what possible motive could Foscarini have for making up such a remark? See D. Stevenson, *Scotland's Last Royal Wedding. The Marriage of James VI and Anne of Denmark* (Edinburgh, 1997), 75.

[14] K. Sharpe, *The Personal Rule of Charles I* (London, 1992), 196.

[15] J. Morrill, 'The Scottish National Covenant in its British Context', in J. Morrill ed, *The Scottish National Covenant in its British Context* (Edinburgh, 1990), 22.

[16] A. I. Macinnes, *Charles I and the making of the Covenanting movement 1625-1641* (Edinburgh, 1991), 1. Professor Macinnes has subsequently recanted on this point and now accepts that 'British' is a far better description for Charles than English.

[17] J. Wormald, 'James VI and I: Two Kings or One?', in *History*, vol. 68, no 223 (1985), 209.

[18] K. M. Brown, *Kingdom or Province? Scotland and the Regal Union 1603-1715* (London, 1992), 99.

[19] C. Petrie, *The Letters, Speeches and Proclamations of King Charles I* (London, 1935), ix.

half-Danish'.[20] The consistent conclusion here would be to transfer the same description to her brother Charles. But Charles is referred to in the same book as an Englishman and English king where 'king of England' would have been more accurate and appropriate. On the whole the assessments of Charles's identity are made in spite of either his country of birth or his parentage and upbringing and usually miss out his Danish pedigree all together.

Charles continued to receive a Scottish education even in England. The prince had several Scottish tutors including William Alexander, first Earl of Stirling, and Thomas Murray. In his Bedchamber, Charles employed seven Scots grooms but only one Englishman.[21] Being surrounded by these Scots may have prompted the request from Prince Charles to his father in 1617 'to let me see the country where I was born and the customs of it'.[22] James unfortunately refused and Charles was left with a limited insight into the workings of Scottish government and the traditional relationship between the King of Scots and his subjects.[23] Despite this, Charles continued to foster his Scottish friendships and developed close associations which affected the way he thought about Scotland and his relationship to that kingdom. In 1618, a contemporary foreign source wrote that 'having been born in Scotland and his attendants being mostly Scots, he is naturally more inclined to that nation, a matter which is very distasteful to the English'.[24] The Scottish element of Charles's character filtered through in his letters, proclamations and actions. His Scottish identity was expressed in his use of the Scots language and in his repeated identification with the Scottish nation even when in conflict with them.[25] It is also worth reiterating that it was during

---

[20] G. M. D. Howat, *Stuart and Cromwellian Foreign policy* (London, 1974), 18. Fischer also mentions the national identity of the Princess Elizabeth; 'Was not the queen of the unfortunate King of Bohemia, on whose account the war arose, a Scottish Princess, Elizabeth, born in the old castle of Falkirk and educated in West Lothian among her own people?', Fischer, *Scots in Sweden*, 88.

[21] C. Carlton, *Charles I, the personal monarch* (London, 1983), 26 and 37; G. E. Aylmer, *The King's Servants: The Civil Service of Charles I, 1625-1642.* (London, 1974), 317.

[22] Carlton, *Charles I*, 17.

[23] D. Stevenson, 'The English devil of keeping state: elite manners and the downfall of Charles I in Scotland', in R. Mason and N. Macdougall eds, *People and Power in Scotland: Essays in Honour of T C Smout* (Edinburgh, 1992).

[24] *CSPV*, XV, 1617-1619, 393. Antonio Foscarini's 'Relation of England', 19 December 1618.

[25] Examples of Charles's Scots writings can be found in several places, especially the *Register of the Privy Council of Scotland*, second series, *passim*. Non-governmental examples can be found in *The Miscellany of The Spalding Club*, vol 1 (Aberdeen, 1841), 233. Charles I to The Lords of Session, 16 May 1634, and vol 2 (Aberdeen, 1842), 11. Charles I to Robert Gordon of Straloch, 8 October 1641. For an example of Charles's identification with the Scottish nation

the reign of Charles I that the highest number of Scots held places on the English Council and not during the reign of the more overtly Scottish James.[26]

In August 1604, Charles left Scotland for London where he continued to foster a close relationship with his Danish mother, staying at her residence for protracted periods of up to several months throughout her life. One contemporary observer, Antonio Foscarini, certainly believed that Anna felt more attached to Charles than she had ever been to her other children and reported as much to the Venetian senate.[27] Anna taught her children a sense of pride in their ancestry and in doing so must have made them very aware of their Scottish and Danish heritage.[28] In addition, Charles met his Danish uncles, Duke Ulrik and King Christian IV, on several occasions.[29] Charles's Danish cousin, Prince Ulrik, also stayed with him incognito in 1630 and Crown Prince Christian (V) likewise allegedly visited him in April 1639.[30] Charles was also frequently surrounded by Danes from his uncle's Court and maintained a regular correspondence with his Danish family throughout his life. In addition to Scandinavian influences from Denmark-Norway, Charles spent time in

from a hostile source see J. F. Larkin ed, *Stuart Royal Proclamations volume II: royal proclamations of king Charles I, 1625-1646* (Oxford, 1983), 662-667. Charles I from Whitehall, 27 February 1639, *A proclamation and declaration to inform our loving subjects of our kingdom of England of the seditious practices of some in Scotland, seeking to overthrow our regal power under false pretences of religion.* 'We take God and the world to witness, we hold our self forced and constrained to arm, not onely to reclaim them, and to sett our kingly authority right again in that our ancient and native kingdom, but also for the safety of this kingdom [...] Again they say, that some of power in the hierarchie of England have been the cause of our taking arms to invade our native kingdome, and of medling their religion'.

[26] Wormald, 'James VI, James I and the Identity of Britain', 159.

[27] *CSPV*, XV, 1617-1619, 393. Antonio Foscarini's 'Relation of England', 19 December 1618. There is ongoing debate about the relationship between Charles and his mother. Charles Carlton suggests that Charles was Anna's favourite child only because she disliked her other children more than him. See Carlton, *Charles I*, 7; E. C. Williams, *Anne of Denmark, wife of James VI of Scotland, James I of England* (London, 1970); P. Gregg, *King Charles I* (London, 1981) and F. M. G. Higham, *Charles I* (London, 1932) all provide more sympathetic accounts of the Queen's nature and her relationship to Charles.

[28] Williams, *Anne of Denmark*, 104.

[29] The first being on Christian IV's visit to Britain in 1606 recorded in H. R., *The most Royall and Hounarable entertainment of the famous and renowned King, Christian the Fourth, King of Denmarke & C. who with a fleet of gallant ships, arrived on Thursday the 16. Day of July 1606 in Tylbery Hope neere Gravesend* (Hall Gate, 1606). Anna's children's awareness of their Danish heritage was revealed in a letter by Princess Elizabeth regarding support for her family in their war with the Holy Roman Empire; 'The king of Sweden offers as much as can be desired; I woulde my uncle woulde doe soe too; but he is more backwards than so neere a kinsman should be'. Elizabeth Stuart to Sir Thomas Roe quoted in Miss Benger, *Memoirs of Elizabeth Stuart* (2 vols., London, 1825), II, 224. See also *DNB*, I, 437-439. Gregg, *King Charles I*, 21, 24 and 41.

[30] *CSPV*, XXII, 1629-1632, 435-436. Giovanni Soranzo, 8 November, 1630; *CSPV*, XXIV, 1636-1639, 544-545. Giovanni Giustinian, 3 June 1639.

Spain and married the French princess, Henrietta-Maria. European influences on Charles were therefore extremely powerful. Indeed, Keith Brown argues that many of the presumed 'Anglicisations' of James and Charles's reigns were in fact European influences arriving in Scotland via the Stuart Court.[31] From the age of 4 until the age of 11, Charles was put in the care of Sir Robert and Lady Carey and must also have absorbed from them a perspective on English life impossible to gain from either of his parents. Understanding all the formative elements in the personal identity of Charles Stuart is vital to the interpretation of his later behaviour. Charles's mother was the sister of the reigning Danish monarch, making him Christian IV's nephew by blood. As the following pages reveal, that relationship was made much of by both Charles I and Christian IV.

There has been a consistent failure by historians to adequately determine the identity of King Charles. This is quite remarkable given that such an investigation could go along way in explaining the attitude and actions of the king. Barry Coward, for example, points out that early seventeenth-century England was as remote from the Stuart Court as was Scotland. He has argued that it 'witnessed the development of a Court culture under the patronage of Charles I, which most articulate English people found alien and abhorrent, and which is inextricably interwoven into the process by which the Crown in the 1630s became politically isolated from the majority of its subjects'.[32] Allan Macinnes has highlighted James's error in denying the Prince's request to visit Scotland when he tells us that Charles 'had no appreciation of the ready familiarity between Scottish monarchs and their leading subjects prior to 1603. Charles's concern [...] entailed the deliberate distancing of the king from his subjects and, simultaneously, compounded his remoteness from Scotland'.[33] Historians from Scotland and England seem to agree that Charles and most of his subjects were not harmonised in their perceptions of each other. The usual Scottish answer is to blame this on the Anglicisation of the king, while many Englishmen accept the same point of 'distance', but cannot seem to understand why. Charles Stuart was born neither English nor British, and unless he is to be considered a Scot for the duration of his life, his identity must have, after crossing the

---

[31]   K. M. Brown, 'Courtiers and Cavaliers: Service, Anglicisation and loyalty among the royalist nobility', in J. Morrill ed, *The National Covenant in its British Context 1638-1651* (Edinburgh, 1990), 156.

[32]   B. Coward, *The Stuart Age: A History of England, 1603-1714* (London, 1980), 2.

[33]   Macinnes, *Charles I*, 2.

Tweed in 1604, evolved into something else. To refer to Charles as a Scottish, Anglo-Scottish or a Scottish-Danish king would be as inaccurate as to call him an English king. Given his upbringing, Charles was in fact the first 'British' king of Scotland and England. If both nations found Charles an 'alien' king it might be because, for most of his life, that is what he was. He was, however, not alien for being 'an Englishman at Holyrood and a Scot at Westminster', but for being king of Great Britain in both.

British Political History

The failure to appreciate the continued Scottish and Danish elements of the House of Stuart has been one factor in impairing our understanding of relations between Britain and Denmark-Norway. Another factor has been the lack of appreciation of the nature of Scottish political and diplomatic history after 1603. Many studies of British history confuse or integrate Scottish politics and international relations with those of England – or ignore them altogether. This is particularly true of the role of the Scottish Parliament which met on occasions when Charles I exercised his 'personal rule' in England. Such meetings of the Scottish Estates could either be with royal permission, as in 1633, or without it such as in 1639 (albeit under the names of *The Tables*) and 1640 as a fully fledged gathering of the Scottish Estates 'in defiance of royal prorogation'.[34]

While the independent actions of the Scottish Parliament are all too often overlooked, a further complication arises because many historians have mistaken prominent Scottish individuals in Denmark-Norway, and indeed elsewhere in Europe, for Englishmen.[35] The reasons for this are numerous but one of the most obvious is that many, if not most, printed sources on the subject are often inaccurately translated or indexed, so that where an original document might read 'Great Britain' a modern translation often reads 'England'. The error is applied to the populations of the three Stuart kingdoms, hence Scotsmen become known as English agents, soldiers or diplomats and are therefore presumed to be working for the benefit of England rather than Scotland or indeed greater 'Britain'.[36] This is perhaps best exemplified in the study of English Baltic

---

[34] Munck, *Seventeenth Century Europe*, 78; Macinnes, *Charles I*, 86-89 and 186-189.

[35] In one example, J. V. Polisensky wrote that in the year 1600, Prague 'was full of foreigners, and from England alone there were present at one time three groups of secret agents: one the "official" envoys of Cecil, another the "Essexmen" and a third the Scots from the court of James VI'. See J. V. Polisensky, *The Thirty Years' War* (London, 1971), 16.

[36] Examples from Danish sources include *KCFB, passim*. The index of volume 1 describes Robert

trade by J. K. Fedorowicz. He noted that 'all three of the agents known to be active in Poland from 1606 to 1642 were Scotsmen, serving the Stuart dynasty more than the English government'.[37] After making this important point, Fedorowicz returns to the routine notion of a singularly 'English' policy set by King James and specifically singles out two important Scots, Sir Robert Anstruther and Patrick Gordon, as mediators of the 'English' government.[38] By so doing he fails to recognise the significance of dynastic diplomacy or the pan-British agenda set by the House of Stuart to which these Scottish diplomats wholeheartedly subscribed.

This combination of erroneous labelling and an abundance of Anglocentric historiography has resulted in a belief that there was little or no diplomatic or political relationship between Scotland and other countries.[39] David Stevenson finishes his book on the marriage of James VI and Anna of Denmark with the conclusion that after 1603 'the heyday of personal contacts between Scottish and Danish élites was over' since Scotland no longer had a royal court.[40] The Danish historian, Thomas Riis, has stated that after 1603 'the political relations between the two countries have not been studied, because in most respects British foreign politics furthered the interests of the larger country, viz. England'.[41] These statements demonstrate that there is scope for widening the investigation into the post-1603 political relations between Britain and Denmark-Norway – if only to find out if furthering England's interests was really the intention of the many Scottish diplomats and other individuals operating overseas. Foreign relations were not, in fact, conducted in England's interests, but in the interests of the House of Stuart, and

Anstruther as an 'Engelsk Gesandt' yet the text refers to him as a British envoy e.g. footnote 85-87. In the same volume, the very first letter is directed to James VI of Scotland in 1589, yet indexed under 'Jacob I af England'. A. G. Hasso and E. Kroman, *Danish Department of Foreign Affairs until 1770.* translated by M. Møller (Copenhagen, 1973), section A II, 7 provides an adequate example of equally erroneous indexing: The 'Letters from various English Government and Court officials' 1588-1670 include the important Scots; James King, Lord Eythin and Kerrey (1627), Francis Gordon (1635), Sir George Hay, 1st Earl of Kinnoull (1632), The Lennox Family (1613-24) and Robert Maxwell, Earl of Nithsdale (1615-44).

[37] J. K. Fedorowicz, *England's Baltic Trade in the Early Seventeenth Century: A Study in Anglo-Polish Commercial Diplomacy* (Cambridge, 1980), 17.

[38] Fedorowicz, *England's Baltic Trade*, 150-151. See also G. M. Bell, *A Handlist of British Diplomatic Representatives 1509-1688* (London, 1990), 10-11 and M. P. Jansson, P. Buskovitch and N. Rogozhin eds, *England and the North: the Russian embassy of 1613-1614* (Philadelphia, 1994), *passim*.

[39] For an argument against Anglocentric history see Murdoch, The House of Stuart and The Scottish Professional Soldier, 38-43.

[40] Stevenson, *Scotland's Last Royal Wedding*, 76.

[41] Riis, *Should Auld Acquaintance*, I, 8; See also D. Stevenson, *The Covenanters: The National Covenant and Scotland* (Edinburgh, 1988), 11-16.

frequently by Scottish ambassadors such as Sir Robert Anstruther, Sir James Spens, Ludovick Stuart 2nd Duke of Lennox and James Hay, Earl of Carlisle.[42]

Scottish domestic and foreign policy frequently differed from its English counterparts in the seventeenth century, which had a direct impact on the relations between the two kingdoms and continental powers. In one particular major area of disagreement during the reign of James VI & I – the marriage arrangements of the Princess Elizabeth to the Elector Palatine, Frederick V – the political interests of Scotland challenged those of England. In April 1611, the French ambassador urged the marriage of Elizabeth to Frederick and in doing so he apparently backed Scottish preferences over English ones. Marc' Antonio Correr noted as much when he wrote to Venice that 'in this he [the French ambassador] is supported by the Scottish Nation [...] all the same he knows quite well that the desire of the Queen and of the English Nation is against him'.[43] The Scots were also backed by intervention from Christian IV who sent Jonas Carisius as early as 1611 to support the match.[44] With French and Danish diplomatic pressure being applied, the Scottish interest eventually won over English desires and the Scottish princess married her German prince in 1613.[45]

To counterbalance this Protestant marriage King James sought a Catholic bride for Prince Charles. Initially James considered a marriage of Princess Christina of France to his son. This was dropped in favour of a Spanish match not least because Christina had been the intended bride of the late Prince Henry.[46] James, thereafter, pursued a Spanish bride for Charles, but after years of frustration attention focused on another French princess, Henrietta-Maria. The Earl of Warwick believed that the English Parliament would never consent to marriage 'without due consideration for the English [Anglican] religion' and that further, should Elizabeth Stuart move from Holland to London, James would flee to Scotland and Elizabeth 'would be left mistress in England'.[47] Alvise Valaresso also

[42] *DNB*, XII, 265-267; *DNB*, XIX, 107-108; S. Murdoch, 'Robert Anstruther, A Stuart Diplomat in Norlan Europe', in *Cairn*, no. 1, March (1997).

[43] *CSPV*, XII, 1610-1613, 133-4. Marc' Antonio Correr, 14 April 1611.

[44] *KCFB*, I, 67, Christian IV to Earl of Salisbury, 24 October 1611, and footnote.

[45] James's concern at the growing links between France and Spain which led him to believe that such a marriage was necessary can be found in G. P. V. Akrigg ed, *Letters of King James VI* (London, 1984), 323-325. James VI and I to Sir Thomas Edmondes, 27 August 1612.

[46] Sir Thomas Edmondes prevented James from making a diplomatic blunder by suppressing his instructions since he believed them insensitive so soon after the death of the Prince. James soon after concurred and thanked Edmondes for his discretion. See Akrigg, *The Letters of King James*, 328-330. James VI and I to Sir Thomas Edmondes.

[47] *CSPV*, XVIII, 1623-1625, 57. Valerio Antelmi, Venetian Secretary in Florence, 8 July 1623.

heard rumours from the Scotsman, James Hay, Earl of Carlisle, that a French marriage would split the Scots and English, implying Scottish support for the project, or at least for the wishes of their king.[48] The French marriage went ahead, and for the second time in James's reign the foreign policy favoured by the Scots won over that of the English, and in both these cases that policy proved crucial to developments across Europe.[49]

When the perceived pro-English policies of Charles I were seen to threaten the integrity of the Scottish nation in 1638, the resulting turmoil eventually led to direct conflict between the two countries. It is a mistake to believe that during that period the two nations pursued similar foreign policies. Rather, both attempted to use their various relationships with other nations to win support for their particular cause, and Scotland proved extremely successful at this. One need only look to the debate in the Swedish *Riksråd* discussing the support to be given to the Scottish Covenanters rather than the English Parliament or 'British' government for evidence of this.[50]

The formation of the Stuart-British State

Despite occasional differences between the agendas of Scotland and England, there were attempts to unite the Stuart kingdoms into a single political entity. James VI & I was determined to use his personal dynastic union of the three kingdoms to push for a more complete political union. Political and peaceful union had already been advocated in the sixteenth century by several Scots, including the historian John Major and the Highland cleric, John Elder.[51] Yet it was King James who, for the first

---

[48] *CSPV*, XVIII, 1623-1625, 414. Alvise Valaresso, 16 August 1624.

[49] As Conrad Russell said of the marriage of the Princess Elizabeth in particular, 'it had political consequences which could not be foreseen at the time'. See C. Russell, *The Crisis of Parliaments: English History 1509-1660* (Oxford, 1982), 281 and 297-298; E. Thomson ed, *The Chamberlain Letters: A selection of letters of John Chamberlain concerning life in England from 1597-1626* (Toronto, 1966), 299-318.

[50] *SRP*, VII, *1637-9*, 252-343. June-October 1638. *SRP*, VIII, *1640-1641*, 93-245. July-August 1640. I express my thanks to Dr Alexia Grosjean for these references. She discusses them in far greater detail in A. Grosjean, 'Scots and the Swedish State; Diplomacy, Military Service and Ennoblement 1611-1660' (unpublished PhD thesis; University of Aberdeen, 1998), 159-173. Other distinctly Scottish orientated support from foreign countries came from Russia towards the end of the seventeenth century. See S. Murdoch, 'Soldier, Sailor, Jacobite Spy; Russo-Jacobite relations 1688-1750', in *Slavonica*, no. 3, 1, Spring (1997).

[51] John Major, *Historia Majoris Britanniae tam Angliae quam Scotiae* (Paris, 1521); John Elder, 'A proposal for Uniting Scotland with England, addressed to Henry VIII', in the *Bannetyne Miscellany, I* (Edinburgh, 1827); R. A. Mason, *Kingship and the Commonweal: Political Thought in Renaissance and Reformation Scotland* (East Lothian, 1998), 243-269; Indeed, the

time, took up the concept of 'Great Britain' with any serious prospect of realising it. In April 1604, the English House of Commons received a proposal from James that England and Scotland should henceforth be known as Great Britain, and he proclaimed himself 'James by the grace of God, king of Great Britain, France and Ireland'.[52] He claimed to have chosen the name 'Britain' since it was ancient, already appeared in maps and charts, and was used by previous kings of England though 'having not had so just and great cause as we have'.[53] The Scottish Parliament accepted and adopted the name of Great Britain in its proceedings with the king, albeit reluctantly. At its first meeting after the king's proclamation, James's new title was in place and no objection was raised to its use during the parliamentary session.[54] However, 'King of Great Britain' is not necessarily how James was perceived by many of his subjects. His English Parliament rejected the new title, possibly seeing it as a grossly Scottish concept or else simply because they felt it endangered the very integrity of England. Certainly English merchants abroad ignored the new title and continued to describe James as king of England, even when addressing him after the directive to use his British title had been given.[55]

It cannot be denied that the 1603 succession of the Scottish House of Stuart was a bitter pill for many Englishmen to swallow. It clearly led to a lingering resentment that lasted into the Cromwellian period. This is vouched for by the attack the institution sustained from Cromwellian propagandists who challenged the whole Stuart succession when they wrote:

> Observe this also, viz. That forty years were the English under the government of two Scottish kings, even just as many yeares as the

concept of a Scottish-British identity found expression in a poem celebrating the birth of Prince Henry in 1594 under the title *Principis Scoti-Britannorvm Natalia* (Edinburgh, 1594).

[52] J. R. Tanner ed, *Constitutional Documents of the reign of James I* (Cambridge, 1930), 34. Proclamation of Union, 20 October 1604; See also Akrigg, *Letters of King James*, 224.

[53] Tanner, *Constitutional Documents*, 34.

[54] *APS*, IV, 1593-1625. The Scottish Parliament opened on 7th June 1605 as 'Parliamentum excellenissimi principis Jacobi dei gratia Magne Britannie regis' 276. This title was used thereafter when referring to the king or queen, though the Scottish Parliament specifically used the titles of the kingdoms in the course of its business. See for instance the 'Act anent the King's Prerogative', 9 July 1606, 281.

[55] See R. M. Meldrum ed, *Transactions and facsimiles of the original Latin Letters of King James I of England (VI of Scotland), to his Royal Brother in Law, King Christian IV of Denmark* (1977), 33. A petition from the English merchants trading in Stade directed to 'the High and Mightie Prince James by the grace of God King of England, Scotland, France and Ireland.' included in a letter from James VI to Christian IV, 20 October, 1604. 30-35.

Children of Israel did wander in the Wildernesse [...] The difference betwixt them is this, that wee having cast off their king, it is their designe to settle hime upon us againe, by force, they proclaimed him king of Great Brittaine, etc. But wee have more reason to breake this succession, made up of tyranny, cruelty and oppression [...] our late Tyrant king CHARLES [...] by vertue whereof his father K.James, by the unhappy policie of some Courtiers, did obtaine the crowne, who was then attended with a heavy curse, and terrible plague, into England, if it were no more but the weake and unjust title of the usurping pretenders, the English Nation have sufficient cause to cast off this accursed Monarchie.[56]

This clearly shows the opinion of many Englishmen that King James, Charles I and even Charles II retained a Scottish identity nearly fifty years after the House of Stuart had arrived in England. Jenny Wormald argues that James pressed the idea of 'Great Britain' as a device to deflect his English subjects' attention away from that fact. Even today, some English historians ignore where the House of Stuart came from, or in any case trivialise it. Conrad Russell for one argues that as far as the English were concerned, if James 'chose to be king of Scots in his spare time, that was nothing to do with them'.[57] The alternative way of looking at this of course is that the Scots could go along with the concept of Great Britain so long as that actually meant that Scotland, through the Scottish Royal House, gained in prestige. If this meant that they had to call their Scottish king 'British', then so be it.

Conrad Russell is not alone in his Anglocentric stance. John Morrill has written that 'Wales and Scotland were being institutionally and constitutionally Briticised' and discusses why the Irish were not assimilated to the British state in the same way as the Welsh and Scots.[58] But Morrill, like Russell it seems, has missed the fundamental point. During his reign, James took on possessions in the Americas, claimed Greenland and Spitzbergen from his brother-in-law the king of Denmark-

---

[56] J. L. Philalethes, *Old Sayings and Predictions Verified and fulfilled, touching the young king of Scotland and his gued subjects* (London, 1651). Reprinted in F. Maclean, *A Concise History of Scotland* (London, 1983), 132.

[57] Russell, 'Composite monarchies in early modern Europe', 146.

[58] Morrill, 'The British Problem', 3. On 17, Morrill continues that 'Whatever many Scots and Welsh might wish for their future, they cannot escape a past in which their ancestors in the period in and after that covered by this book were Scots *and* Britons or Welsh *and* Britons'. Of course what he neglects to add is 'English *and* Britons'.

Norway, and even considered the annexation of northern Russia for a time.[59] When James VI left Scotland for England, it was not to assimilate Scotland into England under the guise of Britain, it was to assimilate England into his personal portfolio. As Scotland had been for centuries, England, Wales and Ireland were to be institutionally and constitutionally Stuartised.[60] More than that, the process initially brought peace and prosperity to all the Stuart kingdoms. This at least was how continental observers saw the Stuart take-over. In 1635 Vincenzo Gussoni wrote of Britain that:

> The whole island abounds in ports and rivers; the climate is healthy, the country rather hilly than flat, well populated with a people anciently barbarous and fierce, who lived more in the woods than in well ordered and constructed cities. After eight changes of rulers it has now, by recent and final change, become a happy and most flourishing monarchy under the House of Stuart, of Scottish origin. [...] James the native king of Scotland, succeeded Elizabeth as the nearest of kin, and thus saw his poor little kingdom enriched and aggrandised by the united vassalage of the three kingdoms.[61]

From 1604 onwards, the Stuart monarchs continued to refer to themselves as kings of Great Britain and Ireland even after their hopes for political union had been dashed. But throughout the Union debates, the Scots backed the British experiment. The Marquis of Huntly's address to James

[59] For James's claims to Greenland and Spitzbergen from his brother in law see DRA, TKUA England A I, 2. James VI & I to Christian IV, 9 October 1621; Meldrum, *The Letters of King James*, 222-3; *CSPV*, XV, 1617-1619, 179. Piero Contarini, 21 March 1618. The proposal for the annexation of Russia is discussed in I. Lubimenko, 'A Project for the acquisition of Russia by James I' in *English Historical Review*, XXIX (1914), 246-256; PRO SP91/2, ff.196-199 quoted in S. Konovalov ed, 'Thomas Chamberlayne's Description of Russia, 1631', in *Oxford Slavonic Papers*, 5 (1954), 107 and 112-116; E. Thomson ed, *The Chamberlain Letters. A selection of letters of John Chamberlain concerning life in England from 1597-1626*, 209. Letter from John Chamberlain, 29 April 1613; Fedorowicz, *England's Baltic Trade*, 10; Jansson, *et al*, eds, *England and the North*, 64-68.

[60] B. Ó Buachalla, 'Na Stíubhartaigh agus an t-aos léinn: cing Séamas', in *Proceedings of the Royal Irish Academy*, 83, c, no.4 (Dublin, Royal Irish Academy, 1983) and B. Ó Buachalla, 'James our true king: the ideology of Irish royalism in the seventeenth century', in D. G. Boyce et al, *Political thought in Ireland since the seventeenth century* (London, 1993). Dr Eamonn Ó Ciardha kindly brought these references to my attention. See also N. Canny, 'The attempted Anglicisation of Ireland in the seventeenth century: an examplar of British history', in R. G. Asch ed, *Three Nations - a common history? England, Scotland, Ireland and British History, c.1600-1920* (Bochum, 1993); R. M. Armstrong, 'Protestant Ireland and the English Parliament 1641-1647' (unpublished PhD thesis, Trinity College Dublin, 1995).

[61] *CSPV*, XXIII, 1632-1636, 361-370. Relation of England of Vincenzo Gussoni, 13 April 1635.

as 'his most excellent, most michtie and imperiall Majesty, king of Greit Britain, France and Yrland' in 1607 encapsulates well the Scottish hopes for next stage of the British project after the Union of Crowns.[62] Even after the collapse of the Union project in 1608 it was left to Scotsmen to continue to promote 'Great Britain' at home and abroad, regardless of the attitude of the English Parliament. This they managed quite successfully throughout the reign of King James although the change in title could often confuse James's European neighbours. For example, in a German broadsheet from 1621, King James is portrayed as king of Great Britain, France, Scotland and Ireland.[63] This tells us that, in some circles, Great Britain was understood to mean England. In other words, Britain was not seen to be a composite monarchy, but it was simply assumed that England had changed her name to Britain while Scotland remained a separate entity. In 1627, Gustav II Adolf of Sweden requested that he be allowed to levy troops in England, Scotland, Ireland *and* Great Britain suggesting he was not entirely sure what Great Britain meant.[64] However, it was not just the British title that caused confusion. In one Russian document from 1617, James is referred to as King of England, Scotland, France, Hibernia and Ireland. Not only does this show the Tsar or his advisors believed Hibernia and Ireland to be two separate places, but also that in Russia the British message had simply not been pressed home accurately by the English diplomats there.[65]

Amongst all this diplomatic confusion, most Englishmen had little choice but to tolerate the change of title of the monarch as the king insisted that all his diplomats and allies use his British title. Yet even on the very day of King James's death in 1625, certain Englishmen saw a chance to reinstate the name of England. Thomas, Earl of Kellie noted that within half an hour of the king's death:

Morton and Rosborowche, went to the Prince and dispatched a letter. The subject did not dislyke me, but not to acquent us with it was not

---

[62] Abbotsford Club, *Letters and State Papers during the reign of king James the sixth chiefly from the manuscript collections of Sir James Balfour of Demlyn* (Edinburgh, 1837), 99-100 and 122-123.

[63] J. R. Paas, *The German Political Broadsheet 1600-1700* (Wiesbaden, 1991), III, 73. The confusion was passed on Charles I who was also portrayed as king of Great Britain, France, Scotland and Ireland. See ibid., IV, 213.

[64] SRA, Anglica I/IV, f.44. Gustav II Adolf to James Spens, 21/31/March 1627.

[65] S. Konovalov, 'Seven Russian Royal Letters (1613-23)' in *Oxford Slavonic Papers*, 7 (1957), 23. Tsar Mikhail to King James, August 1617. I would like to thank Carol Mackillop for translating the Russian for me.

weill done; but if I had not bein at the Counsell at the very instant, the proclamatione had past in sutche termes that theye had pitt in Ingland before Scotland. But I remembered them our leat Master had done sume thing upone that subject for the Unione in calling it Great Britain, whitche all the consell and nobillmen yieldet too freelye, nather was I earnest in desyring it, but tould them that if theye did soe we would do the lyke in Scotland; whereupon it was resolved it shuld be Great Brytane. And withall if I had not direktlye gone to my Lord of Morton thaye had send you worde to have pitt Scotland first, and not Great Britane, whitche wold have mated all when it had bein knowen heir.[66]

Despite this attempt by Kellie to save the idea of 'Great Britain' at the start of the reign of Charles I, the notion of a single polity lost favour in Scotland soon after. In 1630, the Scottish Privy Council commanded Sir John Scott, the Director of the Chancellery, to avoid the usage in treaties after the Stuart Court had advocated a common fisheries project which overrode the rights, privileges and vested interests of the Scottish landed and commercial classes in Scotland.[67] Scott believed the term 'Great Britain' misrepresented Scotland and England which he argued were 'twa free and distinct estates and kingdomes and sould be differenced by thair particular names and not confoundit under the name of Great Britane'.[68] The Council continued that:

The Lords of the Secreit Counsell recommends to the commissioners anent the treatie of associatioun for a common fishing with England to represent to our soverane Lord the predudice whiche this kingdome susteanes by suppressing the name of Scotland in all the infeftments, patents writts and records thairofe passing under his Majesteis name and confounding the same under the name of Great

[66] H. Patton ed, *HMC Supplementary Report on The Manuscripts of the Earl of Mar and Kellie* (London, 1930), 226.
[67] Macinnes, *Charles I*, 108-113.
[68] *RPCS*, second series, IV, 56-57. Several other contemporary Scottish sources describe Charles Stuart's realms without mention of 'Britain'. In one such case he is described as 'oighre nan tri rioghachdan' See the poem 'An Cobhernandori' (1648). Allan Macinnes discusses this poem in detail in his article 'The First Scottish Tories?', in *The Scottish Historical Review*, LXVII, no. 138 (1988), 56-66. See also C. O Baoill ed, *Gair nan Clarsach: The Harper's Cry, An Anthology of Seventeenth Century Gaelic Poetry*. Translated by M. Bateman (Edinburgh, 1994), 116-120. Charles's various wars are described by Niall MacMhuirich in 'The Book of Clanranald', as 'cogagh sa na tri Rioghachtuibh' see J. Kennedy and A. MacBain eds, *Reliquae Celticae* (2 vols., Inverness, 1894), II, 176.

Britane, altho there be no unioun as yitt with England nor the style of Great Britane receaved there, bot all the public writts and records of that kingdome ar past his Majesties name as King of England, Scotland, France and Ireland; and thairfoir humblie to intreate his Majestie to give warrand to his Majesteis Counsell that all infeftments, patents, letters and writts passing herafter under his Majesteis name be conceaved under the name and style of Scotland, England, France and Ireland, defender of the faith, and that the style of Great Britane be forborne.[69]

This instruction from the Scottish Privy Council is symptomatic of a general distancing by Scottish institutions from Stuart politics which would eventually lead to the Bishops' Wars and the temporary demise of the Stuart-British political state.

Agents of the British State

The various debates over seventeenth-century 'Britain' and 'Britishness' are lengthy and as yet unresolved.[70] John Morrill has argued that 'the British Isles existed as a geographical term; but there was no term for, and no concept of, a single polity, entity, state incorporating the islands of Britain and Ireland'.[71] For the majority of the subjects of the intended British state, that may well have been the case. Yet, despite the lack of recognition for the new title and the failure of 'union' plans, mutual citizenship for James's Scottish and English subjects born after he gained the English throne was eventually agreed in 1608.[72] The judges in this debate concluded that a king with multiple kingdoms could only have one 'ligeance' and that anyone born within the king's 'ligeance' was his natural-born subject, and no alien in the others. It follows then that, by English law, this judgement must also have made 'post-nati' Irishmen simultaneously citizens of both Scotland and England. So long as the citizens of these nations remained within the British Isles, there was little confusion about their national identity. However, once outwith the British Isles a Scottish, Irish or English diplomat or agent found that he

---

[69]   *RPCS*, second series, IV, 56-57.
[70]   C. Russell, 'The British Problem and the English Civil War', in *History*, 72, no.236, October (1987); Morrill ed, *The National Covenant*; Asch ed, *Three Nations - a common history?*; Grant and Stringer eds, *Uniting the Kingdom?*; Bradshaw and Morrill, *The British Problem*; C. Russell, *The Fall of the British Monarchies 1637-1642* (Oxford, 1991).
[71]   Morrill, 'The British Problem', 5.
[72]   Tanner, *Constitutional Documents*, 24.

represented none of these nations but the Crown of Great Britain and
Ireland and the short-hand term for the polity was often *Britain*.

The establishment of a single polity had important political
implications in foreign relations. The Englishman Joseph Averie, Stuart
chargé d'affaires in Hamburg, noted that the diplomatic treaties that
existed between Denmark-Norway and the Stuart kingdoms were
'agreements between kings' and not between national legislative bodies.[73]
This view received support from Edinburgh when Field Marshal
Alexander Leslie tried to broker a confederation between Great Britain
and Sweden through his old friend Chancellor Axel Oxenstierna in
Stockholm. Leslie saw the federation in terms of one between Charles I
and Queen Christina, 'sanciri possit artissimum foedus inter Regem
nostrum et Reginam Sveciae' and thus the confederation, through the
person of Charles I, would encompass all his realms and subjects.[74] In
diplomatic terms, Charles embodied the polity of Great Britain and
Ireland, albeit that ratification of such a confederation would require the
assent of the Scottish Estates and the English Parliament.

Perhaps because Scotsmen, Englishmen and Irishmen worked for the
same employer abroad, the concept of a single 'British state' did emerge
among many members of the expatriate community, especially among
Scotsmen. Lieutenant-General James King stated this most explicitly in
1641 when he wrote that 'Briteannia ist mein patria, darin ich geborn
sey', revealing that he had a distinct concept of and attachment to a single
British political entity.[75] Other Scots made reference to the single state of
Great Britain. Sir Robert Anstruther came from Fife in Scotland and also
had a strong connection to England through his marriage to a daughter of
Sir Robert Swift. Perhaps because of his familial ties, he found no
problem in serving the combined Stuart nations as a single polity in his
diplomacy. He certainly demonstrated this attitude when he wrote in April
1630 to the Englishman, Lord Dorchester, on the matters 'betwixt our
state [Great Britain] and this king [Christian IV]'.[76] This is a clear
example of a Scotsman writing to an Englishman about the single political
entity to which Anstruther believed they both belonged.

[73]   PRO SP 75/16, f.25. Averie to Roe, 1/11 March 1641.
[74]   *RAOSB*, II, 9, 486-488. Alexander Leslie to Axel Oxenstierna, 4 October 1641.
[75]   *RAOSB*, IX, 958-961. James King to Axel Oxenstierna, 9/19 July 1641.
[76]   PRO SP 75/11, f.70. Anstruther to Dorchester, 24 April 1630. A very positive reference to
      Anstruther and his relationship to Swift can be found in John Taylor's *The Pennyless
      Pilgramage* (1618), printed in full in P. Hume Brown, *Early Travellers in Scotland*
      (Edinburgh, 1978 reprint), 129.

In military parlance as well we find the belief in a unitary political entity. In Henry Brereton's description of the Swedish army in Russia, from 1610 to 1614, we find reference to 'the memorable occurrences of our owne National forces, English and Scottes, under the Pay of the now King of Swethland'.[77] Robert Baillie, subsequently Principal of Glasgow University, must also have believed in some form of entity strong enough to field a unified fighting force. When talking about the restoration of the Palatinate in the 1640s, he noted 'that if the Swedds and confederats can keep the fields till the nixt Spring, it is lyke the British Army may appear in Germany for some better purpose than hitherto'.[78]

Englishmen employed in Stuart business abroad routinely found themselves working for Scotland or the Scottish interest. On one occasion this saw Joseph Averie acting on behalf of a Scottish privateer, Captain Robertson, via an envoy of the Scottish Privy Council, Mr Colville, on the orders of the English Secretary of State.[79] To an astute businessman like Averie this would not have seemed a paradox. He could liken Scotland and England to subsidiaries of a single overarching institution, the House of Stuart – his own employer. Confirmation of Averie's belief in a single polity can be found in his description of the Swedish campaign in Germany. In a letter detailing the success and exploits of Lieutenant General Patrick Ruthven, a Scotsman, Averie lamented 'how poore a recompentce those of our nation are like to receive for their true and faithful service to the Crowne of Sweden'.[80] Knowing General King as he did, when Averie said *our nation* he can only have meant the 'British nation' in an early example of the plural identity common in the United Kingdom today.

Loyalty or association with the House of Stuart aside, certain diplomatic situations sometimes led Stuart agents to work beyond the remit of their 'British' employment. The reason was simply that in many areas the agendas of the House of Stuart and Great Britain were not always the same. Sir John Coke, the English Secretary of State, provided evidence for this when he observed that Christian IV would use his credit

---

[77] H. Brereton, *Newes of the present Miseries of Rushia: Occassioned By the late Warres in that Countrrey [...] together with the memorable occurrences of our owne National forces, English, and Scottes, under the Pay of the now King of Swethland* (London, 1614).

[78] D. Lang ed, *The Letters and Journals of Robert Baillie, Principle of the University of Glasgow MDCXXXVII-MDCLXII* (2 vols, Edinburgh, 1841), I, 357. 15 July 1641.

[79] PRO SP 75/16, ff.233 and 235. Averie to Coke, 2/12 and 31 December 1634.

[80] PRO SP 75/16, f.270. Averie to Coke, 12/22 November 1635; PRO SP 75/16, f.303. Averie to Coke, 12/22 March 1636.

and power to help restore Charles Louis, Prince Palatine, because of 'the ancient interest betwixt these two Houses'.[81] The politics surrounding the German electorate of the Palatine were not directly a Scottish, English or Irish issue, but Charles Louis was Charles Stuart's nephew (and great nephew of Christian IV). The English Secretary of State clearly acknowledged that this was a fundamental issue for the House of Stuart. That fact in itself did not make the Palatinate a British concern. However, it did draw the component nations of the multiple Stuart monarchy into the wider circle of European politics through the person of the constitutional head of state, the Stuart king.

Non-Regal Relations

Having established the strong Scottish, and indeed Danish, credentials of the House of Stuart, there are still further complicating factors to be addressed before proceeding with this study of Stuart-Oldenburg relations. While Denmark-Norway consistently prosecuted her foreign policy via the agents of the House of Oldenburg, the same cannot be said of Scotland, England, Ireland or Great Britain. Between 1603 and 1661, the House of Oldenburg agreed a series of treaties with the House of Stuart (1621, 1625, 1639, 1640 and 1661).[82] However, during the same time period they also held official diplomatic negotiations with the representatives of institutions directly opposed to, and/or in open arms against, the House of Stuart. During the Bishops Wars (1639-1640) between the Scottish Covenanters and Charles I, the Scottish Estates received ambassadors from Christian IV and sent their own ambassador to Copenhagen.[83] From 1643 to 1646, the Parliaments of Scotland and England formed a pan-British council, the Committee for Both Kingdoms, which met to discuss domestic and foreign concerns which affected both Scotland and England.[84] However, as the council representing the two legislatures met, the constitutional British head of state, Charles I, sent his own ambassadors to Denmark-Norway to try to win support against the

[81]   PRO SP 75/13, f.88. Coke to Anstruther, 25 September 1633.
[82]   *Danmark-Norges Traktater*, IV, 14, 380 and 638; V, 119 and 217.
[83]   PRO SP 81/46, f.51. Christian IV to Roe, 18/28 January 1639; *CSPV*, XXIV, 1636-1639, 512. 25. Giovanni Giustinian, 25 March 1639; DRA, TKUA Scotland A I, 4. f.79a. Scottish Estates to Christian IV, 24/14 April 1640; DRA, TKUA Scotland A I, 4. f.79b. Christian IV to the Scottish Estates, 10 November 1640.
[84]   This committee called itself Concilii Amborum Magnae Britanniae, a clear example of confederation in a British context. See DRA, TKUA A I, England. Charles I to Christian IV, 30 June 1645. See also the letters from the Committee to Sweden contained in SRA, Anglica 521, May 1645 to May 1647.

British parliaments. Nonetheless, Christian IV concluded a personal treaty with the English Parliament in 1645 despite his alliance with the House of Stuart.[85] Frederik III also conducted negotiations with the English Parliament between 1649 and 1653 and concluded a confederation with the English Protector, Oliver Cromwell, in 1654 after he assumed power from the English Parliament.[86] That was despite the attempt of Charles II to invoke 'the ancient amity and alliance between your Majesty's [Frederick III] dominions and the Crown of Great Britain' in 1649.[87] On the departure from politics of Richard Cromwell, the English Parliament once more entered negotiations until the Restoration of Charles II in 1660 who, in turn, re-negotiated his own confederation with Denmark-Norway on behalf of the Stuart kingdoms.

Given the above perspective and information, it becomes clear why it is impossible to talk in the usual simplistic terms of Scottish-Danish, Anglo-Danish, or even British-Danish relations after 1603. Instead, this book seeks to address all the main contesting political interests within the British Isles wherever they impacted on the relationship between the various Stuart and Oldenburg kingdoms. How successful it is in doing so will ultimately be for others to decide. Yet if it draws attention to this much-neglected aspect of history and stimulates debate among scholars, it will have achieved its purpose.

---

[85] DRA, TKUA England II 15, f.49b. A printed version in English can be found in M. Sellars ed, *The Acts and Ordinances of the Eastland Company* (London, 1906), 159-165.

[86] *Danmark-Norges Traktater*, V, 134. 15 September 1654.

[87] *HMC, Report on the Pepys Manuscripts preserved at Magdalene College, Cambridge* (London, 1911), 249-251. Charles II to Frederik III, February 1649.

CHAPTER ONE

The Northern Alliance 1589-1618

Relations between Britain and Denmark-Norway in the seventeenth century can be traced to the medieval period and particularly the Scottish-Norwegian Treaty of Perth in 1266. Ratification of the treaty followed in 1312 and again in 1426 after the formation of the Scandinavian Kalmar Union. These ties were reinforced when Margaret, daughter of Christian I of the Kalmar Union became the queen of James III of Scotland in July 1469.[1] As well as improved trade relations, the marriage produced specific diplomatic and military opportunities for individual Scots in Scandinavia.[2] The marriage also saw the transfer of the Orkney and Shetland Islands to the Scottish Crown from the kingdom of Norway as a pledge for the 4/5ths of Margaret's dowry that remained unpaid.[3] As will be seen in due course, this aspect of the marriage alliance would have repercussions well into the seventeenth century.

The Scottish-Scandinavian agreement came to include France in 1499 through the confirmation of the Auld Alliance and the treaty of Denmark. After 1521, however, Scandinavia entered a period of internal turmoil, which ended with Gustav Vasa establishing himself as king of an independent Sweden and Frederik I ruling over the rump of the Kalmar Union, that is to say the kingdom of Denmark-Norway. From this period on, Scottish political connections with Denmark lost any real significance until a new royal wedding became a genuine prospect towards the end of the sixteenth century. Relations improved when a Danish embassy arrived in Scotland in 1585 and negotiations for a new marriage alliance were mooted.[4] Sir Peter Young, a schoolmaster of

---

[1]   For accounts of the early period of Scottish-Danish relations, see T. L. Christensen, 'Scots in Denmark in the Sixteenth century', in *Scottish Historical Review*, XLIX (1970); Riis, *Should Auld Acquaintance*, I, 5-34; *Danmark-Norges Traktater*, III, 1.

[2]   A certain Master David was sent by the king of Denmark-Norway as his ambassador to Muscovy in the 1490s. He has become known to posterity as the first named Scot in Russia. In another example, King Hans of Denmark-Norway, the nephew of James IV of Scotland, sent four Scottish metalworkers who specialised in the production of artillery to Moscow at the start of the sixteenth century. See J. W. Barnhill and P. Dukes, 'North-East Scots in Muscovy in the Seventeenth century', in *Northern Scotland*, 1, (1972), 50; Riis, *Should Auld Acquaintance*, I, 18-19.

[3]   *Danmark-Norges Traktater*, III, 1.

[4]   *Danmark-Norges Traktater*, III, 5; *DNB*, I, 431. Section on Anna of Denmark-Norway. The embassy had also come to refute the erroneous conception of Orkney's legal status that had appeared in the recent Scottish historical works of Hector Boece and George Buchanan; Riis, *Should Auld Acquaintance*, I, 18-35.

James VI, became the Scottish envoy sent to Denmark-Norway in 1586 to discuss the marriage negotiations. While he was there another Scottish resident in Denmark, Sir William Stewart, discussed the more sensitive details of the proposals with the Danes.[5]

James VI did not come of age until 1587 and embassies continued to be exchanged until 1589 when the marriage agreement was concluded. Under the terms of that treaty, Scottish commissioners tried to ensure that Scots would enjoy the same status as Danes and Norwegians in those countries while Danes and Norwegians would gain similar rights in Scotland. This, the Danes responded, was already the case under existing agreements between the countries, and they added that there was no need for any new agreement on the subject.[6] Anna married James VI by proxy in Denmark in 1589. The young groom then set off to collect his new bride, arriving in Norway on 28 October 1589 and marrying Anna in person in Oslo soon after. In December they travelled from there to Denmark where James spent much of his time exchanging ideas with Danish scholars and generally being entertained by Christian IV.[7]

The royal couple returned to Scotland on 1 May 1590 accompanied by a Danish embassy that had been sent to finalise the negotiations regarding the queen's dowry. As part of the marriage treaty, Anna was to receive the secularised monastic lands of Dunfermline Abbey, annexed to the Crown in 1587. There were almost immediate disputes as to how much of the land should actually be transferred to the queen, and in 1592-1594 more Danish embassies arrived in Scotland to settle the affair.[8] Coupled to that there were still the unresolved issues over

---

[5] Riis, *Should Auld Acquaintance*, I, 110-111.
[6] DRA, TKUA Skotland A II 5. Scottish proposal to the Danish commissioners, 9 July 1589; DRA, TKUA Skotland A III 7. Danish response to the Scottish proposals, 10 July 1589; *Danmark-Norges Traktater*, III, 10, 14-21. 'Ægteskabstraktat mellem kong Jacob VI af Skottland og kong Frederik II's datter princesse Anna'. For more details of the various embassies during the marriage negotiations, see G. Donaldson ed, *The Memoirs of Sir James Melville of Halhill* (London, 1969), 129-146; D. Stevenson, *Scotland's Last Royal Wedding. The Marriage of James VI and Anne of Denmark* (Edinburgh, 1997), 1-16.
[7] J. T. Gibson Craig ed, *Papers relative to the marriage of King James the Sixth of Scotland with the Princess Anne of Denmark, A.D. MDLXXXIX. And the form and manner of Her Majesty's coronation at Holyroodhouse, A.D. MDXC* (Edinburgh, 1828), v-ix; Donaldson, *The Memoirs of Sir James Melville*, 147-150; J. Spottiswoode, *The History of the Church of Scotland* (London, 1655, 1972 reprint), 377-381; Stevenson, *Scotland's Last Royal Wedding*, 17-39.
[8] See Gibson Craig, *Papers relative to the marriage of King James the Sixth*, 17-18, 'Grant by the King to the Quenis Grace, of the Lordship of Dumfermling, in Morrowing Gift at Upslo, 24 Nov. 1589'. Details of the annexation of Dunfermline by the Crown and the gift of the same to the Queen in 1593 can also be found in *APS*, 4, 1593-1625, 23-24. A further act in favour of the Queen was passed in 1607, see 543; Riis, *Should Auld Acquaintance*, I, 121-130; Donaldson, *The Memoirs of Sir James Melville*, 132 and 167; Stevenson, *Scotland's Last Royal Wedding*, 65-66.

Denmark's territorial aspirations to regain the Orkney and Shetland Islands and frustration over the continued imposition of taxes on Scottish goods passing through the Sound. Yet despite these tensions, the new dynastic connection was of the greatest importance to both monarchs who always referred to their close relationship in their letters.[9]

The new relationship between the royal families of Denmark-Norway and Scotland was enhanced by the fact that the two kings met in person on several occasions. The first visit to Denmark-Norway by James was crucial in establishing this relationship and it was further advanced by Christian's subsequent visits to Britain. Christian IV never reached Scotland though it was often mooted that he had plans to do so or indeed that he was on his way.[10] The closest he came was probably during the period between 1597 and 1600, particularly for the baptism of Prince Charles. Events in the Baltic, especially relations with Sweden, were to prevent his arrival. However, Christian did reach Britain on two occasions. These visits are important since it can be surmised that some of the most intimate and frank exchanges between the two monarchs took place during their face-to-face encounters. In July 1606, Christian IV arrived near Gravesend where King James and Prince Henry met him. Thereafter they resided variously at Queen Anna's lodgings at Greenwich and at Theobalds, home of Robert Cecil, Earl of Salisbury. They spent the next few weeks engaged in hunting and various other entertainments. A state progress to London followed along with visits around the English capital, before the royal party arrived back at Greenwich for the farewell festivities. The Danish king had firmed up his family bond with James, his sister Anna, Princess Elizabeth and the two young princes, Henry and Charles. Christian IV had ensured that the relations between the British and Danish monarchies remained on the warmest of terms.[11]

The Danish king's second visit came in July 1614, when he returned to London incognito and surprised his sister at Denmark House, her

[9] DRA, TKUA, England II and Skotland V. See also R. M. Meldrum ed, *Transactions and facsimiles of the original Latin Letters of King James I of England (VI of Scotland), to his Royal Brother in Law, King Christian IV of Denmark* (1977).

[10] *CSP*, XIII, 16. Advices from Scotland, A Letter From the Master of Gray, 14 June 1597; 1003, George Nicolson to Sir Robert Cecil, 5 December 1600. Also 137-8, Thomas Douglas to Sir Robert Cecil, 12 June 1602.

[11] H. R., *The most Royall and Hounarable entertainment of the famous and renowned King, Christian the Fourth, King of Denmarke & C. who with a fleet of gallant ships, arrived on Thursday the 16. Day of July 1606 in Tylbery Hope neere Gravesend* (Hall Gate, 1606); B. White, 'King Christian IV in England', in *National Review*, LXII, 1939, 492. White gives an estimate of the cost of the trip to James of £453,000. Christian is supposed to have given various gifts including a warship to Prince Henry, complete with a Vice-Admiral, of a value of £25,000. He also gave out sundry other gifts including a sword worth over 20,000 marks.

residence there. Anna immediately sent for James who was on a hunting trip. Christian had left Denmark-Norway without revealing the purpose of his visit to his subjects. It was speculated in London that he had come to visit James for several important reasons.[12] Some people believed Christian hoped to secure James's support in some secret venture. Sir James Spens, the Scotsman serving as Swedish ambassador in London, tried to establish the precise nature of the Danish king's journey and had several meetings with Christian IV in England.[13] Christian did not reveal his plans to Spens and contemporary opinion was that they were probably an attempt to strengthen his position against his northern European Protestant opponents, notably the Swedes and the Dutch – strong military and trading rivals to the Stuart and Oldenburg kingdoms. In a letter to his sister, Elizabeth of Brunswick, Christian mentioned that he and James had discussed the current dispute between the Duke and state of Brunswick and that James would help to mediate.[14] It is possible that this intervention formed the basis for the visit of his brother-in-law, but it is unlikely to have been the only reason for the visit. Whatever his exact political agenda, Christian had a variety of matters to settle in London. Not least of these was the growing domestic unrest between James and Anna. After all, their marriage provided the basis for the entire Stuart-Oldenburg alliance and had to be saved if possible. If it failed then all the military and mercantile benefits to both states could be in jeopardy.

Trade

Trade was of great importance to both Stuart and Oldenburg monarchs. Much of British-European trade was directed towards the Baltic and the hinterlands that fed commerce to the coastal cities. The Baltic and northern Europe were the principal sources of the raw materials required to sustain the European sea-borne trading nations. Not least of these trading goods were the basics required for shipbuilding such as tar, pitch, hemp, flax and timber – especially timber for masts – and obtained by naval agents such as William Girdler and James Lister.[15] Also essential were Swedish iron and copper and Polish corn, not just for Britain but for the rest of Europe. In return the Scots offered wares such as hides,

[12] *CSPV*, XIII, 1613-1615 (London, 1907), Letter nos. 346, 355, 356 and 375; White, 'King Christian IV in England', 492; Williams, *Anne of Denmark*, 179.
[13] SRA, Anglica 3. Spens to Gustav II Adolf, 25 July 1614; ibid., Anglica 5. Spens to Axel Oxenstierna, 3 August 1614.
[14] *KCFB*, I, 82-3. Christian IV to Elisabeth of Brunswick, 15 August 1614.
[15] 'The Jacobean commissions of enquiry 1608 and 1618', in *Publications of the Navy Records Society*, 116 (1971), 37 and 40.

cloth, salt, cured fish and coal.[16] Baltic trade also formed the basis of Dutch commerce; the Dutch relied on it to support their colonial trade as they could not maintain their business in the Indies without the ability to build ships. The Spanish adopted copper coinage in 1599 and needed supplies of Swedish copper in addition to the usual requirements for their navy. Spain and the Dutch States also both coveted the prospect of controlling Baltic ports, and this was to contribute significantly, though indirectly, to the Stuart-Oldenburg alliance.[17]

Many historians working on British trade with northern Europe either neglect Russia or only focus on the activities of the English Eastland and/or Muscovy companies. However, there were Stuart concerns in the region which had an impact on Stuart subjects from outwith these two trading bodies. Christian IV sent Henry Ramelius to King James as an ambassador in 1605 to discuss a variety of trade-related issues ranging from Sound taxes, fishing rights and the 'Russian navigation'.[18] While there had been Scottish merchants in Russia for quite some time, the Scots had nothing like the presence and reputation of the resident English community. Indeed, Muscovy Company traders sought to prevent 'interlopers in the shape of Scottish and Dutch merchants, as well as those from Hull and York, attempt to break their self-awarded monopoly'.[19] If nothing else, this shows that the Muscovy Company did not even represent the trading rights of all Englishmen, let alone the Scots, and this went against the pan-British agenda of the House of Stuart.

The resources of Russia were comparatively under-exploited and competition was developing between the trading nations to gain access to them. Denmark-Norway was one of the competitors and even tried to

---

[16] Scottish trade with the Baltic is discussed by D. MacNiven, 'Merchant and Trader in Early Seventeenth Century Aberdeen' (unpublished M.Litt, University of Aberdeen, 1977). Also S. G. E. Lythe, 'Scottish trade with the Baltic, 1550-1650', in J. K. Eastham ed, *Economic Essays in Commemoration of the Dundee School of Economics 1931-1955* (Dundee, 1955); Riis, *Should Auld Acquaintance*, I, 39-80; J. Lisk, *The Struggle for Supremacy in the Baltic* (London, 1967); J. K. Fedorowicz, *England's Baltic trade in the early seventeenth century: A study in Anglo-Polish commercial diplomacy* (Cambridge, 1980).

[17] Lisk, *The Struggle for Supremacy*, 16-17.

[18] DRA, TKUA England A 1, 2. James VI to Christian IV, 22 January 1605; Meldrum, *The Letters of King James*, 37.

[19] Evidence of Scottish-Russian trade in the sixteenth century came when the Swedes wrote to Scotland seeking support against Russia and asking that Scottish shipping and trade there be stopped. See *Calender of Scottish Papers*, II, 1563-1569, 683, Randolphe to Cecil, February 6, 1562-63; G. P. Herd, *General Patrick Gordon of Auchleuchries - a Scot in Seventeenth Century Russian Service* (unpublished PhD thesis, University of Aberdeen, 1994), 20; S. Konovalov ed, 'Anglo-Russian Relations, 1617-1618', in *Oxford Slavonic Papers*, I (1950), 72 and 87. Konovalov notes that the English East India Company and the Muscovy Company joined forces to have Sir James Cunningham's patent for a Scottish East India Company revoked.

establish a marriage alliance to secure her position. As mentioned in the Introduction, it had been proposed that King James consider the annexation of northern Russia before Tsar Michael Romanov assumed control in 1613.[20] Despite the potential for British commercial growth as a result of such a scheme, James declined the proposal in order not to upset his existing relationships with Gustav II Adolf and Christian IV.[21] He also realised that he could not break the Muscovy Company monopoly and more or less resigned Russia to this select group of London merchants.

On the southern Baltic coast more British communities flourished. An integrated Scottish and English trading company had been established in Elbing as early as 1578.[22] Numerically, if not commercially as well, the Scots dominated the British presence in the region. Two separate contemporary documents allege that there were some 30,000 Scots (or Scottish families) in Poland alone in the year 1620.[23] These migrants spread out across Poland and the East Prussian coastal cities. True, these Scots did not have a mercantile monopoly like the English Eastland Company. However, this was to their advantage. They had no company to restrict their exports to one staple and Scottish traders went wherever markets were best. Scottish merchants, particularly those in Elbing and Danzig, have thus been singled out as having played an important role in Swedish mercantile growth.[24] In Sweden, the Scots also held a dominant position in the fledgling city of Gothenburg. Throughout the seventeenth century 22 Britons became burgesses in the city; 21 of these were Scots and one was an Englishman.[25] Scotsmen frequently acted in senior positions in the Gothenburg trade council and counted among their number John Maclean, son of Hector Maclean, fifth Baron of Duart, who

---

[20] I. Lubimenko, 'A Project for the acquisition of Russia by James I', in *English Historical Review*, XXIX (1914), 246-256; Konovalov, 'Thomas Chamberlayne's Description of Russia, 1631', in *Oxford Slavonic Papers*, 5, 1954, 107 and 112-116; Thomson, *The Chamberlain Letters*, 209. Letter from John Chamberlain, 29 April 1613; Fedorowicz, *England's Baltic Trade*, 10; M. Jansson, P. Buskovitch and N. Rogozhin eds, *England and the North: The Russian Embassy of 1613-1614* (Philadelphia, 1994), 64-68.

[21] Jansson *et al*, eds, *England and the North*, 68.

[22] T. Fischer, *The Scots in Germany* (Edinburgh, 1902), 18n, 52-53; A. Tønnesen, 'Skotterne og englænderne', in *Helsingørs udenlandske borgere og indbyggere ca.1550-1600* (Ringe, 1985), 21. Most sources refer to this as the English Merchant Company in Elbing. The Swedes more accurately call it "brittiska köpmansförsamlingen i Elbing". See B. Hildebrand ed, *Svenskt Biographiskt Lexicon* (Stockholm, 1918 - ongoing), XI, 581.

[23] *CSPD*, 1619-1623, 237. Chamberlain to Carleton, March 24, 1621; William Lithgow, *The Totall Discourse of the Rare Adventures and Painefull Peregrinations of long Nineteene Yeares Travayles from Scotland to the most famous Kingdomes in Europe, Asia and Affrica* (Glasgow, 1906), 368.

[24] Tønnesen, 'Skotterne og englænderne', 22; Fedorowicz, *England's Baltic Trade*, 82-83.

[25] Source, S. Murdoch and A. Grosjean, *Scotland, Scandinavia and Northern Europe 1580-1707* [hereafter *SSNE*]. Published at <www.abdn.ac.uk/history/datasets/ssne>.

traded under the name of Johan Macklier. He achieved the enviable status of being the richest merchant in Sweden and the owner of at least five major Swedish estates.[26] Elsewhere in Scandinavia, the Scots can also be shown to have held dominant or influential positions in terms of trade and commerce.

By the first half of the seventeenth century Copenhagen, Elsinore, Helsingborg, Halmstad, Malmø, and Marstrand all supported considerable British (mostly Scottish) trading communities. The research into these communities by Thomas Riis has clearly demonstrated the importance of Denmark to the Scots and, conversely, of Scottish merchants to Denmark.[27] Despite this, Scottish trade with Denmark has traditionally been viewed as less important than that with Sweden, Poland or the coastal Prussian cities. However, that is often because the trade is based on a 'present day' view of Denmark and Norway which considers the kingdoms separately instead of counting the sum of the two parts. Danish historians tend to ignore the Scottish-Norwegian trade as irrelevant to them. Norwegians on the other hand can easily discuss the Scottish trade without reference to the alliance between the houses of Stuart and Oldenburg.

Instead of thinking in terms of modern nation states, we should think of British trade with both countries, if only to give a background to later diplomatic activity. There have been many detailed works relating to the Scottish merchant communities in Norway engaged in *Skottehandelen* (the Scottish timber trade).[28] Indeed, one of the richest men and largest landowners in Norway at that time was Axel Mowatt, a Norwegian born Scot. He developed his property in Hovland into an important economic trading centre and is considered to have sold more timber to the Scots than any other landowner.[29] Sir Thomas Urquhart of Cromarty thought so highly of Mowatt that he wrote in *The Jewel* of 'Mouat living in Birren, in whose judgement and fidelity, such trust is reposed, that he is

[26] *SAÅ*, V, 142 -143; J. N. M. Maclean 'Montrose's preparations for the invasion of Scotland, and Royalist mission to Sweden, 1649-1651', in R. Hatton and M. Anderson eds, *Studies in Diplomatic History* (London, 1970), 8.

[27] Riis, *Should Auld Acquaintance*, I, 39-80 and II, 148-277.

[28] A. Næss, 'Skottehandelen på Sunnhordland', in *Sunnhordland Tidskrift*, VII (1920), 23-55. I would like to thank Nina Østby Pedersen for this reference. See also E. Vaage, *Kvinnherad* (Bergen, 1972), 206-213; A. Lillehammer, 'The Scottish-Norwegian Timber Trade in the Stavanger Area in the Sixteenth and the Seventeenth Centuries', in T. C. Smout ed, *Scotland and Europe 1200-1850* (Edinburgh, 1986), 97-111.

[29] Næss, 'Skottehandelen på Sunnhordland', 41-43; A. Espelland, *Skottene i Hordaland og Rogaland fra aar 1500-1800* (Norheimsund, 1921), 31; Vaage, *Kvinnherad*, 2-3; A. M. Wiesener, 'Axel Movat og hans slegt', in *Bergens Historiske Forening Skrifter*, no. 36 (1930), 98; F. Tennfjord, *Stamhuset Rosendal* (Oslo, 1949), 7-8.

as it were vice-king of Norway'.[30]

Apart from individuals like Mowatt in the major trading centres, evidence of Scottish communities can also be found in other Norwegian towns such as Vardø in Finmark.[31] Trondheim also became a focus of British migration and trade throughout the sixteenth century. Despite one author's belief that the Scots must have disappeared by the 1620s, he is contradicted by two letters from Christian IV written in 1638 and 1639. In these, Scottish and English merchants in Trondheim were specifically mentioned in regard to the future payment of the Rosenobel Toll.[32] While there is evidence of small pockets of English communities in Norway, the Scots were easily the most significant group from the British Isles to reside there.

Fig. 1.
Number of Scottish burgesses in
Scandinavian and Baltic towns, 1600-1660

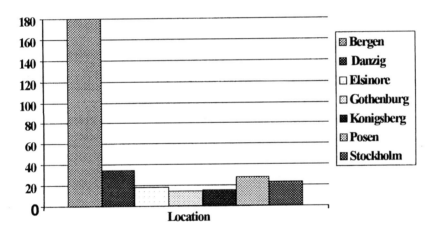

(Source: *SSNE* database)

[30] S. D. Stirling ed, *The Works of Sir Thomas Urquhart of Cromarty, Knight* (Edinburgh, 1834), 215. Birren/Birrane is the proper Scots name for Bergen.

[31] H. Sandvik and H. Winge eds, *Tingbok for Finmark 1620-1633* (Oslo, 1987), *passim; Norske Rigs-Registranter,* VIII, 491. Letter dated 4 October 1652; R. Fladby, *Hvordan Nord-Norge ble styrt: NordNorske administrasjonshistorie fra 1530-åra til 1660* (Tromsø, 1978), 65.

[32] *Norske Rigs-Registranter,* VII, 467 and 502. Christian IV to Eiler Urne, 22 November 1638 and Christian IV to Oluf Parsberg, 3 February 1639; S. Supphellen, *Trondheims Historie 977-1997* (2 vols., Trondheim, 1997), II, 50, 58, 81 and 106.

By undertaking a comparison of the numbers of Scotsmen who became burgesses in a sample of seven major Scandinavian and Baltic trading communities, the importance of Bergen to Scottish trade becomes apparent (Fig. 1). One hundred and eighty Scots served as burgesses in that city alone between 1600 and 1660.[33] The other six trading centres combined only totalled one hundred and thirty.[34] Only a minority of foreign merchants trading in a town were ever likely to become burgesses, therefore a large number of Scottish burgesses in a particular area provides evidence of an even greater trading community.

Figure 1 above clearly demonstrates that the Norwegian timber trade was of considerable significance both to Scotland and to Denmark-Norway. Not only would these burgesses have to pay Norwegian taxes, but their colleagues in the other trading towns noted would also have to pay tax to the king of Denmark. Denmark-Norway's geographical location meant that anyone who wanted to trade with Russia via Archangel had to pass through Danish-Norwegian waters to the north of Norway and pay tolls for the privilege.[35] Similarly any trader wishing to conduct business with Sweden or the Baltic ports had to pass through the Danish Sound and again pay tolls. Denmark-Norway's position of monopoly was to cause much frustration amongst the trading nations and eventually lead to the loss of the Danish provinces on the east of the Sound.[36]

Problems in Trade and Commerce

Christian IV and the English shared a turbulent history. Specific problems just prior to 1603 had been the result of a policy introduced by Queen Elizabeth in 1598. This forbade Danish-Norwegian traffic from using the most direct route to the Iberian Peninsula through the English Channel because of her ongoing war with Spain. The Danes responded by letting it be known that they, and their Polish allies, intended to block the Sound and seize English ships as prizes, presumably until the English lifted their ban. This policy simply further provoked the English, especially the merchants from the City of London, who responded by supplying the Turks, who were then at war with Poland, with

---

[33] During the same period there were ten Englishmen who became burgesses in Bergen. See N Nicolaysen, *Bergens Borgerbog 1550-1751* (Kristiana, 1878), 16-87.

[34] Danzig, Elsinøre, Gothenburg, Königsberg, Posen and Stockholm. See *SSNE* database.

[35] Danish policing of these waters is illustrated in a diary entry of 1618 that recorded the attention an English ship received from a Danish warship off Vardøhus. See 'John Tradescant's Diary of a Voyage to Russia June - September 1618', in S. Konovalov ed, 'Two Documents concerning Anglo-Russian Relations in the Early Seventeenth Century', in *Oxford Slavonic Papers*, II (1951), 132.

[36] Lisk, *The Struggle for Supremacy*, 31-33.

ammunition and powder.[37] Christian IV was outraged and by 1599 he vowed to do the Londoners 'great hurt' for their actions.[38]

James tried to ease the underlying troubles by using his long-term relationship with Christian to smooth matters. In 1605 he wrote, 'Indeed we do not doubt in the least that the past disputes (whatever they might have been) can easily be put to rest and thoroughly removed owing to our mutual friendship'.[39] To cement their friendship, James made Christian a member of the Order of the Garter. In one letter referring to Christian's elevation to the Order, James once more mentioned the recent Danish-English disputes and again showed his desire to have them resolved:

> Since this order was given deservedly by the most serene princess Elizabeth (who recently left this life) to your father, a most serene king, on behalf of their mutual good will, it is right for this honour to be held now by your serene highness for more deserved reasons, namely for the sake of the closest friendship and greatest kinship between us [and] although in the past (before we came into the possession of this kingdom) this inclination was interrupted and somewhat impeded by certain controversies and matters which were not sufficiently and properly understood and perceived, nevertheless there are now many very just reasons why it can and should be achieved most advantageously.[40]

Not least amongst the 'very just reasons' that James mentioned in his letter was his own position as the new monarch of England. Yet despite the long-standing friendship between the kings, Christian IV did not always foster a positive trading relationship in the post 1603 period. Within a year of the Union of Crowns, a dispute arose between Christian IV, King James and the English Merchant Adventurers based in Hamburg. At the request of the citizens of the city, Christian made the English merchants uproot their headquarters and transfer it to the town of Stade. Not content with this disruption, he continually tried to get them to relocate to Krempe, near Glückstadt, between 1604-1614, but without

---

[37] *CSP*, XIII, 127-129. George Nicolson to Sir Robert Cecil, 9 December 1597; 130-132. Roger Aston to Sir Robert Cecil, 12 December 1597; 154-155, Roger Aston to James Hudson, 20 January 1598.

[38] *CSP*, XIII, 546. George Nicolson to Sir Robert Cecil, 1 September 1599.

[39] DRA, TKUA England A 1, 2. James VI to Christian IV, 6 May 1605.

[40] DRA, TKUA England A 1, 2. James VI to Christian IV, 24 June 1603; Meldrum, *The Letters of King James*, 15. The subject was raised again a year later when James wrote to Christian saying: 'Previously, many controversies have existed between the subjects of this our English kingdom and your subjects', 29. James VI to Christian IV, 3 May 1604.

success. This was because, as Christian put it, the citizens of Hamburg had 'rubbed his nose in it' by facilitating the return of the English to the city by the end of 1611.[41] The relationship between the English merchants and the Danish king went a long way in souring the relationship between Christian IV and King James. As king of Scots, James and Christian had little to argue about other than the status of the Northern Isles, and even that debate was temporarily silenced under the terms of the 1589 alliance. However, as king of Great Britain, James often found himself engaged in arguments with his brother-in-law due to a series of specifically English-Danish altercations. Christian IV saw these only in terms of disputes between monarchs and frequently failed to discriminate between Stuart subjects. The dynastic union of 1603 therefore often saw Scots being dragged into essentially English-Danish disputes.

One major bone of contention between the kings centred on the North Sea and Atlantic fisheries. In March 1603, James wrote to Christian requesting permission for two of his subjects to engage in fishing and trading activities in Iceland and suggesting that a favourable response would foster positive relations between the two kings.[42] This was to no avail and the fisheries claimed by Christian IV, especially those around Greenland, proved to be a recurring thorn in the side of Stuart-Oldenburg relations. In January 1615, Sir Robert Anstruther travelled to Copenhagen to discuss an agreement between Great Britain and Denmark-Norway over the contested whaling grounds.[43] When the subject was raised by the Danish *Rigsråd* in April, Christian seemed undisturbed by foreign fishers and whalers, even saying that so long as they paid taxes they were welcome. But there was to be no special dispensation for Stuart subjects.[44] Yet in February of the following year, he wrote to King James, Louis XIII of France, Philip III of Spain and other potentates announcing that he had banned all foreigners from whaling near Norway and its provinces, especially Iceland and the Faeroes, as well as fishing near Greenland.[45] James strongly protested against the ban, arguing that English ships had been in the region since 1553 while seeking a north-east passage to Cathay. He claimed the region as a 'legitimately acquired possession of our English crown' since English sailors had remained in the region without competition before

[41] DRA, TKUA England A 1, 2. James VI to Christian IV, 20 October 1604; Meldrum, *The Letters of King James*, vii and 32; *KCFB*, I, 70-2, 22 December 1611. Christian IV to Henrik Julius of Brunswick; SRA, Anglica 3. Spens to Gustav II Adolf, 25 July 1614.
[42] DRA, TKUA England A 1, 2. James VI to Christian IV, 18 March 1603.
[43] *Danmark-Norges Traktater*, III, 369.
[44] *KCFB*, I, 85-89. Christian IV to *Rigsråd*, 5 April 1615.
[45] *Danmark-Norges Traktater*, III, 370.

the year 1578. In the ongoing debate over fishing rights, James eventually yielded to Christian in the disputes regarding Iceland, Faeroe and Spitzbergen, but not Greenland, and he continued to press his claim to it. Following soon after a letter from Christian IV rejecting Stuart claims to Spitzbergen, Dr Jonas Charisius arrived in London in 1618 to pursue the issue of Danish sovereignty over Greenland and Spitzbergen. Specifically he desired British whalers to pay taxes to Christian IV. James did not accept their arguments, although a concord of sorts was eventually reached between the two monarchs in 1621.[46]

Beyond the issues of contested sovereignty lay other sources of tension. On 12 March 1618, James and his Scottish Council issued a proclamation to deal with Scottish fishing activities near Faeroe.[47] This was in response to complaints received from Christian IV who claimed that by pursuing their craft in Danish waters, the Scots had seriously interfered with the rights of Danish citizens. The supposed result of this Scottish infringement was that Danish fishermen were so impoverished that they were unable to pay Christian IV his royal dues. James agreed that the continued practice of fishing in these areas by Scots was in breach of the laws of nations and inconsistent with his special desire to keep on good terms with Christian. This, however, seems to be in direct contravention of the 1589 alliance that hinted at parity of national status of Scottish, Danish and Norwegian subjects in each other's countries. None the less, penalties were to be severe and fishermen risked confiscation of their equipment and 'further punishment'.[48] One way round this ban for Scottish fish traders could be found through the privileges granted to individual Scots resident in Denmark-Norway to catch and deal in fish. In particular John Cunningham, governor of Finmark, had total control over the fishing rights in the waters under his jurisdiction.[49] Though James eventually yielded to Christian on the issue of fishing rights, he also showed that he did not intend simply to let the Danes get away with impeding British interests in the Danish-Norwegian kingdom. In response to ongoing disputes with the Dutch and the Danes over maritime issues, King James exhorted John Seldon to produce his

---

[46] *Danmark-Norges Traktater*, III, 370-371 and 387-389. James VI & I to Christian IV, 9 October 1621; Meldrum, *The Letters of King James*, 222-3; *CSPV*, XV, 1617-1619, 179. Piero Contarini, 21 March 1618.

[47] *RPCS*, XI, 1616-1619, 320-330 Proclamation, 12 March 1618; Macinnes, *Charles I*, 108-113.

[48] In defence of his slow actions to Christian on the subject James added: 'Concerning the complaint about fishing near the Faeroe Islands, we could not reply so quickly because we had to wait until the councillors of the kingdom of Scotland, whom this matter especially concerned, could be consulted'. Also Meldrum, *The Letters of King James*, 187 and DRA, TKUA England A 1, 2. James VI to Christian IV, 27 March 1618.

[49] See *Norske Rigs-Registranter*, V, 59-60. Christian IV to John Cunningham, 11 December 1619.

work *Mare Clausum*, and by so doing he staked his claim to his rights in the seas around his coast.[50] James also had cause to put pressure on Christian on several other occasions regarding what appeared to be harsh treatment of his subjects.

The fisheries were not the only areas of dispute that arose between the two monarchs. In September 1605, James interceded on behalf of some Scots after he received complaints that a ship and its cargo had been seized by Christian IV's ministers. James asked for restitution and for Christian to remind his ministers about the implementation of international law.[51] James soon after mediated on behalf of William Duncan, a shipbuilder who had completed a ship in Norway but was not allowed to remove it. On his return to Scotland, Duncan had explained the matter to Scottish officials before going on to London to seek compensation. The case eventually concluded when Duncan, and another Scottish shipbuilder, Richard Weddel, received permission to collect their ships in September 1606 after intervention from Britain. Of course Christian IV added the condition that they had to pay the costs incurred in impounding the ships and transporting them to Copenhagen.[52]

In 1611, the Scottish Privy Council asked James to use his good offices with Christian IV on behalf of the Scot, Thomas Watson, whose ships had been seized as prizes in the Sound by the Danes. Watson had been a regular trader with Sweden and had simply been in the wrong place when the Danish-Swedish Kalmar war had broken out.[53] Sir James Spens, the Swedish and British ambassador, also fell foul of the Danish authorities, finding his ships blocked up in the Sound. James VI wrote to the Scottish Privy Council to tell them that he had asked Christian to allow uninhibited passage for Spens's goods through the Sound in order that he might pay off his debts in Scotland.[54] Christian had suspected, correctly, that Spens was actually recruiting troops in Scotland for

---

[50]   J. Wormald, 'The Union of 1603', in R. A. Mason ed, *Scots and Britons: Scottish Political thought and the union of 1603* (Cambridge, 1994), 35.

[51]   Meldrum, *The Letters of King James*, ix-x.

[52]   DRA, TKUA England A 1, 2. James VI to Christian IV, 4 April 1606; Meldrum, *The Letters of King James*, 75. Christian IV had been complaining about the Scottish practice of building ships in Norway since July 1604 when he fined Christopher Dall 2,000 *rigsdaler* for allowing Scots to build ships on his property. In August 1605 he ordered Styring Boel to confiscate two Scottish ships belonging to Jacob Clerk which had been built in Listerlen in Norway. See *Norske Rigs Registranter*, IV, 79. Christian IV to Laurits Krus, 24 July 1604 and 123. Christian IV to Styring Boel, 3 August 1605; *Kancelliets Brevbøger, 1606*, 460. Missive to Brede Rantzau anent the Scots William Dunker (sic) and Richard Weddel, 29 September 1606.

[53]   *RPCS*, IX, 1610-1613, 620, 20 June 1611.

[54]   PRO SP75/4, f.240. James Spens to the Earl of Salisbury, 31 March 1611; *RPCS*, IX, 1610-1613, 626-627.

Sweden and hit back where he could against his ships.[55]

In another incident the same year, an Orkney vessel and its cargo belonging to Robert Scoula had also been arrested in Bergen. The ship had been carrying hides, butter and oil and was the centre of complex litigation for several years, not least since many of the goods on board belonged to King James. It was not until 1618 that Christian ordered that the complaint of the Scottish Privy Council be listened to.[56] The incentive for this order was perhaps the attacks on Norwegian shipping and harbours by Orkney privateers which had been ongoing between 1612 and 1617 and which Christian IV did not want repeated.[57]

In 1619 James interceded again with Christian IV on behalf of Scots who had suffered theft at the hands of Danish officials. The first incident involved one Thomas Lothian who had had his ship and cargo impounded.[58] The second incident involved Robert Baillie of Edinburgh who had bought some gunpowder for King James. The powder was confiscated in Copenhagen by Christian IV's ministers, while Baillie was roughly handled and narrowly escaped imprisonment. Whether the Danish king knew of this remains unclear. Certainly in his statement to the Scottish Privy Council, Baillie said that the Danish officials had indicated that their actions were being carried out at 'the King's pleasure'. The Council wrote to Christian asking him for the return of the powder, but the letter was 'disdainfullie refusit'.[59] Needless to say, the Scots took this as a snub. They then asked James to intervene and he both wrote a letter and sent James Spens as ambassador to the Danish king to demand his powder back. The Council gave Baillie a promise to cover his expenses and he was sent on a mission of remonstrance in 1620 with a personal letter from King James to Christian IV concerning the return of the powder and additional compensation for Baillie himself.[60]

The interference in shipping was not always a one-way process, although as the Scots and English were more often in Danish waters than

[55] SRA, Anglica 4, f.11. Gustav II Adolf to James Spens, 16 November 1611.

[56] *Norske Rigs Registranter*, V, 728. Christian IV to Knut Urne, 28 August 1618.

[57] PRO SP75/4, f.314. Anstruther to James VI, 8 June 1612; *Norske Rigs Registranter*, V, 662. Christian IV to Knut Urne, 9 September 1617; *RPCS*, XI, 1616-1619, 629-630. Letter from the Privy Council to Christian IV in favour of Robert Scoula, and against the privateer Simon Stewart, 18 June 1618. See A. Grosjean, 'Scottish-Scandinavian Naval Links: A case study for the SSNE database', in *Northern Studies*, no. 32 (1997), 111-112; S. Murdoch, 'Simon Stewart: Privateer, Admiral, Orcadian?', in *The Orkney View*, no. 82 (1999), 20-22.

[58] DRA, TKUA England A 1, 2. James VI to Christian IV, 12 March 1619; Meldrum, *The Letters of King James*, 199; SRA, Anglica 5. James VI's instructions to Sir James Spens, 30 July 1619.

[59] *RPCS*, XII, 1619-1622, 77.

[60] SRA, Anglica 5. James VI's instructions to Sir James Spens, 30 July 1619; DRA, TKUA England A 1, 2. James VI to Christian IV, 26 November 1619; Meldrum, *The Letters of King James*, 203-4; *RPCS*, XII, 1619-1622, 217-219. Council to Baillie, 2 March 1620.

vice versa, obviously they bore the brunt of it.[61] Despite the various individual disputes that went on, the bulk of Scottish trade with Denmark-Norway continued undisturbed during the reign of King James. The Scottish merchant who experienced difficulties with the Danish authorities seems to have been the exception rather than the rule. The English, however, had different problems to contend with in their relationship with the Danes. On the whole their situation improved after the accession of James to the English throne, but there is also little doubt that the transitional period proved difficult.

The Stuart Corps Diplomatique

On becoming king of England, James had to deal with new factors in his contact with the European monarchies. He did not simply assume the English throne in 1603, he also inherited a war with Spain and had to contend with the often conflicting agenda of his English subjects, including their near xenophobia of Catholic countries.[62] James immediately set about redefining the relationship of his new kingdoms with the European powers.[63] He believed that the grounds for hostility with Spain had ended with the death of Elizabeth I and were at any rate 'irrelevant to a king from Scotland'.[64] By August 1604, peace with Spain had been established and he had won the right of his subjects to trade in Spain and the Spanish Netherlands. This new friendship and the renewed association with France were confirmed by public proclamations in 1605. In short, the Stuart policy of striving for a united and pacified Christian Europe was to be continued.[65] In order to achieve that end, James looked to his most trusted diplomats and in doing so he restricted English diplomatic input in Scandinavia throughout his reign.

As king of Scotland, James employed Scottish ambassadors throughout Europe. After 1603 the Stuart monarch also inherited the former diplomatic corps of Elizabeth I. In many countries this meant James had a duplication of diplomatic representation. He undertook a

---

[61]   In 1608, however, Christian had cause to complain to James that one of his ships had been seized by English privateers. Meldrum, *The Letters of King James*, ix-x.

[62]   J. V. Polisensky, *The Thirty Years' War* (London, 1971), 95. Spain was seen as 'the sworn enemy of a whole generation of Englishmen'; Williams, *Anne of Denmark*, 93. Williams relates that Anna 'did not, like many of her subjects, look upon hatred of Spain as a patriotic duty'.

[63]   James VI and I, *By the King, Although we have made it knowen by publike edict, that our entrance into these our kingdomes of England and Ireland, we stood, as we still doe, in good amity and friendship with all the Princes of Christendom* (London, 1603).

[64]   G. M. D. Howat, *Stuart and Cromwellian foreign policy* (London, 1974), 17.

[65]   James VI and I, *By the King, Whereas the King's majestie hath always bene ready to imbrace and cherish such a perfect amitie betweene him and the King of Spain* (London, 1605); Anon., *Articles concluded at Paris the XXIIIJ of February 1605 stylo Angliæ* (London, 1606); Jansson, et al, *England and the North*, vi.

rationalisation of resources which effectively meant the withdrawal of many English diplomats, leaving his own tested Scottish diplomatic corps – who had often worked in direct competition with English interests – to conduct diplomacy for all of the Stuart kingdoms. Direct English representation in Denmark-Norway terminated after the withdrawal of the English diplomats Roger Manners and Robert Naughton in August 1603. Scotsmen, like Andrew Sinclair, who had been long-term residents in the country, filled the diplomatic vacuum.[66] Richard Lee's four-year Swedish residency also terminated in 1604. The removal of the Englishman left Swedish diplomacy to be conducted in an *ad hoc* manner by soldiers and merchants until the Stuarts established formal political relations with Karl IX in 1609. Two Scots found work as diplomats to Sweden that year, Sir James Spens and Sir Andrew Keith.[67]

The first Stuart-British ambassador to Poland, Henry Lyall, left Britain in April 1603 to replace the English agent Sir George Carew.[68] On the conclusion of Lyall's embassy, William Bruce replaced him as a permanent resident ambassador in 1604.[69] A doctor of law, he had also served as a soldier in Poland against the Turks since 1595. Bruce was well versed in the indigenous language and returned to Scotland in 1602 in time to escort the Polish ambassador to London the following year. He was subsequently appointed ambassador to Poland, a post which he filled for the next five years. When Bruce left in 1610, another Scot, Patrick Gordon, took up the royal appointment and continued intermittently in Poland until at least 1624.[70] Patrick ensured that his nephew Francis took over as Polish agent in 1625, in which capacity he served until the 1640s.

The transitional period after the Union of Crowns in 1603 led to a similar role for the Scots in diplomatic missions to France. Ludovick Stuart, Duke of Richmond and 2nd Duke of Lennox, spent part of his childhood in France and was next in line to the Scottish throne after the royal children. In 1601 he returned to France with John Spottiswoode, future Archbishop of St Andrews. Their mission, as Spottiswoode recorded, proved more 'for confirming the old amity and friendship, then (sic) for any busines else'.[71] Given his high social status and intimate knowledge of the French Court, it is unsurprising that he was chosen to assist the English resident ambassador to France, Sir Thomas Parry.

---

[66] *DBL*, XIII, 399-400.
[67] PRO SP95/1, ff.158-158v. James VI to Karl IX, 22 September 1609.
[68] Fedorowicz, *England's Baltic Trade*, 15; Bell, *Diplomatic Representatives*, 213.
[69] Fedorowicz, *England's Baltic Trade*, 17; *SSNE* no 4384.
[70] Bell, *Diplomatic Representatives*, 215; Fischer, *The Scots in Germany*, 33 and 255; *RPCS*, XI, 174-178; A. F. Steuart ed, *Papers relating to the Scots in Poland, 1576-1793* (Edinburgh, 1915), xv-xix and 103-107.
[71] Spottiswoode, *Hisory of the Church of Scotland*, 465.

Between November 1604 and March 1605 they negotiated a new treaty between the French and British kings.[72] This mission followed within months of another British embassy led by James Hay, Earl of Carlisle. Hay proved to be the most influential and consistent British ambassador to France in the post-1603 period. He conducted seven embassies there between 1604 and 1629 and also took on diplomatic roles elsewhere, notably to the Spanish Netherlands in 1619 and Spain in 1623.[73]

In northern Europe, it was only in Muscovite Russia that Englishmen continued as the majority diplomatic representatives from James's Court. This was due largely to the impact of the Muscovy Company whose employees provided the House of Stuart with most of their agents.[74] Fabian Smith's dual capacity has been highlighted as 'providing the framework through which diplomacy for the rest of the seventeenth century was to be conducted' in Russia.[75] Following on from Smith, the main envoy throughout the Jacobean period was Sir John Merrick who had been raised in Russia and eventually became the governor of the Muscovy Company.[76]

The very process of Scottisisation in the new British diplomatic corps must be seen as a challenge to the prevalent notion that the Scots in Stuart service were somehow Anglo-British in outlook. These men were not Scots courtiers trying to fit into an English diplomatic agenda but individuals at the very heart of a new British diplomacy to which the English appeared unwilling to subscribe. The transition from Scottish to Stuart diplomat must have been relatively easy for the Scots since they continued to represent the same king at the same courts as they had before 1603. England on the other hand was now often represented in negotiations at European courts by diplomats from a foreign country. The Scottish diplomatic monopoly in Scandinavia was reinforced by the fact that Scottish ambassadors representing the Stuart interest also formed an integral part of the diplomatic institutions of the countries to which they were accredited. During James's reign, Andrew Sinclair conducted at least seven diplomatic missions to the Stuart Court on behalf of Denmark-Norway and Anstruther several more. The latter

---

[72] *DNB*, XIX, 107-108; Bell, *Diplomatic Representatives*, 203; Anon., *Articles concluded at Paris the XXIIIJ of February 1605 stylo Angliæ* (London, 1606).

[73] *DNB*, IX, 265-266; Bell, *Diplomatic Representatives*, 103-109 and 259.

[74] A knowledge of language and customs as a prerequisite is noted by several authorities. See Herd, 'General Patrick Gordon', 18; Jansson *et al*, eds, *England and the North*, 68.

[75] Herd, 'General Patrick Gordon', 21.

[76] Konovalov, 'Anglo-Russian Relations, 1617-1618', in *Oxford Slavonic Papers*, 1 (1950), 64-103; Konovalov, Two Documents concerning Anglo-Russian Relations in the Early Seventeenth Century', in *Oxford Slavonic Papers*, 2 (1951), 128-129; Konovalov, 'Anglo-Russian Relations, 1620-1624', in *Oxford Slavonic Papers*, 4 (1953), 71-131.

ambassador also acted as Danish ambassador to other countries. In 1624, Christian chose him to represent Denmark-Norway to Frederick V of the Palatinate at The Hague and in 1625 Anstruther was accredited as the Danish ambassador both to and from John George of Saxony.[77] Sweden also employed Stuart subjects as their own ambassadors. The Swedes sent Andrew Stewart and Hans Stewart as legates to Russia in 1611.[78] They strove to negotiate a Swedish military intervention in support of the first false Dmitrii, Vasilii Shuiskii. In return the Swedes sought Russian recognition of Karl IX, an end to claims on Livonia and Estonia and Russian guarantees not to ally with Poland.[79] More importantly for Scottish and British interests, Sir James Spens acted as the ambassador both to and from the Swedish Court from 1609 until his death in 1632 and had intimate knowledge of Danish diplomacy through his half-brother Sir Robert Anstruther. This helped Spens immensely when he interceded on behalf of Sweden with Christian IV in 1612-1613 and 1618.[80]

The dual diplomatic role the Scots played in Scandinavia led to perhaps the classic example of Scottish diplomacy in the early modern period. There is a tale that before the fall of Kalmar to the Danes in 1611, the Swedish garrison had a vision of angels. This was interpreted by Sir Ralph Winwood to relate to the diplomatic intervention of King James where the vision involved the 'angels of England'.[81] Winwood was wrong since these 'angels' were actually bred in Fife. During the peace negotiations which followed, Sir James Spens and Sir Robert Anstruther discoursed with each other on behalf of the warring nations, Spens for Sweden, Anstruther for Denmark-Norway.[82] There was more at stake in these negotiations for the Stuarts than simply aiding two potential allies, since the implications of this war stretched beyond the confines of Scandinavia. Despite James's desire to unite Scotland and England into one political entity, there remained a significant mutual resentment between the populations of these countries. In 1610, Marc Antonio Correr intimated to the Venetian Senate that in the city of London hatred of the Scottish race was universal.[83] The feeling was mutual: from Edinburgh, another Venetian, Giovanni Batista Lionelli,

---

[77] E. Marquard, *Danske Gesandter og Gesandtskabs Personale indtil 1914* (Copenhagen, 1952), 27.

[78] *SAÄ*, VII, 782; J. Berg and B. Lagercrantz, *Scots in Sweden* (Stockholm, 1962), 21.

[79] Grosjean, 'Scots and the Swedish State', 44.

[80] SRA, Anglica 3. Spens to Gustav II Adolf, 8 December 1618.

[81] PRO, SP84/68, f.111. Sir Ralph Winwood to Salisbury, 20 August 1611; Jansson *et al*, eds, *England and the North*, 55.

[82] PRO SP75/5, f.3. Christian IV to Sir Robert Anstruther, 8 August 1612.

[83] *CSPV*, XII, 1611-13. Marc Antonio Correr, 31 December 1610, 101-103.

recorded that most Scots did not 'look upon the English too favourably'.[84] This hostility did not diminish when Scots and Englishmen migrated to Scandinavia and occasionally threatened to test the British regal Union. In July 1612, Anstruther wrote a letter to Spens regarding the Kalmar conflict that included a message on Anglo-Scottish relations:

> honourible brother, if this mater be not speedelie looked unto, it is lyk to breed a graite inconvenience betuix the contries of England and Scotland, and it is to be feared at if ther be a day of battell, at then the English and Scots will cout on [an]others throths, and by report afore my coming unto the leager, ther haith passeth some message alreadie betwixt some of the nations.[85]

Given the large numbers of Scots serving in the Swedish army and the recruiting drive underway in England for the Danes, these concerns had a very real foundation. Fortunately the levy from James arrived just before the cessation of hostilities in August 1612 and there was no major bloodletting by Stuart subjects in either army.[86]

King James, however, believed that Christian IV was deliberately stalling the peace process. He informed James Spens that, should his brother-in-law continue to refuse his intervention to establish a peace with Sweden, he would allow Gustav II Adolf to recruit more soldiers from Great Britain.[87] Whether Christian was also made aware of this condition remains unclear. Nonetheless, formalised peace came in January 1613 at Knäred in a settlement negotiated by Spens and Anstruther and guaranteed by James. Both Scandinavian monarchs formally thanked James for his mediation and particularly his diligent ambassadors.[88]

---

[84] *CSPV*, XIV, 1615-1617. Giovanni Batista Lionello, letter no. 785, 8 June 1617, 515-517. The difficulties of being a Scot in London are also discussed in SRA, Anglica 5. James Spens to Axel Oxenstierna, 26 May 1615.

[85] SRA, Anglica 5. Anstruther to Spens, 18 July 1612.

[86] Estimates of levies for Danish service varied at the time from between 4-6,000. They are discussed in greater detail in chapter eight.

[87] SRA, Anglica 3. Spens to Gustav II Adolf, 21 July 1612.

[88] O. S. Rydberg ed, *Sverges Traktater med Främmande Magter*, vol. 5:I, 1572-1609 (Stockholm, 1903), 223-224. Kon. Jakob I:s af Storbritannien garanti af den mellan Sverge och Danmark slutna traktaten. Westminster, 1613, April 2; PRO SP75/5, f.63. James VI guarantee of Danish-Swedish peace, 26 January 1613; PRO SP75/5, f.73. A copy of the contract of peace procured by the King's most Excellent Majestie of Greate Brittaine and betwixt the Kings of Denmark and Sweden, 26 January 1613; Anon., *The Joyful Peace, concluded between the King of Denmarke and the King of Sweden, by the means of our most worthy Soveraigne, James, by the Grace of God, King of Great Britaine, France and Ireland* (London, 1613); M. Roberts, *Gustavus Adolphus; A History of Sweden, 1611 - 1632* (2 vols.,

During his next embassy in 1615 Anstruther conducted negotiations between Christian IV, King James and the representatives of Lübeck. Once again Stuart diplomatic intervention proved influential with Christian in resolving issues peacefully.[89] The diplomats themselves also exchanged sensitive letters to ensure the negotiations would be speeded up. The transfer of information was greatest between Anstruther and Spens, particularly during the Knäred conference. One example is found in the transcript of a letter from Christian IV to Gustav II Adolf, translated into Scots by Anstruther and dated 17 July 1612.[90] Another letter from Anstruther to Spens, noting the safe receipt of a copy of a letter from the Prince of Sweden to the king of Denmark-Norway, exposes the trade in royal letters as a two-way affair.[91] The brothers also occasionally passed restricted information to each other months before it was to be made public.[92] The Scotsman, Andrew Stewart, Swedish envoy to Russia, sent diplomatic letters to both King James in London and Andrew Sinclair in Denmark.[93] Sinclair in turn passed the information on to Christian IV, and it has to be concluded that this was part of Stuart policy. By exchanging information, the Stuart diplomats could better inform James on the correct strategy in dealing with particular leaders at any given moment.

Perhaps because the traffic in correspondence was known, the Scots were sometimes used as 'unofficial' links between the Danish and Swedish kings. When Gustav II Adolf sought to retrieve his bride from Brandenburg, Swedish ships had to cross Danish waters and challenge Danish claims to *Dominium Maris Baltici*.[94] Gustav II Adolf had been informed by a Stuart agent that the Danish *Rigsråd* had advised Christian not to be confrontational – and devise a system for the Scandinavian ships to salute each other should they meet.[95] This information probably reached Sweden via Sir Robert Anstruther or Andrew Sinclair. Sinclair is the more probable since he now sat as a member of the Danish *Rigsråd*. Both these theories are compatible with an official 'leak' tacitly approved by Christian IV himself.

Despite the more covert function of Stuart diplomats, their role

---

London, 1962), I, 70.

[89] SRA, Anglica 3. Spens to Axel Oxenstierna, 4 June 1614; SRA, Anglica 5. Spens to Axel Oxenstierna, 1 March 1615 and 26 May 1615; *CSPV*, XIII, 369-370. Antonio Foscarini, 6 March 1615.

[90] SRA, Anglica 5. Anstruther to Spens, 17 July 1612.

[91] SRA, Anglica 5. Anstruther to Spens, 18 July 1612.

[92] SRA, Anglica 5. Anstruther to Spens, 1 August 1624.

[93] KCFB, I, 63-65. Christian IV to Anders Sinclair, 16 September 1611.

[94] Lisk, *The Struggle for Supremacy in the Baltic*, 30-38; Bellamy, 'Danish Naval Administration', 15-39; Lockhart, *Denmark and the Thirty Years' War*, 250.

[95] KCFB, I, 180-181. Christian IV's speech to the *Rigsråd* and footnote, 17 August 1620.

increasingly centred on the growing tensions in mainland Europe. Importantly, James's letters included a prediction concerning the inflammatory nature of the German principalities and the wisdom of restraint:

> Tiny sparks sometimes produce dangerous fires, especially if they are neglected, if, when the city of Lübeck is compared with your forces, it is of little or no importance, by which your justice will be more advantageous: let not the peace of Germany be disturbed if it wishes to withdraw somewhat according to its own law [...] we must urge your serene highness to be willing to assign so much importance to public tranquillity that you will relinquish that entire matter, however great it may be, to be settled by a decision of your common friends.[96]

Despite the efforts of King James, a constant shower of sparks occurred which were eventually bound to ignite the explosive tensions of Europe. The Stuart kingdoms and Denmark-Norway were to play crucial roles in the coming conflagration, and within their respective roles the *corps diplomatique* continued to exercise considerable influence.

The years of the post-1589 period had witnessed a flourishing of the relationship between the royal houses of Scotland and Denmark-Norway. One might even call it a re-forging of the 'Northern Alliance' of the fifteenth century. This was exemplified by the ennoblement of several Scots into Danish-Norwegian society and the improved opportunities for trade, commerce and cultural exchange for the populations of both nations. However, after 1603 the Union of Crowns complicated Scottish-Danish relations. Serious disputes between English merchants and the Danish crown occurred in 1604 and 1611, causing problems which were left to Scottish diplomats to try to resolve. Contesting English and Danish claims to fisheries around Greenland led to further confrontation and the eventual banning of all foreigners from those grounds by Christian IV. This ban extended to the Scots who, as a nation, were supposed to enjoy equal citizenship with the Danes. The period had also witnessed an escalation in tit-for-tat exchanges in relation to trade and commerce in which the Scots in particular paid a high price. It is

---

[96]   DRA, TKUA England A 1, 2. James VI to Christian IV, 16 July 1615; Meldrum, *The Letters of King James*, 164. As early as September 1614 James had been writing to Christian expressing concern over 'the peace of all Germany and the safety of our kingdom'. James VI to Christian IV, 21 September 1614.

possible that Christian used James's affinity for his Scottish subjects as leverage in what were actually diplomatic disputes with England. Certainly the three major cases between 1611 and 1613 – involving Thomas Watson, James Spens and Robert Scoula – all occurred at a time when Christian had, in his own words 'had his nose rubbed in it' by English traders and the citizens of Hamburg. It was also at a time when Christian was at war with Sweden and wanted James's support. Both Watson and Spens were involved in Swedish trade, and perhaps Christian also wished to remind James who was in charge of the Sound, with all that implied for trade from the British Isles.

The application of diplomatic pressure through the erection of trading obstacles became a feature of Christian IV's policy. He used it against his brother-in-law frequently between 1611 and 1618, seizing goods belonging to James personally. The 1618 incident occurred at a period of little consensus between the two monarchs regarding the growing tensions in Europe and with a general simmering in Stuart-Oldenburg relations. The years between 1614 and 1618 had also seen James fall out with, and separate from, his Danish queen. The Danish king failed to rectify his sister's domestic relations, even after his personal visit to Britain. These years had even apparently seen James deceiving Christian with false promises regarding Anna's servants.[97] James was also furious with Christian IV for trying to renege on the peace treaty between Sweden and Denmark-Norway of 1613 for which the Stuart king was the guarantor. Sir James Spens noted that King James promised to avenge this insult by aiding Gustav II Adolf against the king of Denmark, as he would against a deadly enemy.[98] Yet for all that the Stuart-Oldenburg relationship was in difficulty, it remained stronger than British relations with other nations at that period. The two royal houses had remained in a constant state of alliance after 1589, with the trade and military agreements being renewed and built upon. The unresolved debate over the Orkney and Shetland Islands remained undisturbed by Christian IV and the right of the Danes to levy Sound tolls continued unchallenged – at least for the time being. However, the Stuart-Oldenburg alliance eventually found its most serious test in James's reign during the dangerous escalation of confrontational politics in Europe.

---

[97] Chamberlain relates that promises of pensions relating to the late queen's servants by James remained unratified. The reason given by Chamberlain is that the promises were only made to keep Christian off the king's back since Christian IV had written in strong terms over the issue. *CSPD*, 1619-23, 70. Chamberlain to Carleton, 10 August 1619.

[98] SRA, Anglica 3. James Spens to Gustav II Adolf, 9 February 1618.

CHAPTER TWO

Denmark-Norway, Great Britain and the 'Protestant Cause' 1609-1625

The conflicts in central Europe fought between 1618 and 1648 are the subject of ongoing historical debates as to the causes and consequences of the Thirty Years' War.[1] There had been tensions within the German *Reich*, or Holy Roman Empire, long before 1618, which revealed itself through frequent political, social and religious unrest. The Peace of Augsburg in 1555 had brought about a temporary settlement between the Protestant and Catholic powers. Despite a degree of good will by many on both sides, the terms of Augsburg had not been adhered to and, by 1608, many Protestants feared a Jesuit led Catholic counter-reformation. To deal with the perceived threat, some of the Protestant princes formed an 'Evangelical League' under the leadership of Frederick IV of the Palatinate. In response to this, a Catholic League formed soon afterwards under Maximillian Duke of Bavaria. Just over a decade later, a kaleidoscope of struggles had evolved which pitched Catholic against Protestant, Lutheran against Calvinist, co-religionists against each other, princes against the Holy Roman Emperor and prince against prince. Adding to the complexity of the conflict, various powers outwith the *Reich* manipulated the unrest for their own ends.

During the Julich and Cleves dispute of 1609-1614, various proposals were made to strengthen the Protestant Union of 1608. At the Diet of Halle, it was suggested that Christian IV should become the leader of the Union. Christian declined the offer, saying that he did not want to offend King James and that 'such a title and authority belong to that Crown'.[2] When the Union between James VI & I, Christian IV, the united princes of Germany and the United Provinces was eventually finalised in 1613, James was indeed recognised as its leader. His position had been

---

[1] See for instance J. A. Fridericia, *Danmarks Ydre Politiske Historie* (2 vols., Copenhagen, 1876 and 1972); S. H. Steinberg, *The Thirty Years' War* (London, 1966); T. K. Rabb, *The Thirty Years' War: Problems of Motive, Extent and Effect* (Boston, 1967); Polisensky, *The Thirty Years' War* (Prague, 1971); G. Parker, *Europe in Crisis: 1598-1648* (New York, 1980); G. Parker et al. *The Thirty Years' War* (London, 1997); P. D. Lockhart, *Denmark in the Thirty Years' War, 1618-1648. King Christian IV and the decline of the Oldenburg State* (London, 1996); R. Asch, *The Thirty Years War The Holy Roman Empire and Europe, 1618-1648* (Basingstoke, 1996). As early as May 1648, the term 'the Thirty Years' War' had found both expression and a degree of definition within Europe. See Asch, *Thirty Years' War*, ix; Parker, *The Thirty Years' War*, xii.

[2] *CSPV*, XIII, 1613-1615, 115. Antonio Foscarini, 23 January 1611. For a Dutch take on these events see J. I. Israel, *The Dutch Republic: Its Rise, greatness and Fall 1477-1806* (Oxford, 1995), 407.

strengthened through the marriage of his daughter Elizabeth to the Elector of the Palatinate, Frederick V that same year.[3]

The royal wedding of the Scottish princess to the German prince was greeted with enthusiasm in Britain since it was seen as a positive move for European Protestantism. As discussed above, the match had been vigorously supported by Christian IV.[4] Yet despite the euphoria that surrounded the union, Elizabeth's marriage was only a part of a Stuart plan to establish an equilibrium in the power structure of Europe. It was to be counterbalanced by a proposed marriage between Prince Charles and a Catholic princess, either Princess Christina of France or the Spanish Infanta.[5] The Spanish proposal was strongly opposed by Christian IV who had himself long favoured a French marriage for his nephew.[6] James vacillated between the two options, finding the conditions attached to both quite unreasonable. The Scotsman, James Hay, future Earl of Carlisle, undertook a mission to France in 1616 to try to gain the hand of Princess Christina for Prince Charles. Hay probably knew from the outset of his mission that the conditions accompanying the proposal would be rejected. Nonetheless, he apparently acquitted himself well during his embassy. After the rejection of the French match, James turned his attention back to the possibility of an alliance with Spain.[7] In the summer of 1618, Christian IV tried to use his family relationship to 'speak freely' with James in relation to the planned treaty with Spain. He told James that such an alliance was equivalent to the sacrifice of Charles for political ends. James was quite offended by this and replied that, with all respect for the prudence and wisdom of the king of Denmark, he chose to dispose of his children according to his own fancy.[8]

[3] Francis Yates argues the importance of this marriage vigorously. See F. A. Yates, *The Rosicrucian Enlightenment* (New York, 1996 edition), 16 and 36; Howatt, *Stuart and Cromwellian foreign policy*, 18-19; *CSPV*, XIII, 1613-1615, 10-12. Gregorio Barbagio, 15 July 1613.

[4] Jonas Carisius was in England in 1611 to work for the Elector's marriage to Elizabeth Stuart. See *KCFB*, I, 67, Christian IV to Earl of Salisbury, 24 October 1611, and footnote. The Scots were keen to show their approval of the marriage and the Scottish Parliament voted to raise 100,000 crowns towards the cost of the wedding of their Princess, which equalled about a sixth of the cost. *CSPV*, XII, 1610-1613, 491-492 and 439-440. Antonio Foscarini, 26 October 1612 and 8 February 1613,.

[5] Polisensky, *The Thirty Years' War*, 95; Howatt, *Stuart and Cromwellian foreign policy*, 19-28.

[6] *KCFB*, I, 29-30, Christian IV to Anders Sinclair, 4 May 1610.

[7] *DNB*, IX, 266; Howatt, *Stuart and Cromwellian foreign policy*, 23-24.

[8] *CSPV*, XV, 1617-1619, 205-207. Piero Contarini, 4 May 1618. Prince Charles himself was not initially keen on the Spanish marriage proposals and made his position on that subject quite clear in two letters to Buckingham. C. Petrie ed, *The Letters, Speeches and Proclamations of King Charles I* (London, 1968), 5-6. Charles to Buckingham, 3 November 1621 and second letter, n.d. In the first he declared that he felt that the English Parliament's

In July 1617, Archduke Ferdinand II of Austria succeeded to the throne of Bohemia as king-designate, having been elected by the Bohemian and Hungarian Estates. This move actually unsettled Bohemia's protestant nobility, and their bitterness increased in the lead-up to his election as Holy Roman Emperor in August 1619. Frederick V was raised to the kingship of Bohemia by her nobles in place of Ferdinand whom they had solemnly deposed. His election made the Scottish princess Elizabeth the new queen of Bohemia and thus involved the House of Stuart directly into the unfolding events in the *Reich*. This was a quandary for James since he felt that he could not really approve of a rebellion against the claims of a legitimate succession. However, Frederick was still his son-in-law and could not be abandoned totally.

The Spanish king, Philip III, asked James to try to reconcile the Bohemians and the Emperor early in 1618, with further attempts being made through the meeting of the Spanish ambassador and James Hay, Earl of Carlisle, in Frankfurt in 1619.[9] Ferdinand II also sent an ambassador to London to seek an accommodation, although the embassy was aborted when his envoy received erroneous information relating to the Emperor's death.[10] In the meantime, James pursued his complex policy, instructing James Hay to meet with the Emperor at Salzburg, during which embassy he also visited the United Provinces. While doing his utmost to appease the Spanish king and the Emperor, he continued negotiations with the Bohemians and northern potentates. As Carlisle travelled south, Sir James Spens prepared to conduct embassies to Christian IV of Denmark-Norway and Gustav II Adolf of Sweden.[11] The Venetian ambassador in London, Antonio Donato, reported that James had offered to find 200,000 crowns for their cause by May 1619. By mid-February, James's support for Bohemia became public when a new league was initiated, as the Spaniards put it, 'between the heretics of Germany, the kings of England and Denmark and the Palatine', and there were rumours of Stuart military aid. This included a verbal promise of

---

attitude to his father was seditious and added that 'I should have him [James] command them not to speak any more of Spain, whether it be of that war, or my marriage'. In the second letter he mentions his support for Sir Edward Cecil's proposals for entering a war in defence of the Palatinate. His position altered once he arrived in Spain, though his initial excitement soon faded in the face of Spanish stalling and the unrealistic conditions they wished to impose upon him. See the same volume, 7-30.

9   James Hay, in *DNB*, IX, 266-267; *CSPV*, XV, 1617-1619. Letters No.515, 587, and 600; T. Fischer, *The Scots in Germany* (Edinburgh, 1902), 33 and 255.

10   SRA, Anglica 5. James Spens to Axel Oxenstierna, 28 March 1619.

11   SRA, Anglica 3. Spens to Gustav II Adolf, 8 December 1618; SRA, Anglica 5. James IV's instructions to James Spens, 30 July 1619; *DNB*, XVIII, 789-790; *SAÄ*, VII, 428-9; *RPCS*, XI, cxli.

4,000 infantry 'of his own subjects' to be backed with a further 2,000 more hoped for from the United Provinces and Germany although issues still had to be resolved between the parties.[12]

Frederick V sent an embassy to London in 1619 with the goal of extracting firm support for his cause from his father-in-law. However, after much soul-searching James officially condemned the Bohemian revolt as illegal and implied that his son-in-law was a usurper. James had been joined in his condemnation of Frederick V by John George of Saxony who, though Lutheran, initially remained faithful to the Emperor against the Palatinate party. This denunciation did not alter the fact that Frederick was part of the Stuart royal family, and James indicated that if Frederick did accept the Bohemian Crown, then he would grudgingly lend him support limited support. Representatives of the Elector Palatine, the Stuart kingdoms and the United Provinces entered into protracted negotiations. Intensive bargaining failed to significantly strengthen the Elector's political position and only limited finances were secured for his cause from Britain. The Dutch, through Frederick's uncle, Maurits of Nassau, offered a monthly subsidy of 50,000 *guilders* monthly, but few troops initially. Despite his lack of resources, Frederick marched to the Bohemian border with only 1,000 troops and 150 coaches and was crowned king of Bohemia in November 1619.[13]

The Bohemian embassy reached Christian IV in January 1620 and was coolly received, despite the blood relationship of the Danish king to the Bohemian queen. Christian had done well to keep out of the central European conflict, and even turn it to his advantage. In the spring of 1619 there had been a rumour of Christian IV himself being offered the Bohemian throne, but the Danish king was not foolish enough to accept such an offer even if it were genuine.[14] He viewed the Bohemian war and unrest in the *Reich* purely from the perspective of his position as a *Reichsfürst*, or Prince of the Holy Roman Empire. Beyond the German possessions he already had, Christian also had other dynastic ambitions in north Germany, particularly the establishment of his over-lordship over Hamburg. To the non-specialist of Danish politics the myriad of alliances Christian IV maintained as a *Reichsfürst* are extremely

[12] *CSPV*, XV, 1617-1619, 443-445, 459-460 and 426-424. Antonio Donato to Venice, January and February 1619; Polisensky, *The Thirty Years' War*, 104; Howatt, *Stuart and Cromwellian foreign policy*, 28. Ongoing discussions between King James and the Dutch over the proceedings at the Synod of Dordrecht undoubtedly slowed procedings. See J. V. Polisensky, *Tragic Triangle* (Prague, 1991), 94-95; Israel, *The Dutch Republic*, 460-462.
[13] Polisensky, *The Thirty Years' War*, 107; Israel, *The Dutch Republic*, 469; C. Russell, *The Crisis of Parliaments: English History, 1509-1660* (Oxford, 1982), 291; Howatt, *Stuart and Cromwellian foreign policy*, 27.
[14] Roberts, *Gustavus Adolphus*, I, 197.

confusing.[15] The Danish *Rigsråd* could protest against his actions all they wanted, but the king took a holistic view to the protection and expansion of his territories. Whatever actions he took as *Reichsfürst* impacted directly on Denmark-Norway. However, his aspirations, especially in Brunswick, also made it imperative for him to keep, or at least be seen to keep temporarily, on good terms with the Emperor.[16]

In February 1620 his Council advised the Danish king against any attempt to champion the Protestant cause, a position they maintained even after hostilities became inevitable.[17] Christian IV intended to take a balanced approach, and while rejecting military assistance for Frederick, he also declined to join the Emperor. However, in April, Sir Robert Anstruther was back at the Danish Court having been sent by James to try to raise money for the Elector Palatine. Anstruther spent some days negotiating with Christian IV for a loan of £100,000. Christian claimed he could not afford that amount, but promised 200,000 *rigsdaler*, which he would hold to prevent the opponents of the Stuarts becoming suspicious.[18] One condition attached was that James would try to prevent the United Provinces working with Hamburg or Bremen against Christian IV's interests. In his desire to establish his over-lordship of these towns the Danish king needed to avoid being hemmed in by an alliance between the north German states, the United Provinces and Sweden and through this policy contributed to growing divisions in Stuart and Dutch policy.[19] A servant of Anstruther's was dispatched from Denmark-Norway to tell James that Christian was well disposed to Frederick V and the amount he was prepared to pay. By 1621 he had in fact lent the Stuarts £100,000 at a cost to James of £6,000 per annum in interest payments alone.[20]

King James sought to remain aloof from the conflict, publicly at least. He claimed that any support given to his family and friends was intended

---

[15] They are explained well in Fridericia, *Danmarks Ydre Politiske Historie* and Lockhart, *Denmark in the Thirty Years' War*.

[16] Fridericia, *Danmarks Ydre Politiske Historie*, I, 24-25; T. Munck, *Seventeenth Century Europe: State, Conflict and Social Order in Europe, 1598-1700* (London, 1990), 13. Christian IV was particularly talented at keeping up appearances. Even as late as May 1625, long after Christian had decided on war with the Empire, the Emperor believed himself to have enough influence with Christian to ask him to use his good offices with the Stuart king to impede anything which would obstruct the Emperor's plans. *KCFB*, I, 436-437. Christian IV to Frederick Gunther (draft letter to Emperor), 14 May 1625.

[17] Parker, *The Thirty Years' War*, 73; Munck, *Seventeenth Century Europe*, 13.

[18] SRA, Anglica 5. Spens to Axel Oxenstierna, 20 April 1620.

[19] *KCFB*, I, 171-3, Christian IV to Christian Friis, 4 May 1620. In July 1620, Christian handed over another 100,000 *rigsdaler*; See Israel, *The Dutch Republic*, 469; Munck, *Seventeenth Century Europe*, 13.

[20] *CSPD*, 1619-23, 437. Warrant authorising payment of £6,000 interest, 5 August 1622.

to promote peace not war. James wrote to Christian in early June 1620 to ask that money given to his allies should:

> not be used to support a war in Bohemia but only to protect our son-in-law's inherited lands in the Palatinate and our grandson's there [...] for we do not want to commit ourselves to do anything by which we may be rendered useless for the purpose of conciliating peace in some way between the parties.[21]

Though James and his English ministers may have officially been pursuing a peaceful policy there were rumours that his agents were not. Sir Robert Anstruther was one who was felt to be covertly working on behalf of Frederick V under the direction of the Prince of Wales.[22] Given his influence at the Danish Court and the reported attitude of Christian IV to the Bohemian situation, it is quite possible that the ambassador had brought the Danish king round to more positive support for his Scottish niece and her family.

James at last countenanced limited military support from his kingdoms in 1620, organised initially by the Scottish Catholic, Sir Andrew Gray.[23] He arrived in London in February 1620 having been sent by Frederick V to muster 2,000 foot in Britain. His orders were to raise a regiment composed equally of Scots and English. By March he had been granted permission to raise his levy, though he was to do so quietly and not to 'beat the drum'.[24] This restriction was later lifted and the drums started beating in London on the very day and close to the hour of the arrival of the Spanish ambassador, resulting in an official complaint being registered. In Scotland orders were issued to those who had enrolled to fight in the Bohemian wars to assemble in Edinburgh in May to await transportation to Hamburg.[25] Toward the end of the month, Colonel Gray's 1,500 Scottish volunteers set sail for the continent

---

[21] DRA, TKUA England A 1, 2. James VI to Christian IV, 3 June 1620; Meldrum, *The Letters of King James*, 206.

[22] *CSPV*, XVI, 1619-1620, 276-7. Girolamo Lando, 11 July 1620.

[23] *RPCS*, XII, 1619-1622, 257-261; SRA, Anglica 5. Spens to Axel Oxenstierna, 20 April 1620; J. Taylor, *Taylor his travels: From the city of London in England, to the city of Prague in Bohemia* (London, 1620) B4; Anon., *Certaine Letters declaring in part the Passage of Affaires in the Palatinate from September of this present moneth of April* (Amsterdam, 1621) B2-B3; S. R. Gardiner, *History of England from the Accession of James I to the Outbreak of the Civil War 1603-1642* (10 vols., London, 1883-1884) III, 358; J. V. Polisensky, *Anglie a Bílá hora* (Prague, 1949), 164 and 201.

[24] *CSPD*, 1619-23, 125. 26 February 1620; SRA, Anglica 5. Spens to Axel Oxenstierna and to Gustav II Adolf, 20 April 1620; *CSPV*, XVI, 1619-1621, 204-7. Girolamo Lando, 19 March 1612.

[25] *RPCS*, XII, 1619-1622, 255. 19 April 1620.

followed by 1,000 English recruits who left from London the next day.[26] By July, Gray had arrived in Lusatia 'with his Brittans'. One Dutch report noted that 'They are so well governed, and so good discipline amongst them, they are praised by all men above all other nations that are there'.[27] Similar commentaries on the good spirit of 'every Brittaine' with Gray were reported by the traveller, John Taylor, on his arrival in Mansfeld's camp soon after.[28]

After the departure of Gray to the continent, recruitment in Britain continued. Sir Horace Vere left for the Palatinate from Rotterdam in August 1620 with other English troops under the Earls of Essex and Oxford totalling over 2,000 men.[29] In October 1620, Sir Henry Bruce returned to Britain from Imperial service to levy another 2,000 men for the anti-Habsburg coalition. Bruce began his recruiting drive too late for them to have been ready to leave Scotland before the start of 1621.[30] However, Colonel Gray's regiment were joined by other Scottish volunteers in Bohemia, though not enough to ensure them victory in the campaign. These units, or those under Vere, were never pulled into one British army. Gray and his men were engaged in Count Mansfeld's alliance of around 7,000 men while another 1,000 Scots in Colonel John Seton's regiment formed part of Frederik V's army proper in southern Bohemia.[31]

In both Mansfeld's and Frederick's service the Scots appeared to be more committed to the fight than their counterparts from England. Some 500 Englishmen deserted for lack of pay and grievances with their officers before they reached their destination, whereas Scottish troops apparently had better relations with their officers.[32] The combined forces of the Protestant Union faced a huge Imperialist army on 8 November 1620. The outcome of the battle is a matter of record, Frederik V fled and the British troops blamed his cowardice for the loss of the battle and this sentiment was echoed by his uncle Maurits in The Hague.[33] Colonel

[26] *RPCS*, XII, 1619-1622, lxxvii and 257-258; *CSPV*, XVI, 1619-1621, 262-263. GirolamoLando, 28 May 1620.

[27] Anon., *A most true relation of the late Proceedings in Bohemia, Germany and Hungaria, dated the 1, the 10 and 13 of July this present yeere, 1620. And the Happie Arrivall of Sir Andrew Gray into Lusatia* (Dort, 1620), 10.

[28] Taylor, *Taylor his travels*, D2.

[29] Taylor, *Taylor his travels*, B4; Anon., *Certaine Letters*, A4.

[30] *CSPV*, XVI, 1619-1621, 432-435. Girolamo Lando, 11 October 1620; Polisensky, *Tragic Triangle*, 181; Ferguson, *The Scots Brigade in Holland*, 224.

[31] J. V. Polisensky, *Anglie a Bílá hora* (Prague, 1949), 202; Polisensky, *The Thirty Years' War*, 125-126.

[32] Polisensky, *Anglie a Bílá hora*, 164; For the disorder and desertion of English troops see Anon., *Certaine Letters*, B2-B3.

[33] Anon., *Certaine Letters*, B1; Israel, *The Dutch Republic*, 471.

Seton chose not to flee with the rest of the army. Instead, his regiment retired into the town of Trebon in southern Bohemia, which they managed to hold until February 1622 after a siege of one and a half years.[34] Gray's regiment also occupied a Bohemian town after White Mountain, but only for two months. An English observer noted that they 'did in three assaults repulse the enemie bravely' but by January 1621 they had been reduced in number to only 300 men. These remnants joined up with the English force under Lord Essex in the garrison of Frankenthal.[35]

Despite the efforts of Gray, his colleagues from the United Provinces and the army of Count Ernst von Mansfeld, the conflict continued to go badly for Frederick V. When the focus of the war shifted from Bohemia to the Palatinate, public opinion demanded firm action. It was obvious that more military support was required and James summoned the Scottish nobility to a convention in Edinburgh between 24-27 November 1620 where they discussed voluntary contributions to the defence of the Palatinate.[36] The nobles remained unaware that the Elector's forces had been defeated at White Mountain when they convened, the news not reaching Britain until December.[37] They felt that it would be impossible to raise the required voluntary contributions to equip further military expeditions without Scottish Parliamentary approval. In January 1621, after news had reached Scotland of the capture of Prague, further meetings of the Council and the nobility were held.[38] Again the convention requested that a full Parliament should be called since only that body could raise the contributions required from Scotland for the war effort. The Archbishop of St Andrews, John Spottiswoode, set off for London with the request for James to call a Scottish Parliament.

Upon his arrival in London, Spottiswoode convinced King James that a full Scottish Parliament was required to discuss the financing of future expeditions to Germany. James not only agreed to call a Scottish Parliament, but also ordered that an English Parliament should be convened as well.[39] In June 1621, the Scottish Parliament assembled and

---

[34] John Seton to General Marradas c.25 November 1621. Letter translated from Italian and reproduced in Polisensky, *Tragic Triangle*, 254; Polisensky, *The Thirty Years' War*, 159.

[35] Anon., *Certaine Letters*, B3-5; Count Mansfeld, *More News From the Palatinate* (London, 1622), 18

[36] Spottiswoode, *History of the Church of Scotland*, 541; *RPCS*, XII, 1619-1622, 366 and 379-381. It is interesting to note that James called together the nobility but not a full Parliament. It is likely that he was in fact trying to circumvent such a Parliament in order to achieve his goals without the obstructions that a Parliament might have raised.

[37] Polisensky, *Anglie a Bílá hora*, 203.

[38] Spottiswoode, *History of the Church of Scotland*, 541; *RPCS*, XII, 1619-1622, lxxx and 367.

[39] Russell, *The Crisis of Parliaments*, 292.

the discussion of the Palatinate issue was set for July.[40] The new Taxation Act was passed relatively easily, despite mild alarm once the extent of the tax-raising and investigative powers sought by the Council was understood. This was especially true of the Scottish burghs that successfully sued for lump-sum payments instead. In this way the king raised just over £42,000 in ready cash, the bulk of it coming from Edinburgh and destined to support a more aggressive war effort.[41] These were helped by Sir Robert Anstruther who had also returned to the continent, officially to give Queen Elizabeth £20,000 to make up for the loss of her household goods in Bohemia.[42] He also had instructions to speak to the States Council of the United Provinces to try and encourage them to furnish the necessary arms to support a greater military campaign which Maurits of Nassau seemed willing to do. By March 1621 he was back in Denmark seeking a full military alliance between Denmark-Norway and Great Britain. In response to this proposal, Christian IV sent his ambassador, Andrew Sinclair, to the Stuart Court to clarify the proposals.[43]

As Sinclair left for London, pro-Habsburg forces advanced north, and Christian IV began to take measures to protect his interests in northern Germany. Members of the Lower Saxon Circle were invited to meet Christian in the Danish town of Segeberg at the end of February to discuss the measures to be taken for their common interest. Delegates were also invited to represent the House of Stuart and the king of Sweden. Not surprisingly, James sent Sir Robert Anstruther as his representative. At the conference, a military alliance between Denmark-Norway and Great Britain remained central to the talks. Christian IV chose to discuss the matter with Anstruther in private during the negotiations, perhaps wishing to talk more candidly than he could in open session. The other conference delegates included Frederick V, Christian of Lüneburg and Frederick Ulric of Brunswick-Wolfenbüttel who all had differing agendas to that of the Stuart-Oldenburg alliance. Increased military action was seen by many as the only response to the reverses suffered at White Mountain and the fall of Heidelberg. The

[40] Spottiswoode, *History of the Church of Scotland*, 541.
[41] For more information on the raising of cash from Scottish burghs, see *RPCS*, XII, 1619-1622, 591-593, 689-691,704 and 747.
[42] The origin of this money is usually ascribed to James VI & I, but Anstruther also had instructions to receive that same amount from Queen Sofia of Denmark, Elizabeth's grandmother. The Danish money was to be sent via English merchants to Amsterdam. See PRO SP75/5, ff.241 and 253. Anstruther to Sir George Calvert, 31 March and 12 April 1621. Anstruther also noted James's instructions to pass on £20,000 to Elizabeth in his 'Relation of Expenses', SP75/5, f.261, October 1621.
[43] *Danmark-Norges Traktater*, III, 375.

convention agreed to raise an army of 30,000 men and to form a new Protestant League to restore Frederick V to his hereditary possessions in the Palatinate. Christian IV asked Anstruther to inform him how many men James had ready to contribute to this force, to which Anstruther could not reply. He did, however, suggest that if Frederick V would submit himself totally to James's counsel, the king would be prepared to commit a large force if all peaceful avenues had been exhausted.[44] In the end, the scheme to raise 30,000 men amongst the Segeberg allies failed since it depended on major support from Great Britain and the continued resistance of the Protestant Union to General Ambrosio Spinola, commander of the Spanish army in Flanders. The financial obligation from James could not be fulfilled and the conference failed to meet its objectives. Despite this setback, the House of Oldenburg agreed a treaty with the House of Stuart on 29 April 1621, undoubtedly on the back of the private negotiations between Anstruther and Christian IV.[45]

Christian IV's vigorous diplomatic endeavours also brought additional political dividends. In July Hamburg finally submitted to Danish terms for over-lordship and in September Christian's son Frederik was accepted as coadjutor of Bremen. Verden followed suit in November, giving the Danes political control of the rivers Elbe and Weser.[46] But the alliance with James encountered problems since he failed to effectively pursue the agreed course of action. Throughout the summer of 1621, James still hoped for peace in Europe through some rather complex, and perhaps unrealistic, diplomacy. Christian IV again sent Andrew Sinclair to London to press James into a firm commitment for military aid.[47] The Prince of Wales also sent his own envoy, John Wentworth, to negotiate with Christian on a supplementary mission.[48]

James's apparently contradictory attitudes over the Palatinate made him quite unpopular in Britain.[49] While emphasising his desire for peace,

---

[44] PRO SP75/5, f.235-8. Anstruther to Secretary of State, 10 March 1621; *KCFB*, footnotes 186-9.

[45] *Danmark-Norges Traktater*, III, 380-411. It is interesting to note that this document was signed by Scots representing both parties: Andrew Sinclair for Denmark-Norway, and the Dukes of Lennox and Hamilton, among others, for Great Britain. Apparently Sir Robert Anstruther had impressed Christian IV sufficiently during his negotiations that he invested the Scot with the Crown of Denmark-Norway for the duration of the celebratory festivities. See A. H. Millar, *Fife: Pictorial and Historical: It's people, Burghs, Castles and Mansions* (Edinburgh & Glasgow, 1895), 406-407.

[46] Munck, *Seventeenth Century Europe*, 13.

[47] PRO SP75/5, f.235-8. Anstruther to Secretary of State, 10 March 1621.

[48] *KCFB*, I, 215-9, Christian IV to Christian Friis, 2 July 1621.

[49] One of his Scottish knights, Sir John Ramsay, was apparently so angry at his policy that he allegedly declared that; 'if his majesty did not do what he professed for his religion he would throw out of the pulpit the first preacher whom he heard call him Defender of the Faith'. See *CSPV*, XVII, 1621-3, 56. Girolamo Lando, 28 May 1621.

he also appeared to recognise the need for war to defend his daughter's interests in Germany. This was not helped by the fact that the king and his English Parliament were divided on how best to proceed.[50] James quite clearly saw that the Bohemian crisis was a political as well as a religious matter. On the one hand, paternal feelings and a desire to support the Protestant cause inclined him to the Palatinate. On the other he remained opposed to the political principles behind the Bohemian revolt and could not subscribe to the contempt for legality that marked Frederick's conduct and continued intransigence. James believed his son-in-law's attitude spoiled the prospects of a settlement which the 1621 Vienna negotiations between Frederick V and Ferdinand II had promised.[51]

The English Parliament simply did not see the issues in the same terms as the king. According to Michael Roberts, he was up against 'an ignorant and obstreperous parliament, exacerbated by misgovernment and petty tyrannies, which thought only of a freebooting war in the old style and [which] kept a tight grip on supplies'.[52] This is, of course, quite a partisan account, but one that undoubtedly reflects the perspective of the king. Representatives of the English Parliament claimed they wanted stronger action in support of the Palatinate, yet seemed to place obstacles in the way of the king's desire to achieve it. They pushed for stronger action to be taken against Spain rather than supporting the northern Protestant league. James viewed foreign policy as his personal field and still held out hopes of a Spanish marriage to solve the Palatinate problem diplomatically.[53] The king furthered his control of foreign policy by concluding the treaty of confederation between Denmark-Norway and Great Britain in November 1621.[54] In the same month, members of the English Parliament gave James their conditions for providing the finances for his various schemes, including his unequivocal support for Frederick V on their terms. Rather than do so, he rebuked his southern Parliament for speaking ill of the king of Spain and debating foreign policy.[55] In retaliation, the English Parliament demanded an open stand against Spain, which enraged James so much that he dismissed them, leaving himself in a political and diplomatic quandary. He continued to

[50] Howatt, *Stuart and Cromwellian foreign policy*, 28; Russell, *The Crisis of Parliaments*, 294-296.
[51] Roberts, *Gustavus Adolphus*, I, 200; Russell, *The Crisis of Parliaments*, 291.
[52] Roberts, *Gustavus Adolphus*, I, 185-186.
[53] Polisensky, *The Thirty Years' War*, 163; Parker, *The Thirty Years' War*, 65; Howatt, *Stuart and Cromwellian foreign policy*, 33; Russell, *The Crisis of Parliaments*, 294-296; *RPCS*, XII, 1619-1622, 633, footnote.
[54] PRO SP75/5, f.262. Confirmation of the treaty with Denmark, 11 November 1621.
[55] Polisensky, *The Thirty Years' War*, 163; Russell, *The Crisis of Parliaments*, 294-296.

receive particularly strong remonstrances from his English MPs and privy councillors over his course of action. Despite these, the same people would not allow the king the resources to carry out stronger measures when he proposed them. For example, when James submitted a plan to collect 14,000 foot and 4,000 horse for the defence of the Palatinate, his English councillors whittled the number down by almost half.[56] James once more turned to Christian IV and begged his intervention for his daughter's family concluding that;

> the matter seems to have reached such a point that force must be repelled by force and that, which cannot be preserved by friendly and peaceful means, must be protected by arms, we earnestly implore your serene highness to provide aid to our son-in-law; we ask this on behalf of our mutual and many-sided relationship and on behalf of that bond of nature which exists between our serene daughter and her children and, finally on behalf of the justice of his cause as much as its necessity, whether we consider religion or the political situation of Germany, so that he might be better able to defend his remaining territory and regain and recover what has been taken from him.[57]

His request was not totally in vain but events were unfolding which caused serious concerns for the Protestant allies. This support took on ever increasing urgency when, in 1622 Spinola's forces and the soldiers of the Catholic League under Tilly moved in to attack the remainder of the Palatinate. King James had agreed to the sending of more troops from the British Isles once it had become clear that the Spaniards had no intention of leaving the Palatinate unoccupied. The Palatinate forces now consisted of the armies of Count Mansfeld (including Gray's regiment), the Margrave of Baden-Durlach and Christian of Brunswick, Elizabeth Stuart's cousin.[58] Baden-Durlach's army were quickly defeated by Tilly at Wimpfen and Brunswick suffered the same fate at Hochst. The English regiments found themselves in great difficulty with many soldiers deserting and others dying of cold and disease in their garrisons.[59] In Mannheim, Sir Horace Vere received orders to surrender

---

[56] *CSPV*, XVII, 1621-1623, 197-200. Girolamo Lando, 6 January 1622.
[57] Meldrum, *The Letters of King James*, 225-6. James VI to Christian IV, 31 December 1621.
[58] Mansfeld, *More News From the Palatinate*.
[59] A. M., *A Relation of the Passages of our English Companies from time to time, since their first departure from England* (London, March 1621/22), 1 and 4; Anon., *Certaine Letters*, B.2 and B.3.

his forces by mid October 1622.[60] With that capitulation, the Palatinate was effectively lost to Frederick V. Maurits of Nassau also found himself unable to help his nephew through internal Dutch politics and personal physical weakness. Only the Anglo-Scottish garrison at Frankenthal clung on until the following year.[61]

By the end of 1622 some 8,000 soldiers had left the British Isles to engage in the war.[62] Rumours that Mansfeld had disbanded his forces were quashed by Colonel Gray who sought to increase this number. He returned to Britain to levy 3,000 more men and told the king he needed £100,000 for the support of Mansfeld's troops, including the British regiment at Frankenthal. According to the ambassador of Venice, Gray had been told he would not get this support and so he returned to the continent.[63] However, in November Sir James Spens informed Axel Oxenstierna that Gray had authority to use an army of 6,000 fresh British troops to reinforce Bergen-op-Zoom *en route* to Mansfeld's army.[64] It appears these did not arrive immediately, but Mansfeld did not give up hope of support from King James. In December he sent Colonel Seton to negotiate with him, while also sending one Colonel Carpson to ask for direct assistance from Christian IV.[65]

There was no immediate prospect of support from either Denmark or Britain. The allies of Frederick V had been so badly thrashed militarily that he was ready to renounce his claims to Bohemia if he was allowed to keep the Palatinate. In this piece of political backsliding he had the full support of James and Christian IV even after he had lost his territories.[66] Frederick had seriously misjudged the military and political situation in Europe, and Ferdinand II was in no mood for reconciliation. An Imperial embassy, led by Count Schwarzenberg, arrived in London to explain the Emperor's desire for peace.[67] In reality this mission was

[60]   Polisensky, *The Thirty Years' War*, 164; *More News From the Palatinate* (London, 1622), 18.
[61]   Israel, *The Dutch Republic*, 482-483; A. W. Ward et al. eds, *The Cambridge Modern History, IV; The Thirty Years' War* (Cambridge, 1907), 83.
[62]   *CSPV*, XVI, 1619-1621, 327 and 617. Girolamo Lando, 9 July 1620 and March 1621.
[63]   *CSPV*, XVII, 294-6. Girolamo Lando, 22 April and 16 June 1622.
[64]   DCJS, 188, Spens to Axel Oxenstierna, 3 November 1622.
[65]   *CSPV*, XVII, 532-3. Christofforo Surian, Venetian secretary in The Netherlands, to Venice. 26 December 1622.
[66]   See *KCFB*, I, 382-387, Christian IV to Count Oldenburg (draft), 8 July 1624.
[67]   Sir Robert Anstruther, *The Oration or Substance of that which was delivered before his Majestie of Great Brittaine by the Emperours Ambassador, the high and excellent Lord, Count Schwarzenburg, at his day of Audience, being the seventh of Aprill in the Parliament Chamber. This is the True Copie of the Ambassadours speech, delivered by him in high Dutch; and repeated in English by Sir Robert Anstruther Knight, Gentleman of his Majesties Privie Chamber* (London, 1622).

simply to let King James know that Ferdinand had the upper hand in Germany and did not need to negotiate. This became clear when, at the Diet of Ratisbon in February 1623, the Emperor transferred the Palatinate Electorate to Maximillian of Bavaria while Bohemia became a Habsburg territory. James could do little to alter the situation other than to write to Christian IV urging him to pressure Saxony not to recognise the transfer.[68] Under a separate agreement made with the Infanta Isabella, King James ordered the Anglo-Scottish garrison to withdraw from Frankenthal for a period of 18 months while a diplomatic settlement could be reached.[69] Gray arrived back from The Netherlands the following month whereupon James confirmed his permission to levy 6,000 more troops in Scotland. The ongoing Spanish-Dutch truce meant that recruiting had to be undertaken quietly and schemes were hatched to try to make it look as if the levies were going to the service of The Netherlands or Denmark-Norway. These complicated arrangements continued until August. Although James was keen on the project, the Council of the United Provinces were not.[70] The undertaking was subsequently shelved until the following year. With the military option once again stalled, James thereafter returned to the difficult search for a diplomatic solution, and again a Spanish marriage alliance returned to the top of the agenda. This culminated in the infamous, and ultimately futile, covert expedition to Madrid by Prince Charles and the Duke of Buckingham in 1623 under the guardianship of James Hay, Earl of Carlisle.[71]

Hope for European Protestants now shifted firmly to the Scandinavian powers: Denmark-Norway and Sweden. As a member of the Lower Saxon Circle Christian IV was bound to be drawn into the German hostilities as they moved northwards. In February 1623, the officers of the Circle forbade troops to pass through its territory in a bid to preserve its neutrality. It is unlikely that many people, especially Christian, believed that such neutrality could be maintained. He therefore took a definite step towards war when he persuaded his *Rigsråd* to approve the levy of troops to repel any attack on the Lower Saxon Circle. The

---

[68] DRA, TKUA England A 1, 2. James VI to Christian IV, 20 February 1623; Meldrum, *The Letters of King James*, 231; Russell, *The Crisis of Parliaments*, 297-298.

[69] Ward et al., *The Cambridge Modern History*, IV, 83.

[70] *CSPV*, XVII, letter nos. 800, 824, 845; *CSPV*, XVIII, letters 2, 15 and 20.

[71] Carlisle was sent in haste to Paris to ensure that no harm came to the Prince as he travelled through France on his way to Spain. Carlisle accompanied Charles and Buckingham all the way to Madrid and acted in the capacity of ambassador extraordinary while there. See *DNB*, IX, 266; Bell, *Diplomatic Representatives*, 106 and 259. The correspondence of Charles and Buckingham from and regarding Spain is contained in Petrie, *The Letters of King Charles*, 7-31; Thomson, *The Chamberlain Letters*, 299-318.

military and political situation deteriorated dramatically for the Protestant princes when General Tilly's Catholic army defeated Christian of Brunswick on 27 July at Stadtlohn. Frederick V found that, without sustained help from his German allies or the prospect of Stuart or Danish intervention, he could do little but sue for peace and therefore concluded an armistice with the Emperor in August 1623. The Protestant Union was finally ruined, and in an effort to attract a new sponsor, Frederick V offered to make over his army to Gustav II Adolf of Sweden. There followed many difficult negotiations involving Spens, Anstruther and Sinclair shuttling between London and the Scandinavian monarchs in an attempt to bring Denmark-Norway and Sweden into an alliance with Great Britain.

In autumn 1623, Gustav II Adolf encouraged the formation of yet another Protestant League independent of Denmark-Norway and backed by Swedish arms. It was hoped that British forces in Dutch service might be used as a focal point for any future alliance and the following year the Earls of Oxford and Southampton raised a new force of 6,000 Englishmen for the Dutch army. This force quickly disintegrated after both leaders died of disease within months of arriving. Thereafter the remaining British regiments at Breda, under the command of Sir Horace Vere and Sir Charles Morgan, surrendered to General Spínola.[72] By 1624, the Swedes looked as though they had a clear run to take the place of Britain or Denmark-Norway as champions of the Protestant cause by offering direct intervention in Germany. The Swedish proposal was accompanied by very specific terms. Gustav II Adolf proposed to provide 12 regiments of foot, each of 1,184 men, totalling 14,208 soldiers plus 2,000 horse. In return, the allies were asked to provide 24 regiments of foot to the same numbers totalling 28,416 soldiers and 6,000 horse. In addition, the Swedish offer demanded four months' pay for the allied troops in advance amounting to £311,664, while Danzig had to remain neutral.[73]

Palatine exiles and European Protestants took heart at the prospect of this new 'Evangelical League' and Stuart envoys continued to organise support against the Emperor and Philip IV of Spain. Sir James Spens

---

[72] *APC, 1623-1625*, 249-250 and 258; *CSPD*, 1623-1625, 217, 248, 251, 267, 281 and 295; *DNB*, XX, 235 [Oxford]; *DNB*, XXI, 1060 [Henry Wriothesly, 3rd Earl of Southampton]; *DNB*, V, 890 [Essex]; *DNB*, XX, 237-238 [Vere] and *DNB*, XIII, 910 [Morgan]; Israel, *The Dutch Republic*, 484.

[73] PRO SP75/6, f.32. The military proposals of the Kings of Sweden and Denmark, anno 1624. The Swedes would also provide 66 artillery pieces, 82,800lb of cannon powder, 120,240lb of musket powder and 180,360lb of match; Roberts, *Gustavus Adolphus*, I, 238. Roberts estimated that Gustav II Adolf's requirements would probably have cost England [*sic*] £400,000 per annum, presumably after equipment and transportation were taken into account.

travelled first to Sweden and then to The Hague in his capacity as both British and Swedish ambassador, although the Dutch were in no position to help anyone in 1624.[74] Sir Robert Anstruther, acting as a dual British and Danish ambassador, visited Frederick V at The Hague. Anstruther's instructions from King James allowed him to negotiate with Christian IV, Gustav II Adolf, John George of Saxony (now vacillating in his loyalty to Ferdinand) and the princes of the Lower Saxon Circle. According to his instructions Christian IV should be the focus of northern European support for Frederick V. He was further charged to inform Christian that James wanted a particular union with the Danish king first and that Sweden, the Dutch and French were also being courted to help him.[75] Already, by March 1624, the Earl of Carlisle had been dispatched to Paris to join Lord Kensington on a mission to secure the marriage of Prince Charles to Henrietta-Maria of France.[76] By this time, Cardinal Richelieu had re-entered the French Council of State which pressed stricter terms on the negotiators. A French alliance with the Stuart kingdoms was provisionally agreed by June, although the treaty was not confirmed until September.[77]

Despite the French agreement, Christian IV had well-founded reservations about the Stuart proposals for going to war in the *Reich*. He pointed out that he and his sons in the German Bishoprics were more vulnerable than either Great Britain or Sweden as he could easily be attacked by the forces of the Catholic powers. Sweden and Britain, he argued, were relatively safe since the Emperor did not have a navy.[78] Anstruther also informed Spens that the mistrust the Scandinavian kings had of one another was far from being resolved. Despite his anxiety, Christian promised not to make a final decision on the proposals until Anstruther returned from his German embassy. Gustav II Adolf asked Adolf Frederick of Mecklenburg to ascertain exactly what Anstruther's instructions were in order that he could better understand British

---

[74] PRO SP 95/2, ff.86-88. Instructions to Spens, 6 June 1624; SRA, Anglica VIII, f.54. James Spens to Gustav II Adolf from The Hague, 17 December 1624; Israel, *The Dutch Republic*, 484-485.

[75] PRO SP75/5, f.312-5. Instructions to Sir Robert Anstruther, June 1624; E. Marquard, *Danske Gesandter og Gesandtskabs Personale indtil 1914* (Copenhagen, 1952), 27; Anstruther's orders to support Christian IV over Gustav II Adolf were well known to the Swedes. See *RAOSB*, III, 31. Axel Oxenstierna to James Spens, 10 February 1625. See also T. Sehested, *Cantsler Christen Thomesen Sehested* (Copenhagen, 1894), 33.

[76] *DNB*, IX, 266; *CSPD*, 1623-1625, 203, 207, 243 and 255; Bell, *Diplomatic Representatives*, 106.

[77] *CSPD*, 1623-1625, 269 and 346. 'Lord Carlisle is well received in France and his overtures embraced', Dudley Carlton to Sir Dudley Carlton, 7 June 1624. Dudley Carlton to John Chamberlain, 30 September 1624; Polisensky, *The Thirty Years War*, 166; *DNB*, IX, 266.

[78] *KCFB*, I, 382-387.

intentions.[79] These were beginning to take on a more serious form to European observers who were well aware of a massive British expeditionary force assembling throughout the winter of 1624.

Sir Andrew Gray returned to London in 1624 to organise some 4,000 Scots who were to form part of an army of 13,000 British soldiers for Mansfeld's army.[80] John Chamberlain noted that the Scottish regiments were to be commanded by Colonels Gray and Ramsay. The four English regiments would be under Lord Cromwell, Sir Charles Rich, Sir John Burgh and Viscount Doncaster. Elizabeth of Bohemia seemed most delighted by the news of this new army when she wrote to Sir Thomas Roe announcing 'some certain good news out of England where there is therteene thousand men a levying for Mansfeld. What they are to doe I know not for the king and I are utterlie ignorant of all, though they say it is for our service'.[81]

Most reports record that the soldiers were pitifully supplied in England before boarding ship. John Chamberlain further described them as little more than raw and pressed men who lived off the land in lieu of proper support.[82] Many of the soldiers, trapped in disease infested ships, died of malnutrition and infection before they could be landed in mainland Europe. Indeed, historians usually conclude that the expedition was totally wiped out.[83] The Swedish agent in Denmark-Norway, however, provided evidence of 6,000 men landing at Vlissingen in the United Provinces. Here they were joined by 2,000 cavalry under Christian of Halberstadt in March 1625 and a steady trickle of Scots and English volunteers thereafter.[84] Yet, despite this Stuart military presence, serious hopes for European Protestants centred firmly on the northern powers.

Elizabeth Stuart wrote that 'The king of Sweden offers as much as can be desired; I would my uncle woulde doe soe to; but he is more

[79] SRA, Anglica V. Sir Robert Anstruther to Sir James Spens, 1 August 1624; G. Styffe ed, *Konung Gustaf II Adolfs Skrifter* (Stockholm, 1861), 445-467. Gustav II Adolf to Adolf Frederick of Mecklenburg, 12 October 1624.
[80] E. Thomson ed, *The Chamberlain Letters: A selection of the letters of John Chamberlain concerning life in England from 1597-1626* (Toronto, 1966), 333-334, 9 October 1624.
[81] Mrs Benger, *Memoirs of Elizabeth Stuart, Queen of Bohemia, Daughter of King James the First* (2 vols, London, 1825), II, 233. Copy of a letter from Elizabeth Stuart to Sir Thomas Roe.
[82] Thomson, *The Chamberlain Letters*, 335-338, 18 December 1624.
[83] Howat, *Stuart and Cromwellian Foreign Policy*, 33; Grant, *Memoirs of Sir John Hepburn*, 22. Grant quotes Balfour as saying that most died of cold and hunger.
[84] Tandrup, *Svensk agent ved Sundet*, 546-547 and 550-551. Anders Svensson to Axel Oxenstierna/Gustav II Adolph, 14 and 31 March 1625; *RPCS*, second series, 1625-1627, 50-52.

backwards than so neere a kinsman should be'.[85] Her statement was undoubtedly based on the various reports of support offered by the Scandinavian kings. But despite her scepticism it was her uncle Christian who was the first of the northern monarchs to try his hand against the Emperor. When Anstruther returned to Copenhagen in December 1624, it was to conclude an agreement relating to further subsidies and troops for the proposed alliance.[86] The coalition was set to include George William of Brandenburg, Gustav II Adolf's brother-in-law, and this must have raised hopes for Swedish participation. King James and Christian IV thereafter selected Anstruther as their joint ambassador to John George of Saxony to discuss the political options.[87] Despite continued warnings from his ministers, Christian prepared for war and offered an army at once if James would add 7,000 men to his 5,000, to be built up to 30,000 men with their German allies.[88] Compared with Gustav II Adolf's more expensive proposal, this appeared a financially more attractive offer for the Stuart king. By March 1625, Gustav II Adolf received letters from Christian IV and Anstruther implying strong support for the cause and urging Swedish participation, although the Swedish king remained deeply suspicious of Danish intentions.[89]

Gustav II Adolf was right to be sceptical and Oxenstierna wrote to Spens informing him of the imminent intervention of Christian IV in the European conflict.[90] By the end of the month Swedish plans were formally rejected and James accepted Christian's terms. The Danish scheme was only supposed to cost the Stuart kingdoms £180,000 at most. This was an important consideration for a government which was committed to spending £360,000 as a subsidy to the king of Denmark, £240,000 per annum to Mansfeld, £100,000 to the Dutch and £300,000 on the fleet, out of a parliamentary grant of £300,000 in total.[91] To finalise these measures, a general congress of Protestant powers was scheduled to meet in The Hague in April 1625. Christian at last felt that he had reached a trustworthy agreement with the Stuart kingdoms and he

---

[85]   Benger, *Memoirs of the Queen of Bohemia*, 2, 224.
[86]   PRO SP75/5, f.349. An abstract of Anstruther's negotiations in Denmark, Holstein and Germany, 1624; Sehested, *Cantsler Christen Thomesen Sehested*, 34.
[87]   Marquard, *Danske Gesandter*, 27; *CSPV*, XVIII, 1623-1625, 487-490.
[88]   PRO SP75/5, f.349. An abstract of Anstruther's negotiations in Denmark, Holstein and Germany, anno 1624; PRO SP75/6, f.32. The military proposals of the Kings of Sweden and Denmark, anno 1624.
[89]   *RAOSB*, III, 47. Axel Oxenstierna to Ludvig Camerarius, 13 March 1625.
[90]   *RAOSB*, III, 47. Axel Oxenstierna to James Spens, 13 March 1625.
[91]   Roberts, *Gustavus Adolphus*, I, 238-242; Russell, *The Crisis of Parliaments*, 300. The fleet to be 'loaned' to the Bohemians included 12 royal ships and 100 armed merchantmen and had to be accompanied by 15,000 troops plus sailors. See SRA, Anglica 5. Spens to Axel Oxenstierna, 24 February 1625.

believed that Sweden and Brandenburg also intended to be involved. Denmark-Norway, it seemed, had seized the military leadership of Protestant Europe back from Sweden.[92] In the same month as the meeting of the Lower Saxon Circle, James VI & I died and Charles Stuart became indisputably responsible for foreign policy. His personal agenda would ensure that Stuart-Oldenburg relations were significantly remodelled during the early years of his reign.

At the outset of the Thirty Years' War, Stuart-Oldenburg relations were at a low point brought on by the marital split between King James and Anna and a host of mercantile disputes. However, the troubles of the Elector Palatine and his family, coupled with Christian's ambitions in Germany, combined push the two royal houses back into closer alliance through their confederation of 1621. That treaty was only one of many that sought to bring a peaceful solution to the troubles in Europe. King James consistently tried to avoid Habsburg enmity and sent James Hay, Earl of Carlisle and three other Stuart ambassadors to Ferdinand before concluding his new treaty with Denmark-Norway.[93] Thereafter he looked in vain to Madrid for a solution to his daughter's problems.

The Spanish conditions for a Stuart marriage proved impossible for James to meet and his dreams of permanent peace in Europe were shattered. His policy, as Michael Roberts put it 'was not without a good deal of common sense, but to the Protestant world it inevitably appeared as recreant, heartless and stupid'.[94] It has been argued that the reason for the debate between the king and the English Parliament was that James preferred to debate rather than to fight a war that England could not afford, but that misrepresents the facts.[95] Between 1620 and March 1625 James oversaw the raising and dispatching of over 25,500 soldiers to the continent, either in Bohemian and Dutch service or the various armies commanded by Count Mansfeld.[96] That was a larger actual commitment

[92]   *KCFB*, I, 420-421. Draft of a memorial of intent, 10 April 1625. The Western powers hoped that Gustav II Adolf and Christian IV would join the fight together. However, Gustav II Adolf believed that if Christian IV thought he could defeat the Empire, then he should prove it, allowing him to focus on his own Baltic ambitions for a time. He told Oxenstierna he would back Christian's plan and that he would step in if the Dane failed. See *RAOSB*, III, 47 Axel Oxenstierna to Ludvig Camerarius, 9 April 1625.

[93]   See particularly the entry for James Hay in the *DNB*, IX, 267; *CSPV*, XV, 1617-1619. Letter nos. 515, 587, and 600.

[94]   Roberts, *Gustavus Adolphus*, I, 222.

[95]   C. Russell, 'The Foreign Policy Debate in the House of Commons in 1621', in *The Historical Journal*, vol. 20, no. 2 (1977), 309.

[96]   *APC*, *1623-1625*, 395 and 398; *CPSD*, *1623-1625*, 418, 464 and 551. King James to Andrew Gray, 24 December 1624.

than the two armies offered in 1624 by Christian IV and Gustav II Adolf combined.[97] Professor Polisensky noted that while the English Parliament strove to pursue its own foreign agenda against the wishes of the king, 'the representatives of British public opinion were Gray's soldiers'.[98] Those men came from a country less affluent than England but with a much stronger bond with the House of Stuart. They consistently supported the war effort in a way their neighbours in England simply did not match. Their involvement challenges the prevalent historical notions about Stuart commitment to the war in Germany and show that 'British' and 'English' involvement were not the same thing. This was true also in the sphere of diplomacy.

In the complex realm of European international relations, Robert Anstruther, Andrew Sinclair, James Spens and James Hay represented the premier league of Stuart diplomats. The first three persevered in shoring up old alliances and finding new partners among the northern Protestant powers. Hay found himself engaged in repeated excursions to France, the Spanish Netherlands and the main Habsburg Courts in Spain and Germany looking for solutions acceptable to the Stuart Court. In both northern and southern Europe these men plied their craft, often hindered by the disunity that resulted from conflicting Scottish, English and Stuart agendas. While their task had been hard under James's rule, the accession of Charles I would bring the alliance to breaking point

[97]   These two forces would have equalled 21,208 men. Gustav II Adolf proposed to provide 12 regiments of foot, each of 1,184 men, totalling 14,208 soldiers plus 2,000 horse. Christian IV offered an army of only 5,000 men. See PRO SP75/6, f.32. The military proposals of the Kings of Sweden and Denmark, 1624; PRO SP75/5, f.349. An abstract of Sir Robert Anstruther's negotiations in Denmark, Holstein and Germany, 1624.
[98]   Polisensky, *Anglie a Bilá hora*, 203.

CHAPTER THREE

The Dour Years: Stuart-Oldenburg Relations
1625-1639

The ongoing negotiations in The Hague throughout 1625 cast the die in terms of Danish-Norwegian and British participation in the war the Danes refer to as *Kejserkrig*. Charles I hoped that despite his father's rejection of the earlier Swedish proposals, Gustav II Adolf could be persuaded to join the impending alliance. For the next four years Spens, Anstruther and several other diplomats including Sir Robert Primrose of Culross travelled to Scandinavia with the purpose of bringing Gustav II Adolf into the 'Common Cause'.[1] Charles was mistaken if he thought he could persuade the Swedish king, whose jealousy and doubts over Christian IV's military ability persisted, but undeterred he continued negotiations with the Danes and the Dutch despite Swedish reluctance. By May 1625, Charles committed himself to spending approximately £30,000 per month as a contribution to the military development of Christian IV's army. Indeed some estimates claim that Charles's total expenditure by the end of May 1625 equalled about £1,000,000.[2] What becomes clearer on reading such sources as the *Register of the Privy Council of Scotland* is that these financial obligations actually concerned all the Stuart kingdoms rather than simply England.[3] The Scots were taxed for levying and transporting troops to the continent, ordered to raise taxes to bolster coastal defences and encouraged to find money for the provision of ships and mariners.[4] In November 1625, Charles I completed alliance negotiations with Denmark-Norway and the United Provinces obliged him to pay Christian IV £30,000 per month and the Dutch a further £5,000. An initial instalment of £46,000 had previously been delivered to Christian IV by Sir Robert Anstruther in June.[5] Due to

---

[1]   *RAOSB*, III, 47 and 55. Axel Oxenstierna to Ludvig Camerarius, 13 March 1625 and 9 April 1625; PRO SP 95/2, ff.165-168. Charles I instructions to James Spens, June 1627. For Primrose, see Sir James Balfour-Paul, *The Scots Peerage* (8 vols., Edinburgh, 1904-1911), VII, 213.

[2]   PRO SP 75/6, f.72. Instructions to Anstruther, 10 May 1625; Sehested, *Cantsler Christen Thomesen Sehested*, 44-46; B. Coward, *Early Stuart England, 1603-1640* (London, 1980), 137-138.

[3]   P. Hume-Brown states that 'as part of the United Kingdom Scotland had to contribute its own share in these undertakings, and much of the business of the Council had consisted in raising levies, and placing the country in a state of defence against invasion'. *RPCS*, second series, III, 1629-30, vii.

[4]   *RPCS*, second series, I, 1625-1627, xi-lxxxii, 362-363, 550-553, 578-587 and 599-600; II, 1627-1628, ix-xiii.

[5]   PRO SP 75/6, ff.58 and 72. Instructions to Anstruther, 10 May 1625; *KCFB*, II, 149.

Charles's increasing problems in raising revenue, this payment proved to be his only large cash contribution to the Danish cause. As is revealed in chapter nine below, in terms of the manpower he committed to the war, Charles exceeded his treaty obligations by a significant margin.

The supply of men and the supply of money both involved specific sets of problems. Financial expenditure caused continual friction between Charles and his English Parliamentarians who refused to co-operate with his budget proposals. Rather than approve Charles's plans for prosecuting the war, they sought to give the monarch two subsidies totalling £140,000.[6] The English Commons believed that the foreign policy of the monarch and the Duke of Buckingham was misguided and mishandled and they were quick to point this out. As a result, Charles dissolved his second English Parliament in June 1626 and a third was not called until March 1628. Christian IV could also see that any conflict between Charles and any of his kingdoms would result in a loss of revenue for the king and, therefore, his ongoing commitments to Denmark-Norway. To compound the problems of supporting the war between Denmark-Norway and the Empire, trouble broke out between the Stuart kingdoms and Spain in 1625, and France by 1627.

The Franco-Spanish Diversions, 1625-1630

English Parliamentarians were not the only British subjects to be suspicious of the Duke of Buckingham's foreign policy. Sir James Spens wrote a letter to Gustav II Adolf of Sweden in September 1626 in which he claimed that Buckingham's policy had been engineered to bring down Christian IV while maintaining the appearance of supporting him.[7] Buckingham, he claimed, led the movement seeking to prevent the payment of funds required by Christian to maintain his army. Spens further alleged that Buckingham hoped that the starving of finance and the diversion of military manpower would force the Danish king to sue for a peace with Ferdinand II on his own account and thus allow Charles I to accuse his uncle of breaking the Treaty of The Hague. The background to these extraordinary claims lay in two ill-fated British

Christian IV to Christian Friis, 30 June 1625; PRO SP75/5, f.262. Confirmation of the treaty with Denmark, 11 November 1621; PRO SP75/7, f.66. Ratification of the treaty with Denmark, 9 December 1625; *Danmark-Norges Traktater*, III, 620-637. Alliance between Great Britain, Denmark-Norway and the United Provinces signed in The Hague, 29 November/9 December 1625; Lockhart, *Denmark in the Thirty Years' War*, 125.

6 *RPCS*, second series, I, 1625-1627, 72-73; Coward, *Stuart England*, 138; E. A. Beller, 'The Military Expedition of Sir Charles Morgan to Germany, 1627-9', in *English Historical Review*, XLIII (1928), 528.

7 SRA, Anglica 3, f.64. Spens to Gustav II Adolf, 10 September 1626; Sehested, *Cantsler Christen Thomesen Sehested*, 44-45.

military expeditions of 1625-1626.

On 8 September 1625, at a time when Christian IV had committed himself to war with Ferdinand II, Charles I and the United Provinces concluded the Treaty of Southampton. That document provided for an offensive alliance against Philip IV of Spain and ensured additional British military intervention on the continent over and above existing obligations to Denmark. In Charles's mind, this did not detract in any way from his guarantee to support his uncle against the Emperor. He viewed all his continental campaigns as part of one conflict and considered them useful in diverting Habsburg forces from the German theatre.[8] In the month following the treaty with the Dutch some 80 vessels with 10,000 soldiers and 5,000 sailors under Viscount Wimbledon sailed for Cadiz and a singularly unsuccessful attack against Spain. The failure of this venture is attributed to bad leadership, a lack of supplies and disease. Whatever the causes, Charles I had been seriously humiliated.[9]

The frustration caused in Britain by the defeat of the Spanish expedition was compounded by deteriorating British relations with France. Any prospect of the marriage of Henrietta-Maria to Charles Stuart leading to a stronger alliance between the British and French Crowns was short-lived. Stuart policy became neither more predictable nor reliable because of it and, if anything, became even more confused.[10] A somewhat chaotic expedition had left Britain in 1625 with the task of helping the French government against the Huguenots whom they besieged at La Rochelle.[11] Despite this support for the French government, the Duke of Buckingham deliberately antagonised the French due to a snub he had received at the hands of the new Queen, Henrietta-Maria, and so sought revenge against them. There were further strains relating to the laws concerning Roman Catholicism in England which both Louis XIII and Cardinal Richelieu wanted Charles to reform as part of the recent marriage treaty.[12] Neither Charles nor his councillors would entertain such changes and, to make matters worse, the La Rochelle expedition achieved little other than to irritate the French

---

[8]   PRO SP 75/8, f.213. Instructions to Edward Clarke, 27 July 1627; Sharpe, *The Personal Rule*, 66; *RPCS*, second series, I, 1625-1627, lxxv. Here the comment is made that the sum total of the wars against Spain and the Imperialists was called generally by the name of the 'War for Religion'.

[9]   *RPCS*, second series, I, 1625-1627, xxxix and 209-219; Roberts, *Gustavus Adolphus*, I, 249; Howatt, *Stuart and Cromwellian Foreign Policy*, 34; J. H. Elliot, 'Spain and the War', in G. Parker ed, *The Thirty Years' War* (London, 1997), 92.

[10] Munck, *Seventeenth Century Europe*, 12.

[11] E. L. Petersen, 'The Danish Intermezzo', in Parker, *The Thirty Years' War*, 68-69.

[12] *RPCS*, second series, I, 1625-1627, lxi-lxii; Howatt, *Stuart and Cromwellian Foreign Policy*, 35.

government. As a result of these tensions, public opinion in England turned against the Catholic French government.[13]

Both the pro-French and anti-Spanish expeditions that left Britain between 1625-1626 had hurt the international prestige of the Stuart-British government. But their true shortcoming, from Christian IV's perspective, lay in the fact that Denmark-Norway had been left under-resourced in northern Germany leading, he believed, to his defeat at Lutter in 1626.[14] And worse was still to come. Through a combination of poor judgement and mismanagement Charles I had allowed the Duke of Buckingham's foreign policy to drive France into an alliance with Spain. It became obvious very quickly to Britain's Danish allies that this would lead to war between Britain and France. The Danish Crown Prince, Christian (V), on hearing that armed conflict was inevitable, observed that this would be a 'hard knock' for Denmark if it could not be quickly resolved.[15]

In late 1626, James Spens had clearly stated that Buckingham had a preference for war against one of England's traditional enemies rather than one in support of Britain's main ally. Within months of his letter to the Swedish king, a second expedition under the Duke of Buckingham departed for La Rochelle, this time against the French government and in support of the Huguenots. Charles committed £14,000 in cash and victuals to this enterprise while a mixed British and Irish army of 6,500 men were to be assembled for the campaign. Four hundred troops were to be dispatched in the early summer with 2,000 English troops following on under Buckingham's command. These were joined by a further 2,000 soldiers 'out of Scotland' under Lord Morton and William Balfour and 2,000 more levied in Ireland by Sir Pierce Crosby. Other officers from Ireland, like Captain William Stewart and his cohorts, joined Morton's forces.[16] Further, Charles ordered as many officers out of the Low Countries as could be spared. However, as Spens had predicted, the unsuccessful attempt to relieve the Huguenots at La Rochelle made it extremely difficult for Charles to support Christian IV

---

[13]   Munck, *Seventeenth Century Europe*, 12.

[14]   Howatt, *Stuart and Cromwellian Foreign Policy*, 36; Roberts, *Gustavus Adolphus*, I, 249; Lockhart, *Denmark in the Thirty Years' War*, 138-141.

[15]   E. Marquard and J. O. Bro-Jørgenson eds, *Prins Christian (V)'s Brev. Bind II. Kancellibreve i uddrag 1643-1647 med et tillæg af prinsens egenhændige breve, 1627-1647* (Copenhagen, 1956), 736. Christian (V) to Korfitz Ulfeldt, 7 June 1627.

[16]   *The Earl of Stirling's Register of Royal Letters*, 200-201. Charles I to the Scottish Privy Council, 22 August 1627; C. Petrie ed, *The Letters, Speeches and Proclamations of King Charles I* (London, 1968), 50-51. Charles I to the Duke of Buckingham, 13 August 1627; *RPCS*, second series, I, 606 and II, 1627-1628, ix-xiii; *APC, January-August 1627*, 293-297. 24-27 May 1627; *CSPI, 1625-1632*, 266. 24 August 1627.

financially or logistically.[17] Christian's army was supported by fewer English troops than he had hoped for, only four depleted regiments under the Welshman, Sir Charles Morgan, while less than a quarter of the Scottish troops promised had arrived by July 1627.[18]

In a bid to re-direct Charles's attention towards his Danish obligations, Christian IV advocated peace between the Stuart kingdoms and France. Through the Danish ambassador, Palle Rosenkrands, Christian IV encouraged Charles to call an English Parliament in September 1626. This intervention did not go down well with Charles I who insisted that in his own kingdoms nobody should try to interfere with his authority, regardless of any family bonds they had. None-the-less, Christian briefed two new ambassadors, Christen Sehested and Jørgen Brahe, whom he charged with trying to persuade Charles to avoid conflict with France.[19] They left Denmark in July 1627 and arrived in London in August after first visiting the United Provinces. Charles kept them entertained but uninformed and in October he revealed to Buckingham that he had dismissed the Danes adding: 'I have sent them away well enough satisfied, yet without discovering my intentions; so that I hope my uncle will be content with my proceedings with France'.[20] Sehested and Brahe did not leave. Instead, now reinforced in London by the Danish ambassador to France, Johannes Lobell, they kept up the pressure and only twelve days later Charles again wrote to Buckingham indicating a discernible change of position. The only obstacle in the way of a Stuart accommodation with France now seemed to be Stuart pride. Charles did not want to make the first move but he told Buckingham that 'in case they [the Danes] made a peace between me and France, the army that you command should be ready to serve my uncle, if he desired it'.[21] The Danish diplomats remained at the Stuart Court until the end of November when they got orders to travel to negotiations in the United Provinces. Despite their hopes being raised, they actually left without any tangible advance in Franco-Stuart or Stuart-Oldenburg relations. Once more Danish affairs were left in the hands of the resident agent,

---

[17]   E. A. Beller, 'The Thirty Years' War', in J. P. Cooper ed, *The New Cambridge History IV. The Decline of Spain and the Thirty Years' War 1609-1648/59* (Cambridge, 1970), 325.

[18]   The frustration at the slow arrival of the Scottish troops was noted in a letter of Sir Charles Morgan on 11 July 1627. See PRO SP75/8, f.201.

[19]   *KCFB*, II, Christian IV to Charles I (draft), 21 October 1626, 41 and footnote; Beller, 'The Military Expedition of Sir Charles Morgan', 532.

[20]   Petrie, *Letters of Charles I*, 54. Charles I to Buckingham, 1 October 1627; *APC, September 1627-June 1628*, 59-60. Travel pass for 'Christian Thomasin' [Sehested] and 'George Brickey' [Brahe] for travel to France, granted on 30 September 1627; Sehested, *Cantsler Christen Thomesen Sehested*, 55-59.

[21]   Petrie, *Letters of Charles I*, 55. Charles I to Buckingham, 13 October 1627; *APC, September 1627-June 1628*, 95. Travell pass for Johannes Lobell, 24 October 1627.

Johan Kaspar von Wuffen, who waited in vain for news of a Franco-Stuart peace while Danish and Dutch ambassadors in France kept working to find a solution.[22]

If it was simply Charles's pride that prevented a treaty, it cost both the Stuart and the Danish kings dearly. Christian did not manage to get an accommodation on behalf of his nephew and so toiled to secure the support of the forces of Morton and Buckingham. Charles for his part had squandered money and men on an unsuccessful campaign through which he incurred the wrath of his uncle and the opposition of his own subjects in both Scotland and England.[23] In an effort to regain the favour of his subjects and relatives, Charles sent Sir Robert Anstruther to Denmark to promise Christian IV his choice of money, men or ships for his campaigns. A further motivation for Charles would have been to prevent Christian from concluding a treaty with Ferdinand II. Such an agreement would have placed Charles and his uncle in a situation of virtual conflict. Christian responded by pointing out that he had kept an ambassador in London for the previous year, and on receipt of such an offer from Charles directly, Christian would return a fitting thanks to his nephew.[24] The Dane had every right to be sceptical since such an offer did not materialise, though English Parliamentary policy probably had more to do with this than Charles I's desire to help his uncle.

Charles and Christian both searched for alternative ways out of their military, diplomatic and financial quagmires. To this end they both managed to extract themselves from wars in 1629. The fall of La Rochelle in October 1628 and the assassination of Buckingham removed two of the remaining obstacles to a Franco-Stuart peace.[25] Cardinal Richelieu, keen to rationalise resources and join the anti-Habsburg alliance, also wanted an end to the war with Britain, and a treaty was agreed upon in April 1629.

At the start of the following month, rumours abounded that Christian IV sought to join with Sweden to stop Ferdinand II gaining a foothold in the Baltic.[26] Many conjecture that the purpose of the Danish-Swedish negotiations was to give Christian IV some leverage over Ferdinand II

---

[22]   *CSPI*, 1625-1632, 309 and 324. Lord Conway to Lord Deputy, 13 February and 18 April 1628; *KCFB*, II, 131, footnote.

[23]   A discussion of Scottish, English and British reaction to Charles's policies can be found in Macinnes, *Charles I*, 77-80. The English Parliament passed the 'Petition of Right' which made it very difficult for Charles to raise forces or loans from his subject to subsidise future expeditions. See Petrie, *Letters of Charles I*, 57; Howatt, *Stuart and Cromwellian Foreign Policy*, 36.

[24]   *CSPV*, XXII, 1629-1632, xxxi and 43-44. Alvise Contarini, 4 May 1629.

[25]   K. Sharpe, *The Personal Rule of Charles I* (London, 1992), 65-70.

[26]   *CSPV*, XXII, 1629-1632, 43-44. Alvise Contarini, 4 May 1629.

with which to extract fairer conditions from the Danish-Habsburg negotiations. From another perspective, if Christian was serious about an alliance with Sweden, it could be argued that Ferdinand II offered easy terms to Christian to detach him from Gustav II Adolf.[27] Either way, within only a few weeks Christian IV concluded the Treaty of Lübeck with the Emperor. This restored the Danish monarch to all his pre-war possessions so long as he promised not to interfere with the interests of the Empire again.[28] It was a favourable treaty for Christian, given that he was hardly the military equal of Ferdinand II. The generous conditions of the Treaty of Lübeck aroused the suspicions of Sir Robert Anstruther as to the intentions of the Danes. He complained that the Danish deputies were quite reserved towards him and, therefore, his information regarding Danish policy had to be gleaned indirectly. He was particularly annoyed since, up to that point, the Danes had always consulted him in negotiations with the Emperor. Now they did not even answer his letters, which he felt showed a split in the axis confronting Ferdinand II.[29]

In the months and years following the Lübeck treaty, the issue of Baltic supremacy and the role of Denmark-Norway in this remained unsettled. Paul Lockhart has argued that the defeat of Denmark awakened The Hague allies to the need to keep the Baltic in friendly hands and did much to strengthen Gustav II Adolf's position within the Protestant north.[30] After the treaty hopes grew among the anti-Habsburg protagonists that the Lübeck agreement could be undermined on this point.[31] It remained a widely held belief that Denmark would either have to submit totally to Habsburg domination of the Baltic or press the recently mooted association with Sweden. Even at the end of June 1629, Sir Thomas Roe hoped to be able to prevent Christian IV from actually ratifying the treaty, and his aspirations were bolstered in July by rumours that Christian had not yet done so. The reason for this was felt by some to be because he had been sold out by his own commissioners. They, like the majority of the Danish nobility and people, were determined to

---

[27] M Roberts, 'Sweden and the Baltic, 1611-54', in Cooper, *The New Cambridge History IV*, 391; P. D. Lockhart, 'Denmark and the Empire; A Reassessment of Danish Foreign Policy under King Christian IV', in *Scandinavian Studies*, 64, 3 (1992), 410; A. W. Ward 'Gustavus Adolf 1630-32', in A.W. Ward, G.W. Prothero and S. Leathers eds, *The Cambridge Modern History IV. The Thirty Years' War* (Cambridge, 1906), 191.

[28] *Danmark-Norges Traktater*, IV, 77-86. Treaty between Christian IV and Emperor Ferdinand, 12/22 May 1629; Munck, *Seventeenth Century Europe*, 64. Analysis of the treaty is given in Fridericia, *Danmarks ydre politiske historie*, 38-60; Lockhart, *Denmark in the Thirty Years' War*, 198-207.

[29] *CSPV*, XXII, 1629-1632, xxxii, 71-71, and 119-121. Giovani Soranzo, Venetian Ambassador to the United Provinces, 28 May 1629 and Alvise Contarini, 6 July 1629.

[30] Lockhart, *Denmark in the Thirty Years' War*, 214.

[31] *CSPV*, XXII, 1629-1632, 67-71. Alvise Contarini, 25 May 1629.

establish peace regardless of the wishes of their king.[32]

Christian's failure to sign the Treaty of Lübeck immediately led many to hope that an alliance between the Stuart kingdoms, the Dutch and the Swedes would encourage him to abandon the treaty. Even among the Danish diplomatic community there were rumours that their king would break the treaty with Ferdinand II should such a scheme be pressed. The Danish ambassador in the United Provinces, Scultetus, told Vicenso Gussoni that, since Christian believed the treaty prejudiced the rights of the Danish princes to the coveted north German Bishoprics, he could use one of several pretexts to break the treaty should an alliance be established.[33] Even as late as January 1631, the Stuart ambassador Donald Mackay Lord Reay, described Christian IV's growing embitterment with Ferdinand over the Bishoprics. Reay suggested that the Danish king and princes were again coming round to the Stuart position, though he also noted that the Danish Estates feared the growing power of the Swedes.[34]

In July 1631, Charles I requested Christian IV's permission for the Marquis of Hamilton and his troops to be allowed to pass through Danish waters and territory.[35] It was hoped that Hamilton's appearance in Denmark, *en route* to Gustav II Adolf, might tempt Christian back into the war against Ferdinand. Yet despite Hamilton's arrival, the Danes opted out of any negotiation with Sweden. Gustav II Adolf embarked on a new phase of the Thirty Years' War without an alliance with Denmark-Norway and with only limited support from the Stuart government.[36]

Sir Robert Anstruther left Christian IV's Court in January 1630 and travelled to Hamburg. Perhaps as a result of his treatment by the Danish negotiators during the Lübeck negotiations and his general distrust of Danish intentions, Anstruther conducted much of his business from Hamburg during his remaining 'Danish' residency, though even there he expressed his desire to be back home.[37] This relocation signalled a

---

[32] *CSPV*, XXII, 1629-1632, 112-121. Various letters of Alvise Contarini June-July 1629.

[33] *CSPV*, XXII, 1629-1632, 122-123. Vicenzo Gussoni, Venetian Ambassador in The Netherlands, 8 July 1629.

[34] PRO SP 75/12, f.26. Lord Reay to Dorchester, 22 January 1631.

[35] *CSPD*, 1631-33, 110. Marquis of Hamilton to Secretary Dorchester, 15 [?] July 1631; DRA, TKUA England A1. Charles I to Christian IV, 16 July 1631; PRO SP 75/12, f.156. Charles I to Christian IV (copy), 16 July 1631.

[36] *CSPV*, XXII, 1629-1632, 537-538. Giovanni Soranzo, 29 August 1631; C.G. Styffe, *Konung Gustav II Adolfs Skrifter* (Stockholm, 1861); D. Norrman, *Gustav Adolfs Politik mot Ryssland och Polen Under Tyska Kriget, 1630-1632* (Uppsala, 1943); M. Roberts, 'The political objectives of Gustavus Adolf in Germany 1632', in *Transactions of the Royal Historical Society*, 5th Series, 7 (London, 1957); M. Roberts, *Gustavus Adolphus: A history of Sweden 1611-1632* (2 vols., London, 1953, 1958); G. Göransson, *Gustav II Adolf och hans folk* (Stockholm, 1994).

[37] PRO SP 75/11, f.5. Anstruther to Charles I, 25 January 1630 and f.7. Anstruther to Roe, 28

expressed his desire to be back home.[37] This relocation signalled a change in the nature of diplomacy in the area as, for the first time since the 1590s, the Stuarts had no direct permanent representation at the Danish Court in Copenhagen.

Anstruther's disillusionment with the Danes continued to grow and by the spring of 1630 he wrote to Roe that unless directed by Charles I to do so, or personally summoned by Christian IV, he had no intention of visiting the Danish king. Instead he intended simply to conduct all his diplomatic business by letter.[38] Long gone were the days when, in 1620, Christian and Anstruther had such an implicit trust they could conduct negotiations verbally and without witnesses.[39] When he ratified the Lübeck treaty Christian had not only alienated his closest allies, the Stuart kingdoms and the United Provinces, but also a personal friend.

Claims and Counter Claims: Stuart-Oldenburg divisions.

After the Treaty of Lübeck, Stuart and Danish diplomats found difficulty in finding common ground over any political issue. While Charles sought to concentrate on the subject of the restoration of the Palatinate, Christian IV chose rather to steer clear of it, offering advice or mediation only when he saw a personal advantage in doing so. Christian still retained some significant open wounds around which the majority of diplomatic contact between him and Charles would focus for several years. In July 1629, the Danish ambassador to the United Provinces told his Venetian opposite number that Charles's failure to support Denmark-Norway provided the main reason why Christian had signed the Treaty of Lübeck. The conviction that Charles, through his French campaign, had cost Christian the war found expression in a letter from the Danish king himself to Frederick Gunther.[40]

On conclusion of the Danish-Norwegian war against Ferdinand II in 1629, there still remained the problem of the alleged outstanding Stuart subsidies to the Danish Crown. To add to these financial allegations, Christian had amassed a substantial body of complaint with which he was to confront Stuart envoys for the next decade. He bemoaned the low number of troops received from 'England' compared to those that Charles had offered.[41] There was also a series of specific complaints

---

[37]   PRO SP 75/11, f.5. Anstruther to Charles I, 25 January 1630 and f.7. Anstruther to Roe, 28 January 1630; Bell, *Diplomatic Representatives*, 33.

[38]   PRO, SP 88/7.2, f.232-235. Anstruther to Roe, 11/21 March 1629 (1630).

[39]   *KCFB*, I, Christian IV to Christian Friis, 4 May 1620, 171-173.

[40]   *CSPV*, XXII, 1629-1632, 122-123. Vicenzo Gussoni, Venetian Ambassador in The Netherlands, 8 July 1629; *KCFB*, II, 230-233. Christian IV to Frederick Gunther, 3 December 1629; Lockhart, *Denmark in the Thirty Years' War*, 249.

[41]   *KCFB*, II, 230-233. Christian IV to Frederick Gunther, 3 December 1629; Fridericia,

against the behaviour of General Morgan's troops in Danish service. A royal petition, dated July 1629, detailed Christian's various dissatisfaction and that Morgan would have to be contented by Charles I as he would receive no money from Denmark. The degree to which Christian really felt embittered towards the General and his abilities is unclear. It is possible that Christian simply used Morgan's outstanding wages as a method to get back at Charles I.[42]

It is hard to validate the Danish accusations against Charles. The agreement relating to the numbers of troops Charles would provide had been made with the Stuart Crown and not the English Parliament. Charles was in a strong position to argue that, including the Scots levy, the Danes obtained between 18,000 and 20,000 troops from Britain. This far exceeds the 7,000 troops King James had agreed to in February 1625. Sir Thomas Roe sought to find some more flaws in Christian IV's arguments against Charles I. Roe's grounding in Danish-Norwegian politics was insufficient for such an undertaking and he carefully probed Anstruther regarding various aspects of Danish, Lower Saxon and Habsburg negotiations and particularly questioned Christian's commitment to the Palatine cause. Roe also sought information on any irregularities resulting from the recent peace with Ferdinand II. Anstruther addressed each point in turn and, despite his personal opinion of the king of Denmark, steadfastly defended the integrity of Christian IV.[43]

Anstruther travelled from Hamburg to the Danish Court in November 1629 and brought with him a message from the English Secretary of State, Lord Dorchester, in which he defended the Stuart subsidy to the Danish king. Anstruther further denied the inclusive obligations and binding character of Stuart-Oldenburg arrangements. The agreements referred to were of course part of The Hague Treaty of 1625. Anstruther further claimed that the Treaty of Lübeck, which was concluded without Charles's agreement, had invalidated all agreements – fulfilling James Spens's prediction in 1626 defining this as Charles I's tactic to avoid payment to his uncle.[44] According to some historians Christian IV never actually got a copy of The Hague Treaty. Instead, Christian had bound himself to the promises made by Charles in a letter of 2 March 1626 in which the Stuart king had promised to abide by The Hague agreement.[45]

---

[42] The Danish Crown Prince later asked Morgan to train one of his courtiers, Envold Kaas, in the art of war. He probably believed Morgan was not the military incompetent his father claimed. Marquard, *Prins Christian (V)'s Brev*, I, 408. Missive to Charles Morgan from Christian (V), 31 March 1638.

[43] PRO, SP 88/7.2, ff.232-235. Anstruther to Roe 11/21 March 1630.

[44] SRA, Anglica 3, f.64. Spens to Gustav II Adolf, 10 September 1626; *KCFB*, II, 233, footnote.

[45] Dk. RA. TKUA A1 3, Charles 1 to Christian IV, 2 March 1626.

himself to the promises made by Charles in a letter of 2 March 1626 in which the Stuart king had promised to abide by The Hague agreement.[45] Christian's ratification of that promise in good faith actually predates Charles's letter by a few days, but did not take into consideration several secret articles which had been built into the treaty, and on which grounds Charles found reason to clear himself of any obligation to his uncle.[46]

Regardless of the 'hidden clauses' of The Hague Treaty, it remained clear that during the French and Spanish campaigns of the late 1620s, Charles was still obliged to help his uncle in his fight against the Empire. To this end he sought to find financial solutions which would not drain his dwindling coffers. In a bid to escape direct cash payment of the moneys owed to Christian, Charles presented his uncle with an expensive jewelled necklace in March 1627 which was partly to offset the wages of Morgan's troops.[47] Christian gave every impression of being happy with the necklace, which he accepted and made no attempt to return as unsuitable payment. The problem with this ornate present was that the jewels were simply too precious to be converted into cash. Christian IV himself put an estimated price on the necklace at 700,000 'DK' and declared that no other such necklace had been made in 500 years.[48] The jewels were so valuable that no one could afford to buy them and so the necklace became a recurring feature of grievance between Charles and Christian. By June, and only after he had failed to pawn the piece, the Danish king argued that the necklace could not pay the troops and so he wrote to Charles demanding 'for Gods sake assist us with this money...thus you dear nephew and brother shall help us to add to our old age some honour'.[49] Christian further wrote to Charles complaining of the non-payment of money asking to 'let God and the whole world judge whether this be answerable or Christian like dealing'.[50]

Of course, to Charles, the necklace had been sent and Christian had accepted it in good faith, and it was only when he found he could not sell it that he became angry. By September 1627, Christian was trying to get the necklace to Sir Robert Anstruther so that he could arrange for money

---

[45] Dk. RA. TKUA A1 3, Charles 1 to Christian IV, 2 March 1626.
[46] For a description of these articles see PRO SP75/7, f.68, 'Consideration upon the ratification of the secret articles at The Hague, December 1625'; *KCFB*, III, 151.
[47] Beller, 'The Military Expedition of Sir Charles Morgan', 529.
[48] *KCFB*, II, Christian IV to Christian Friis, 27 March 1627, 65; Fridericia, *Danmarks Ydre Politiske Historie*, I, 30.
[49] PRO SP75/8, f.143. Christian IV to Charles 1, 2 June 1627; P. Chapman, *History of Gustavus Adolphus and The Thirty Years' War* (London, 1856), 176; *KCFB*, II, footnote, 84.
[50] PRO, SP 75/8, f.16 and 18. A Statement to Charles I from Christian IV. 26 February/8 March 1628.

money against it in Holland.[51] Charles felt that when he had given his uncle the ruby necklace he had fulfilled his financial obligations to him. Christian strongly disagreed and made it quite clear that he would have few dealings with Charles or his representatives until the matter was resolved. To add to his already hostile feelings, Christian became angered by Roe who let slip that Charles I had referred to Gustav II Adolf as the 'strongest king' in Christendom. Christian said that if Charles had indeed given the Swede that title then all other kings should call Charles '*Fortissium omnium stultorum in toto mundo*' or 'the greatest fool in the world'.[52]

In a bid to circumvent this growing diplomatic exclusion Charles now faced, he selected diplomats and individuals he knew Christian respected. On his return from the Diet at Ratisbon in 1631, Anstruther spent some private time with Christian IV where they no doubt sought to rediscover their mutual trust and work out a solution to the Stuart-Oldenburg ill feeling.[53] Colonel Donald Mackay, Lord Reay had proved to have been one of Christian's most loyal soldiers during *Kejserkrig* and his regiment had at times formed the bodyguard of the king. He assumed a diplomatic role to Denmark in 1631 serving as an itinerant ambassador on his journeys between Britain and Sweden.[54] Mackay was probably also chosen due to the great respect the Danish king had for this former officer. The softening up tactic, if indeed it was deliberate, failed to impress, although Reay was well entertained.

Sir Henry Vane arrived in Denmark in September 1631 to end the royal dispute, re-establish the Stuart-Oldenburg confederation of 1621 and settle all debts.[55] Despite his efforts to gain an audience with Christian IV, Vane was refused access to the Danish king. He departed leaving specific instructions with Joseph Averie to pursue Christian IV on the same issues with which he himself had been charged.[56] Christian simply responded by writing to Lord Dorchester, arguing that he had always abided by the confederations of 1621 and 1625 and that Charles

[51] *KCFB*, II, Christian IV to Frederick Gunther, 8 September 1627, 95 and footnote. The investors are given as Hans and Jacob Morse; Ditlev, Anton and Daniel von Buchwald. Perhaps in a bid to emphasise his financial discomfort to his nephew, the same month saw Christian ask that Charles I should acquire him some clothes, but insisted that these should be acquired on credit. *KCFB*, II, Christian IV to Frederick Gunther, 19 December 1627, 131.

[52] *KCFB*, II, 270-272. Christian IV to Christian Friis and Frands Rantzau, 20 May 1630.

[53] Fridericia, *Danmarks Ydre Politiske Historie*, I, 198-201; *KCFB*, II, 354.

[54] *HMC 21*; *11th Report*, 70-72.

[55] In addition to dealing with the Stuart-Oldenburg rift, Vane also sought to reconcile Christian IV and Gustav II Adolf. PRO SP 75/12, f.198. Charles I to Christian IV, 22 September 1631; ibid., ff.204-209, Instructions for Sir Henry Vane, 22 September 1631.

[56] PRO SP 75/12, f.232. Instructions to Joseph Averie from Sir Henry Vane, 1631; Bell, *Diplomatic Representatives*, 34.

simply responded by writing to Lord Dorchester, arguing that he had always abided by the confederations of 1621 and 1625 and that Charles clearly owed the Danes a large sum of money. Dorchester's response could not have been less favourable for Christian. He included a list of counter claims which seriously challenged the king of Denmark's integrity, especially in his dealings with the freezing of Queen Sofia's estate of which, as her grandchildren, Charles I and Elizabeth of Bohemia were entitled to a share.[57]

Charles I was furious that Christian IV withheld his inheritance. He attempted to address the situation, appointing the Earl of Leicester as his ambassador to Denmark-Norway. Leicester's instructions from Charles I included orders to convey his condolences for the death of Christian's mother, Queen Sofia, to the Danish royal family. As all the children and grandchildren were entitled to a share of the queen's estate, Charles hoped that Leicester might be able to collect the Stuart share estimated at £160,000. Christian insisted to Leicester that Charles would be denied his share of the estate until he gained satisfaction for the debts he believed Charles still owed him.[58] The Danish king also held back Elizabeth Stuart's portion of the inheritance for several years, insisting that she could only receive it once Charles had settled with him.[59] It was the constant referral to these debts that proved the primary focus for Leicester's trip to Copenhagen.

Charles I carefully described to Leicester the two sorts of debt his Danish uncle claimed from him.[60] One of these debts Charles strongly denied, while another one he acquiesced to. Charles outlined his position on the debt, with a detailed description of the flaw in the Danish argument relating to it. He further developed his arguments relating to the ruby necklace that Christian had first accepted as payment, then pawned and now refused to give back. Charles left discussions regarding the necklace open depending on the outcome of negotiations relating to

Diplomatic Representatives, 34.
[57] PRO SP 75/12, ff.286-288. Christian IV to Dorchester, c.1631 with Dorchester's reply.
[58] PRO SP 75/12, f.396. Instructions for the Earl of Leicester from Charles I, 16 August 1632; Marquard, *Prins Christian (V)'s Brev*, I. 67. Missive to King Charles I from Christian (V) thanking Charles for the condolences delivered by the Earl of Leicester, 8 October 1632; PRO SP 75/12, f.282. The legacy claimed by Charles I from the estate of the Queen Dowager of Denmark. c.1631; *KCFB*, III, 52-54. Christian IV to the Earl of Leicester [draft], 13-14 October 1632.
[59] Elizabeth's agent, Rusdorf, arrived in Denmark in October 1633 to secure from Christian IV the inheritance left to her by Queen Sofia, but he received no satisfaction. *CSPV*, XXIII, 1632-1636, 159 and 191. Antonio Contarini, Venetian Ambassador to The Netherlands, 31 October 1633 and 6 February 1634.
[60] PRO SP 75/12, f.396. Instructions for the Earl of Leicester from Charles I, 16 August 1632; Instructions are also reproduced in R. Cant, 'The Embassy of the Earl of Leicester to Denmark in 1632', in *English Historical Review*, LIV (1939), 252-262.

Instead of further audiences with Christian IV, Leicester had to be content with several letters from him discussing the Swedish tolls in the Baltic. These had been introduced in 1630 in ports controlled by the Swedes and had been a recurring source of discontent for Stuart and Oldenburg subjects.[61] The only concession Charles I obtained from his uncle entailed a joint remonstrance against Sweden in respect of the new tolls. Leicester also recorded that, 'although he asked many questions he never spoke of England or enquired after the king or queen'.[62] The Venetian ambassador, Vicenso Gussoni, reported that Leicester took such offence at Christian IV's attitude towards him and his monarch that he refused the gifts offered him by the Danish king.[63] He returned to England thoroughly disgruntled at the failure of his first diplomatic mission. After Leicester's departure in December, Stuart-Oldenburg relations were once more placed in the care of Sir Robert Anstruther, newly returned to Hamburg on the conclusion of his embassy to the Emperor.

Stuart-Oldenburg Diplomacy in the Post Lübeck Era

Denmark-Norway, in theory at least, remained the Stuart kingdoms' closest ally after 1629, since Christian IV insisted that the two states were still bound by previous alliances.[64] The cessation of hostilities between Charles's kingdoms, France and Spain coupled with the withdrawal of Denmark-Norway from the German wars, led to a shift in diplomatic emphasis by Charles's diplomatic corps. Denmark-Norway verged on becoming the diplomatic pariah of Europe after Lübeck, and immediately sought rehabilitation. Christian IV attempted to re-invent himself as a credible international arbiter between Emperor Ferdinand II, Charles I and Gustav II Adolf of Sweden. The Stuart government, however, remained sceptical about the offer of this intervention due to Christian's jealousy of the Swedish king and the Swedes' distrust of the Danes.[65] Because of this, Charles pondered alternative support in the quest for a Palatinate settlement, particularly from Sweden and her German allies.[66] These negotiations initially revolved around Arthur Hopton in Madrid, Sir Robert Anstruther in Vienna and Balthasar

---

[61] *KCFB*, II, 270-272. Christian IV to Christian Friis and Frands Rantzau, 20 May 1630; *KCFB*, III, 48-52. Christian IV to Frederick Gunther, 7 October 1632, Christian IV to Leicester (drafts), 7-14 October 1632.

[62] Cant, 'The Embassy of the Earl of Leicester', 259.

[63] *CSPV*, XXIII, 1632-1636, 59-60. Vicenso Gussoni, 20 January 1633.

[64] *KCFB*, III, 157-158. Christian IV to Frederick Gunther, 28 August 1633.

[65] PRO SP 75/11, f.18-19. Anstruther to Dorchester, 28 February 1630.

[66] For more on these negotiations see S. Murdoch, 'Scottish Diplomats and the Thirty Years' War', in S. Murdoch ed, *Scotland and the Thirty Years' War 1618-1648* (Brill, 2001).

German allies.[66] These negotiations initially revolved around Arthur Hopton in Madrid, Sir Robert Anstruther in Vienna and Balthasar Gerbier in Brussels.[67] Yet Denmark continued to play a role in the Palatine cause.

As part of his policy, Christian IV chose to avoid overt relations with most of his former 'Hague' allies. Indeed, as Paul Lockhart has argued, he remained deliberately vague in his foreign policy to avoid conflict with anyone.[68] Christian played cat and mouse with Sweden and the Empire hoping to use his position to gain the best advantage for his kingdoms. On his return from the Swedish-Polish negotiations in 1629, Roe sought Christian out at Glückstadt, where the Danish king quizzed him on the nature of the Swedish negotiations with the House of Stuart. One of the features of the conversation that fascinated Christian IV concerned the apparent lack of a mention of the Palatinate in these talks. Roe responded that the Palatinate had formed no part of the discussions since he had not been instructed to include the issue. However Roe, according to Christian, continued that, should Gustav II Adolf not do anything regarding the Palatinate by summer, then 'we will help him break his neck'.[69] What remains unclear here is whether Roe meant 'we' to mean the Stuart kingdoms (which is more likely) or 'we' to mean the Stuart kingdoms and Denmark-Norway together. Whichever, it is apparent that the Palatinate was the key feature in Charles's foreign policy.

Christian IV was also determined to settle the Palatinate issue, using it as a tool to gain prestige with both the Empire and Sweden as well as Charles I. Indeed he quickly tried to orchestrate talks in Danzig between the Swedish Chancellor, Axel Oxenstierna, and Albrecht Wallenstein in April 1630. From Oxenstierna's perspective the engagement in such talks were seen as an excellent stalling opportunity. The Swedish commissioners eventually arrived late and the meeting ended in fiasco with the Imperial delegates refusing to acknowledge the validity of Swedish claims in Germany.[70] Undaunted, Christian continued to look for ways to gain advantage from Wallenstein and Oxenstierna. Both parties offered Christian similar proposals in order to secure his support

---

[66] For more on these negotiations see S. Murdoch, 'Scottish Diplomats and the Thirty Years' War', in S. Murdoch ed, *Scotland and the Thirty Years' War 1618-1648* (Brill, 2001).

[67] For more on the Spanish and Palatine negotiations see Sharpe, *The Personal Rule*, 70-75 and 92-97.

[68] Lockhart, *Denmark in the Thirty Years' War*, 218.

[69] *KCFB*, II, 270-272. Christian IV to Christian Friis and Frands Rantzau, 20 May 1630.

[70] *RAOSB*, V, 253. Axel Oxenstierna to Gustav II Adolf, 3 April 1630; ; Sehested, *Cantsler Christen Thomesen Sehested*, 69; Roberts, *Gustavus Adolphus*, II, 412-413; Lockhart, *Denmark in the Thirty Years' War*, 218.

March 1632, Christian IV was widely believed to have broken off his negotiations with Spain, which had been ongoing since 1629.[71] This action undoubtedly helped him apply pressure on Ferdinand II by implying an improving relationship with the Swedes. The image Christian wished to project of a warming of Scandinavian relations soon hit problems. In the spring of 1632, Gustav II Adolf rejected Danish mediation. Consequently, if unsurprisingly, Christian thereafter came to favour Wallenstein's position over the Swedes. This made Stuart-Oldenburg relations more complex as Charles I distrusted Christian's vacillations between the Habsburgs and Sweden. Perhaps the familiarity of such diplomacy, not dissimilar to that practised by Charles himself, allowed him to see through the thin veil of good intentions Christian espoused for the Palatinate cause.

None-the-less, Charles sought to satisfy Christian's evident desire to be seen as the main arbitrator of peace. He made it quite clear that a main thrust of the 1632 Leicester embassy would be 'the publicke peace, and the interest of our brother and deare sister depending thereupon'.[72] The Venetian ambassador Vicenzo Gussoni, among others, still believed that the Danish king's blood relationship to Elizabeth Stuart and her children would prevent him from acting in any way against their interests.[73] Charles was keen to discover with whom, if anyone, Christian was negotiating. He encouraged Leicester to intimate to Christian that Charles was willing to join any scheme that would ensure the 'full restitution of our brother and sister to their patrimonial dignities and estates (being the only interest of our engagement)'.[74] Charles also indicated that he believed the war might continue for a long time and that Christian IV should promote peace using his influence with Ferdinand II.

Christian cultivated his correspondence with Ferdinand II, who wrote to him in early 1632 empowering Wallenstein to conduct further dialogue with the Danish king.[75] Such talks did not always find favour in the Stuart kingdoms. There was some anxiety in Stuart circles regarding Christian's intentions of involving himself in the Palatinate issue with the Emperor. It was widely believed that such action had a selfish motivation, particularly to gain some advantage in the Danish-Hamburg dispute and to strengthen his position over the north German

---

[71] A Searle ed, *Camden 4th series, vol. 28; Barrington Family Letters 1628-1632* (London, 1983), 230. Sir Gilbert Gerard to anon., March 1632. For Danish negotiations with Spain see Fridericia, *Danmarks Ydre Politiske Historie*, I, 151.

[72] Cant, 'The Embassy of the Earl of Denmark', 253.

[73] *CSPV*, XXIII, 1632-1636, 89-91 and 101-103. Vicenzo Gussoni, 1 April and 6 May 1633.

[74] Cant, 'The Embassy of the Earl of Denmark', 255.

[75] *DBBTI*, V, 75. Ferdinand II to Christian IV, 21 February 1632.

Christian's intentions of involving himself in the Palatinate issue with the Emperor. It was widely believed that such action had a selfish motivation, particularly to gain some advantage in the Danish-Hamburg dispute and to strengthen his position over the north German Bishoprics.[76] Such anxieties were exacerbated when an envoy carrying letters relating to a treaty between Christian IV and Ferdinand II was captured by the Swedes as they occupied Segeberg, a territory of the Danish king. Swift diplomacy on the part of Christian meant that a few individuals were held to have 'miscarried themselves' and the threat of trouble between the two Scandinavian kings melted away.[77]

Several observers continued to believe that Christian displayed a 'perverse disposition' in his dealings with Charles regarding the Palatinate.[78] He seemed unable to decide which side, if any, he was going to support. His inconsistency probably cost him any credibility that his intervention might have given him. In an apparently decisive move, Christian wrote to Wallenstein in November to excuse himself for not having initiated the mediation he had promised between Sweden and Ferdinand II.[79] The likely reason for the delay might be explained in a letter Christian IV wrote to his secretary, Frederick Gunther, the month before. In it he declared his desire to be on good terms with the Swedish king, probably for similar motives to those of Charles I – leverage over the Emperor.[80] Christian IV, like the other protagonists, probably wished to see how matters progressed before committing himself as the international arbitrator.

Fickle or otherwise, Christian's policies sometimes looked like they might pay off. In March 1633, a Stuart agent in Dresden notified the Marquis of Hamilton that Christian IV still offered mediation in Germany.[81] Joseph Averie informed John Coke that Ferdinand II and the Duke of Saxony had accepted the Danish king as the main arbitrator for peace in Germany and that Christian had been given permission to summon a Diet for that purpose.[82] However, in the interim, Anstruther and Oxenstierna had held consultative talks during which Christian's intervention had been discussed. Anstruther indicated that Christian was

---

[76]   PRO SP75/13, f.34. Averie to Coke, 8/18 May 1633; *CSPV*, XXIII, 1632-1636, xi and 89-90. Vicenso Gussoni, 1 April 1633.
[77]   PRO SP75/12, ff. 351-353. Averie to Dorchester, 20/30 March 1632.
[78]   *CSPV*, XXIII, 1632-1636, 150-151. Vicenso Gussoni, 30 September 1633.
[79]   *DBBTI*, V, 111. Christian IV to Wallenstein, 11 December 1632.
[80]   *KCFB*, III, 49. Christian IV to [?], 9-11 October 1632; Cant, 'The Embassy of the Earl of Leicester', 256.
[81]   J H McMaster and M Wood eds, *HMC; Supplementary Report on the Manuscripts of His Grace the Duke of Hamilton* (London, 1932), 27-28. M Curtius to the Marquis of Hamilton, 14/24 April 1633.
[82]   PRO SP 75/13, f.34. Averie to Coke, 8/18 May 1633.

that he would like to break Swedish control in the Baltic. Oxenstierna noted that despite being a long-time servant of Christian IV, he trusted Anstruther's words on these matters.[83] Perhaps knowing that his position had been given away to the Swedes, Averie thereafter noted that Christian turned down Charles I's offer to act as a joint mediator. The official reason given was that that he did not want to make the negotiations any harder for Ferdinand. Regardless of Christian's rejection of this offer, the French believed that Charles actually held this role as Christian IV claimed that he treated in the name of himself and his nephew.[84] This angered both Charles and Anstruther, neither of whom understood where Christian thought he had gained such authority.

Anstruther travelled back to Holstein to clarify this point with Christian and to advance the relations developing between Denmark and the Emperor. He was encouraged in his task by the fact that Ferdinand himself had recently instructed Wallenstein to prosecute this relationship more vigorously.[85] Anstruther met with Christian in the Duchy of Olsacia where the Danish king told him no business could be conducted outwith his kingdom and so far from his councillors. Given Christian's humour towards the Stuarts at this juncture, he probably sought to prolong the negotiations until a settlement could be found in the Stuart-Oldenburg dispute. The two men travelled back to Denmark together where Antonio Contarini reported that the talks got off to a poor start, though he did comment that Anstruther had brought the king round a little by their second meeting.[86] Despite another sharp lecture being delivered to Sir Robert on the nature of the Stuart debt to Denmark-Norway, Charles wanted to keep Anstruther as his representative at the Danish Court.[87]

Sir Robert Anstruther worked ceaselessly to get Christian to accept Charles I's view of the obligations to Denmark-Norway and he suggested that a way to proceed might be to ratify the existing treaty between the two kings.[88] He kept up the diplomatic pressure on several fronts. He sent his agent, Major Borthwick, to visit the Danish crown prince, a meeting in which Christian (V) was reminded of Charles I's

[83] *RAOSB*, III, 688. Axel Oxenstierna to the Riksråd, 13 May 1633. He actually said that despite 'Därtill medh att Amstrytter altijdh haver varit godh Dansk', he trusted him.
[84] PRO SP 75/13, f.40. Averie to Coke, 6/16 June 1633; PRO SP 75/13, f. 61-63. Anstruther to Coke, 3/13 August 1633.
[85] *DBBTI*, V, 172-175. Ferdinand II to Wallenstein, 30 June 1633.
[86] *CSPV*, XXIII, 1632-1636, 146. Antonio Contarini, Venetian Ambassador to The Netherlands, 17 September and 22 September 1633. The apparent resolve of the Danish king to rejoin the fight came after his son Ulrich was murdered during an armistice in Schleswig in September.
[87] *CSPV*, XXIII, 1632-1636, 150-151 and 175-176. Vicenso Gussoni, 30 September and 23 December 1633.
[88] *KCFB*, III, Christian IV to Frederick Gunther, 28 August 1633, 157-8.

suggested that a way to proceed might be to ratify the existing treaty between the two kings.[88] He kept up the diplomatic pressure on several fronts. He sent his agent, Major Borthwick, to visit the Danish crown prince, a meeting in which Christian (V) was reminded of Charles I's continued peaceful intentions. The prince in turn offered Charles reassurances that he was sincere in his intentions on behalf of the Elector's family.[89] While Christian (V) remained open to such approaches, his father gave a reserved response. Anstruther continued pressing Christian IV for ratification of the disputed Hague Treaty of 1625, although Christian seemed to believe that the treaty remained in place despite the ongoing difficulties between the two kings.[90]

Anstruther received a fresh set of instructions from Sir John Coke towards the end of September 1633.[91] These orders varied little from those to the previous ambassadors. Coke insisted, however, that Anstruther had to convey Charles's belief that Christian IV had deserted his obligations to the House of Stuart. The reasons Coke gave were that Christian had entered into a confederation with the Elector of Saxony, taken a commission from Ferdinand II to assemble the German princes, and refused to accord the Electoral title to Charles Louis. Perhaps most importantly of all, Christian had used Charles's name as a joint negotiator with the Emperor without permission or commission to do so. Ferdinand aggravated the situation by opting to stay out of the peace talks directly, preferring to leave matters in the hands of the Danish ambassador.[92] None-the-less, Anstruther had to give assurances that Charles believed his uncle was acting in the best interests of the Palatine and should, therefore secure the 'ancient interest betwixt these two Houses'. As usual, before any new confederation could be ratified, the issues of outstanding debts had to be settled.[93]

When Anstruther caught up with Christian IV in November he was apparently graciously treated despite the fact that ill-health prevented the Danish king's participation during the business meetings. Instead, Anstruther negotiated with members of the *Rigsråd*, who eventually conceded to his arguments that there was a need for a new confederacy. On the issues of debt, however, the Danes insisted that Charles I had betrayed Christian with regard to subsidies. Indeed, Anstruther reported that they became very personal in their attacks and he seems to have

---

[88]   *KCFB*, III, Christian IV to Frederick Gunther, 28 August 1633, 157-8.

[89]   Marquard, *Prins Christian (V)'s Brev*, I, 116. Missive to Anstruther, 8 October 1633.

[90]   *KCFB*, III, 151 and footnotes. Christian IV to Christian Friis, 9 August 1633; *KCFB*, III, 157-158. Christian IV to Frederick Gunther, 28 August 1633.

[91]   PRO SP 75/13, f.88. Coke to Anstruther, 25 September 1633.

[92]   *DBBTI*, V, 191. Ottavio Piccolomini to Francessco del Carretto, 26 September 1633.

[93]   PRO SP 75/13, f.88. Coke to Anstruther, 25 September 1633.

Though diplomatic links with Denmark remained cool, they had at least thawed slightly. Charles I received an invitation to the Danish prince's wedding in 1634 to which all the crowned heads of Europe were invited.[95] Christian IV used the occasion to place himself at the centre of European diplomacy though Charles I himself stayed away. The proposed coming together of so many heads of state presented the chance to offer up agenda suggestions for the forthcoming Diet which was to be held at Frankfurt. Christian used the opportunity afforded by the Diet to once more offer his intercession in Germany to the Swedish Chancellor.[96] Axel Oxenstierna wrote to the Marquis of Hamilton proposing the items he would like discussed at the meeting and querying how best to make use of the king of Denmark's offer of mediation.[97] The United Provinces also eventually decided that Danish mediation with Ferdinand II would be beneficial and in June they directly requested Danish involvement at the Frankfurt Diet.[98]

Charles I again selected Sir Robert Anstruther to serve as his representative at the Diet of Protestant Princes in 1634. During the Diet, which ran from April to September, official Stuart relations and diplomatic input with Denmark-Norway were conducted mainly between Anstruther and the Danish delegates at the conference rather than by further embassies between the two kings.[99] Christian offered to arrange another meeting to discuss a peace though, due to his illness and his son's wedding, this had to be scheduled for 1635.[100] In the interim, one of the main Swedish armies had been soundly thrashed in the two day battle of Nördlingen. That event led to the collapse of the League of Heilbronn and some of the allies looking to make their peace with the Emperor.[101] By the Treaty of Prague in May the following year, the most important of the combatant German princes, John George of Saxony, gave up his alliance with the Swedes and made peace with Ferdinand II.

[95] *KCFB*, III, 217. Christian IV to Frederick Gunther, 11 January 1634.
[96] SRA, Anglica 532. Proposition to Charles I of Johan Oxenstierna, 12 April 1634.
[97] McMaster and Wood, *HMC, Hamilton Manuscripts*, 34-35. Axel Oxenstierna to Marquis of Hamilton, 28 January 1634. Interestingly, Axel Oxenstierna had been the first person, and indeed for a while the only person, to invite Christian IV to send an agent to this Diet. See *KCFB*, III, 224, footnote.
[98] *CSPD*, 1634-35, 96. John Durie to Roe, 28 June 1634.
[99] There was also indirect contact with the Danish intellectual elite via Robert Anstruther's chaplain, Sampson Johnson. He communicated with John Durie and ensured that Oliger Rosencrantz, the father-in law of the Danish Chancellor, had Durie's irenicist ideas distributed at the Danish Universities of Søro and Copenhagen. These teachings, if adopted, by their very nature had to impact on the political outlook of the Danish-Norwegian state. Turnbull, *Hartlib, Dury and Comenius*, 161.
[100] *CSPD*, 1634-35, 338. Roe to Wentworth, 1 December 1634; Lockhart, *Denmark in the Thirty Years' War*, 243.
[101] Polisensky, *The Thirty Years' War*, 214.

Heilbronn and some of the allies looking to make their peace with the Emperor.[101] By the Treaty of Prague in May the following year, the most important of the combatant German princes, John George of Saxony, gave up his alliance with the Swedes and made peace with Ferdinand II. Christian IV seized the opportunity of the Peace of Prague to once more offer mediation between Sweden and the Emperor. His approaches were met with suspicion by Oxenstierna who felt uncomfortable at placing Sweden's future into Danish hands.[102] Moreover, Ferdinand II no longer needed to rely on Christian's benevolent neutrality, and his desired position as international peacemaker became obsolete.[103]

Charles I, Christian IV and the post-Prague Embassies

Despite the setback of Prague, Charles still sought his uncle's friendship. Direct Stuart diplomacy with Denmark continued with the return of Anstruther to Hamburg in 1635 and was further bolstered by the missions to Copenhagen of Joseph Averie and Sir Henry de Vic in 1636 and 1637. De Vic's orders were explicit. He was to point out the failure of the Earl of Arundel's recent embassy to Ferdinand II, and that the only purpose of that embassy had been to gain the restitution to the Charles Louis to his Electoral dignities.[104] As always, Charles remained optimistic that Christian IV, by virtue of his blood relationship, would be willing to 'join us with his best councils for opposing the wrong' done to his sister's family. Christian IV was, after all, reported to have been building a large army to be commanded by Count Henry Vandenberg.[105] Obviously, Charles hoped that Christian's intention for this army included the interests of the Count Palatine. Charles instructed de Vic to inform Christian that he hoped for the support of the king of France 'and other friends' to act for Charles Louis's interest.[106] However, Charles I's hopes for his family came to naught. Interestingly, Charles also begged forgiveness should any of his ministers have previously given offence to Christian. It is possible that Charles hoped that Christian might be willing to ascribe the differences between the two monarchs to one of Charles's subjects, in a similar way to that by which Christian had

---

[101] Polisensky, *The Thirty Years' War*, 214.
[102] Roberts, 'Sweden and the Baltic 1611-54', in Cooper, *The New Cambridge History*, IV, 400.
[103] Lockhart, *Denmark in the Thirty Years' War*, 243.
[104] PRO SP 75/13 f.311. Instructions to Averie, 1 April 1636; ibid., f.347. Instructions for Henry de Vic from Charles 1, 1636; PRO SP 75/13 f.347. Instructions for Henry de Vic, 1636. PRO SP 75/14, f.5. Instructions to Henry de Vic, 22 January 1637.
[105] *CSPD*, 1635-36, 188. John Durie to Roe, 25 January/4 February 1636.
[106] PRO SP 75/13 f.347. Instructions for Henry de Vic from Charles 1, 1636. The 'other friends' were the Swedes who, through Field Marshal Alexander Leslie had pledged 'to keep the field until a more honourable peace could be obtayned'. See PRO SP 75/13, f.295. Averie to Coke, 15/25 February 1636.

foundations of dialogue to be conducted by commissioners chosen to settle differences between Christian IV and Charles I.[108] These talks would form part of the multi-national negotiations that were about to commence in Hamburg. Although Sir Robert Anstruther was once more selected to represent Great Britain he declined the mission.[109] As it transpired Sir Thomas Roe was appointed instead.[110] Anstruther, correctly, predicted that the conference would come to naught and, as Roe found to his cost, representing the Stuarts could prove both futile and frustrating.[111] While the main thrust of the negotiations centred round seeking the ratification of a treaty drawn up by Cardinal Richelieu, a secondary purpose was the settling of the Stuart-Oldenburg debt.[112] While the former issue proved beyond him he had some success with the latter. Christian IV finally settled the issue of the debt over the ruby necklace Charles I had given him in the 1620s by agreeing to sell it back at a much reduced price.[113] A new treaty between the two kings was ratified in April 1639 and the 'dour years' of the Stuart-Oldenburg rift was apparently at an end.[114] Christian allegedly drank numerous toasts to his nephew and fired guns in celebration at the treaty.[115] But by the time Charles's relations with his uncle were normalised, his conflict with the Covenanters in Scotland had become far more pressing than his alliance with Denmark-Norway, or indeed any other foreign power.[116]

---

[108] PRO SP 75/15, f.150. Abstract of business between Christian IV and Vane, 15 April 1638.

[109] PRO SP 75/15, f.168. De Vic to Secretary of State, 3/13 May 1638.

[110] PRO SP 75/15, f.194. De Vic to Secretary of State, 21/31 May 1638. De Vic expressed great surprise at hearing that Anstruther was no longer coming to Hamburg, and resentment at having to hear the news from the French ambassador. See also *CSPV*, XXIV, 1636-1639, xviii, 399-401 and 409-411. Francesco Zonca, 23 April and 14 and 21 May 1638; Rumours of Anstruther's unsuitability for the negotiations in Hamburg in 1638 seem to appear only after he turned down the royal appointment. Indeed, by the end of May the unfounded rumour at Court circulated that Anstruther had been dismissed and replaced by Roe, the King's second choice diplomat. Perhaps this snub to the King prompted such rumours in the first place. Perhaps Anstruther's refusal to accept the appointment had more to do with the fact that he was a Scot rather than any particular frustration with Stuart politics. Indeed, one of the rare mentions of Anstruther specifically as a Scot in diplomatic dispatches came in April 1638 in a letter largely concerned with the background and progress of the Scottish Covenanting revolution. The author, Francesco Zonca's, actual attack on Anstruther's ability came in the same letter in which he reported that the Scotsman wished to resign his position as Stuart resident in Hamburg. It is surprising given the timing of the letter and the developments in Scotland that no-one appears to have connected Anstruther's resignation with his nationality and the Covenanting revolution in his native country.

[111] E A Beller, 'The Mission of Roe to the Conference at Hamburg, 1638-40', in *English Historical Review*, XLI (1926), 71.

[112] Beller, 'The Mission of Roe', 61-77.

[113] *KCFB*, III, 195. Christian IV to Frederick Gunther, 26 November 1638; *CSPD*, 1639, 143 and 206. Coke to Windebank, 9 and 27 May 1639; Beller, 'The Mission of Roe', 74.

[114] *Danmark-Norges Traktater 1523-1750*, 4, 191-199.

[115] PRO SP 81/45, f. 244. Roe to Coke, 12 April 1639.

[116] Elliot, 'The Year of the Three Ambassadors', 166-167.

his nephew and fired guns in celebration at the treaty.[115] But by the time Charles's relations with his uncle were normalised, his conflict with the Covenanters in Scotland had become far more pressing than his alliance with Denmark-Norway, or indeed any other foreign power.[116]

Stuart diplomacy with the Oldenburg state in the post-Jacobean era is indicative of the cooling relations between the two Courts. Indeed, for those employed in Scandinavia, it proved absolutely fundamental in ensuring a continued dialogue was maintained with Christian IV, especially after Charles declared war on Spain and France. It was through their work that a total breach in communication between London and Copenhagen was prevented. Though this was not said explicitly by Christian IV, his actions over the next ten years were proof of his growing differentiation between the Scots and Englishmen who represented the House of Stuart in Denmark. Even the visit to London of Prince Ulrik in 1630, Charles's cousin and a son of Christian IV, did not ease relations.[117] Though Charles appeared happy to entertain his cousin, the visit had no obvious diplomatic significance. Crown Prince Christian (V) did not even know how the relationship with the two kings stood. In October 1633, the prince thanked Sir Robert Anstruther for passing on the good wishes of Charles I to himself and added tellingly that he 'assumed' that there would be a similar message for his father.[118] The tentative nature of the 'assumption' highlights the prince's awareness of the tension in the family. Perhaps, realising his father's intransigence, and in a bid to keep links with the Stuart Court alive, Christian (V) sent a stream of royal servants, including cooks, chemists, hunters and musicians to the Stuart Court for their education between 1632 and 1635.[119] If nothing else these men would serve as a reminder of the blood link between the two Courts and hopefully re-spark a positive relationship.

When Christian IV did send an ambassador to the Stuart Court in 1632, he apparently had no instructions to discuss the politics of northern Europe.[120] The Stuart-Oldenburg relationship was rather neatly summarised by the Venetian, Vicenso Gussoni, in April 1635 when he noted that:

> with the King of Denmark he [Charles I] has rather a close blood

---

[115] PRO SP 81/45, f. 244. Roe to Coke, 12 April 1639.

[116] Elliot, 'The Year of the Three Ambassadors', 166-167.

[117] *CSPV*, XXII, 1629-1632, 435-436. Giovanni Soranzo, 8 November 1630; A J Loomie ed, *Ceremonies of Charles I, The Notebooks of John Finet 1628-1641* (New York, 1987), 315.

[118] Marquard, *Prins Christian (V)'s Brev*. I, 116. Missive to Anstruther, 8 October 1633.

[119] Marquard, *Prins Christian (V)'s Brev*. I, 30, 52, 108 and 230

[120] *CSPV*, XXII, 1629-1632, 603-604 and 613-4. Vicenzo Gussoni, 2 April and 7 May 1632.

used to do.[121]

Only as the frost which had covered Stuart-Oldenburg relations slowly thawed did ambassadors and agents from Denmark-Norway reappear at the Stuart Court. Even the ageing William Below, Danish resident at the Stuart Court from 1606-1626, was briefed by Charles to undertake fresh duties between the Oldenburg and Stuart states in 1639.[122] Like Christian IV, Charles opted not to keep a resident ambassador in his kinsman's Court. Whether this was a direct response to the withdrawal of any permanent Danish resident from London is unclear.

Charles I conducted a different sort of diplomacy to that of his father. Resident ambassadors with a strong cultural and political understanding of a given country gave way to the 'one off' ambassador favoured by Charles and other European leaders.[123] Few of these new men had the chance to develop the understanding and personal relationships between monarch and resident which marked the diplomacy of the Jacobean diplomats. In a way this continued unofficially after the Treaty of Lübeck. It was, after all, the personal friendships that Donald Mackay and Robert Anstruther had with Christian IV that allowed them access to the Danish king. Compare the embassies of the Scots and reception with those of the new English agents in Scandinavia. The Scottish colonel in Swedish service, Sir James Ramsay, had to reconcile a serious "mistake" which Sir Thomas Roe had made with Gustav II Adolf at their first meeting in Prussia in 1629.[124] Sir Henry Vane could not get an audience in Copenhagen and the Earl of Leicester left believing he had been snubbed. Through sheer perseverance Anstruther eventually gained the concessions that Leicester had failed to achieve basically through his long term relationship with the king. Other men also laid the groundwork for the Stuart-Oldenburg treaty of 1639. Donald Mackay Lord Reay and Alexander Master of Forbes both helped to keep lines of communication

---

[121] *CSPV*, XXIII, 1632-1636, 361-370. Relation of England of Vicenzo Gussoni, 13 April 1635.

[122] *CSPD*, 1638-1639, 618. William Below's petition for payment of arrears, 27 March 1639. Below claimed unfair financial treatment which the Council decided to rectify 'so that after 50 years toil and travail he may bring his wearied bones to the grave without curse and disgrace'. This occurred in March 1639 only days before the new treaty with Denmark was signed, and with the acknowledgement that Charles was about to employ Below in some important business.

[123] Charles's preference for extraordinary ambassadors for extraordinary occasions and residents, secretaries or such ministers for ordinary ones was noted by Gussoni. The problem for Charles was that he lived in extraordinary times. See *CSPV*, XXIII, 1632-1636, 361-370. The Relation of England of Vicenzo Gussoni, 13 April 1635.

[124] Roe had to be reminded about this in 1633 when he became a bit full of himself. See John Durie to Sir Thomas Roe, 28 January 1633, reprinted in G. Westin, *Negotiations about church unity 1628-1634; John Durie, Gustavus Adolphus, Axel Oxenstierna* (Uppsala, 1934-36), 230-233.

snubbed. Through sheer perseverance Anstruther eventually gained the concessions that Leicester had failed to achieve basically through his long term relationship with the king. Other men also laid the groundwork for the Stuart-Oldenburg treaty of 1639. Donald Mackay Lord Reay and Alexander Master of Forbes both helped to keep lines of communication open between the courts in London and Copenhagen. Joseph Averie and Henry de Vic also played their part though only Roe is usually given credit for the treaty.

Though the Jacobean *corps-diplomatique* had proved a reasonably successful organisation but, by the end of the 1620s, it had become quite anachronistic. The *corps-diplomatique* did not have the same vision of Britain or the House of Stuart that either Charles I or most of his subjects had. There had been a degree of disillusionment with the monarchy since the start of the Bohemian crisis in 1618, which vented itself in outbursts against the lack of support by 'Great Britain' for the cause of Elizabeth Stuart. With the death of James Stuart in 1625, Great Britain faced the new challenges. Despite attempts thereafter to save the concept of 'Great Britain', the notion of a single polity state continued to lose favour in England, but also in Scotland as well. When the Scottish Privy Council commanded Sir John Scott to avoid the usage of the name Great Britain in domestic treaties, they effectively conceded that 'Great Britain' had failed as anything other than a convenient label for foreign relations. The instruction from the Scottish Privy Council was symptomatic of a distancing of Scottish institutions from Stuart politics in general which would eventually lead to the first Bishops' War in 1639.

Indeed there are many examples of Scotsmen seeking to promote their own particular cause outwith the official Stuart aegis, even while being employed as Stuart ambassadors. James Spens sought to impede Francis Gordon's official mission to Poland since any Stuart contact with the Polish court ran contrary to the agenda of the Swedish government. Spens saw to it that another Scottish agent, Hugh Mowatt, was planted in the Polish Court with the explicit brief of destroying both Gordon's mission and reputation. This appointment saw Mowatt contract himself to the Swedish government and Spens requesting Axel Oxenstierna to conceal the receipt of delicate information from Sir Robert Anstruther during his Swedish embassy.[125]

The Roman Catholic Earl of Nithsdale sent one Friar Aston, described as a 'Scottish Religious' in a diplomatic capacity, with the Danish

---

[125] SRA, Anglica 5. Spens to Axel Oxenstierna, 8 March, 12 and 29 July 1626; SRA, Anglica 3. Spens to Gustav II Adolf, 8 August 1626, including Hugh Mowatt's letter binding himself to Swedish service.

ambassadors to the French treaty negotiations in 1629.[126] The Vatican agent to the Stuart Court in 1636 was a Scotsman, Father George Con, while the Stuart agent in the Vatican was the Scottish Catholic, Sir William Hamilton.[127] Another Scottish cleric, John Durie, sought to unify the various Protestant denominations throughout the whole of northern Europe.[128] To this end he followed a path which often led to his playing a diplomatic role. Durie accompanied Anstruther to the Frankfurt diet in 1634 against the express wishes of Laud, the Archbishop of Canterbury, though Anstruther covertly supported him. Durie met frequently with both Gustav II Adolf and Axel Oxenstierna of Sweden in his efforts to promote a Protestant union. His intellectual ideas, although frequently challenged for their radical nature, reverberated through the minds of the European intellectual and diplomatic elite including Christian IV.[129]

In the light of the confusion and distrust that many felt during the reign of Charles I, it should perhaps not be surprising that the form of 'independent' diplomacy practised by Durie and Aston should be that employed by the Covenanters on behalf of the Scottish nation. During this time a new, aggressive, Scottish diplomacy proved very successful indeed, though it had little to do with the dour years of Stuart-Oldenburg relations. When centralising Stuart-British policies (erroneously perceived as pro-English policies) threatened the liberties of the Scottish nation, the resulting turmoil eventually led to direct conflict between the Scottish Covenanters and the Royalist army of King Charles. The Covenanting revolution occurred at exactly the time that the Stuart and Danish royal houses officially returned to a full diplomatic relationship. As such, the Stuart and Scottish association with Denmark-Norway began to follow, for a time at least, somewhat separate paths -- paths that sometimes crossed but frequently collided.

---

[126] *CSPV*, XXII, 1629-1632, 2-3. Zorzi Zorzi in France to Alvise Contarini, 3 April 1629.

[127] M. F. S. Hervey, *The Life, Correspondence and Collections of Thomas Howard Earl of Arundel* (New York, 1969), 381. The Earl of Arundel to Sir William Hamilton, 6/16 September 1636, Arundel to Rev. W. Petty, 4 November 1636: 'I wrote unto you formerly to be acquainted with Sir William Hamilton who represents at Rome for our Queen'; C. V. Wedgwood, *The King's Peace, 1637-1641* (New York, 1991 reprint), 122.

[128] Brown, *Itinerant Ambassador*, 199-208.

[129] DRA, TKUA General Part 141, 1634-39, 'Letters with enclosures from the clergyman John Durie (Johannes Duraeus) to King Christian IV'; A. Milton, 'The Unchanged Peacemaker? John Dury and the politics of irenicism in England, 1628-1643', in M. Greengrass et al., eds, *Samuel Hartlib and Universal Reformation. Studies in Intellectual Communication* (Cambridge, 1994), 95-117; S. Mandelbrote, 'John Dury and the Practice of Irenicism', in N. Aston ed, *Religious Change in Europe 1650-1914* (Oxford, 1997), 40-58; *Svenskt Biografiskt Lexikon*, IX, 581-585.

CHAPTER FOUR

Agendas at Odds: Stuart and Covenanter Diplomacy with Denmark-Norway 1638-1641

The previous chapter highlighted that, by April 1639, diplomatic relations between the House of Stuart and Denmark-Norway had returned to a state of amicable confederation based on the Stuart-Oldenburg treaty of 1621. Charles I now set about cementing the alliance into a firm commitment for the young Elector Palatine. Events were to prove, however, that there were too many conflicting agendas at work to resolve the Palatine issue. Although Charles I had managed to renew his alliance with his uncle, he had effectively lost control of power within his own native kingdom of Scotland. From the drafting of the National Covenant in February 1638, few people could doubt that Charles I faced the prospect of a rebellion in Scotland. Ostensibly Scottish reaction was triggered by the threat of religious uniformity being imposed by Charles I onto the Calvinist traditions of the Kirk in Scotland. But the Covenanting movement represented more than just the grievances of the Kirk. Allan Macinnes has summed up the movement as 'a revolutionary alliance of the landed and commercial classes intent on redressing constitutional and nationalist grievances in the State as well as upholding the Presbyterian version of the Reformed tradition in the Kirk'.[1]

In order to suppress the Covenanting movement, Charles I embarked on a course of military action and he issued circular letters to the soldiers serving on the continent to return and support his military preparations. His pleas went largely unheeded by his Scottish subjects. Their response to Charles's request was epitomised by the answer he received from Sir John Seaton, a colonel in the Swedish army, who replied that he could not bring himself to serve the king against his native kingdom.[2] The minority of Scottish officers in continental service still loyal to the Stuart crown preferred to remain abroad rather than get involved in a civil war in Scotland.[3] The extent of the shift in loyalty by the Scottish

---

[1] A. I. Macinnes, *Clanship, Commerce and the House of Stuart, 1603-1788* (East Lothian, 1996), 88. See also D. Stevenson, *Scottish Covenanters and Irish Confederates* (Belfast, 1981); M. Lee jr., *The Road to Revolution: Scotland under Charles I 1625-37* (Illinois, 1985); Morrill, *The National Covenant*; M. C. Fissel, *The Bishops' Wars; Charles I's campaigns against Scotland 1638-1640* (Cambridge, 1994).

[2] D. Lang ed, *The Letters and Journals of Robert Baillie, Principle of the University of Glasgow MDCXXXVII-MDCLXII* (Edinburgh, 1841), 72; Burton, *The Scot Abroad*, 226.

[3] PRO SP 81/47, f.102. Certificate of General King upon arms sent to England, 28 June 1639. Lt General Sir James King, Colonel Francis Ruthven, Lt. Colonel James King, Colonel John Leslie, Lt Colonel John Chamberlain and Lt. Colonel Gladstone were all loyal 'British'

professional soldiering class became evident when Colonel Robert
Monro commanded the first Covenanting regiment in the field in 1639.
Lord Reay, his former colonel in chief, followed him into the field in
May 1639, and numerous other officers streamed home from the
continent in defiance of their king.[4] One observer noted that:

> there came home so many commanders, all gentlemen out of
> foreign countrayes as would have seemed to command one armie of
> fytie thousand and furnish them with all sorts of officers, from a
> generall doun to a sergeant or corprall.[5]

Sir Thomas Roe witnessed the exodus and noted that there was no way
to prevent them shipping from Bremen. He did however suggest to the
English Secretary of State that the deployment of ships to prevent their
landing might serve as a powerful example to others that tried to get
home.[6]

As the Scots prepared for war against their king they looked to their
European neighbours for the weapons and ammunition to enable them to
do so. The desired diplomacy reached fruition through the personal
friendship and correspondence of Alexander Leslie and the Swedish
Chancellor, Axel Oxenstierna.[7] In June 1638, Leslie wrote to the
Swedish *Riksråd* regarding the nature of the Scottish Covenant and
seeking Swedish support. The Swedes agreed to the furnishing of some
artillery which was granted as an advance on Leslie's salary. This was
backed within a fortnight by an arrangement to supply 2,000 muskets,
through the Scottish merchants, John Maclean of Gothenburg and his
uncle James Maclean in Stockholm. This measure had been taken to
avoid giving Charles the impression that the Swedes were sanctioning
rebellion.[8] The Marquis of Hamilton also knew about the Covenanters'
military preparations noting that 'they ar still sending for more armes
and amunitioun not onlie from Hollen but lykuys from Hamburg, Breme,
Lubick, Dansick, and Sued, that if one part should faill they may be
suppleud from ane other'.[9] This goes a long way toward indicating the

---

subjects that associated with Sir Thomas Roe but chose to remain on the continent during the
first Bishops' war.

4   Furgol, *A Regimental History*, 35.
5   Burton, *The Scot Abroad*, 226.
6   PRO SP 81/45, ff.113 and 117. Roe to Secretary of State, 15 and 19 February 1639.
7   *RAOSB*, IX, 480-519; D. Stevenson, *The Scottish Revolution 1637-1644; The Triumph of the
    Covenanters* (Newton Abbot, 1973), 137-138; Grosjean, 'Scots and the Swedish State', 154-
    165.
8   *SRP*, VII, 274-9. 2, 9 and 10 August 1638; Grosjean, 'Scots and the Swedish State', 166-172.
9   NAS, GD 406/1/10491, 24 June 1638; S. R. Gardiner ed, *Hamilton Papers: Being selections
    from original letters in the possession of His Grace the Duke of Hamilton and Brandon*

degree to which the Scottish community had infiltrated the Baltic ports as well as highlighting the persuasive nature of Scottish diplomats and agents. Not only were ships transporting officers and men arriving from northern Europe, but the English Secretary of State was informed that 20 to 30 Dutch ships were being fitted for war. They were to be manned by Scots and Dutchmen, sailed under Scottish colours and ready to attack English ships as soon as war was declared.[10] The problem for the Scottish Covenanters was that they had to transport their soldiers and weapons across waterways controlled by two of the strongest navies in Europe, the Stuart navy and the maritime forces of Denmark-Norway. Both states were united under their confederation of April 1621, and that alliance was renewed in April 1639, binding them closer once more than any of their other allies.[11]

Denmark-Norway and the Bishops' Wars 1638-1641

While the general background to the Covenanting conflict is well known, the degree of involvement of Denmark-Norway in the conflict, both politically and militarily, has remained obscure. At least three nations were overtly thought to be supportive of the Covenanters; the United Provinces, France and Sweden. As a state that had rebelled against its king because he had tried to impose a uniform confession of faith upon them, it is perhaps unsurprising that the United Provinces should feel sympathy for the Covenanting movement. For Sweden, the analogy to the Covenanters was not so obvious in terms of religion, but as Axel Oxenstierna pointed out to the *Riksråd*, Sweden too owed her independence to an uprising against the tyrannical rule of a foreign power, Denmark.[12]

France proved supportive of the Scottish Covenanters for a variety of reasons, not least due to the 'Auld Alliance'. Secretary Coke persuaded Charles of the fact that the French were helping the Scots.[13] Indeed a survey of Cardinal Richelieu's diplomatic correspondence of shows that there certainly were covert overtures from the French to see how they

---

relating to the years 1638-1650 (London, 1880), 17. Marquis of Hamilton to Charles 1, 24 June 1638.

[10]   *CSPD*, 1639, 234. Mr Bogan to Secretary Windebank, 26 May 1639

[11]   PRO SP 81/45, f.244. Roe to Coke, 12 April 1639; *Danmark-Norges Traktater*, IV, 14, 191-209. 'Fornyelse af den 29 April 1621 mellem Danmark-Norge og Storbritannien sluttede Alliance og Handelstraktat; med dertil hørende Biakter, 6 April 1639'.

[12]   *SRP*, VIII, *1640-41*, 160. 27 July 1640.

[13]   Elliot, 'The Year of the Three Ambassadors', 167; Stevenson, *Scottish Covenanters and Irish Confederates*, 91; *CSPD*, 1638-39, 143. Coke to Windebank, 9 May 1639. 'you will understand what heavy burden the French begin to lay upon our merchants, and how they favour the Scots after the old manner'.

could help.[14] These letters were well known of in both the United Provinces and Sweden, as the Dutch and Swedish agents discuss them freely.[15] Ironically, one of the French agents trying to help the Franco-Covenanter accord was the Scottish Jesuit agent, Thomas Chambers, known in France as Abbot Chambre.[16]

The previous chapter showed that during the early phases of the Covenanting build up, Denmark-Norway, or at least the Danish king, still retained an active grudge against Charles I. Additionally, Christian IV would not necessarily have been rigid in his condemnation of any movement similar to the Covenanters. After all he had himself, as Duke of Holstein, supported challenges to the accepted legal order of superiority when he declared war against the Habsburg Empire in 1625. Yet for all the live animosity between himself and Charles I, the concept of Christian IV actively lending supporting to a group challenging the authority of an anointed king descended from the Danish royal house, must have been considered remote. However, the Scots exercised a considerable influence within the Danish-Norwegian merchant communities, which in turn could conceivably have an effect on Danish revenue should they withhold taxes or disrupt trade. Perhaps because of this mercantile influence rumours reached the Stuart Court that Christian IV might actually assist the Covenanters.[17]

In addition to trying to gain the friendship of Christian IV, the Covenanters may well have thought of approaching various well-placed Scots in Danish society for help in their cause. If such moves could not

[14] M V Hay ed, *The Blair Papers* (London, 1929), Appendix VI, Richelieu and the Covenanters, 250-253 where Hay argues for French intervention as early as 1637-38; M Avenel ed, *Lettres, Instructions Diplomatiques et Papiers D'Etat du Cardinal Richelieu* (Paris, 1867), VI, 688-691. 3 letters, one pre 4 May, one 4 May and one 5 May 1640, Richelieu to M de Chavigni. In the footnote of the second letter it is mentioned that attached to the original manuscript there is a folio with a translation of the instructions given to William Colville, representative of the gentlemen and lords of Scotland. It is dated 17 April 1640 and signed by 'Leslee, Mar, Louden, Forester, Rothes, Montrose and Montgomeri'. The letters themselves discuss how to avoid accusations from Charles I now that Colville has been arrested in London, and how to tip off the other Scottish agent [Erskine] without arousing suspicion.

[15] B. L. Meulenbroek ed, *Briefwisseling van Hugo Grotius* (The Hague, 1981), XI, 251 and 256. Grotius to J. Salvius, Swedish Envoy to Hamburg, 5 May 1640 and same to L. Camerarius, Swedish agent in The Hague, 12 May 1640.

[16] *CSPD*, 1640, 100-101. Anon., 22 April 1640. This letter observed that the brother of Thomas Chambers, Friar and Almoner to Richelieu had noted the Abbot's intervention between the French government and the 'nobility' of Scotland although the author did not state in which capacity. See also Avenel, *Lettres, Instructions Diplomatiques et Papiers D'Etat du Cardinal Richelieu*, 688. The footnote notes Coleville to be the intermediary between the Scots and Chambers for the secret correspondence between the two parties. Consult also Hay, *The Blair Papers*, 250-253. Disappointingly, while using Avenel for Richelieu sources, Hay failed to discuss the presence or role of Colville or Erskine in France.

[17] *CSPD*, 1639, 264. Thomas Harrison to Charles I, 1 June 1639.

guarantee support for the movement, they might have hoped that such individuals could exploit the extant ill feeling of Christian IV toward Charles I to guarantee Danish-Norwegian neutrality. Whether through the influence of such men, or simply in a bid to avoid getting wrapped up in Charles's domestic conflicts, foreign powers including Denmark-Norway and Sweden sent ambassadors to mediate between the Stuart king and the Scots. Despite ten years of harbouring a public grudge against Charles I, Christian IV voiced concerns about the political situation in the British Isles. He let it be known to his nephew that he wished to act as a mediator between him and the Scottish Estates. To add weight to Christian's desire to be confirmed in his role as international peace broker, a Danish ambassador was to be dispatched immediately for Scotland, and was due to arrive in London in March 1639.[18] The Venetian Ambassador doubted that the Danish representative would even be given an audience by Charles since the Danes had travelled to the Scottish Estates before they arrived at the Stuart Court in London.[19] The Archbishop of Canterbury noted that Charles had turned down Christian's offer of mediation and Secretary Windebank confirmed this to Roe at the beginning of May.[20] Regardless of this snub, rumours circulated that Denmark would contribute a large combat force to back the king's campaign in Scotland. This chatter proved unfounded and no armed intervention from Denmark-Norway occurred. Christian did not consider such a military operation as viable. In Scotland it was believed that the reason for this was because the Swedish Chancellor, Axel Oxenstierna, had diverted Danish attention from Scotland with some posturing with his army close to the Danish border.[21]

Charles I's decision to attack Scotland proved to be a costly mistake for the House of Stuart. Although fighting had been avoided in most areas outwith the Northeast of Scotland, the truce of Berwick in June 1639 left the Covenanters in effective control of Scotland. Sir John Coke took great care to relate the positive terms of the truce Charles had secured from the Scots to Sir Thomas Roe in Hamburg, adding:

and soe with infinite honour to His Majestie the nations are reunited in obedience and affection, which may give just hope that our neighbours will not hereafter undervalue us and that His Majesties

[18]   PRO SP 81/46, f.51. Christian IV to Roe, 18/28 January 1639; *CSPV*, XXIV, 1636-1639, 512. 25. Giovanni Giustinian, 25 March 1639.
[19]   *CSPV*, XXIV, 1636-1639, 512. 25. Giovanni Giustinian, 25 March 1639.
[20]   PRO SP 81/46, f.244. Archbishop of Canterbury to Roe, 17 April 1639; PRO SP 81/47, f.7. Windebank to Roe, 3 May 1639.
[21]   P. Gordon, *A Short Abrigement of Britane's Distemper* (Aberdeen, 1844), 6-7.

affairs abroad will proceed with reputation, according to this evidence of His wisdome and power.[22]

In truth, Charles had been humiliated militarily and had expended a great deal of money on his failed expedition. Further, the effectiveness of Charles's control in his other two kingdoms had been challenged by the actions of the Scots. In order to redress this situation Charles used the time provided by the truce to prepare again for war with the intention of reasserting his authority. In April 1640 he summoned the English Parliament hoping for a subsidy equal to the £150,000 'bullied' from the Irish Parliament by Lord Wentworth.[23] Charles was unsuccessful, dissolved the Parliament in May and resolved on war with Scotland without its backing.

Between the end of 1639 and the end of 1640 a Scottish veteran of Swedish service, General Sir James King, based himself in Hamburg where he maintained contact with both the Swedish and Danish Courts. It is likely that King had been recruited by Charles I to help him build an army of trained officers and soldiers from abroad in 1640. Sir Thomas Roe and James King both visited Christian IV looking for soldiers and promising money in advance. Christian intimated that if that was the case he could gather men from Hamburg, Lübeck and the surrounding areas although there was a distinct tone of scepticism in his words. General King specifically sought 3,000 Danish cavalry. Although Christian did not allow that levy, he ordered his Foreign Secretary, Frederik Gunther, to divert horses destined for Spanish service to England.[24] It has been claimed that Danish troops were to be used simply because they could ride roughshod over native troops. The family relationship between the two kings and a desperate need for professional forces are more probable reasons for Charles seeking Danish help. However, Charles did mention that should there be peace with the Scots, the Danes would be handy for bringing under control the 'Commons of *this kingdom,* who in these times of his majesty's necessity have shewed too much disaffection'– and by this he must have meant England.[25]

Rumours circulated that the English Lord Treasurer had been instructed to issue Sir James King with £50,000 to purchase arms, but no merchant could be found to make up this money. Christian IV noted his

---

[22] PRO SP 81/47, f.85. Coke to Roe, 20 June 1639.

[23] Brown, *Kingdom or Province*, 119.

[24] *KCFB*, IV, 300-301, 358 and 361. Christian IV to Korfitz Ulfeldt, 10 February, 19 June and 20 July 1640; DRA, TKUA England A1 3; *CSPD*, 1640, 365 and 450. 30 June and 4 July 1640; Fissel, *The Bishops' Wars*, 172.

[25] Quoted in Fissel, *The Bishops' Wars*, 172-173 (my italics).

arrival in a letter to his son-in-law, Korfitz Ulfeldt, the Danish Chancellor. He informed Ulfeldt that the Scot brought news of Charles's dire position in both England and Scotland.[26] Sir James King met Christian soon after and urged his support. Christian expressed his willingness to help Charles but asked for a written proposal which, for secrecy's sake, the General could not comply with. General King was granted a further audience with Christian IV in mid-July during which meeting Christian offered some of his own troops for the Stuart army. He further gave permission for Charles I to levy in Danish territory at his own expense but added that Charles would be responsible for supplying ships to transport these men.[27]

The Covenanters were fully aware of Charles's intentions and continued to seek allies and support on the continent. They pre-empted Charles's military operation by co-ordinating their continental network of agents and diplomats to ensure they were always a step ahead of their Royalist counterparts. Colonel Sir John Cochrane, a former Stuart diplomat, travelled to Scandinavia and Germany as the ambassador of the Scottish nation in April 1640. He first visited Sweden where he reiterated the Scottish perception of the conflict. Cochrane vigorously argued that the Scots feared something akin to the Spanish Inquisition should Charles I gain the upper hand. Most importantly, from the point of view of the Scottish nation, he concluded that the polity of Scotland itself was being changed by the king. Scottish laws and liberty were being dismantled and the kingdom of Scotland reduced to a province by the Stuart monarch.[28] Cochrane insisted that the Scots required neither money nor troops, as Scotland was well supplied with both. Rather he sought only ships, arms and relevant munitions which he promised would be returned to Sweden once the struggle was over. The Swedes were duly persuaded and responded with arms through the familiar route of John Maclean in Gothenburg.

Cochrane's diplomacy in Denmark pressed a more peaceful message than that of the Swedish mission, asking only for the Danish king's intervention to maintain peace.[29] By convincing Christian IV to act as

---

[26]   *KCFB*, IV, 367-368. Christian IV to Korfitz Ulfeldt, 13 July 1640; Fissel, *The Bishops' Wars*, 172.

[27]   NAS, GD 406/1/1146 and 1147. Sir James King to the Marquis of Hamilton, 19 July 1640; Fissel, *The Bishops' Wars*, 172-3.

[28]   In this they had some justification for their beliefs, since suggestions had been mooted that Scotland should be governed as a dependency of England by the English Privy Council; Russell, 'The British Problem' 400; *SRP*, VIII, 1640-41, 97-99 and 118. July 1640. Cochrane's mission to Sweden is discussed in greater detail in Grosjean, 'Scotland and the Swedish State', 166-172.

[29]   DRA, TKUA Scotland AI 4. f.79a. Scottish Estates to Christian IV, 24/14 April 1640.

arbiter, Cochrane averted outright condemnation of the Covenanters by emphasising the just nature of their actions. He claimed that it was only due to the 'treacherous peace' of the King that the Scots continued in their defiance of Charles I. Through written requests and the physical presence of Cochrane, the Covenanters had neutralised Christian IV in the dispute between Charles I and the Scottish Estates. In his response to them, Christian declared that, after long consultations with Cochrane, he understood the situation in Scotland and could see the Scottish nation's 'evident virtues', knowing they only desired the situation to be resolved to ensure peace in the 'united kingdoms'.[30] Christian IV interceded by letter with Charles and ordered his ambassadors Korfitz Ulfeldt and Greggers Krabbe to 'fix' the misunderstandings that existed between his dear nephew the King of Great Britain and his royal [Scottish] subjects. These ambassadors arrived at Court in September and had three meetings with the king. At each they insisted that they were only in Britain to arrange a compromise between the Scots and Charles I and would not engage in any other business.[31]

The quest for peace in Scotland had not been the only desire of the Danish king. Christian IV had issued his ambassadors with a letter requesting a private audience for them with Charles I. At that meeting the Danes were to discuss the conditions by which Christian IV would take possession of the Orkney and Shetland islands in return for Danish assistance to the Stuart cause. Christian was well aware that under his agreements with the Stuarts in 1621 and 1639 he had agreed not to broach this subject during his lifetime. However, he argued that, since the Scots had taken up arms against their king and Charles would gain benefit from his offer, it was worth breaking his undertaking.[32] Of course, the commercial benefit to Denmark-Norway of a whaling and fisheries centre on the Northern Isles – as well as a strategic point to defend their northern fisheries – cannot have been overlooked by Christian IV. It has been said that the plan fell through because Charles remained unwilling to cede the Orkneys and that this in turn left the Royalists under-armed, undermanned and incapable of mounting an effective campaign in Scotland. However, Charles did not directly reject his uncle's offer. Indeed he offered to pawn the Scottish islands to Christian IV for 50,000 gold guilders. The plan fell through because the

---

[30] DRA, TKUA Scotland AI 4. f.79b. Christian IV to the Scottish Estates, 10 November 1640.

[31] *KCFB*, IV, 378. Christian IV to Korfitz Ulfeldt and Gregers Krabbe, 9 August 1640; *CSPD*, 1640-1641, 120. Nicholas to Roe, 30 September 1640; ibid., 128, Secretary Vane to Windebank, 1 October 1640.

[32] *KCFB*, IV, 379. Christian IV to Charles 1, 9 August 1640; Fissel, *The Bishops' Wars*, 172-3; Fridericia, *Danmarks Ydre Politiske Historie*, II, 316; Lockhart, *Denmark in the Thirty Years' War*, 255.

Danish king remained unconvinced that the islands were worth that sum of money.[33]

Christian IV responded that the islands were worth nothing to the House of Stuart owing to the fact that the sitting laird supported the Covenanters. Since Charles could not collect one 'dalers' worth of revenue from the islands, Christian's revised proposal involved a waiving of the pawn price in return for direct military action. He claimed that once in possession of the Orkneys he could occupy and fortify them and gain a foothold in Scotland from which he could apply further pressure to the Covenanters. He additionally offered to promote the use of foreign troops in this process and, using the combination of Danish occupation and mercenary support, force the Scots to re-evaluate their course of action against their king.[34] Christian's immediate schemes however came too late for Charles I. In August 1640, 18,000 Scottish soldiers crossed the border into England under Field Marshall Alexander Leslie. They defeated the Royalist forces at Newburn on 22 August and occupied Newcastle by the end of the month. Charles had little prospect of subduing them militarily and was forced to come to terms with the Scots. A truce was agreed at Ripon in October which eventually resulted in peace being formalised by the Treaty of London in August 1641.

The Stuart-Oldenburg alliance 1639-640: an evaluation.

While Christian IV attempted mediation between Charles I and the Scots, he also appeared to have been undertaking practical measures to prevent war from breaking out. If the Covenanters were deprived of the means to conduct a war, then theoretically they would have to come to terms with Charles I. As early as June 1638, the Marquis of Hamilton suggested that the Stuart allies should be contacted in order that all shipping bound for Scotland be stopped and searched for supporters of the Covenant or military supplies for them.[35] Christian IV in particular was to be prevailed upon to prevent movement of shipping through the Sound. Christian had pre-empted this request and in April 1638, Admiral Axel Mowatt received orders to leave his winter anchorage in Trondheim to scour the coast for enemies of the Danish king and anyone smuggling forbidden goods. His fleet was to be kept at sea until the end of September after which he had instructions to bring all his ships to Copenhagen.[36]

[33]   Fridericia, *Danmarks Ydre Politiske Historie*, II, 316; *SRP*, VIII, 3 July 1640, 81-82; Fissel, *The Bishops' Wars*, 173.

[34]   *KCFB*, IV, 378. Christian IV to Korfitz Ulfeldt and Gregers Krabbe, 9 August 1640.

[35]   Gardiner, *The Hamilton Papers*, 17. Marquis of Hamilton to Charles 1, 24 June 1638.

[36]   E. Marquard, *Kancelliets Brevbøger, 1637-1639* (Copenhagen, 1949), 338. Orders to

In addition to the employment of the Danish-Norwegian navy, the Marquis of Hamilton suggested that Charles could place one of his own ships at Elsinore to intercept vessels from Lübeck, Sweden or Danzig. In October 1638, Charles I deployed his navy to search Scottish merchant craft, ostensibly in a bid to discover clandestine cargoes of armaments, but in reality trying to try to capture Field Marshall Alexander Leslie on his return from Swedish service.[37] The following month Hamilton suggested that Charles keep between 8-10 warships in the Firth of Forth and a further 3-4 on roving patrol between the Firth and Aberdeen. This, he argued, would cripple Scottish commerce, defeating the Covenanters within the year 'without further charge to Your Majesty', as the Scots were so dependent on trade.[38] Hamilton was clear on this point: blockade Scottish trade and prevent the import of victuals and thereafter Scotland would succumb to the Crown. He did add, however, that all those who submitted to the King's favour should have the economic blockade against them lifted and given royal protection. One contemporary English report recorded that, by April 1639, there were:

> 20 Scotch ships stopped in the Thames. In most of the ports of England and Wales and in some ports of Ireland, there are Scotch ships arrested, so that the King has in his custody most of the ships which belong to Scotland. It may be concluded that all their traffic by sea is already cut off.[39]

Scottish losses continued in May 1639 when the Stuart navy captured a ship that had sailed from Bremen with many of Leslie's former officers from Swedish service. Indeed by the second Bishops' War, several more Scottish supply vessels had been taken into Berwick with at least 5,000 muskets on board.[40]

The Danish king also intercepted several Scottish ships laden with arms which attempted to pass through the Sound and apologised for any

Admiral Mowatt from Christian IV, 11 April 1638.

[37] Gardiner, *The Hamilton Papers*, 17. Marquis of Hamilton to Charles 1, 24 June 1638; NAS, GD 406/1/685. Earl of Roxburghe to Marquis Hamilton, 1 October 1638.

[38] J. B. Hattendorf, et al. eds, *British Naval Documents 1204-1960* (London, 1960), 152-153.

[39] *CSPD, 1639*, 70-71. Edmund Rossingham to Viscount Conway, 23 April 1639.

[40] NAS GD 406/1/924. Marquis Hamilton to Eleazer Borthwick, 20 May 1639, and NAS, GD 406/1/1193. Marquis Hamilton to Sir Henry Vane, 21 May 1639. *CSPD*, 1639, 225-7. 24 May 1639; PRO SP 81/46, f.117. Roe to Secretary of State, 19 February 1639; *CSPD*, 1640, 154, 244, 260 and 273. The Royalists did not have things all their own way when it came to seizing ships carrying arms. Alexander Jaffray of Aberdeen noted that 'My Lord Carnegies armes puder and and ball [is] tane cuming be sea from Kircaldie to Montroiss so that thair is no assurance be sea evin'. See L. B. Taylor ed, *Aberdeen Council Letters* (Oxford, 1950), II, 215. Alexander Jaffray to Provost Patrick Leslie, anno. 1640. Lord Carnegie was the Earl of Southesk and imprisoned by the Covenanters in 1640 due to his support for the Royalists.

shipments which had run the blockade without his knowledge.[41] By July 1639, the city of Edinburgh lobbied the Danish Chancellor, Christian Friis, for the return of *The George* of Leith which had been impounded for trying to pass the Sound with gunpowder and lead. The Edinburgh burgesses argued that the edict of Christian IV banning such trade had not been in place when the skipper, Captain Downie, had headed east through the Sound, therefore the edict should not apply on his return journey westward.[42] Another Leith ship, *St. Peter*, had also been impounded for trying to pass through the Sound with a cargo of gunpowder. The skipper of this ship, Jacob Douin, did not receive permission to retrieve his command until July 1641.[43]

Sir John Coke complimented Sir Thomas Roe for his part in preventing the transportation of arms through the Sound. Some ships carrying Scottish weapons were refused permission to complete their journeys, while some found their cargoes impounded. Christian IV himself bought some of these intercepted weapons and allowed Sir Thomas Roe to buy some of the rest for the use of Charles I.[44] These, however, proved to be the worst of those seized and some 30 muskets acquired in this way exploded on their first discharge.[45]

The main targets of Mowatt's navy appear to have been the Dutch and the Swedes and not the Scots. Danish-Dutch relations had been strained since Christian had increased the Sound Tolls in 1638. One ship, belonging to the Dutch entrepreneur Louis de Geer, was arrested for carrying arms and munitions, though permission to pass eventually came from Christian IV. The Dutchman argued successfully that the weapons were destined for service against the Habsburg Empire and not for use in Scotland.[46] De Geer was fortunate. In June 1640, Sir Thomas Roe described an additional facet to Christian's policy in the Sound whereby

---

[41]   PRO SP 81/45, ff.307-311. Roe to Coke, 7/17 December 1638.

[42]   M. Wood ed, *Extracts From the Records of the Burgh of Edinburgh 1626-1641* (Edinburgh, 1936), 222.

[43]   *Kancelliets Brevbøger, 1637-1639*, 511. Christian IV to Sten Beck, 15 July 1641.

[44]   PRO SP 81/46, ff.15-16. Coke to Roe, 10 January 1639; The amount of weapons stayed in the Sound of Swedish origins in early 1639 reveals the extent of Swedish support to the Covenanters. There were 4,400 forks and bandoleers in Denmark and 1,000 horsemen's arms and 1,000 pikesmen's arms in Sweden amongst other goods already in Hamburg. See also PRO SP 81/46, ff.128, 230, 236, 238 and 266. Various inventories of armaments bought and shipped by Sir Thomas Roe from Hamburg, April 1639.

[45]   PRO SP 81/47, f.87. Archbishop of Canterbury to Roe, 21 June 1639; PRO SP81/47, f.102. Certificate of arms sent to England, 28 June 1639; See also *CSPD*, 1640, 374-375.

[46]   Israel, *The Dutch Republic*, 543; A. Fryxell, *Handlingar rörande sverges historia ur utrikes arkiver* (Stockholm 1936), 67; *SRP*, VII, 412, 19 January 1639; This is also interesting for the fact that De Geer was friends with both John Maclean and Jacob Macklier. In 1640 he sent a sack of money via both John and Jacob for delivery to a third person. See E. W. Dahlgren, ed, *Louis De Geers Brev och Affärshandlingar 1614-1652* (Stockholm, 1934), 416-7.

he gave the Dunkirkers a Danish island where they could live and, at their pleasure, 'annoy, persecute and surprise the Hollanders'.[47] This attack on Dutch commerce looked as though it would lead to open war, especially after Swedish craft were also targeted for harassment. In July 1640, the Scottish cleric, John Durie, wrote to Roe to inform him that 'a fire is like to break forth betwix the Swedes and the Danes; some four or five Swedish ships are kept up at the Sound which the Swedes resent very much', proving the ability of the Danish-Norwegian navy to close the Sound at will.[48]

Yet, for all the efforts of both the Stuart and Danish-Norwegian navies, a remarkable number of weapons, munitions and personnel arrived safely in Scotland from the continent. Obviously, the Marquis of Hamilton's fleet in the Firth of Forth was ineffective in preventing the landing of supplies in Leith, right under the guns of his ships.[49] Many of these supplies came from areas outwith Danish control, such as the United Provinces, indeed 11 out of the 13 ships sent by Thomas Cunningham of Campvere arrived safely in Scotland.[50] Many more, however, successfully negotiated the Sound blockade. The Sound Toll records show that 29 Scottish vessels passed eastward through the Sound in 1639 and 31 successfully returned westward.[51] The skippers paid Sound duties on, among other things, quantities of ammunition and lead from Danzig.

---

[47]   *CSPD*, 1640, 364-365. George Rodolph Weckherlin to Viscount Conway, 30 June 1640. Continued harassment of the Hollanders by the Danes were also noted by Queen Elizabeth of Bohemia to Roe in August. *CPSD*, 1640, 582-583, 12/23 August 1640; Lockhart, *Denmark in the Thirty Years' War*, 254.

[48]   *CSPD*, 1640, 510-512. John Dury to Roe, 24 July 1640. The tolls which had proved to be the cause of so much trouble in the Sound eventually had to be reduced in spring 1641 in order to avoid conflict with all the trading nations. See Lockhart, *Denmark in the Thirty Years' War*, 254.

[49]   Jane Ohlmeyer has noted that 'in the Forth Hamilton, fearing the Covenanters would confiscate his estates, dallied'. See J. Kenyon and J. Ohlmeyer eds, *The Civil Wars. A Military History of England, Scotland and Ireland 1638-1660* (Oxford, 1998), 20. Other reasons to avoid interfering with Scottish shipping might be attributed Hamilton's healthy respect for Dear Sandy Hamilton's shore battery or, indeed, his mother who patrolled the banks of the Forth and 'rode with her Horse troop and a loaded pistol to shoot her son should he land'. References to Dear Sandy Hamilton's shore battery, and the Covenanting leadership's refusal to let him engage the Royalist fleet in the Firth can be found in Sir W. Fraser ed, *Memorials of the Earls of Haddington* (Edinburgh, 1889), I, 31.

[50]   E. J. Courthope ed, *The Journal of Thomas Cuningham of Campvere 1640-1654. With his Thrissels-Banner and Explication Thereof* (Edinburgh, 1928), 54. In July 1639, *the Marie* of Leith deposited 50 tons of swords, muskets, pistols, pikes, gunpowder and cannon balls in Leith along with 6 brass cannon, all from Amsterdam. John Carse arrived in Leith in September with a shipment of arms from Campvere. In December, an Englishman observed yet more boxes of muskets, bandoleers and pistols being landed at Leith. See S Mowat, *The Port of Leith, Its History and its People* (Edinburgh, 1997), 175.

[51]   N. Bang ed, *Tabellen over Skibsfart og Varetransport gennem Øresund 1497-1660* (Copenhagen, 1906), I, 314-319.

Field Marshall Alexander Leslie arrived with 200 muskets from Swedish service in January 1639 and must have crossed Danish waters. By November the remainder of Leslie's armaments arrived in Leith harbour in two Swedish ships. This shipment included up to 15 brass cannon, 4,000 corslets and 1,800 muskets.[52] In addition to arms, material for making arms also came past the Danish navy such as iron, copper and brass from Danzig and Königsberg. The shipping manifests from Gothenburg from 1638 indicate that John Maclean had shipped 6,746 lasts of iron to Scotland, which was no doubt destined for the arms trade.[53] Given the strength of Danish-Norwegian maritime forces and the narrowness of the Sound, questions must be asked about the efficiency of that navy, or at any rate their commitment to capturing Scottish supplies coming from the Baltic ports, German rivers or Gothenburg.

One as yet unexplored avenue that might help to shed light on the motivation and actions of the Danish-Norwegian fleet may be found in the composition of its higher command. During the Bishops' Wars, Axel Mowatt was the commander of the flottila dispatched in April to scour Danish-Norwegian waters for enemy shipping. He was a Scot and held the position of top operational admiral in the Norwegian fleet.[54] Another Scottish admiral, John Cunningham, was stationed in Vardøhus in the north of Norway. Cunningham had long since ceased sea-borne operations. However, as governor of Finmark, he controlled the sea route to Archangel in Russia and exercised considerable influence in Danish-Norwegian naval and civic society. This status is of great significance in the investigation of Danish-Norwegian involvement with the supply of weapons and ammunition to the Covenanters. There were several other

---

[52]   PRO SP81/45, ff.307-311. Roe to Coke, 7/17 December 1638. Roe notes Leslie's artillery to have been 10 field pieces, 2 half cannon and 100 iron bullets for each, ordered from Gothenburg in July. The November shipment included 15 brass cannon, 4,000 corslets and 1,800 muskets, exactly the right number of muskets to make up the 2,000 given to Leslie and the two reports probably refer to the same shipment. See Beller, 'The Mission of Sir Thomas Roe to Hamburg 1638-1640', 73.

[53]   *CSPD*, 1640, 98-100. Information given to Charles I from Scotland, 22 April 1640: 'They [the Covenanters] have good provision of great ordnance, as battery pieces, field pieces, and field pieces of new invention, and are daily casting of ordnance of all sorts; of copper and brass they have good store from Holland and the Sound, also sundry engines to be shot out of great ordnance besides great store of powder and shot, so that who soever leads your majestie to believe that they are not well provided does not inform you the truth as it is'. See also Göteborg Landsarkiv, ref. 801 'Göteborgs Drätselkammare 1638', nos. 90, 92 and 97. The largest recipients of iron from Maclean were the Amsterdam merchants who received 16,640 lasts, the English got 2,418 lasts. One last equals 2 tons or 4,000lb. See H. F. Morland-Simpson ed, 'Civil War Papers 1643-1650', in *Miscellany of the Scottish Historical Society* (Edinburgh, 1893), I, 157.

[54]   *KCFB*, IV, 333. List of Warships and Crews, 7 May 1640. L. Tandrup ed, *Svenske agent ved Sundet; Toldkommissær og agent i Helsingør: Anders Svenssons depecher till Gustav II Adolf og Axel Oxenstierna 1621-1625* (Aarhus, 1971), 525-526. footnote.

Scottish naval captains in Christian IV's service at this time. All were in a position to either hinder the passage of Scottish victuals through the Sound, or Danish attempts to intercept them, depending on their personal allegiance. Most notable of these men were Vice Admiral Christopher Mowatt, captain of the 54-gun *Spes*, Captain Alexander Arrat, who commanded the 28-gun *Merkatten* and Albert Jack in command of the 26-gun *Gabriell*.[55] It is not apparent whether or not these men held particularly strong views on the struggle developing in Scotland. If they did not, they were certainly in the minority of Scots at the time.[56]

The Scots were not alone in the Danish-Norwegian navy in having a strong Scottish interest. The Norwegian, Eric Ottesen Orning, had married Axel Mowatt's sister, Karen Mowatt. The marriage was considered illegal in Norway as the couple were first cousins once removed, and they had spent eighteen years in Scotland before they were allowed back to Norway in 1627. Orning became an Admiral in 1630, and by 1640 he had been promoted to the *Rigsadmiral's* 'under admiral' – second in command of the combined Danish-Norwegian fleets. Another Danish Admiral, Borg Juel was married to the sister of Axel Mowatt's wife.[57]

While these particular men may not have actively supported the Covenanters, they have, thus far, not been proven to be vigorous supporters of Charles I either. Indeed the Scots, including the admirals, had previously shown their contempt for Charles I by ignoring a royal directive for all seamen in foreign navies to return home for service in the Stuart navy in 1634 and a similar order during the build-up to the Bishops' Wars.[58] John Cunningham also chose this time to break with his custom of wintering in Bergen which he had done since 1622. Instead, he received permission from Christian IV to leave Norway for a prolonged visit to Copenhagen during the winter of 1638-39 to settle 'some business there'.[59] Cunningham therefore had direct access to Christian IV and other influential persons in the *Rigsråd* and the navy. This would have included Axel Mowatt and his kinsmen, whom

---

[55]   *KCFB*, IV, 334. List of Warships and Crews, 7 May 1640.
[56]   Charles I even noted that most Scots were Covenanters when he sent a gentleman, probably Henry Bruce, to Lord Wentworth in June 1639 saying of him 'That though he be a Scottishman, yet he is no Covenanter, nor ever was; which indeed is not the ordinary'. Petrie, *The Letters of King Charles I*, 103-104. Charles I to Lord Wentworth, 30 June 1639.
[57]   Espelland, *Skottene i Hordaland*, 31-32; Wiensener, ' Axel Movat og Hans Slegt', 93-100.
[58]   J. F. Larkin ed, *Stuart Royal Proclamations, 2, Royal Proclamations of King Charles 1 1625-1646* (Oxford, 1983), 417-418. 'From the King. A Proclamation commanding all Our Subjects, being Seamen and Shipwrights, in the service of any forreigne Prince or State, to returne home within a certaine time'. Greenwich, 5 May 1634.
[59]   *Norske Rigs-Registranter*, VII, 423. Christian IV to John Cunningham, 19 July 1638; Espelland, *Skottene i Hordaland*, 19.

Cunningham knew from his stays in Bergen, and who also remained in Copenhagen with the Danish-Norwegian fleet that same winter.[60]

Mowatt's naval squadron was perfectly placed to hamper the movement of Covenanters or their supplies through the Sound. Charles I thanked Christian IV for his endeavours in preventing Swedish armaments passing through his waters.[61] Christian, in turn, wrote to Sir Thomas Roe in January 1639 confirming his belief that blocking the Sound acted as a positive means of ensuring peace in Great Britain.[62] However, in February, within only a few weeks of this letter, the Danish Chancellery issued a set of orders on Christian IV's instructions which made a farce of Charles I's requests to impede the supply of Covenanting weapons and personnel. On the 19th of February 1639 Frederik Urne received the following instructions:

> Efter Begæring af Dronningen af Sverrig har Kongen for denne Gang tilladt, at Monroe og Stuart maa passere gennem Sundet med deres Rekrutter og ligeledes øverste Flitwitz med 1 Regimenter Englænder og øverste Hammelton med 2 Regimenter Skotter, og endvidere 30 Læster Krudt, 30 Skippd. Lunter og 2,000 Par Pistoler.[63]

> ['At the request of the Queen of Sweden the King has this time permitted that Monroe and Stuart may pass through the Sound with their recruits and equally Colonel Fleetwood with one English regiment and Colonel Hamilton with two Scottish regiments, and further 30 lasts of gunpowder, 30 ship's pounds worth of match and 2,000 pairs of pistols'.]

It is conceivable that Christian allowed these troops through in good faith since they were accompanied part of the way by an English regiment under George Fleetwood's command. After all, for several years before this, he had allowed the transport of Scottish and English troops in Swedish service through to Pomerania.[64] Christian may have believed, therefore, that these soldiers were merely continuing in that established pattern but for the fact that they were travelling in the other

---

[60]   *Kancelliets Brevbøger, 1637-1639*, 338. Orders to Admiral Mowatt from Christian IV, 11 April 1638.

[61]   DRA, TKUA England Al. Charles I to Christian IV, 31 January 1639.

[62]   PRO SP 81/46, f.51. Christian IV to Roe, 18/28 January 1639.

[63]   *Kancelliets Brevbøger, 1637-1639*, 672-673. Missive to Frederik Urne, 19 February 1639.

[64]   *Kancelliets Brevbøger, 1637-1639*, 171, 213 and 348. Various missives to Frederik Urne allowing Scottish soldiers through the Sound to Pomerania for Swedish service between May 1637 and April 1638.

direction. However, given his distrust of the Swedes, and requests by Charles to keep a look-out for Scotsmen bearing arms, the favouring of Monro and his volunteers through the Sound with weapons toll-free is quite remarkable. Just over four weeks later, on 21 March 1639, Colonel Monro and his regiment of 2,000 men took part in the successful action by the Covenanters against Edinburgh Castle.

Undoubtedly aware of these recent developments in Scotland and the fact that most Scots were indeed very hostile to his nephew, Christian IV committed another breathtaking act against the interest of Charles I. During the course of spring 1639 the Danish fleet had impounded a ship belonging to John Maclean of Gothenburg. On board the ship were 600 muskets, 2,000 bandoliers and 2,000 pieces of armour. These were openly manifested as being destined for Scotland and should, in theory, have been impounded or confiscated. Christian IV in his infinite wisdom chose rather to accept the petition of Maclean's servant, Thomas Gilmour, that if the Danes released the goods the Scots promised that they would be sent directly to The Netherlands and not back to Gothenburg or any other state. Christian's only guarantee that they would not be directed to Scotland thereafter lay in the Swedish resident's promise of the same![65] Clearly these weapons were now destined for the Scottish staple at Veere, but none-the-less this shipment signalled the end of overt Scottish arms shipments through the Sound for over a year.

At the end of August 1640, Sir John Cochrane completed his negotiations in Sweden for fresh supplies of arms for the Covenanters. The very next day the Swedish *Riksråd* mentioned five of the Crown's ships being moved from Gothenburg to Stockholm, which were to register with the Danish coastguard as containing material belonging to the Swedish Crown. The ships were then used to transport the munitions and copper requested by Cochrane to the United Provinces, from where they would be shipped to Scotland.[66] The squadron remained under orders not to engage in any action against the Danes, but if challenged they were to lower their colours and put into the nearest Danish port to

---

[65] *Kancelliets Brevbøger, 1637-1639*, 722-723. Missive til Frederik Urne, 26 April 1639. 'Kongen tillader denne Thomas Gilmour at føre samme Munition genem Sundet til Nederland efter hans eget Tilbud og ikke til Gottenborg, som først nu omtales og aldrig er omtalt. Den svenske Resident skal kavere for, at samme Munition ikke føres til andre Steder end til Nederland'.

[66] It is unclear if these arms formed part of the 12 cannon of 24 and 18lb ball, 15,673 muskets, 6,965 swords and 52 pairs of pistols along with 123,098 lb. of match, 95,620 lb. of powder and 15,416lb of refined saltpetre sent to Scotland from the United provinces by Thomas Cunningham at the Scottish Staple at Veere to the Covenanting army during the Bishops' Wars, or if they represent the bulk of later shipments. See Courthope, *The Journal of Thomas Cuningham*, 53-54; M. P. Rooseboom, *The Scottish Staple in The Netherlands* (The Hague, 1910), 175.

protest. The Swedes received no Danish challenge. They recorded the return of their five ships from Holland to Gothenburg and thence to Stockholm in early September. Admiral Claes Flemming reported that thery had safely come through the Sound without incident, and he pointed out that this had never been achieved before.[67]

Surprisingly, no complaint appears to have been made by the Danish king to the Swedish authorities regarding this free passage of the Swedish warships through Danish waters. A Swedish naval squadron passing through the Sound unhindered should be construed as a serious blow to Danish claims over *Dominium Maris Baltici* unless Christian IV had issued orders to allow them through. Only in July, John Durie had reported Swedish merchant ships being blocked in the Sound, yet in August these warships went unhindered.[68] And this at a time when the Danish navy had orders not to allow munitions through the Sound and had escalated the naval presence in and around those waters.[69] No proof has come to light to suggest collusion between Admiral Mowatt and the Swedish navy. However, the senior *Holmadmiral* of the Swedish navy at this time was a fellow Scotsman, John Clerk. Indeed, during the Bishops' Wars, the Swedes employed three Scottish admirals – John Clerk, Simon Stewart and Andrew Stewart – and a plethora of Scottish naval captains including 'Holm Major' Richard Clerk who commanded the naval squadron to Amsterdam through the Sound in 1640.[70] It should also be noted that the man responsible for the distribution of military supplies to Scotland once they reached the United Provinces was Thomas Cunningham, Scottish conservator at Campvere. Further, a long-serving Scottish officer in Swedish service, Hugh Mowatt, acted as the Scottish Resident in Stockholm and Swedish envoy to both Scotland and England throughout the duration of the later Solemn League and Covenant.[71] Communication between the senior officers in both navies has not been proved, but neither can it be ruled out. The sort of sensitive communications required to prove collusion rarely survive to damn their authors.

The Danish king added to the confusion over his personal involvement

[67] *SRP*, VIII, 217, 243-245 and 299. 18 and 28, 29 August and 22 October 1640; Grosjean, 'Scots and the Swedish State', 165-172.

[68] *CSPD*, 1640, 510-512. John Durie to Roe, 24 July 1640.

[69] Lockhart, *Denmark in the Thirty Years' War*, 253.

[70] *Svenskt Biografiskt Lexicon*, VIII, 619; A. Grosjean, 'Scottish-Scandinavian Seventeenth Century Naval Links; A Case Study for the *SSNE* Database', in *Northern Studies*, no. 32, 1997, 116-119.

[71] Given the nature of the Scottish expatriate community and the confines of the Baltic it is unlikely that these men did not know each other. The possibility also exists that the Mowatts and Cunninghams involved may even have been be related. Hugh Mowatt's diplomatic correspondence can be found in SRA, Anglica E. 514.

and the role of his navy in Covenanting affairs by apparently sponsoring the illegal movement of saltpetre to Scotland through his waters. One thing that the Scots actively sought was saltpetre to make gunpowder, especially after the instructions from the commissioners of the shires in September 1639 who ordered the instigation of indigenous gunpowder production.[72] Certainly the Scots received 15,416 lb. of saltpetre during the Bishops' Wars from the United Provinces, which probably originated in the Baltic.[73] Christian IV recorded that there were two main sources of saltpetre production in 1639-40 outwith Denmark. One of these was the trade in the East and West Indies while the other was Russia. Christian introduced a huge tax on saltpetre, some 78% of its market value, quadrupling its net price.[74] A correspondent of Sir Thomas Roe in Danzig detailed the new Danish taxes and information relating to a declaration by Christian IV that no more saltpetre would pass through the Sound but that he would keep it for himself. Christian IV said that he intended to use the new tax as the main method for preventing saltpetre and ammunition from passing through the Sound.[75]

There are a lot of contradictions in Christian's declarations and actions in regard to his saltpetre policy which also attach themselves to the Scot, Francis Gordon, Stuart and Danish factor in Danzig. Gordon's correspondence from 1639 indicates that he strove to fulfil his orders from Secretary Windebank to inform the Danish customs of the names of ship's masters and merchants carrying munitions through the Sound.[76] When his words are analysed, however, he is really giving nothing away that would damage the Scots. The customs officers in the Sound were unlikely to miss the ships as they neared Danish waters. After all Christian IV fitted out a fleet of ships in 1639 to sail to Danzig to challenge the imposition of taxes by the king of Poland and the Elector of Brandenburg.[77] All Gordon had done was to inform the Danes of something they would already have known in regard to Scottish ships. In Gordon's correspondence to Roe there is no information relating to the Scottish individuals involved in the ammunition trade, only the

---

[72] L. B. Taylor ed, *Aberdeen Council Letters* (Oxford, 1950), II, 144. Instructions to the representatives sitting at the September Parliament by the Commissioners of the schires, September, 1639.

[73] Courthope, *The Journal of Thomas Cuningham*, 53-54.

[74] *KCFB*, IV, 269-270. Christian IV to Korfitz Ulfeldt, 20 December 1639; Lockhart, *Denmark in the Thirty Years' War*, 252.

[75] PRO SP 81/46, f.166. J. Westphal to Roe, 11 March 1639.

[76] PRO SP 81/48, ff.60 and 98. Francis Gordon to Roe, 20/30 September 1639 and 8/18 October 1639.

[77] This fleet is variously numbered at between 16 and 50 ships. See PRO SP 81/46, f.166. J. Westphal to Roe, 11 March 1639; *CSPD*, 1639, 2. Edmund Rossingham to Viscount Conway, 1 April 1639.

continental merchants selling to them. In combination with other evidence, Gordon's loyalty to Charles I becomes less than certain.

The Danish king observed that, in addition to the manufacturing countries, there were large quantities of saltpetre stockpiled in Danzig and on the river Weser. Christian said that shipments from the Danzig stockpile were not being sent through the Sound as an unspecified 'they' were afraid that the Sound was blocked to such traffic. This was understandable since Christian himself had stated that this was the case, certainly with regard to Sweden.[78] Yet in his correspondence with Korfitz Ulfeldt, Christian suggested that his agent, Francis Gordon, perhaps misunderstood the situation and should 'they' pay the additional toll, then the saltpetre could 'go wherever it needed to'.[79] Danzig had been specifically highlighted as a port of supply targeted by the Covenanters for weapons in 1638 and it is apparent that the individuals involved believed the Sound would be barred to them.[80] Further, it should not be overlooked that on both occasions Gordon married he did so in a Presbyterian church in Danzig, the second time to the daughter of a Scottish Presbyterian minister.[81] He had also been accused of treason only two years before and had been forced to return to the Stuart Court to explain himself.[82] Given this information Gordon may be considered as a potential hostile to the Stuart Crown and the Covenanters as being a possible recipient of the saltpetre.

The Danzig store of saltpetre formed only one of several supplies of the material over which Christian exercised control. John Cunningham had long since been able to monitor and prevent cargoes of saltpetre leaving Russia via Vardøhus in Finnmark. But in 1640, the Scottish skipper, Albert Jack, in command of the warship *Gabriell*, was also ordered to the river Weser in order to ensure the payment of customs duties on saltpetre to the Danish Crown.[83] In fact, in 1640, Christian

[78] J. A. Fridericia, *Danmarks Ydre Politiske Historie, II; i tiden fra Freden i Prag til Freden i Bromsebro, 1635-1645* (Copenhagen, 1972), 219; Lockhart, *Denmark in the Thirty Years' War*, 252. Lockhart only notes that Christian banned the sale of saltpetre to ports *east* of the Sound.

[79] *KCFB*, IV, 269-270. Christian IV to Korfitz Ulfeldt, 20 December 1639. 'Der ligger Nu En stor *quantitet* aff Saltpeiiter tiil dantzig, som dy Inted tør søge sundiid med, udaf arsag at dy biller dem ind, at ded maa inted ygennom, Huorfor du skaldt lade den Engelske *Resident Gordon* uyde, ded Inted at uerre myn mehning, Mens naar di Erlegger den paabødne toll, daa maa den gaa, huordthen dii den begehrer'.

[80] NAS, GD 406/1/10491, 24 June 1638; Gardiner, *Hamilton Papers*, 17.

[81] T. Fischer, *The Scots in East and West Prussia* (Edinburgh, 1903), 63 and 223-225. Gordon first married Anna Wegner, apothecary to the king of Poland. His second marriage was to Margaretha, the daughter of the late James Porteous, a minister of Scotland.

[82] *CSPV*, XXIV, 1636-1639, 271. Anzolo Correr, 18 September 1637.

[83] Riis, *Should Auld Acquaintance*, II, 225; *KCFB*, IV, 333-336. List of Warships and Crews, 7 May 1640.

gave Scots direct authority, or a significant degree of control over three major sources of accessible saltpetre. Further, the Scotsman, Thomas Skotte, held a quarter share in the gunpowder factory at Christiansstad, adding to the potential supply of gunpowder from Denmark to Scotland.[84]

As if to underscore the doubts cast on the Sound toll diplomacy conducted by Christian IV one need only look to the till receipts. In February 1640, it was noted by Herman Holstein and Godert Braem, that the Scots, English and Irish had all paid more in Sound Tolls in 1639 than in 1638. This was true for all the trading nations. Indeed between 1636 and 1639, Sound Toll revenue had increased from 226,000 to 620,000 *rigsdaler* per annum.[85] Had Christian simply increased the tolls on the Scottish ships not carrying restricted cargoes, this increase would have been understandable, but the increases applied equally to the English, Royalist Scots and the Irish.[86] This leads to a rather unsavoury question in relation to diplomacy in the Sound. Did Christian want to help his nephew or simply make a profit?

It cannot be overlooked that there is an uncanny series of coincidences that took place surrounding the naval blockade during the Bishops' Wars. Christian IV, either in an innocent blunder, or for some unscrupulous motive, had issued Danish Royal missives to armed Covenanters to pass through the Sound under the command of Colonel Robert Monro. He displayed a remarkable trust, or great naiveté in maintaining Scotsmen to seal the Sound, the German rivers and northern approaches to Russia against fellow Scots.

A similar position might also have applied to some aspects of the Danish merchant fleet trading with the British Isles. Christian's 'tax blockade' had many problems. On at least two occasions, December 1638 and March 1639, Crown Prince Christian (V) issued protection passes to one David Melville, a naturalised Danish subject from Dundee. The passes were to ensure that Melville, his ship and crew, would not be

---

[84] Riis, *Should Auld Acquaintance*, II, 148.
[85] *KCFB*, IV 305, fn.5. Specifically the editors note payment from the Stuart kingdoms of 210 Rosenobler and 34,364½ rigsdaler. They do not state if this is the total for the year or the difference since the previous one; Lockhart, *Denmark in the Thirty Years' War*, 253.
[86] PRO SP 81/48, f.249. Information on His Majestie of Great Britain's subjects injuries in the Sound in 1639; Edinburgh University Library Special Collection. Transactions of the Committee of Estates of Scotland from August 1640 to June 1641. Scottish Commissioners to the English Peers, 29 March 1641, 90. Article 8 of the document concerning commerce and trade talks of the 'exorbitan customes exactiounes & vther rigous deallings...taken & vsed be the king of Denmark both of the Scottis Inglisch and Irische and vthers his Maties subjectis passing the sound'. See also *APS*, V, 603. Article by the Burrows to the Estates, 27 September 1639; Taylor, *Aberdeen Council Letters*, II, 147. Instructions to the representatives sitting at the September Parliament by the Commissioners of the schires, September, 1639

treated any differently to other Danish subjects trading with Britain due to the rising unrest in that country.[87] Certainly the Covenanters made use of 'legitimate' traders such as Melville to circumvent blockades against arms. In 1640, a captured Irish soldier told his English inquisitors that the St Andrews vessel he travelled in from Dunkirk to Scotland carried a cargo of wine with 300 muskets hidden under the ballast.[88]

It is unlikely that Christian IV would have been informed of such smuggling activities. However, his blockade was compromised by his own civil servants. One of his factors in Danzig had obtained some royal passes which he was selling to anybody that wanted to pass by Pillau, en route to Königsberg.[89] This city was noted by Francis Gordon as a source of Covenanting arms and a general trading centre for Scottish, Dutch and English merchants.[90] While the actions of a civil servant could not be used as evidence of foul play by the Danish king, Christian IV did later prove himself capable of allowing contraband through the Sound for use by the enemies of his nephew. In 1645, Christian told Richard Jenkes that the only reason the English Parliamentarian ship *Rebecca,* carrying a cargo of gunpowder, had been confiscated in the Sound in 1642 was due to the fact that the Danes had not received the required 'additional' toll.[91] He added that once that had been paid, the ship and cargo would be released.

And what of the Palatinate?
The partial success of the negotiations of Sir Thomas Roe between 1638 and 1640 with Christian IV led many Stuart optimists to believe that a concerted political and military effort by the Stuart and Oldenburg nations would lead to a satisfactory settlement for the Palatine party. As early as October 1638, Christian IV noted the arrival of 'eight or nine' ships on the Weser full of English soldiers which the English noble, William, Lord Craven, had brought at his own expense to serve the Elector Charles Louis in an alliance with the Swedes.[92] However, any

[87] Marquard, *Prins Christian (V)'s Brev,* I. 446 and 466, 12 December 1638 and 31 March 1639; Riis, *Should Auld Acquaintance,* II, 218-219, 235 and 245. Melville (recorded by Riis as Melvin) had become a burgess of Elsinøre. Melville had links with Admiral Cunningham, eventually renting his house in Elsinøre in 1648. He also had links with Sweden, a country shown to have supported the Covenanters. Along with one Albert Douglas he bought a ship from a resident of Stockholm in 1640. Should there have been any attempt to smuggle contraband, a ship belonging to a 'Dane' would have had a much simpler passage through the Sound than a Swedish or Scottish flagged vessel.

[88] *CSPD,* 1640, 63. The interrogation of Peter Melch, 22 April 1640.

[89] PRO SP 81/48, f.186. Gordon to Roe, 28 November/8 December 1639.

[90] PRO SP 81/48, ff.98 and 186. Gordon to Roe, 8/18 October and 28 November/8 December 1639.

[91] *Danmark-Norges Traktater,* IV 408-410.

[92] Dutch sources note that he arrived in Zeeland with fully 15-17 companies. See J. A. Worp ed,

hopes that Charles had of Craven's expedition arriving in Danish waters bringing the Danes back into the fight for the Palatinate were short lived. Charles Louis was defeated at Vlotho on the Weser and his brother Prince Rupert, Field Marshall Ferentz and Lord Craven were all taken prisoner. Nevertheless, the very fact that Craven had mounted an expedition was hoped to convince Christian IV that the Stuarts were serious about escalating the war for Charles Louis. Such optimism was soon retarded during the two Bishops' Wars. There was little prospect of raising an army for the Palatine cause while Charles concentrated his military forces towards his campaigns in Scotland.

No doubt in part due to the ongoing military action within the British Isles, Charles Louis repeatedly pressed Sir Thomas Roe to pay attention to Christian IV's various offers of mediation. He further urged Roe to dispel the rumours that Charles I had turned over Charles Louis' cause entirely to Christian IV, preferring to press the notion that the intervention of the Dane should be supplemental to Stuart diplomacy.[93] Christian IV, however, insisted that Charles had written to him on 25 October 1639 transferring all matters of the Palatinate to 'our love and wisdom' and argued vehemently that he continued to press the Emperor and the Electoral College on the subject at every opportunity.[94] Elizabeth Stuart believed that her uncle sought the removal of the Palatine matter from the agenda of the Hamburg negotiations, ironically, since the settling of the Palatinate issue had been one of the main items on the agenda. Indeed, she pointed out that her cousin, Christian Ulric, an illegitimate son of Christian IV, now worked for the Spanish interest in The Hague. She believed that her uncle grew ever more hostile to the Dutch which, she added, 'makes me fear him [Christian IV]'.[95] Christian Ulric raised a troop of Danish cavalry in September for service in the Spanish Netherlands with Christian IV's approval. This move placed the Danish Royal house perilously close to the anti-Palatine military camp, though the Prince was killed by the Dutch soon after.[96] Despite the death of his son, Christian IV offered to arrange safe conducts for Charles Louis through Imperial territory to the Ratisbon Diet, the new venue for talks relating to the Palatinate, after they had been jettisoned from Hamburg. Indeed this appeared to be Christian's main contribution until the Treaty of Westphalia in 1648. Sir Robert Anstruther was selected to

De Briefwisseling van Constantijn Huygens 1634-1639 (The Hague, 1913), 485; *KCFB*, VIII, 121. Christian IV to Korfitz Ulfeldt, 23 October 1638.

[93] *CSPD*, 1640, 535-536. Charles Louis to Roe, 31 July 1640; *CSPD*, 1640-41, 120-121. Charles Louis to Roe, 30 September/10 October 1640

[94] PRO SP 75/16, ff.13-15. Christian IV to Charles I, 6 February 1641.

[95] *CSPD*, 1640, 582-583. Elizabeth Stuart, Queen of Bohemia to Roe, August 12/13, 1640.

[96] Lockhart, *Denmark in the Thirty Years' War*, 246.

return to Denmark to press the Palatine message and Sir Thomas Roe was to join Charles Louis in Ratisbon.[97]

Christian IV insisted that the Palatine issue should be dropped from the Ratisbon agenda and moved to a specific treaty negotiation to be scheduled in May 1641.[98] He also believed that before any fresh attempt to challenge the Empire was made by Sir Thomas Roe, Charles I should ensure that his countrymen were brought firmly under royal control. This, Christian argued, would prevent Sir Thomas being laughed out of the Diet for threatening the Emperor while Charles could not even keep order in his own kingdoms. These comments followed a rash speech by Roe to some members of the English Parliament during which he apparently disputed the rights of the Danish king within the Sound. Christian felt that was the concern of no man, but only God. Angered, Christian used Roe's speech against the next Stuart agent to visit him, Joseph Averie. Christian also declared he wanted no dealings with the English Parliament after that, only with Charles himself.[99]

Charles, for his part, tried to build a strong Parliamentary, Stuart and Danish alliance to represent his nephew, Charles Louis, at Ratisbon.[100] The Danish king was dismissive about this attempt. The English Parliament, he concluded, had never been interested in the Palatinate, though without its help Charles I could not possibly intervene in support of that cause.[101] Indeed, when Christian received news that Roe had tried to threaten the Emperor at the end of July he expressed his belief that Roe's mission was futile. What Christian, with some justification, wanted to know was by what means Charles could possibly mount an expedition against the Empire when he could not even pay the Scottish soldiers occupying Newcastle what he owed them.[102] Roe, meanwhile, heard from the Scottish Imperial Count, Walter Leslie, that had there not been a Stuart representative at the Diet, Christian IV would have

[97] *CSPD*, 1640-41, 120-121. Charles Louis to Roe, 30 September/10 October 1640; *CSPD*, 1641-1643, 436. Charles Louis to Roe, 2/12 January 1643; *CSPV*, XXV, 1640-1642, 135. Giovanni Giustinian, 5 April 1641. For Roe's mission see R. B. Mowat, 'The Mission of Sir Thomas Roe to Vienna, 1641-1642', *in English Historical Review*, XXV (1910), 264-275.

[98] PRO SP 75/16, ff.13-18. Christian IV to Charles I, 6 February 1641 and Averie to Roe, 9/19 February 1640/1.

[99] *KCFB*, V, 107. Christian IV to Korfitz Ulfeldt, 21 July 1641; HP 45/3/22A-22B. Christian IV's answer to the 2nd Proposition of Averie, 2 December 1641.

[100] *CSPD*, 1641-43, 572. Charles I speech to Parliament asking for their co-operation with the Danes in the Palatinate representations at Ratisbon, 5 July 1641.

[101] *KCFB*, V, 108-109. Christian IV to Korfitz Ulfeldt, 28 July 1641; 'Hiidintil haffuer Parlamendtit liidit bekymrit sig om Paldtzgreffuens dondt. Huad hiielp konningen kan *apart* gørre Paltzgreffuen, ded er uel bekendt'.

[102] *KCFB*, V, 75-76. Christian IV to Korfitz Ulfeldt, 30 July 1641; 'ty dy kan ingen myddel finde y Engeland tiil at betale ded Skodske folck, dii haffuer, Huoraff er at Erfare, huad middel der kan uerre til at Effectuere M: Roes truen med'.

'worked to further his own agenda' at the expense of the Stuart interest.[103]

By November 1641, Christian heard of plans for Alexander Leslie to visit Chancellor Axel Oxenstierna in Sweden with the intention of forming a confederation between Charles I and Sweden to reinstate Charles Louis to his father's possessions in the Palatinate.[104] Christian voiced his concerns stating that before Charles attempted any such scheme he should sort out his affairs in his kingdom of Ireland.[105] Charles, optimistically, hoped that Christian might wish to consider joining the new league. From Scotland, Charles ordered Roe to try to persuade Christian IV to get involved in just such a scheme to restore the Palatinate. He also sent Joseph Averie from Hamburg to Copenhagen as his envoy. In his *First Proposition* to Christian IV, Averie once more pressed a request from Charles that Christian act as mediator for the Palatinate dispute. Further he wanted the issue raised at Vienna and that Christian should begin re-conscripting soldiers in case the war should reach his territories. Christian replied that he had both particular and universal negotiations in mind, but that other remedies were also to be sought. The evasiveness of this reply alerted Averie to the king of Denmark's attitude. He focused the remainder of his mission on issues of Sound Toll commerce on behalf of the Scottish and English parliaments.[106] He was probably right to do so. Only the day before the *First Proposition*, Christian had informed a correspondent that the answer the Stuart agent would get 'would be easy to guess' and from that we can deduce he had no interest in getting involved.[107] Christian finally voiced his contempt for the Stuart nations when he noted that 'The English, Scots and Irish until now wanted to be masters over others, but now they find themselves isolated so they forget about Germany and Sweden'.[108] Clearly, Christian believed that Charles I no longer had the capacity to get involved in continental European politics and seemed to revel in the troubles of the British Isles.

---

[103] PRO SP 81/52, f.178. Count Walter Leslie to Roe, 17 October 1641. Leslie was a diplomat in Imperial service. He had maintained a correspondence with Roe since 1639.

[104] *RAOSB*, II:9, 488. Alexander Leslie to Axel Oxenstierna, 4 October 1641, 'et confoederationem inter haec regna et regnum Sveciae ineundum'; PRO SP 81/52, f.221. Scottish Parliament's Statement on the Palatinate [extract], 12 November 1641.

[105] *KCFB*, V, 143-144. Christian IV to Christen Thomesen Sehested, 14 November 1641.

[106] HP 45/3/19A-20B. 1st Proposition to the King of Denmark, 1 December 1641 with answer; HP 45/3/21A-22B. 2nd Proposition to the King of Denmark, 2 December 1641 with answer.

[107] *KCFB*, V, 147-149. Christian IV to Christen Thomesen Sehested, 30 November 1641. 'Huad suar hand faar derpa ded Er letteligen at gette'.

[108] *KCFB*, V, 148-9. Christian IV to Korfitz Ulfeldt, 30 November 1641. 'Ded ladder siig ansee, At haffuer dii Engelender, Skotter och Irlander Indtildiis wyllit spille Selffuer offuer ander, da haffuer dy nu nock huos dem Selffuer at waare, Saat dii glemmer uel tysland och Suerrig'.

Throughout the early 1640s Christian IV again tried to build his role as an international arbitrator. What he did not understand was that since 1630 the war in Germany centred on two power blocks; that dominated by Sweden and the other dominated by the Empire. Neither the Swedes nor the Imperialists would tolerate a third force.[109] As far as both the Imperial and Swedish governments were concerned Denmark-Norway, like Charles I, could only ever be a spectator in this European power play. The Palatinate question was settled by neither Stuart nor Danish intervention but by the protagonists in the field. Of course the vast numbers of Scots in Swedish, Dutch and French service played their part, but by the 1640s this had little to do with Charles I directly. From the failure of Lord Craven's expedition in 1638 until the Peace of Westphalia in 1648 the Palatinate became a secondary concern in Stuart relations with Denmark-Norway.

Between 1638 and 1640 there were several agendas being played out between Great Britain, the House of Stuart, and Denmark-Norway. These led to a war often described as being between Scotland and England, but in actuality, one that concerned all of Royalist Britain against the Scottish Covenanters. To the latter faction the reality was more simple: The actions of Charles I had threatened the polity of the Scottish nation and they therefore empowered themselves to arm and defend the integrity of their country. As part of that policy they deployed skilled diplomats to secure allies and ensure that pro-Stuart nations, like Denmark-Norway, remained effectively neutral. The Stuart agenda involved trying to secure support for the military action to be taken against the [Covenanter] Scots, and that meant dragging England to war as part of 'Royalist Britain' in a war they were simply not prepared for. However, Charles I also wished to proceed with his continental foreign policy while his 'internal' political situation deteriorated. This agenda seemed to many, including his uncle Christian, to be spreading his resources too thinly. And in this Christian IV was correct.

Likewise, during the Bishops' Wars the motivations of the Danish king were also complex. While reconstituting the old confederacy with Charles I, Christian actually sought to remain aloof from any of the situations in which such an alliance implied he was bound to become involved. In respect to the actions of the Danish king during the Bishops' Wars there is significant evidence of a differing interpretation of the Stuart-Oldenburg alliance between himself and Charles I. It is interesting

---

[109] Lockhart, *Denmark in the Thirty Years' War*, 247.

that Christian IV bought the weapons stopped in the Sound in 1639. That he did not simply confiscate them and lock up the crews as enemies of his nephew raises serious questions. As Christian well knew, Charles remained desperate for arms at this time and it would have been of great value to the Stuart cause to give Charles all the weapons free of charge or on loan. Christian, however, placed his own interest first. By purchasing the arms he could both tax the merchants and get the best weapons for the Danish Crown at the best price. By letting the merchant ships pass they could both convey Danish goods abroad and pass the Sound to be taxed another day. Christian did allow Charles to purchase weapons also, but only the ones left after he had taken his choice of the best.

Charles I faced numerous complaints by Scottish merchants with regard to the exorbitant tolls charged by Christian IV in the Sound. Increased revenue from the Sound tolls during the Bishops' Wars must surely suggest a blind eye being turned to a trade which Christian knew would hurt his nephew. Rather than stop all shipping as requested by Hamilton, Christian simply charged more tax. Furthermore, Christian's application to take possession of the Northern Isles when he had only recently reaffirmed his pledge not to mention the subject in his lifetime poses yet more problems regarding his integrity. His decision to attempt a Danish recovery of these islands at a time when his nephew felt quite desperate can only be described as rank opportunism. The passing of prohibited goods through the Sound on payment of special taxes, and the general rise in taxes four-fold and the role of the Danish-Norwegian navy in not sealing the Sound to munitions ships, especially Swedish ones, all bring the motivation of the Danish king into question. After all, since the Danish navy has been shown to be a major instrument of Christian's foreign policy, its failure to secure the Sound in 1639-1640 can only reflect a royal desire to keep the waterways open.

Perhaps in combination these events are not so strange. Christian IV believed the actions of his nephew were inept. His offers to serve as a mediator were probably sincere. In both 1639 and 1640 he engaged diplomats to travel to Britain to settle the dispute and it was Charles who decided not to accept this mediation. Once rejected as an arbitrator Christian IV had no particular reason to favour his nephew over the Covenanters. After all, the harder the Covenanters pressed Charles, the more chance Christian must have believed Denmark had of regaining the Northern Isles. Had the Danish scheme worked it would have left Christian in possession of the Northern Isles with a military garrison which Charles would have found difficult to dislodge.

The Scottish Covenanters received more, in real terms, than their

Royalist adversaries from Christian IV. As early as 1639 they had established diplomatic links with the Scandinavian countries, which staved off condemnation of the National Covenant or military intervention by Denmark-Norway. They had also been graced by several Danish diplomatic envoys trying to intercede on their behalf with Charles I. These missions went a long way towards the international legitimisation of the Covenanting movement. As if the diplomatic missions were not damaging enough to Stuart prestige, Christian actually had his envoys travel to Scotland before England, and without consultation with Charles I. This breach of etiquette could, and probably was, interpreted by Charles as giving the Scottish Estates political precedence over the Stuart Crown.

Militarily the Covenanters succeeded as the Danish-Norwegian navy and government appear to have tacitly supported Scottish Covenanting supplies passing through their waters, albeit for a financial return to the Danish Crown. Through a combination of Scottish, Dutch and Swedish ships, the collusion of the Swedish authorities, and the neutrality of the Danes, the Covenanters had surmounted their logistical problems. Most military supplies and personnel reached Scotland with ease from the continent, guaranteeing the success of the Covenanting movement during the Bishops' Wars against a humiliated Stuart government. In turn, their success negated Stuart-Oldenburg policy on the Palatinate. This manifested itself by a course of action by Christian IV tantamount to a betrayal of his relative Charles Louis, in a quest to establish himself as a force within central European politics.

CHAPTER FIVE

The Danes and the Wars in the Three Kingdoms
1641-1649

Between the 2nd and 11th of June 1640, the Scottish Parliament, which had been prorogued in 1639, reopened without royal consent and passed a series of acts which were to significantly alter the relationship between the Scottish Estates, Kirk and the House of Stuart.[1] The second act of this Parliament removed the estate of the clergy from Parliament after which the three estates were composed of the nobles, the commissioners of the shires and of the burghs. While the Scottish Estates declared that they had no intention of challenging royal authority with their actions, the Scottish constitutional settlement of 1640-41 had done just that. Some noblemen believed that with these changes the Covenant had now gone far enough. James Graham, Earl of Montrose had become increasingly alienated from the mainstream of the Covenanting movement since the Glasgow Assembly in 1638 and the General Assembly of 1639, despite continuing to maintain a role on Parliamentary committees.[2] He had also conducted ongoing covert communication with the king since the Pacification of Berwick in 1639. This correspondence was indicative that the unity of the Scottish Covenanters was more fragile than their decisive actions in 1639 demonstrated. The fractures that occurred within the movement also spread to Covenanters active outwith Scotland. Colonel Sir John Cochrane remained on the continent between April and July 1640 and so could not have known of the ratification of the radical acts of the June Parliament until after they had been passed. Like Montrose, Cochrane also believed the Covenanting Parliament had moved well beyond the original goals already conceded by Charles I.[3]

During his mission to Denmark-Norway and Hamburg in 1640, Sir James King met with Sir John Cochrane. King described Cochrane to Charles I as 'a gentellman, a contrayman and auld acquaintance of

---

[1] Munck, *Seventeenth Century Europe*, 78; E Cowan, *Montrose, For Covenant and King* (Edinburgh, 1995), 92; J. R. Young, *The Scottish Parliament 1639-1661: A Political and Constitutional Analysis* (Edinburgh, 1996), 10-15 and 20-26.

[2] Rev. G. Wishart, *The Memoirs of James Marquis of Montrose 1639-1650*, [hereafter, *The Deeds of Montrose*] ed, A. D. Murdoch and H. F. Morland-Simpson (London, 1893), 20; Cowan, *Montrose*, 97; Young, *Scottish Parliament*, 7 and 26.

[3] Spalding, *History of the Trubles*, I, 345; C. Russell, *The Fall of the British Monarchies 1637-1642* (Oxford, 1991), 317; M. Napier, *Memoirs of the Marquis of Montrose* (2 vols., Edinburgh, 1856), 303-304; Cowan, *Montrose*, 107.

myne'.[4] The details of this letter are fascinating, coming so soon after Cochrane's meeting with Christian IV and his impassioned speech to the Swedish *Riksråd*, and indeed, military involvement at Newcastle. Cochrane must have been fully aware of the negotiations taking place in Ripon throughout October, and probably also knew that these would lead to an eventual settlement with the king. Sir James King advised Charles that Cochrane held all the secrets of the Covenanting movement, having been sent to Scandinavia and northern Europe to gain support and gather intelligence in the various nations. King took great pains to vouch for Cochrane to Charles, describing him as a loyal subject who wished to have a meeting with one of the king's representatives. The object of the meeting requested by Cochrane appears to have been to offer his services to Charles I. Cochrane said he would wait at Queen Elizabeth's court in The Hague until 20 December 1640 for a reply from Charles I. Sir James King was insistent that Cochrane was serious about helping to settle the king's affairs in Scotland. The extent of Cochrane's powers to conduct such a negotiation or achieve such a position remains unclear. But that it should have been attempted at all is worthy of note.

By October of 1641, any doubts Charles may have had about Cochrane's sincerity to oppose Argyll and the hard line Covenanters were allayed. After Charles I arrived in Edinburgh, Cochrane approached William Murray, a gentleman of Charles's Bedchamber, to discuss the possibility of publicly accusing Hamilton and Argyll of hindering the peace. Cochrane met Charles I privately between the 9th and 12th of October 1641 and became embroiled in the Incident, a blundered attempt to eradicate the power of Hamilton, his brother Lanark and Argyll through their arrest and possible assassination.[5] William Murray acted as one of the main agitators behind the Incident, another was Alexander Stewart, an officer in Cochrane's regiment. On the morning of the 11 of October, Alexander Stewart met with Captain William Stewart, a relative of the imprisoned Sir James Stewart, Lord Ochiltree. Alexander revealed the plan to arrest Argyll, Hamilton and Lanark, and that it had the support of the Earls of Home, Roxburgh and Crawford, amongst others. The plot hinged on Murray inviting Argyll and Hamilton to the king's chambers, where they would be arrested. Crawford proposed that they should be killed on the spot while James Livingstone, Lord Almond, sought their trial and imprisonment. The attempt was unsuccessful,

[4] PRO, SP75/15 f.475. General James King to Charles 1, 24 October 1640.
[5] *HMC Fourth Report*, I, 163-170; *CSPD*, 1640-41, 137-139. Secret account by Nicholas of the pretended plot in Edinburgh against the Marquis of Hamilton and the Earl of Argyll, 14 October 1641; Sir J. Balfour Paul ed, *Scots Peerage*, III (Edinburgh, 1906), 343; Cowan, *Montrose*, 124-126; Russell, *The Fall of the British Monarchies*, 322-328.

largely due to a tip-off to the intended victims by William Stewart and Lieutenant Colonel Hurry's information to Alexander Leslie. The episode ended with Argyll, Hamilton and Lanark withdrawing from the city and Cochrane's officers being dismissed. Sir John Cochrane himself was summoned to appear before the Scottish Parliament and imprisoned. However, Hamilton and Argyll, the intended victims of the plot, petitioned for Cochrane's release, which was duly granted in early November.[6]

The Incident ensured that there would be several vendettas ongoing within the Covenanting movement. On his release from prison, Cochrane had to contend with allegations of the theft and resetting of a Swedish 'copper' ship, a claim that he absolutely denied. Some of his enemies wanted him hanged in effigy in his absence but this was prevented. In response, Cochrane removed himself to the king's camp at York.[7] Regardless of his personal plans, Cochrane had moved firmly into the Royalist camp and, with a number of his colleagues, set about using his talents and overseas connections abroad to promote the Royalist cause.

With the ever growing mire of contesting Scottish, Irish and English interest, Cochrane's duties had become somewhat more complicated. News of the uprising in Ireland quickly spread to northern Europe along with rumours of renewed anti-Stuart conspiracies in Scotland in regard to Scottish support for the English Parliament.[8] Joseph Averie believed that news of these developments reaching Hamburg and Denmark-Norway would undoubtedly retard the Stuart position in those parts. This was not helped by the news that the Irish insurgents had seized the greater part of their kingdom and slain 25,000 Protestants.[9] Averie travelled to Christian IV to ensure that the Danish king could be prevailed upon to dismiss the rumours as being gross exaggerations. He reported back to the Secretary Windebank that Christian was pleased that the stirrings in Edinburgh amounted to particular differences amongst the nobility and had been resolved by the 'high wisdom and presence' of

---

[6]   Balfour Paul, *Scots Peerage*, III, 343; Russell, *The Fall of the British Monarchies,* 328; *The Deeds of Montrose*, 37, footnote; Napier, *Memoirs of Montrose*, 1, 276-277 and appendix lviii, lxii-lxiv.

[7]   D. Lang ed, *The Letters and Journals of Robert Baillie, Principle of the University of Glasgow MDCXXXVII-MDCLXII* (2 vols., Edinburgh, 1841), II, 9. 10 May 1642. Baillie noted 'He was weell received by the King, and sent over sea, for what it is not yet known; there was never a sojour of his years of so great credite and expectation universallie in all our land, and now none universallie in such disgrace'.

[8]   PRO SP 75/16, f.111. Averie to Roe, 13/23 November 1641. For two excellent surveys of Ireland during the 1640s see R. M. Armstrong, 'Protestant Ireland and the English Parliament 1641-1647' (unpublished PhD thesis, Trinity College Dublin, 1995) and M. Ó Siochrú, *Confederate Ireland 1642-1649* (Dublin, 1999).

[9]   PRO SP 75/16, ff.113-114. Averie to Secretary of State, 24 November 1641.

Charles I.[10]

Part of the attempted solution by Charles lay in the reconstitution of the Scottish Privy Council on 13 November. In effect this saw a Council in which the radical nobility dominated and where the conservative/pragmatic royalists were marginalised.[11] After the Treaty of Ripon in 1641, the Scottish Estates and the House of Stuart maintained an uneasy peace as war broke out in England between the English Parliament and Charles I. The radical leadership in Scotland, however, sought to export the Covenanting revolution to England and Ireland on a pan-British basis as a means of attaining security for their Scottish gains.[12] Hence the year 1641 concluded with a proposal from the Scots to send an army to Ireland. An expeditionary force was not actually despatched, however, until 1642. This ultimately saw Scottish military intervention in England on behalf of the English Parliament against the House of Stuart. That in turn led to the signing of the Solemn League and Covenant in September 1643 after which the Scottish Estates pressed for a British confederal commitment to the various wars against Charles I.[13]

Christian IV and the Wars in the three Stuart kingdoms

In response to the growing influence of the Scottish radical leadership throughout 1642, leading Scottish Royalists directed their attentions to aiding their fellow Royalists in England and Ireland by continuing to press a Stuart agenda within the three kingdoms, and abroad. Indeed, a pan-British solution was sought by the opposing factions in England. Both Stuart Royalists and the English Parliamentarians lobbied the Covenanting leadership for support, eventually conveyed to the latter by the Solemn League and Covenant in 1643. In the meantime, the contesting factions dispatched envoys to the continent to secure help for their causes abroad.

In March 1642 Queen Henrietta Maria reported that Christian IV had plans to send a fleet to England in support of Charles I.[14] A resolution attributed to Christian IV was read out in the English Parliament and

---

[10]   PRO SP 75/16, ff.113-114. Averie to Secretary of State, 24 November 1641.

[11]   Young, *Scottish Parliament*, 54-55.

[12]   Russell, *The Fall of the British Monarchies*, 69; Young, *Scottish Parliament*, 68; Armstrong, 'Protestant Ireland', particularly 7 and 107-146.

[13]   A copy of the Solemn League and Covenant dated 25 September 1643 can be found in S. R. Gardiner ed, *The Constitutional Documents of the Puritan Revolution, 1625-1660* (Oxford, 1899), 267-271.

[14]   TT 245 669 f.3 (1-64), no.62. *Copie of the Queen's letter from The Hague, 19 March 1641* [1642] (London, 1642).

subsequently published.[15] It too claimed a Danish fleet was being prepared in support of Charles I. To confirm these reports, new embassies were needed. Sir John Cochrane returned to Denmark-Norway twice in 1642 to seek a firm commitment of support for Charles I from his uncle. To bolster his mission there another Scottish Royalist, Colonel John Henderson also travelled to Copenhagen.[16] Both men brought particular requests for weapons, powder and war material. Henderson specifically asked for 12,000 men, 24 cannons, £100,000 and the loan of some warships for transportation. Further, he sought 3,000 German infantry and 1,000 cavalry under Count Woldomar Christian's command.[17] Christian IV pondered Charles's petitions and eventually gave Cochrane promises of powder and weapons but pleaded ignorance of the full extent of the troubles between the Stuart king and his English Parliament. Christian told Cochrane that, before he responded to his nephew's request, he wished to be better informed of developments in the British Isles. Christian's understanding of the situation did not progress even after the arrival of the English Royalist envoy, John Poley.[18] The Danish king remarked that he was 'as wise as to the reason for the conflict between Charles and his English Parliament as he was after Poley's previous visit' in April which had not clarified anything for him.[19]

In England, military and political posturing had turned to open warfare between the contesting factions. After some minor skirmishes in September, the first major action of the English Civil War took place at Edgehill on the 23 October 1642. Surmising from the increasing military action that such a fight was imminent, Christian IV sent Korfitz Ulfeldt and Sir John Cochrane to London to inform Charles I of the sincerity of

---

[15] TT E.154 (3), Christian IV, *The King of Denmark's Resolution concerning, the King of Great Brittain* (London, 1642).

[16] DRA, TKUA England A II 15. Charles I to Christian IV, credentials for Sir John Cochrane, 10 May 1642 and 19 August 1642; Balfour Paul, *Scots Peerage*, III, 343. Balfour Paul suggests that Cochrane travelled with the English ambassador to Denmark and they were both 'evill entreated and put in prison'; TT 22 E.124 (6). *A Declaration and Protestation of the Lords and Commons in Parliament to this Kingdome, and to the whole world*, 23 October 1642; This is perhaps the Colonel Henderson noted as an acquaintance of Charles Louis, Prince Palatine, in Oldenburg in February 1639. PRO SP 81/45, f.116. Charles Louis to Roe, 13 February 1639.

[17] DRA, TKUA England A II 15. Charles I to Christian IV, credentials for John Henderson, 6 September 1642 with an appendix of requests for the Danish king; J. A. Fridericia, *Danmarks Ydre Politiske Historie, II; i tiden fra Freden i Prag til Freden i Bromsebro, 1635-1645* (Copenhagen, 1972 reprint), 314.

[18] DRA, TKUA England A II 15. Charles I to Christian IV, credentials for John Poley, 10 March 1643; Fridericia, *Danmarks Ydre Politiske Historie*, II, 314-315.

[19] *KCFB*, VIII, 277-278. Christian IV to Korfitz Ulfeldt, 2 November 1643. 'Ieg er bleffuen lyge sa wiis aff hannem dennegang som tylforn, tii hand kan Inted siige mig Arsagen, huorfor konningen och parlamendtit fører med hiinanded'.

the Danish offer of help. A further letter was sent instructing Ulfeldt to deliver guns and ammunition to Charles and to act as mediator between Charles and his English Parliament. Ulfeldt and Cochrane arrived in Newcastle with four Danish ships soon after, bringing with them between 5-6,000 suits of armour and 'a considerable sum in ready money'.[20] They travelled on to London and delivered Christian's new terms to Charles for helping him in his war.

In addition to his earlier requests for the Orkney and Shetland islands, Christian IV now wanted to ensure that he could also gain possession of Newcastle, in pawn, in return for Danish military aid.[21] Again, the motive must have been commercial as Newcastle was renowned for her coal and salt industries. While Charles I considered Christian's offer of help, Cochrane and Ulfeldt visited the English Parliament where they were apparently maltreated and incarcerated. Although the Danish ambassador was released soon after, Sir John Cochrane remained in captivity for several months longer. The imprisonment of Cochrane and the maltreatment of Ulfeldt remained a point of contention between Christian IV and the English Parliament for some years. Christian later instructed Korfitz Ulfeldt that captured Englishmen should be treated in the same way as his own people had been treated in England.[22] Ulfeldt returned to Denmark-Norway having achieved little by way of either mediation or settling the conditions for Danish intervention.

As early as November 1640, rumours of Danish military intervention had circulated in England. It had been hoped that Sir James King would attempt a landing in London with 6-7,000 Danish troops in support of Charles I.[23] Unfortunately for the Royalists these rumours were unfounded: Sir James King did not leave Hamburg for another year. When he arrived in Scotland then, it was only to bring a published declaration regarding Danish negotiations with the Empire after which he returned to Hamburg.[24] News eventually reached Aberdeen in January 1643 that General James King had landed from Denmark-Norway in England with £500,000 for Charles I but without the Danish or German troops the Royalists hoped for. Indeed, Spalding recorded that in total he

[20]   *KCFB*, VIII, 219. Christian IV to Korfitz Ulfeldt, 19 October 1642; *KCFB*, V, 256-257. Christian IV to Korfitz Ulfeldt, 24 October 1642; TT 22 E.127 (25). *The Daily Proceedings of His Majesties Fleet on the Narrow Seas, from the 17 October to the 15 day of November* (London, 1642), 3; *CSPV*, XXVI, 203. Giovanni Giustinian, 26 November 1642; Spalding, *History of the Troubles*, 2, 168-169

[21]   *KCFB*, VIII, 220-222. Christian IV to Korfitz Ulfeldt, 22 October 1642; Fridericia, *Danmarks Ydre Politiske Historie*, II, 315.

[22]   Spalding, *History of the troubles*, II, 99; *KCFB*, V, 398-399. Christian IV to Korfitz Ulfeldt, 23 September 1644.

[23]   Laing, *Letters and Journals of Robert Baillie*, I, 269-270. 5 and 6 November 1640.

[24]   PRO SP 75/16, ff.87 and 89. Averie to Vane, 10/20 and 17/27 September 1641.

only arrived with between 60-80 officers and it is probable that these men were themselves Royalist exiles rather than foreign mercenaries.[25]

In February 1643, Christian IV came up with a cynical plan to cut off Hamburg from both land and sea in order to strengthen his grip on that city. He deliberately spread the rumour that the forces he was gathering were intended for the service of Charles I in England. He gave credence to the deception by writing to a Count Pens as if to secretly ascertain how many ships were available to transport horses supposedly requested by Charles I.[26] The Danish scheme obviously worked and they armed a fleet destined for Hamburg which the citizens of that town did not suspect was directed against them until it was too late.[27] This manoeuvre proved successful for Christian IV and certainly had the attention of the Parliamentarians, who published a letter noting a fleet of 25 Danish ships in the Elbe and believing 'the Designe is for England'.[28] The realisation that the anticipated help from Denmark-Norway might not come after all must surely have lowered morale among the Stuart Royalists. However, they maintained their hope of Danish succour and rumours of its arrival continued to circulate until the end of the year.

Neither the lack of troops accompanying Sir James King nor the Hamburg deception prevented the Parliamentarians from believing that Danish forces would eventually arrive. Between January and July, the English Admiral Robert Rich, Earl of Warwick, received instructions from the English Parliament in which Denmark was listed as one of nations whose ships he was expected to stop and search for Royalist provisions. If such ships contained Royalist stores they were to be either captured, or sunk if they resisted. Warwick himself noted that Captain Batten had requested more ships especially 'for fear of the Danes'.[29] Not all English captains feared the arrival of the Danes, in fact some positively relished the prospect of a meeting with them at sea. One Captain Haddock wrote 'We take divers prizes, pray for the coming of the Danes, with whom we are ready to encounter'.[30] The opportunity did

---

[25] Spalding, *History of the Trubles*, II, 108. Given that this is a Scottish source, it is most probable that the money is pounds Scots. That would equate to about £41,700 sterling; Laing, *Letters and Journals of Robert Baillie*, II, 80 and 105. 26 July 1643 and 17 November 1643.

[26] *KCFB*, V, 299-301. Christian IV to Christen Thomesen Sehested, 10 February 1643. 'At indbylde En eller anden at myn *intentio* gaar pa Engeland, ded kan letteligen skee....'. See also 314, Christian IV to Korfitz Ulfeldt, 4 March 1643.

[27] *KCFB*, V, 340. Christian IV to Korfitz Ulfeldt, 14 May 1643.

[28] TT 19 E.105 (20). *A Coranto from beyond Sea: or True Intelligence from France, Spain, Germany, and Denmark, Amsterdam, 27 May* (London, 1643).

[29] *CSPV*, XXVI, 223, 235 and 249. Gerolamo Agostini, 2 and 30 January and 6 March 1643; J. R. Powell and E. K. Timings eds, *Navy Records Society; Documents Relating to the Civil War, 1642-1648* (London, 1963), [hereafter *NRS Documents*] 53-54 and 68-69, Instructions to Warwick, 5/15 April 1643; *NRS Documents*, 82-83. Warwick to Smith, 19/29 July 1643.

[30] *NRS Documents*, 78-80. Haddock to (?), 3/13 July 1643.

not arise as often as either Haddock or Charles I would have preferred.[31]

The Solemn League and Covenant 1643-1647

During the visits of the English Royalist envoy, John Poley, to Denmark-Norway in 1643, weapons and an army were again requested from the Danish king with the Orkney and Shetland Isles offered as security against them. In response to these requests, Christian sent Charles quantities of weapons and supplies. A manifest of these weapons survives which shows that the Danes intended to supply Charles with enough swords and muskets for about 3,000 men and pikes and other arms for about 2,000 more. Unfortunately for Charles I, the list had been drawn up by a Parliamentarian after the ship had been captured and taken to Portsmouth.[32] The same letter records the seizing of a coal ship bound for Holland by the Earl of Warwick and containing £3-4,000 buried 'deep in the coals' and reported to have been 'happily diverted another and better way'.

Charles had lost both weapons and money within days of each other. Yet he continued to hope that 'German' cavalry sent by the Danish king could form part of a multi-pronged attack planned in response to the Solemn League and Covenant. This plan included the landing of Gaelic troops under Alasdair MacColla in the west of Scotland while soldiers under the Marquises of Newcastle and Montrose were to enter Scotland from the south.[33] Charles had to suffer another disappointment. The loss of the ship and weapons in August apparently 'cooled' Christian's interest in his nephew's affairs.[34] He eventually rejected Charles's offer regarding the Northern Isles since he did not believe that Charles would ever cede the islands or find the capital to pay for the weapons. It is also probable that the re-entry of the Covenanters into the anti-Stuart coalition, meant Christian did not believe Charles had the ability to hand over islands which he did not actually have control of.[35]

---

[31] TT 27 E.150 (26), *The Earl of Warwickes victory over fifty Ships of the King of Denmarkes in the Narrow Seas*, (15 June 1642 or 1643). This document reports a naval engagement between 21 ships under the Earl of Warwick and 50 Danish ships. The report, read to the English Parliament, states that 2 Danish ships were taken and the rest put to flight. This report remains to date unconfirmed by Danish sources.

[32] *NRS Documents*, 85-86. Report of a ship taken near Newcastle, August 1642 or 1643. Barrels of gunpowder 476; Bundles of match 990; Drums 50; Belly pieces of armour 150; Swords 3,040; Muskets 2,977; Pistols 493; Headpieces 3,000; Roundheads or clubs 1,000; Pikes, very good ones 1,500; Musket rests 3,000; Forks to fight against horses 500; Collars of bandoleers 3,000. A sub-manifest records lesser items such as belts, musket moulds and flasks.

[33] *The Deeds of Montrose*, 37; D. Stevenson, *Highland Warrior: Alasdair MacColla and the Civil Wars* (Edinburgh, 1994), 120-199.

[34] Fridericia, *Danmarks Ydre Politiske Historie*, II, 316.

[35] *KCFB*, V, 386 footnote; Fridericia, *Danmarks Ydre Politiske Historie*, II, 316.

The timing of the Solemn League and Covenant between Scotland and England could not have come at a more inappropriate time in relation to hope of military aid from Denmark-Norway. Christian IV allegedly sent a further £60,000 to Charles I in November 1643, apparently still believing that he was not in any imminent danger from the Swedish army, who were well advanced with their plans to overrun his kingdom.[36] Two munitions ships are said to have reached Newcastle from Denmark-Norway in January 1644 along with a prize ship of corn they had taken *en route*.[37] However, when the Danish-Swedish war broke out in December 1643, all realistic hope of significant Danish military or financial support ended.[38]

Throughout the Torstensson War (1643-1645) between Denmark-Norway and Sweden, Stuart envoys continued to try to get Danish help but with little success. Colonel Henderson arrived in Denmark during April 1644 requesting weapons and men, despite the obvious difficulty this would have posed given the Swedish occupation of much of Denmark.[39] Henderson informed Christian that the Royalists had few warships since many naval ships were held in occupied ports. Through Henderson, Charles indicated that he would have to arm merchantmen and use privately provided ships to impede the trade of the 'traitors'. This discussion regarding the weakness of the Stuart naval forces had obviously been designed to prompt Christian IV into firmer action against the anti-Stuart confederacy.[40]

Sir John Cochrane arrived in Copenhagen in May to augment Henderson's mission. Cochrane's instructions were clear. He had to apologise for Charles being unable to intercede in Christian's conflict with Sweden due to the pressures of his own conflict in England. Christian IV had to be informed of how his enemies opposed peace and the 'dangerous combination of his majesty's subjects, who have not only invaded his majesty in his particular rites, but have laid a design to dissolve the monarchy and frame of government, under pretences of

---

[36] Spalding, *History of the Trubles*, II, 168-169.

[37] *CSPV*, XXVII, 21. Gerolamo Agostini, 22 January 1644.

[38] Laing, *Letters and Journals of Robert Baillie*, II, 143. 18 February 1644. Baillie noted simply 'Nothing now expected from Denmark'. See also TT 8 E.45 (7), *Christian IV and Queen Christiana, Two manefestos, or Declarations: The one by the King of Denmarke, the other by the Queene of Sweden, both concerning the present warres* (London, 1644). The invasion of Denmark-Norway by Swedish forces in 1643 is discussed in chapter ten.

[39] DRA, TKUA England, A I. Charles I to Christian IV, March 1644.

[40] DRA, TKUA England, A I. Charles I to Christian IV, March 1644; Two months after this request Charles I issued a proclamation allowing privateers to act on Parliamentary vessels. See Larkin, *Stuart Royal Proclamations*, II, 1034-1035. 'A Proclamation for taking of Prizes at Sea in the Time of this Rebellion'. Oxford, 9 May 1644.

liberty and religion'.[41] Charles wished it to be pointed out to his uncle that the success of his enemies in Britain would carry serious implications for all the monarchies of Christendom.[42] Cochrane was further instructed to convey the jeopardy in which the family of Charles I had been placed by the 'rebels', leading to the Stuarts having to abandon London.

In terms of the military situation Charles remained more upbeat. He declared that on his personal appearance many forts had declared for him and that he now had near six thousand horse and ten thousand foot under arms to help him defeat the rebels. Knowing how to attract his uncle's attention, Charles played on the recent negotiations of confederation conducted by Hugh Mowatt on behalf of Sweden in both Scotland and England.[43] Through Mowatt, and in direct correspondence with the Chancellor of Scotland, John Campbell Earl of Loudoun, the Swedish Chancellor Axel Oxenstierna broached the notion that the Danish commercial monopoly over the Sound had to be broken. He suggested that Scotland might have a role to play in that action in response to the Danish king's negative attitude toward Scottish traders. Charles I urged Cochrane to point out that in the English Parliament it had been mooted that a naval fleet should be sent to the Danish waters to 'take away his customs of the Sound'. These ships were to be joined by a further 2,000 Scottish soldiers and 1,000 Scottish sailors who had been recruited in order to join the Swedes in an attempted occupation of the Sound.[44] Charles determined to press the impact of the Solemn League and Covenant on Denmark-Norway. Cochrane told Christian IV that the naval commissions issued to the Parliamentary fleet had been ordered in response to the communication between the two royal houses. Obviously Charles's intention was to show Christian how unreasonable his opponents were if they could not even accept the intervention of a

---

[41]   T. Park ed, *The Harliean Miscellany: A collection of scarce, curious, and entertaining Pamphlets and Tracts, as well in manuscript as in print. Selected from the library of Edward Harley, second Earl of Oxford. Interspersed with historical, political and critical annotations by the late William Oldy's esq. and some additional notes by Thomas Park, F.S.A.* (London, 1811), VII, 567-570. 'Instructions to Colonel Cockran, to be pursued in his Negotiation to the king of Denmark'. c. 1644-45; DRA, TKUA England A II 15. Proposal of John Cochrane (?) to Christian IV, c. June 1644.

[42]   This is a point which Charles raised frequently. See DRA, TKUA England, A I. Charles I to Christian IV, 26 February 1645.

[43]   For a comprehensive discussion of these see Grosjean, 'Scots and the Swedish State', 193-201.

[44]   Dumfries House: Marquis of Bute's Archives, Loudoun and Rowallow Deeds, Bundle 2/2, Draft of a letter to Axel Oxenstierna, n.d., 1643. Also Bundle 1/1, Axel Oxenstierna to John Campbell, Earl of Loudoun, 26 March 1644. I would like to thank Prof. Allan Macinnes for these references; Park, *The Harleian Miscellany*, 568. Instructions to Cochrane; DRA, TKUA England A II 15. Proposal of John Cochrane (?) to Christian IV, c. June 1644.

neutral party like the Danish king.

After Cochrane had delivered all the just reasons why Christian should help his nephew, he had orders to seek specific forms of help. These were to include a loan of £100,000 which Charles gave his 'kingly word' he would repay and offered 'such of his crown jewels, as are in his disposure' as his guarantee.[45] One of the problems that Charles mentioned to his uncle was that, despite 8,000 Scots apparently having left the Scottish army for the king's forces, he had no means to arm them.[46] This claim by Charles has little historical foundation, but perhaps he hoped to use it as a method to persuade Christian to release arms which he could then supply to fresh English recruits or continental mercenaries. Charles promised to replace all the armaments as soon as he could and offered to help maintain the Danish fleet so that they might uphold Christian's right to levy tolls in the Sound. In terms of arms, Charles specifically asked for 6,000 muskets, 1,500 horse arms and twenty mounted pieces of field artillery.[47] Charles also asked that any manpower offered would only consist of horsemen and that these should be landed at Holy Island or Newcastle. Charles concluded his request by promising that once he had sorted out his own difficulties, he would turn his full attention to aiding Christian IV should he still require help. Cochrane added the further sweetener that he had persuaded some of the Scottish officers in the service of Sweden to reconsider their actions against Denmark-Norway as an act of disloyalty to their own king. He also assured Christian that he had had some success in this matter, hinting of future conversions to come, though again there seems to be little evidence to support Cochrane's claims.[48]

Despite Charles's arguments, Christian IV decided another attempt at mediation would be more appropriate than a military endeavour, given the limitations imposed by the ongoing conflict with Sweden. Christian sent Sir John Henderson back to Charles I to explain the Danish situation and the problems posed in supplying men and munitions. Henderson also carried orders requesting military support from Charles I to his uncle. Christian sought to invoke the clauses in the confederacy between the two royal houses to get Charles to supply him with at least a dozen fully armed and crewed warships and 4,000 soldiers by spring of the following year. Realising that Charles might be unable to comply due to

[45] Park, *The Harleian Miscellany*, 568, Instructions to Cochrane. Two specific sets of Jewels were mentioned as being in Holland at the disposal of the Danish king should he agree to assist Charles. One great collar of rubies (perhaps even the same one that had caused so much friction in the 1630s) and a lesser collar of rubies and pearls.

[46] DRA, TKUA England A II 15. Proposal of John Cochrane (?) to Christian IV, c. June 1644.

[47] Park, *The Harleian Miscellany*, 568. Instructions to Cochrane.

[48] DRA, TKUA England A II 15. Proposal of John Cochrane (?) to Christian IV, c. June 1644.

his internal troubles, the Dane intimated that he could make do with Scottish officers to command German mercenaries instead.[49] In response to this request, Charles released the officers to Christian and wrote a personal letter to him in February 1645 reiterating the points raised in Cochrane's earlier instructions. In this letter Charles emphasised that he could expect help from no other quarter and that, therefore, the fate of the three Stuart kingdoms lay in the Danish king's hands. The scheme that Charles now proposed involved the landing of some 4,000 Danish troops at the end of March – at either Yarmouth or Lynn – in Norfolk where they would be met by Charles's forces.[50] Christian was in no position to comply with this and it appears neither king fully understood the desperate situation of the other.

Still acting in the capacity of a Danish diplomat, Sir John Henderson undertook a mission to the English Parliament during which he was arrested and imprisoned.[51] However the 'Committee of Both Kingdoms' decided to release Henderson on this occasion.[52] They also insisted that in future Christian IV should not employ anybody as an envoy who had actually raised arms against the confederated kingdoms of Scotland and England. At about the same time as Henderson secured his release, Queen Henrietta-Maria wrote to Christian IV asking that ships belonging to the Duke of Courland be allowed to pass through the Sound 'toll free'. She argued that they were crucial to the Royalist war effort since they carried powder and lead acquired by John Cochrane and destined for the Marquis of Montrose's Royalist army in Scotland.[53] The Royalists hoped that even more support could be brought from Denmark if only Christian IV could be persuaded to land 500 horsemen, some arms and money now that it was generally believed that peace could not be far off between Denmark-Norway and Sweden.[54]

---

[49]   DRA, TKUA England, A II 15. Instructions to John Henderson from Christian IV to be related to Charles I, 28 November 1644. See chapter ten for further discussion on this point

[50]   DRA, TKUA England, A I. Charles I to Christian IV, 26 February 1645.

[51]   DRA, TKUA England, A I. Letter from the English Parliament to Christian IV, 25 June 1645; *KCFB*, VIII, 352, footnote.

[52]   This was the body established to run the affairs of state and foreign policy which affected Scotland and England. A copy of the ordinances appointing the committee can be found in Gardiner, *Constitutional Documents*, 271-273 (first committee) and 273-274 (second committee). For the specific business mentioned see *CSPD*, 1644-1645, 392-3. Proceedings of the Committee of Both Kingdoms, 8 April 1645.

[53]   *CSPD*, 1644-1645, 387. Dr Stephen Goffe to Henry Lord Jermyn, 6/16 April 1645; Laing, *Letters and Journals of Robert Baillie*, II, 310. c.1645. Baillie noted that the arms had been acquired by Sir John Cochrane; At least one of the Courland skippers was a Scot by the name of Teyrfull, see H. F. Morland-Simpson ed, 'Civil War Papers 1643-1650', in *Miscellany of the Scottish Historical Texts Society*, vol. I (Edinburgh, 1893), 151. Agent of the Duke of Courland to Charles I, c.1645. Also 155, Abraham de Vicqfort to Duke James of Courland, 30 August 1645.

[54]   DRA, TKUA England A II 15. Charles I to Christian IV, 20 July 1645. Credentials for Sir

The Scandinavian powers finally ended their war with a treaty signed in Brømsebro on the 13 August 1645, by which Denmark-Norway had to cede the provinces of Gotland, Herjeland and Jemtland to the Swedes who were also to occupy Halland for thirty years.[55] Liberated from this war, Christian IV hoped he could now seriously act as 'middleman' between the contesting parties in the British Isles.[56] In September 1645, Henderson brought Christian news of the dire situation of the Royalists in England after the battle of Naseby in June, and the disintegration of Goring's army at Langport in July.[57] Through Henderson, Charles informed Christian that he earnestly desired peace. On 10 September, Henderson returned to England carrying a written offer of Danish mediation between the king and Parliament.[58] He arrived in Britain in time to hear of three more Royalist defeats. Oliver Cromwell had recently captured Bristol, and Montrose's Royalist army had been destroyed by David Leslie at Philiphaugh on 13 September. Langsdale's Royalist Cavalry had also been defeated at Rowton Heath on the 24th of the same month. Reports abounded that Christian IV and other European leaders were going to intervene to help Charles. Both Englishmen and Scots believed the Danes had mustered seven or eight regiments to be led by Count Woldomar, Christian IV's son, and a naval squadron to transport them had been arranged. As so often before, the imminent arrival of continental allies turned out to be mere rumour.[59] Sir John Cochrane struck east in search of firmer supplies than those offered by the Danes. He arrived in Danzig where he entered into negotiations for muskets, powder, match and lead with James Duke of Courland. Cochrane had some success, and on his return to Lübeck he learned that Duke James intended to supply a dozen cannon in addition to the muskets he had requested.[60]

By May 1646, Charles's political fortunes had seriously deteriorated.

John Cochrane; *CSPD*, 1645-1647, 55-60; Henry Lord Jermyn to George Lord Digby, 26 July/5 August 1645. Henry Lord Jermyn to George Lord Digby, 12/22 August 1645.

[55] *Danmark-Norges Traktater*, IV, 437-474.

[56] *KCFB*, VI, 62-63. Christian IV to Christen Thomesen Sehested, 25 August 1645.

[57] *KCFB*, VI, 68-69. Christian to Korfitz Ulfeldt, 2 and 3 September 1645.

[58] *CSPV*, XXVII, 21. Advices from London, 19 October 1645; *KCFB*, VI, 63 and 69, footnotes. Christian paid Henderson 400 *rigsdaler* for his journey back to Britain.

[59] *CSPD*, 1645-1647, 189-190. Sir Robert Honeywood to Sir Harry Vane, 13/23 October 1645; Laing, *Letters and Journals of Robert Baillie*, II, 338-339.

[60] Morland-Simpson, 'Civil War Papers 1643-1650', 158-159, 160-161 and 163-165, various letters from Cochrane to James Duke of Courland. The specific request amounted to a consignment of lead for Scotland, 1,000 muskets with bandoleers, 100cwt of powder and as much match and lead bullets as could be spared. The cannon and muskets caused some problems since initially they were to arrive without carriages and when they did arrive, they were mounted for use at sea rather than land. The muskets were also considered to be nearly worthless and had to be exchanged.

The king contemplated going to Scotland to meet up with Montrose and the remnants of his force. Should that fail, Charles told Henrietta-Maria he would either make for Ireland, France or Denmark-Norway. Charles also thought of sending the Prince of Wales to Denmark for safety.[61] The conceptual Stuart 'British' kingdom had all but evaporated and on 5 May Charles decided to entrust himself to the Earl of Leven's Covenanting army at Newark. At exactly this moment, Sir John Cochrane was engaged in another mission to try to solicit aid for Charles from Denmark-Norway. Crown Prince Christian (V) wrote to Charles expressing his concern at the news Cochrane brought regarding the king's present situation.[62] However, he asked Cochrane to inform his cousin that the recent war with Sweden had left Denmark-Norway so militarily and financially ruined that the only thing he could send to Charles was his prayers. Cochrane reacted strongly to this letter. Within a week of the letter being sent to Charles I, Prince Christian sent another letter to Cochrane denying that he had tried to place any distance between himself and his kinsman. The letter to Cochrane included, according to the prince, proof of his complete sincerity and the affection he bore for Charles I. He further hoped that Cochrane would emphasise the total commitment to Charles's interest that the prince had demonstrated in his audience with the Colonel.[63] The Danes continued to give the impression that they were about to transfer their resolution into firm actions. Certainly Cochrane thereafter collected weapons and ammunition to the value of 29,300 *rigsdaler* from the Danish armoury in Glückstadt via the Berns & Marselis company in Hamburg. The Scottish Commissioners in London also believed that Christian IV was 'using all diligence to sett for 28 saill of shippes for assistance of the King'.[64]

Unfortunately for Charles I, Prince Christian's prayers did not prevent the situation worsening for the Stuart forces and the weapons Cochrane gathered are so far unaccounted for in Scotland. Additionally, the main Danish fleet of ships, if they were ever actually being prepared to assist

[61] *CSPV*, XXVII, 21. Advices from London, 15 February 1646; J Bruce, *Charles I in 1646. Letters of Charles the First to Queen Henrietta-Maria* (London, 1856), 38-39. Charles I to Henrietta-Maria, 15 May 1646, 45-46. *Charles I to Henrietta-Maria*, 3 June 1646. Charles told Henrietta-Maria that plans to send Prince Charles to Denmark-Norway have changed since France would be a better place for him; Lockhart, *Denmark in the Thirty Years' War*, 255.

[62] E. Marquard and J. O. Bro-Jørgenson eds, *Prins Christian (V)'s Brev*, II. *Kancellibreve i uddrag 1643-1647 med et tillæg af prinsens egenhændige breve 1627-1647* (Copenhagen, 1956), 516-517. Prince Christian (V) to Charles I, 28 May 1646.

[63] Marquard and Bro-Jørgenson, *Prins Christian (V)'s Brev*, II, 516-517. Prince Christian (V) to Charles I, 28 May 1646 and 532-533. Prince Christian (V) to Cochrane, 5 June 1646.

[64] J. T. Lauridsen, *Marselis Konsortiet* (Århus, 1987), 88 and 132; H. W. Meikle ed, *Correspondence of the Scots Commissioners in London 1644-1646* (Edinburgh, 1917), 199. Scots Commissioners to the Committee of Estates at Edinburgh, 9 July 1646.

Charles, did not arrive. It is also unclear exactly what happened to the ship that left Copenhagen carrying the muskets and cannon from the Duke of Courland, for by the time it would have reached Scotland there could have been few places able to receive the munitions for the Royalists.[65] John Poley again travelled to Denmark bearing an urgent message from the Prince of Wales to Prince Christian at the end of September. Despite being told of the imminent exile of the Prince of Wales, Prince Christian could only reiterate the sincerity of his sympathies. He again pointed out that Denmark-Norway had still not recovered from the previous war and could therefore not send any succour to the Stuarts. The prince added that his father had already recently rejected the idea of such support despite being sympathetic to the Stuart royal house.[66]

In October 1646, now with confirmation that there would be no Danish intervention, Charles described his personal paradox to Henrietta-Maria:

> That my remaining in these kingdoms, though I be not a direct prisoner, is the only means, in my mind, to secure the Scots, and settle a new Government here, without a breach between the two nations. For as long as I remain as I am, though in Scotland, I (being but a cipher as to power) shall be no impediment to the change of government. And yet the English will not dare to break with the Scots, lest they, setting me up to claim my right, should raise a great party for me in England; whereas if I were in a secure freedom any where else, I believe the two nations must needs fall out, and so give me an opportunity, either to join with the weaker party, or frame one of my own; for then men will begin to perceive that, without my establishing, there can be no peace.[67]

This letter implies that, at that particular juncture, the securing of the Scots (Covenanters) was of primary importance to Charles. Obviously this is because it suited his plans at that time to do so. However, it also suggests that if Charles was to join any of the two sides in an all-out war

---

[65] Morland-Simpson, 'Civil War Papers 1643-1650', 165-166. John Cochrane to Duke James of Courland, 16/26 July 1646. Cochrane simply notes here that the ship had been dispatched to Scotland.

[66] Marquard and Bro-Jørgenson, *Prins Christian (V)'s Brev*, II, 584-585. Prince Christian (V) to Charles I, 30 September 1646.

[67] Petrie, *The Letters of King Charles I*, 210. Charles to the Lords Jermyn, and Culpepper, and Mr John Ashburnham, October 27, 1646.

between Scotland and England he would either join the Scots (unless of course anyone believes that Charles saw England as the weaker party) or raise a third force. Such an army would possibly have meant employing his Irish supporters or a disaffected 'mixed British' force with Irish and mercenary support. The letter came as a reaction to the growing power in England of the New Model Army, established in early 1645. This military development heralded a new phase of military independence for the English Parliamentary forces from their Scottish Covenanting allies who had, anyway, become disillusioned at the failure of English Presbyterians to secure a pure church settlement in England. This disappointment had led to a split in the Scottish political nation between those conservatives who sought a quick and peaceful settlement and Covenanting radicals who strove for a true Covenanter Kirk settlement rather than political reforms or guarantees.[68] This division ultimately cost the Scottish nation its political independence.

The complaint against Denmark of the Solemn League and Covenant

Throughout the mid-1640s the Solemn League and Covenant conducted its own diplomacy with Denmark-Norway. The bulk of these negotiations centred on Danish-Norwegian operations against trade passing through the Sound. Charles I had frequently asked that Christian IV intercept shipping in the Sound whenever hostilities loomed with his Scottish subjects or the Parliament in England.[69] Christian eventually responded to these requests and kept his navy busy with their operations in the Sound. He claimed himself, however, that his actions were mainly in retaliation for the seizure of a Royal Danish ship, *Arken*, loaded with ammunition which had been captured on the English coast in August 1643. By September, *Arken* had been returned to Denmark-Norway though stripped of her cargo estimated by the Danes at a value of 45,555 *rigsdaler* plus 12,000 interest.[70] Joseph Averie reported to Sir Thomas Roe that Christian IV had been so outraged that he ordered the crews of English merchant ships to be imprisoned under armed guard and that the taking of 20 English ships could not satisfy his revenge.[71] Christian

---

[68] Munck, *The Seventeenth Century*, 221.

[69] This request came soon after Sir Thomas Roe had spent months negotiating a reduction in the Tolls. Information on these discussions can be found in PRO SP 75/16, *passim*; *KCFB*, V, 121-123, 129 and 170. Christian IV to Korfitz Ulfeldt, 27 August 17 September 1641 and the 19 January 1642.

[70] TT 12 E.68 (3), no. 36, 7. *Certaine Informations from several parts of the Kingdome and from other places beyond the Seas*, 23 September 1643; PRO SP 75/16, f.168. Averie to Roe, 1/11 September 1643; *CSPV*, XXVII, 7. Gerolamo Agostini, 13 August 1643; *KCFB*, VIII, 269-270. Christian IV to Korfitz Ulfeldt, 28 September 1643; *Danmark-Norges Traktater*, IV, 406.

[71] PRO SP 75/16, f.168. Averie to Roe, 1/11 September 1643; *KCFB*, V, 399, footnote; *CSPV*,

issued orders to the naval squadrons in the Sound, and around the coast of Norway, to stay all goods belonging to the City of London which passed by his dominions. Some Englishmen believed that *Arken* had only been bait in order that Christian could do exactly that and arrest the goods of the Merchant Adventurers.[72] Whatever the case, the governor of Glückstadt seized a cloth ship sailing up the Elbe with a cargo valued at £30,000.[73] The navy was told to keep up such pressure until the English granted him satisfaction. Christian allowed many of the confiscated English goods to be sold off to compensate for the losses from his own ships.[74] He also banned the import of any goods from London, although he later rescinded this order until such time as Averie could advise him that Charles would derive a benefit from staying London goods in the Sound.[75]

Christian had clearly grown weary of the traders from the British Isles, regardless of their loyalties. He had, in fact, impeded trade on the Elbe 'without distinction of any persons whatsoever', Scottish Covenanters, English Parliamentarians and Royalists alike.[76] Averie was so desperate to find a solution to the trade embargo that he turned up at the Danish Court without credentials from Charles I. Christian dismissed him until such time as the proper authority to talk arrived from Charles.[77] Christian also forbade Averie from referring to himself as the 'Royal Envoy' until such time as the English Parliament submitted to Charles I.[78] The benefit to Charles I of this move by Christian IV is not clear. Humiliating a loyal envoy of the House of Stuart for the actions of the English Parliamentarians seems quite inappropriate. Averie rather bravely ignored Christian and engaged in negotiations with the Danish Chancellor, Reventlowe, without permission from the Danish king.[79] Christian's contempt for the protagonists of both sides suggests that he was unconcerned about the reaction of the English Parliament or Royalist envoys to his actions.

XXVII, 21. Gerolamo Agostini, 25 September 1643.
[72] TT 12 E.68 (3), no. 36, 8. 23 September 1643
[73] TT 12 E.68 (3), no. 36, 7. 23 September 1643; PRO SP 75/16, f.168. Averie to Roe, 1/11 September 1643.
[74] *KCFB*, VIII, 274 and 276-277. Christian IV to Korfitz Ulfeldt, 12 and 23 October 1643.
[75] PRO SP 75/16, f.170. Averie to Roe, 29 September 1643.
[76] PRO SP 75/16, f.178. Averie to Roe, 10/20 November 1643.
[77] PRO SP 75/16, f.172. Averie to Roe, 6/16 October 1643.
[78] *KCFB*, V, 255-256. Christian IV to Christen Thomesen Sehested, 30 September 1642.
[79] The Englishman tried to secure the release of several trunks belonging to his wife which had been removed from an English cloth ship. The Danish Chancellor promised the trunks would be returned unharmed since they did not constitute merchandise. Averie found the trunks the following day at Christian IV's lodgings where he noted the locks had been forced, the contents ransacked and that many valuable items were missing PRO SP 75/16, f.172. Averie to Roe, 6/16 October 1643.

After the signing of the Solemn League and Covenant of 1643, Danish prizes included both Scottish and English ships. The Scottish Estates viewed the interference with merchant shipping as an act of betrayal by Christian IV. The conservator of the Scottish staple at Campvere in the United Provinces, Thomas Cunningham, received notice that Christian IV's seizure of these vessels breached the 1641 treaty between the House of Stuart and the House of Oldenburg which protected British merchants. This was an accusation also levied by the Englishman, Joseph Averie, in Hamburg.[80] As a result, Cunningham received orders to solicit help from any town or state that would give it should the Danes continue in their actions.

On occasion, the Scots managed to exert sufficient pressure on Christian IV to win back their ships, goods or at least receive compensation for them. Some of the captured Scottish ships were scuttled at the entrance to Gothenburg harbour in an attempt to block it during the Torstensson War.[81] Christian IV soon had cause to regret that particular action. Within days, the Scottish skipper, William Steens, had managed to exact a promise from Christian IV that his ship would be replaced by one of the Danish fleet along with compensation for his cargo. Not only that, but Christian undertook to pay for the transport of Steens and his belongings to Copenhagen in the meantime.[82] On another occasion, an Irish privateer brought a Scottish ship into Bergen as a prize. Given the size of the Scottish community in Bergen at this juncture, this was not a shrewd move by the Irish skipper. After some debate, Christian ordered the restitution of the Scottish ship and cargo. He further declared that if the Irishman turned up in Danish waters again he was to be arrested.[83] Clearly both Steens and the privateer victim managed to bring sufficient legal weight to bear to make Christian IV back down.

Despite the victories by the Scottish merchants over the Danish king, Christian IV could always resort to his favourite weapon in retaliation – the Sound tolls. British merchants claimed that Christian had raised the Sound tolls four-fold since 1637. The motive, they believed, was Christian's economic retribution for Scottish Covenanter and English Parliamentarian action against his nephew.[84] To try to resolve the

---

80 E. J. Couthrope ed, *The Journal of Thomas Cuningham of Campvere* (Edinburgh, 1928), 78 and 87; PRO SP 75/16, f.168. Averie to Roe, 1/11 September 1643.

81 *KCFB*, VIII, 319. Christian IV to Korfitz Ulfeldt, 25 April 1644 and footnote.

82 *Kancelliets Brevbøger, 1644-45*, 73. Christian IV to Korfits Ulfeldt, 26 April 1644.

83 *Norske Rigs-Registranter*, VIII, 433-4. Christian IV to Henrik Thott, 17 July 1646.

84 Spalding, *History of the Trubles*, II, 40. Spalding added 'and none suld pas by Alschoneir without payment to the gryte wrak of our contreis who can not weill leiv without iron, lynt, pis, whyte, ry and sic commodeteis'.

negative situation for British shipping, the English Parliament sent several envoys to the Danish Court between 1643 and 1645. In September 1643, Theodorus Haak and Robert Lowther received their orders to travel to Denmark-Norway to represent the English Parliament. They were followed in November by William Barker and Richard Jenkes.[85] Although sent from England their objective should have been to open the Danish Sound to their Scottish and Irish allies as well since foreign policy formed part of the portfolio of the Committee of Both Kingdoms after February 1644.[86]

The involvement of partisans of the English Parliament constituted a move that Joseph Averie seriously regretted. In a letter to Sir Thomas Roe, Averie maintained that he had always advised the Company of Merchant Adventures to conduct themselves in a way which would not prejudice Charles I. This had been observed by those of all political persuasion within the company. However, in light of Christian's recent actions the English Parliament had received £30,000 from the company executive based in London, in order to send envoys to reach an accommodation with Christian IV regarding the seized ships. Averie noted that the actions of the London merchants to sponsor English Parliamentarian intervention could have been prevented 'had it not been for the harsh proceedings of the King of Denmark'.[87] In essence, Averie argued that Christian IV had pressured the Merchant Adventurers to move from a state of neutrality, in political matters, firmly into the camp of the Solemn League and Covenant. Averie himself received orders from his superiors in London to give advice and counsel to the English Parliamentarian envoys, including both political and trading concerns. Averie refused to deal with the men in any field other than trade. However, as Robert Anstruther once observed, 'Both matters of State, and the trade of the land are intermixed, and cannot well be separated'.[88]

Christian IV authorised a meeting between the English representatives and the Danish *Rigsråd* in Copenhagen. There were three main areas of complaint. The first surrounded the increase in Sound tolls in 1643 which broke the 1641 agreement negotiated by Sir Thomas Roe; the

---

[85] HP 43/15 A-16B. Parliaments Instructions to Theodore Haak and Robert Lowther, 19 September 1643; PRO SP 75/16, ff.186-188. Averie to Roe, 22 December 1643 and 5/15 January 1644; *KCFB*, V, 399, footnote and 425, Christian IV to Korfitz Ulfeldt, 12 December 1643 and footnote; *Danmark-Norges Traktater,* IV, 402.

[86] Gardiner, *Constitutional Documents,* 271-272. The ordinances appointing the First and Second Committee of Both Kingdoms, 16 February 1643/44 and 22 May 1644. These ordinances notes that six people were required to form a quorum 'with power to hold good correspondence and intelligence with foreign states'.

[87] PRO SP 75/16, f.178. Averie to Roe, 10/20 November 1643.

[88] PRO SP 75/11, f.70. Anstruther to Dorchester, 24 April 1630. Anstruther's comments were made in the context of the dispute between Christian IV and Hamburg over the Elbe tolls.

second point concerned the detention of Parliamentary shipping in the Sound, while the third regarded the charging of tolls on the 'free' German rivers under Christian IV's control.[89] Christian IV carefully considered the case presented by the English representatives. In March 1644 he decided that as a gesture of good will he would reduce the Sound tolls to the 1637 rate.[90] Just after he did so, ships loyal to the English Parliament confiscated another Danish vessel that had nothing to do with running supplies to the Royalists. The Danish merchantman *Golden Sun* had been captured and taken to Portsmouth while *en route* between the East Indies and Denmark-Norway laden with pepper and sugar. Admiral Warwick implored the Parliament not to miss the opportunity of using the *Golden Sun* to apply pressure on Christian IV adding that 'if you shall think fit to repair the losses and miseries, received from the King of Denmark by the English merchants, this opportunity might not be omitted'.[91] The Parliament obliged and the *Golden Sun* remained in Portsmouth. The situation remained unresolved between the two parties. Jenkes and Skynner presented a proposition to the Danish *Rigsråd* in October 1644 in a bid to find a solution.[92] Little common ground could be found and the Englishmen were still in Denmark in February 1645 despite Charles's request to Christian to have them removed from Danish soil.[93]

One major point of contention centred on Christian's unwillingness to discuss ships taken by his navy in 1642. The English, for their part, believed the seizing of the *Arken* had constituted a legitimate act of war. In an effort to get past this stalemate, Jenkes pointed out that the English treated the Danish prizes in a different way to that in which the Danes treated English prizes. They argued that the English treated the crews better and had, after all, released the ammunition ship *Arken*. Importantly they also pointed out that the *Golden Sun*, though in Portsmouth, remained under the charge of her skipper.[94] In contrast, English skippers

---

[89] *KCFB*, V, 425. Christian IV to Korfitz Ulfeldt, 12 December 1643; DRA, TKUA England, A
     II 15. See the numerous letters of William Barker and Richard Jenkes throughout the 1640s;
     Danmark-Norges Traktater, IV, 403; Lockhart, *Denmark in the Thirty Years' War*, 254-255.
[90] DRA, TKUA England, A II 15. Christian IV to the English Parliament, 27 March 1644;
     Danmark-Norges Traktater, IV, 407.
[91] TT I E.2 (29), *The true relation of the Queens departure from Falmouth into Brest*, 22 July
     1644; *NRS Documents*, 163. Information contained within 'The Queen Sails from Falmouth',
     14 July 1644 and 164-165. Warwick to C.o.B.K., 17/27 July 1644; *Danmark-Norges
     Traktater*, IV, 404-406.
[92] DRA, TKUA England, A II 15. Jenkes and Skynner to the *Rigsråd* 14 September and 28
     October 1644; *KCFB*, V, 513-514. and footnote. Christian IV to Korfitz Ulfeldt, 13 October
     1644.
[93] Park, *The Harleian Miscellany*, 568. Instructions to Cochrane.
[94] *KCFB*, VI, 14-15. Christian IV to the *Rigsråd*, 5 February 1645 and footnote; *Danmark-
     Norges Traktater*, IV, 402-406.

were arrested and put in prison while their ships were confiscated and cargoes sold. Regardless of a feeling of inequality in certain areas, the English Parliamentarians claimed they only wanted to find a solution. They offered to pay Christian IV 30,000 *rigsdaler* for the ammunition taken from *Arken* before her release.[95] This amounted to a shortfall of some 27,500 *rigsdaler* estimated by Christian IV (including interest). Despite this discrepancy, the two sides agreed on a settlement. After payment for the ammunition the Danes promised to pay the English merchants 174,000 *rigsdaler* for their confiscated goods. As part of the treaty however, the English merchants had to buy the *Golden Sun* for 74,000 *rigsdaler* which left the deficit owed to the English standing at 100,000 *rigsdaler*. The agreement was reached between the parties on the 26 April 1645, whereupon the Danes undertook to pay the English merchants this amount over the following three years.[96]

This treaty marked a major milestone as it included article 15 which lifted the restriction relating to the passage of weapons and ammunition from Hamburg. More distressingly for those Royalists in the Stuart kingdoms anticipating Danish support, Christian IV had effectively recognised the legitimacy of the English Parliament by having his name attached to the agreement. From a Scottish perspective, the treaty represented a distancing of Scottish and English trading concerns. Since King James ascended to the English throne, the trading interests of both Scotland and England had been bound together by commercial treaties made between their mutual monarch. The 1645 agreement between the English Parliament and Christian IV superseded the earlier pan-British treaty of 1641 made by Sir Thomas Roe. That treaty had effectively been ripped up by Christian IV through his actions in the Sound and the Elbe since 1642. The problem for the Covenanters was that the new deal made no mention of the Solemn League and Covenant, Scotland or the Committee of Both Kingdoms. In terms of trade through Danish waters, Scotland had been marginalised on paper by both Denmark-Norway and England, though in reality the Sound was opened to traders of all nations as a result of the English agreement. Crucially for internal British politics, however, Anglo-Irish resentment at the growing power of the Scots in Ulster after October 1644 had manifested itself openly through

---

[95] DRA, TKUA England, A II 15. Propositions of Jenkes and Skynner, 27 April 1645; *Danmark-Norges Traktater*, IV, 406-407.

[96] This agreement can be found in the introductory section of the trade and toll agreement between Christian IV and the English Parliament of 26 April 1645. The original version can be found in DRA, TKUA England II 15, f.49b. A printed version in English can be found in M. Sellars ed, *The Acts and Ordinances of the Eastland Company* (London, 1906), 159-165; A printed German version can be found in *Danmark-Norges Traktater*, 412-418.

the actions of English Parliamentary agents in Denmark in April 1645.[97]

Despite the new trade treaty, the English Parliamentary navy found cause to renew its actions against the Danes in 1645 and captured a Danish man-of-war.[98] Another ship of the Solemn League, an Irish privateer working under a Scottish commission, captured a Stavanger ship and had it taken to England by an English colleague. Perhaps because of this the agreement between the English and the Danes did not last. In retaliation, Christian IV took possession of at least one English frigate in Bergen and ordered all English shipping arriving in Stavanger to be arrested. Despite protestations from the English Parliament, Christian instructed that the frigate be held until Sir John Cochrane revealed Charles I's intentions for the ship.[99]

Richard Jenkes returned to Denmark-Norway in March 1647, ostensibly to bring Christian IV a ratification of a treaty relating to compensation for the English ammunition ship *Rebecca*. These negotiations continued through 1647 by which time Richard Jenkes also wished the Danes to stop searching English ships in the Sound and to find out when the first instalment of the 100,000 *rigsdaler* was to be paid.[100] Christian gave Jenkes repeated assurances but the money had still not been paid by 1648. Richard Jenkes and Henry Taylor returned to Copenhagen complaining to the *Rigsråd* that the Danes had not kept their promise to pay damages to the English.[101] After Christian IV died, Frederik III met the envoys and expressed regret at the lack of payment. He pointed out however that the expense of setting up the new monarchy meant that the debts would remain unpaid for the present. Frederik did ratify Christian IV's obligation to pay, though no money was forthcoming from him.[102]

[97] For the divisions of the Committee of Both Kingdoms over Ireland see Armstrong, 'Protestant Ireland', 121 and 123-125.
[98] *NRS Documents*, 220-221. 'List of ships taken by the Parliament', 18/28 June 1645.
[99] *Statholderskabets Extraict Protokol af Supplicationer og Resolutioner 1642-1652* (2 vols., Christiania, 1896-1901), I, 257 and 271. Søffren Pederszen to Hannibal Sehested, November 1645 and February 1646. This is probably the seized frigate belonging to the Englishman 'Hansz Simenson' who complained to Hannibal Sehested that Colonel Seaton had liberated 60 Spanish pistols from him; *Norske Rigs Registranter*, VIII, 433-434. Christian IV to Henrik Thott, 17 July 1646.
[100] DRA, TKUA England, A II 15. Jenkes to Christian IV, 11 April 1646 and Extract of the proposition of Jenkes 11 May 1647. Memorial to the Danish Commissioners, 18 May 1647 and Jurgen Brahe to R. Jenkes, 1 June 1646; *Danmark-Norges Traktater*, IV, 410.
[101] DRA, TKUA England, A II 15. Complaint of Jenkes and Taylor, 21 June 1648 and 24 July 1648; C R Hansen ed, *Aktstykker og Oplysninger til Rigsradets og Stændermødernes Historie i Frederik III's Tid*, 1648-50 (Copenhagen, 1959), I, 117.
[102] By 1662 the debt amounted to 141, 808 *rigsdaler*. This debt was eventually written off by the Charles II at the treaty of Breda in July 1667. See DRA, TKUA England 132. The Dispatches of Simon de Petkum, no.37. Copies of dispatches regarding the ship Rebbecca; *Danmark-Norges Traktater*, IV, 411-412.

The Rise and Demise of the Scottish Engagers

The 1645 trade agreement between England and Christian IV, with all the implications discussed above for Scotland, followed soon after the establishment of the New Model Army in England. A clear distinction was now possible between the Scots and the English in terms of both commerce and military forces. These two events were indicative of cooling relations between the Parliament of England and the Estates of Scotland.[103] The changing political relationship between the two British kingdoms became more complicated as various factions vied for control of their respective Parliaments. In Scotland this led to a power struggle between the followers of Argyll and Hamilton within the Committee of Estates which John Young noted 'would be resolved in favour of the conservative/pragmatic Royalists and would result in the Engagement of 1647-48'.[104]

In early 1647 the Covenanters handed Charles I over to English Parliamentary forces. Throughout 1647 the New Model Army grew stronger and Charles's negotiations with the English Parliament faltered, for as Sir Charles Petrie puts it, 'his English opponents never allowed for the dour stubbornness of the Scot in his nature'.[105] Charles was effectively kidnapped by agents of the New Model Army in June, and on 6 August 1647 that army marched into London and forced the withdrawal of the Presbyterian leadership from the House of Commons. This move precipitated the final decline in relations between the Scottish and English Parliaments. Charles sent John Henderson once more to Christian IV to enlighten his uncle on the developments in the three kingdoms and his ever more precarious situation.[106]

Towards the end of 1647, Charles came to terms with the Scottish Commissioners and agreed to confirm, conditionally, the Solemn League and Covenant for a trial period of three years. In response the English Parliament subsequently ceased all negotiations with the king. As Charles had earlier predicted, the English Royalists rose and 'the Scots' moved south to protect '*his right*'. A new conservative Scottish Covenanting army, the Engagers, under the Duke of Hamilton, entered England in July. Unlike Montrose who can best be described as a lapsed Covenanter turned Royalist, the Engagers were truly Covenanting Royalists. The Engagement ended in a disastrous defeat for the Scots at Preston on 17 August 1648. Soon afterwards Hamilton was captured and

103   Morrill, 'The National Covenant in its British Context', 20.
104   Young, *Scottish Parliament*, 185.
105   Petrie, *The Letters of King Charles I*, ix.
106   DRA, TKUA England, A II 15. Charles I to Christian IV, 25 October 1647.

executed, though under his English title of Earl of Cambridge.

News of the defeat of the Engagers must have taken time to filter through to the continent. Over a month later a Danish ship with 10,000 arms destined for the Duke of Hamilton arrived in Leith and was immediately siezed by Argyll's supporters.[107] It is not clear from the letter if these arms were lent, given or sold to the Engagers by Christian IV or if they simply represented a business transaction between Hamilton and Danish merchants. Given that no reference to them has been found in the papers of Christian IV, the latter is probably the case. The removal of Hamilton left Argyll's faction as the strongest party within Scotland. Elsewhere, Montrose still had his supporters and a high degree of Royal favour which he put to use on the continent. The defeat of the Engagers ultimately led to the Whiggamore Raid that saw Scotland returned to a radical Covenanting leadership and secure from any follow-up military operation by the New Model Army.[108] Indeed, Cromwell supported the Radicals' seizure of power from the Engagers in the Autumn of 1648 and guaranteed they could hold onto power.[109]

The Cavaliers and Engagers in Scotland had been militarily defeated and driven from political control, especially after the Act of Classes was passed in 1649. On the continent, however, Royalists, especially Scottish Royalists, still retained a substantial degree of influence. During the late summer of 1648, Montrose arrived as a Royalist envoy in Copenhagen where he gained a friendly audience from the new Danish king, Frederik III.[110] While this meeting proved cordial, little tangible benefit derived from it on this occasion. On 24 October 1648, Charles I wrote Frederik III from prison, to pass on condolences for the death of his father, Christian IV.[111] Perhaps realising the futility of his own situation, Charles I expressed his thanks for the late king's endeavours on his behalf. Importantly he asked Frederik III for nothing. While Charles awaited trial in prison, the Prince of Wales wrote an impassioned letter to the new Danish king to save his father and preserve the Stuart monarchy.[112] The prince's request came too late for Charles. Within months of Christian passing away, and only a week after the letter to Frederik, Charles I had been executed. The two stubborn monarchs, Charles I and Christian IV, had frequently frustrated each other's ambitions and failed to give adequate support to one another when they

---

[107] TT E.465 (34), *Good News from Scotland,* 27 September 1648.
[108] Young, *Scottish Parliament,* 210.
[109] Young, *Scottish Parliament,* 210 and 215-7.
[110] *The Deeds of Montrose,* 227; Napier, *The Memoirs of Montrose,* II, 670-671.
[111] DRA, TKUA England, A I. Charles I to Frederik III, 24 October 1648.
[112] DRA, TKUA England, A I. Charles, Prince of Wales to Frederik III, 23 January 1649.

needed it. Yet there would be little scope for their passing to lead to a new flourishing of the relationship between Britain, Denmark-Norway and the House of Stuart as the next decade held deeply troubled times for all three political entities.

Having staved off incorporation into England as a region, and become the driving force of British politics between 1638 to 1645, contesting groups formed in Scotland between the radicals and conservatives who strove to win control of the country. During the Royalist conflict against the Covenanters and the English Parliament, Charles I found himself supported by a small, but significant number, of 'Royalist Scots' who included high profile Covenanters such as Sir John Cochrane and the Marquis of Montrose. They joined those members of the Scottish-Stuart elite who had always remained Charles's most loyal supporters.[113] Indeed, for the remainder of his life, Charles I once more relied heavily on Scottish ambassadors to undertake missions both to, and from, his continental allies. Sir John Henderson became a regular Stuart envoy to Christian IV, as did Sir James King. Having left the Covenanting movement, Sir John Cochrane undertook repeated missions throughout the 1640s for both Charles I and Charles II and was joined on the continent by James Graham, the Marquis of Montrose. Christian IV in turn employed Scots as his envoys to the Stuart Court and English Parliament, trusting these Scottish Royalists to the same degree as Charles I himself. Even Robert Anstruther, acting once more as a Danish envoy, conducted a final mission for Christian IV to the Stuart Court in 1644. As in the previous four decades, the Scots proved to be the constant link on which Stuart-Oldenburg bonds were maintained. Cochrane and Henderson in particular endured being jailed and the constant threat of further imprisonment for the Stuart cause.[114] In contrast, and possibly due to his self-confessed lack of understanding of British politics, Christian IV demonstrated an overt distrust for English agents. None appear to have been accredited as Danish diplomats in the same way as Cochrane, Henderson, Anstruther or King. Additionally, Sir Thomas Roe was on the verge of deportation from Denmark-Norway in July 1641 due to allegations of bringing 'threats' against the Emperor and in deference to the inequality between his king and [the English]

---

[113] Brown, 'Courtiers and Cavaliers', 158.

[114] Interestingly Henderson was described in a letter from Sir Robert Honeywood to Sir Henry Vane as being 'only a spy'. The letter does not make clear who this is for though later Henderson is accused of spying for Cromwell. See *CSPD*, 1645-1647, 188-189, 13/23 October 1645.

Parliament.[115] Joseph Averie, the long-serving Stuart resident in Hamburg, also had to suffer the indignity of having his status as 'Royal Envoy' invalidated by Christian IV, a blow to both Averie and Charles I.[116]

During the wars in the three Stuart kingdoms, as during the Bishops' Wars, the motivations of the Danish king seem more driven by money, or a desire to keep Denmark-Norway out of the 'British Wars', than a determination to help to secure the throne of his nephew. It has been claimed in past histories that Christian IV's loyalty to his sister's son is undoubted.[117] There is enough evidence to raise serious doubts regarding the depth of support the Danish king actually gave. While such material may not prove Christian acted as an actual enemy of his nephew, it challenges the notion that his loyalty remains 'unquestionable'. Throughout the continuing trouble in the British Isles, Christian continued to apply pressure to Charles I to consider pawning parts of his kingdoms. The incentive was usually the promise of Danish military intervention. Because of this there were continuing rumours in Britain that Charles was about to employ Danish soldiers against his enemies. It has also been argued that Christian IV showed a willingness to go to war with the English Parliament in 1643 which was only frustrated by the war with Sweden.[118] When Christian actually offered military succour to Charles in 1643 it was only as a smoke-screen to cover his imperialist designs on Hamburg. Christian never actually committed himself to military support for his kinsman, since perhaps the price was simply not right or the benefits to Denmark-Norway did not equate to the risks involved.

Christian IV is reported to have sent Charles I quantities of money ranging between £45,000 and £60,000.[119] If true, this must have benefited his nephew's cause. He had also sent a munitions ship which, through no fault of his own, the English Parliamentarians captured. But it must not be forgotten that Christian IV lent the money and Charles would have to pay it back with interest. Further, the money actually cost

---

[115] *KCFB*, V, 108-109. Christian IV to Korfitz Ulfeldt, 28 July 1641. 'Naar M: Roe kommer *more solito* fram med hans truen, da bør man at spørre hannem ad, om hand truer nomine *Regis aut Parlamentj*'.

[116] *KCFB*, V, 255-256. Christian IV to Christen Thomesen Sehested, 30 September 1642. It is possible that Charles asked Christian IV to strip the royal title, but that is not substantiated in the text.

[117] Napier, *Memoirs of Montrose*, 656; *The Deeds of Montrose*, 245. 'of the goodwill and favour of the King of Denmark there was no room to doubt'.

[118] *CSPV*, XXVII, 45. Christian IV to John Poley, 30 April 1643; Lockhart, *Denmark in the Thirty Years' War*, 255.

[119] These figures are given on the basis that the £500,000 reported by Spalding would have been in Scots pounds.

Christian nothing in real terms since he had acquired it by charging Royalist, Covenanter and Parliamentarian alike extra tolls in the Sound. When Christian did actually seal the Sound to the supporters of the Solemn League and Covenant, it was usually only for a brief period, such as August to September 1644 and then in reprisal for the seizure of a Danish ship rather than through loyalty to the House of Stuart.

From the point of view of family honour and royal kinship, Christian IV had an obligation to help his nephew in his time of dire need. Had Christian merely stood aloof or adopted a position of benevolent neutrality he would have gone some way to satisfying that commitment. But Christian did neither. He sought to turn Charles I's troubles to his own advantage by taking possession of the Northern Isles and Newcastle (not to mention the money he hoped to make on arms sales and interest payments on loans). He even managed to turn a profit from the English Parliamentarians. Not only did he make them buy an unseaworthy ship from him, the *Golden Sun*, but he got them to pay for the weapons they took from the ship *Arken* rather than have them returned to Denmark-Norway. In effect, Christian sold his nephew's enemies, the English Parliamentarians, weapons to continue their rebellion. As a proof of his contempt for all sides, and of his war profiteering, Christian reneged on his deal to pay the English merchants compensation for the goods which he had confiscated from them and subsequently sold for a profit.

A final point of contemplation when considering the Stuart-Oldenburg relationship lies in the plea from the Prince of Wales to Christian (V) for help. During that correspondence the Prince of Wales explicitly expressed that he was being forced into exile by circumstances in Britain and as late as 1648 he still considered travelling to Denmark-Norway.[120] Christian (V) made it equally clear that he wanted to do all he could to help his cousin in his moment of need. He argued vigorously that had Denmark-Norway not been in such a dire situation he would have given money and perhaps even sanctioned direct military intervention. But not once did Christian (V) offer the one thing his cousin obviously needed – sanctuary. It would seem obvious that when a member of a royal house is being forced into exile that he or she would need somewhere to go. The option was never given and all the Stuarts got from Denmark-Norway after 1646 were courtesies and prayers.

The Scottish and English confederates of the Solemn League and Covenant received more, in real terms, than their Royalist adversaries, just as the Scottish Covenanters had during the Bishops' Wars. Throughout the 1640s, Christian IV openly negotiated with English

---

[120] *CSPV*, XXVIII, 203. Giovanni Battista Nani, 24 March 1648.

Parliamentarians and effectively sold them large quantities of arms originally destined for Charles I. Though the Scots did not figure in the English trade agreement of 1645, the Sound was effectively opened to all trade after it was signed. What is more important, by undertaking the trade agreement with the English Parliament, Christian failed to grasp an opportunity to strangle economically the anti-Stuart forces in England. This single act sent a signal of legitimisation to the English, and other trading nations, that Christian IV believed economics outweighed family loyalties.

CHAPTER SIX

'a hearty detestation of all the villanies which have been acted in England'

Throughout the 1640s, Charles I had warned his neighbours that the success of his enemies would carry serious implications for all the monarchies of Christendom.[1] Charles's concerns remained largely ignored amongst his neighbours. The harsh realities of economics had, however, edged Denmark-Norway into an economic treaty with the English Parliament in 1645.[2] Elsewhere, Sweden remained hostile to the House of Stuart while Russia, Danzig, Hamburg and Poland all enjoyed the relative benefits of a trading relationship with both Scotland and England despite the impact of war. The regicide of Charles I immediately forced a re-evaluation of the degree of co-operation each state was prepared to give the English Parliament or their various enemies. Royalist propagandists began to circulate faked condemnations of the regicide, but the repulsion they expressed was probably genuine.[3] In the United Provinces this shock was felt not only amongst the pro-Stuart Orange faction but even among their hard line Republican opposition.[4] One English Parliamentary envoy described the city of Hamburg as one of England's most cordial enemies.[5] In Russia, the English merchants of the Muscovy Company had their charter cancelled.[6] The Poles allegedly introduced a new tax on all traders making them pay one tenth of all their goods to the new Stuart king, Charles II.[7] The Earl of Crawford wrote to Charles declaring that from the king of Spain's 'own mouth he has heard that

---

[1]   DRA, TKUA, England, A I. Charles I to Christian IV, 26 February 1645.

[2]   *Danmark-Norges Traktater*, IV, 402-412.

[3]   TT E.552 (24) *A declaration to the English nation, from Don John de Austria the 8th. King of Germany, &c. Lewis 11th. King of France and Navarre. Philip the 5th. King of Spain & Aragon, &c. Christern the third King of Denmark, Zealand, &c. Lodowick Duke of Lorain, and Adolphina Queen of Sweden, in detestation of the present proceedings of the Parliament and Army, and of their intentions of coming over into England in behalf of King Charles II. Being translated out of the true copy.* (London, 1649).

[4]   W. C. Abbott ed, *The Writings and Speeches of Oliver Cromwell* (4 vols, Harvard, 1938-1947), II, 267.

[5]   *HMC, Sixth Report*. 430. Bradshaw to Strickland, 16 July 1650.

[6]   PRO SP91/3 f. 77-79 'The humble remonstrance of John Hebdon, 16 March 1660'; L. Leowenson, 'Did Russia intervene after the execution of Charles I', in *Bulletin of the Institute of Historical Research*, XVIII (1940-41), 15; G. P. Herd, 'General Patrick Gordon of Auchleuchries - A Scot in Seventeenth Century Russian Service' (unpublished PhD thesis, University of Aberdeen, 1994), 33.

[7]   F. A. Patterson et al, eds, *The Works of John Milton: State Papers* (Columbia, 1937), XIII, 44-45. English Parliament to the city of Danzig, 6 February 1650.

assistance will be given to punish the traitors'.[8] Needless to say, the execution of a first cousin of Frederik III was also extremely badly received in Denmark-Norway. The Earl of Clarendon noted that in Copenhagen the Marquis of Montrose found 'a hearty detestation of all the villanies which had been acted in England'.[9]

Danish disgust with the judicial murder of Charles was very important as Denmark-Norway had the power to undermine the English Parliamentary Republic by closing the Baltic Sound to English trade. Indeed, the Royalists took delight in publishing a proclamation attributed to Frederik III stating that whoever took up arms against the Parliament of England or captured any of their ships, would have 'free egress and regresse into his harbours'.[10] With a shortage of allies in the area the English Parliament's prospects seemed bleak.

Immediately after news arrived of Charles I's execution, the Prince of Wales was proclaimed king of Great Britain and Ireland in Edinburgh. The Scots endeavoured to ensure that the continental potentates knew that they had no part in the regicide by sending messengers to the continent to announce Charles II as their new sovereign.[11] Members of the expatriate community also sought to press home the message that the actions of the English Parliament had no legality in law and indeed that the entire English Republic had no legal foundation. Only days after Charles I's beheading, *Eikon Basilike*, a work attributed to the late king, had been distributed widely in the British Isles and abroad. Despite attempts to suppress the book by the new English authorities, the work reached 60 editions in the first year, including versions in French, Latin, Dutch, German and Danish.[12] The promotional effect of this work was devastating on home and foreign readership alike. Charles Stuart 'the martyr' became a Royalist icon in the courts of Europe, prompting numerous paintings, prints and eulogies, all feeding more grist to the Royalist

---

[8]   *HMC, Report on the Pepys Manuscripts preserved at Magdelane College Cambridge* (London, 1911), 251. Ludovick, Earl of Crawford to Charles II, 13/23 March 1649.

[9]   Clarendon, *History of the Rebellion*, V, 122; *Danmark-Norges Traktater*, V, 134.

[10]   TT 87 E.564 (8). *A Great Victory obtained by Prince Charles his ships: upon the north Coast of England,* (13 July 1649).

[11]   *APS*, VI, part II, 157; Morrill, 'The Britishness of the English Revolution, 101; Young, *Scottish Parliament*, 223-224; *The Deeds of Montrose*, 235. Sir Joseph Douglas proclaimed Charles II king of Great Britain and Ireland in The Hague on March 4th.

[12]   See F. F. Madan, *A new bibliography of the Eikon Basilike of King Charles the First* (London, 1950); W. R. Parker, *Milton a biography* (Oxford, 1968), 360-361; E. Skerpan, *The Rhetoric of Politics in the English Revolution 1642-1660* (University of Missouri Press, 1992), 110-112; D. Hirst, 'The English Republic and the meaning of Britain', in B. Bradshaw and J. Morrill eds, *The British Problem, c.1534-1707. State formation in the Atlantic Archipelago* (London, 1996), 7.

propaganda mill.[13] The English Republic was on the defensive in the battle for moral legitimacy. So successfully had the Royalists promoted their message that in the Swedish *Riksråd* Queen Christina recited the Stuart mantra 'that it was of concern to all potentates to see Charles II reinstalled in his kingdoms'.[14] Indeed the Swedish state councillor, General Magnus de la Gardie, advocated sending the Swedish army into England to avenge the death of Charles I, as did several other European leaders.[15]

In an attempt to legitimise the actions of the English Republic, ambassadors were sent to the continent in 1649. Perhaps unsurprisingly their reception was seldom friendly and many were prevented from delivering their message. Indeed, Royalist agents often managed to make a mockery of Parliamentary diplomacy. Even in 1654 Bulstrode Whitelocke had to conduct his business with the Governor of Gothenburg through a Scottish Royalist interpreter, Colonel Sinclair. Similarly, in Moscow, William Prideaux blamed the failure of his embassy on the deliberate mistranslations of his Royalist interpreter, John Hebdon.[16] Royalist obstruction to the Republican message also travelled a more violent path. The evening Dr Isaak Dorislaus arrived in The Hague he was assassinated by a group of Scots in the service of the Marquis of Montrose including Colonel Walter Whiteford, a Scottish Catholic, and Sir John Spottiswood.[17] The following year, Antony Ascham and his secretary were murdered in Madrid by English Royalists.[18] Ascham's death both removed a major Republican propagandist and provided the English government with a minor propaganda opportunity. When news of the assassination reached Hamburg the nationality of Ascham's killers had been altered. Richard Bradshaw noted the death blow 'to be done by the Irish

[13] Skerpan, *The Rhetoric of Politics*, 112; For engravings and paintings see; Anon. 'Endhauptung dess Königs in Engelandt anno 1649' reprinted in F. Maclean, *A Concise History of Scotland* (London, 1970), 131; Scottish National Portrait Gallery, Anon. 'The Execution of Charles I, 1600-1649'.

[14] *SRP*, XIV, 51-2. 20 February 1650.

[15] A. Fryxell, *Handlingar Rörande Sverges Historia* (Stockholm, 1836), I, 87. Peder Juel's report to his Council, 10 April 1649; Leowenson, 'Did Russia intervene', 19.

[16] R. Spalding ed, *The Diary of Bulstrode Whitelocke 1605-1675* (Oxford, 1990), 301; Herd, 'General Patrick Gordon', 38.

[17] A deposition regarding Whiteford's alleged confession can be found in *HMC, Pepys Manuscript*, 266. Deposition of John Christian, 8 November 1651; Edward, Earl of Clarendon, *The History of the Rebellion and Civil Wars in England together with an historical view of the affairs of Ireland* (Oxford University Press, 1849), V, 127; Abbott, *Oliver Cromwell*, II, 76-77; J. T. Peacey, 'Order and Disorder in Europe: Parliamentary Agents and Royalist Thugs 1649-1650', in *The Historical Journal*, vol. 40, no. 4, (1997), 956.

[18] S. R. Gardiner, *History of the Commonwealth and Protectorate* (4 vols., Gloucestershire, 1988), I, 308-309; Clarendon, *History of the Rebellion*, V, 150-156.

villains'.[19] The admission that the assassins were actually Englishmen would have demonstrated that England was not as unified as the Republicans wished to portray. However, the news of an Irish act of violence against an English diplomat could only help to justify English atrocities against Irish garrisons as they fell to Cromwell's army, most infamously exemplified by Drogheda in September 1649.

The ongoing actions of Royalist assassins had a significant effect on English Republican diplomats. Walter Strickland in The Hague felt that he was in danger of suffering a similar fate to his predecessor. Richard Bradshaw, the Parliamentarian envoy to Hamburg and Denmark, constantly wrote to England that he feared being murdered. Bulstrode Whitelocke hesitated about going to Sweden in 1653 believing that he too would be killed as soon as he got there.[20] Violent retaliation against the English regicides was not confined to execution. Colonel John Cochrane had English Republicans beaten up in the streets of Hamburg and orchestrated, with Danish support, the kidnapping of some English merchants who supported the English Parliament.[21] Later, in Sweden, Bulstrode Whitelocke recorded numerous assaults on his associates and entourage. Throughout the 1650s Bradshaw complained that the threat of violence meant he could 'not stir out of doors' and he frequently pondered the assassination attempts on Republicans such as Dr. Elburrow.[22]

Among the heads of state and ruling elites in Europe there were many who felt that the hostile actions against regicides and their supporters had some justification. In September 1650, one captured would-be killer, Halterman, was not only released by the Hamburgers, but the court initially made the English Merchant Company pay his charges and give him 100 *rigsdaler* for wrongful arrest.[23] Five out of six of Ascham's assassins were allowed to escape in Spain. One

[19]   N. Smith, *Literature and Revolution in England 1640-1660* (Yale, 1994), 181; *The Nicholas Papers*, III, 428. Bradshaw to Frost, 25 June 1650.

[20]   Abbott, *Oliver Cromwell*, II, 167; *HMC, Sixth Report*, 427-429. A small sample of Bradshaw's fears are expressed in Bradshaw to Frost, 25 June 1650; Same to Council of State, 29 June 1650; Same to Council of State, 2 July 1650; Spalding, *Bulstrode Whitelocke*, 9.

[21]   J. N. M. Maclean, 'Montrose's preparations for the invasion of Scotland, and Royalist mission to Sweden; 1649-1651', in R. Hatton and M. Anderson eds, *Studies in Diplomatic History* (London, 1970), 14; 'Sir John Cochrane's relation of the particulars that have occurred in his negotiations since his coming to Hamburg', in H. F. Morland-Simpson, ed, 'Civil War Papers 1643-1650', in *Miscellany of the Scottish History Society*, I (Edinburgh, 1893), 175-180; Peacey, 'Order and Disorder in Europe', 962-963.

[22]   Spalding, *Bulstrode Whitelocke*, 337; *HMC, Sixth Report*, 429 and 432. Bradshaw to the Council of State, 9 July 1650; Same to Frost, 1 October 1650.

[23]   *HMC, Sixth Report*, 432-433. Bradshaw to Frost, 1 October 1650; Same to anon., no date; Same to Frost, 8 and 15 October 1650.

Spanish nobleman said of them 'I envy those gentlemen for having done so noble an action', and even the Spanish king declared an interest in having 'such resolute subjects'.[24] The continent of Europe remained fertile ground for Royalist vigilantes and assassinations raised morale amongst the Royalist party. More importantly, the killings removed the main instruments of English Parliamentary promotion at and within foreign Courts – the diplomats themselves.

Stuart Duplicity 1649-51

While Royalist supporters responded with a mix of pro-Stuart publicity and anti-Parliamentarian violence to the regicide of Charles I, his son played a dangerous game. Charles II negotiated with all nations and most competing Scottish, English and Irish factions, promising them all his support in return for their loyalty. Indeed even as he commended Montrose to his cousin, Frederik III, Charles informed the Danish king that he neared an amicable agreement with 'our Scots' from the Scottish Estates – in effect, the radical regime led by the Marquis of Argyll.[25] The effective collapse of the Royalists in England meant that Charles had to decide between courting mainstream Irish or Scottish support to pursue a recovery for the House of Stuart. The dowager Queen, Henrietta-Maria, favoured the Scottish nobles at the exiled Court over the English ones. She also pressed Charles to consider negotiating with the Scottish Covenanters and this was to be done at the expense of any public negotiations with the Duke of Ormond and the various Irish factions. Given her staunch Roman Catholicism it might seem remarkable that she favoured the Scottish Presbyterian option over the Irish, but the Queen was quite pragmatic. Ormonde's fragile alliance in Ireland was failing. Henrietta-Maria therefore wrote to Charles to tell him to go to Scotland as it would be his only realistic refuge.[26]

The principle protagonists of the Scottish factions, Argyll, the 2nd Duke of Hamilton and the Marquis of Montrose, bitterly hated each other. However, the moderate Scottish faction headed by Hamilton and Lauderdale entered into negotiations with Charles and pressed the acceptance of proposals offered by Argyll and the Scottish Estates. This support for Argyll by Hamilton in early 1650 carried a lot of weight with the king since, in the period before the defeat of the Covenanting army at Dunbar in September 1650, there was little

---

[24] Clarendon, *History of the Rebellion*, V, 157.
[25] DRA, TKUA, England, A I. Charles II to Frederik III, 20/30 January 1649/50.
[26] Clarendon, *History of the Rebellion*, V, 41 and 115.

obvious prospect of a patriotic accommodation to unite the nation.[27] The Hamilton-Lauderdale faction, therefore, had the most to lose from Charles accepting the Scottish proposals. Backed by Hamilton, Henrietta-Maria, some English and some foreign support, the only real obstacle blocking Charles's return to Scotland remained the Marquis of Montrose. Charles overtly negotiated with Montrose, cynically using him and his followers to gain leverage over Argyll.[28] His orders to Montrose were deliberately ambiguous throughout his ongoing negotiations with the Scottish Estates in Breda.[29] It must have appeared to foreign observers that there were 'two Scotlands'; one led by Argyll, the other by Montrose and both of whom the king seemed to acknowledge. Charles II published two letters in Paris, one to the Scottish Estates and one directed to Montrose, which were so contradictory that an English commentator noted:

> The publishing of which letters, specially that to Montrosse, must needs be looked upon as a speciall providence of God. There is in it so little of common prudence as to his interest [...] he ought not to have written it at all.[30]

Despite the obvious inconsistency of these letters, Montrose aimed to establish an army which was not going to challenge the regicides in London but whose sole purpose was the destruction of the Argyll faction in Scotland.[31] In essence Montrose sought to re-open the civil war of 1644-45 – something the Estates of Scotland had no intention of allowing.

The Montrosian Expedition
Frederik III of Denmark-Norway was updated on the political developments in Great Britain by Sir John Cochrane who arrived in Copenhagen in 1648.[32] Frederik also had direct written

---

[27] John Young notes that the 'Patriotic Settlement' which led to the repeal of the Act of Classes in June 1651 formed a major component of the Sixth, Seventh and Eighth sessions of the Second Triennial Parliament beginning in November 1650, two months after the battle of Dunbar. See J. R. Young, 'The Scottish Parliament and the Covenanting Revolution: The Emergence of a Scottish Commons', in J. R. Young ed, *Celtic Dimensions of the British Civil Wars* (Edinburgh, 1997), 164; Young, *Scottish Parliament*, 244-261.

[28] J. R. Jones, *Charles II Royal Politician* (London, 1987), 15-18.

[29] The Breda negotiations are variously discussed in Abbott, *Oliver Cromwell*, II, 254; Jones, *Royal Politician*, 15-18.

[30] S. R. Gardiner ed, *Letters and papers illustrating the relations between Charles II and Scotland in 1650* (Edinburgh, 1894), 12. Extract from *A Brief Relation*.

[31] Jones, *Royal Politician*, 15.

[32] *HMC, Pepys Manuscript*, 219. Prince of Wales to Hannibal Sehested, Viceroy of Norway,

communication with Charles II who urged Frederik to provide both support and advice in order preserve the ancient alliance between the two crowns.[33] Charles informed his cousin that the Marquis of Montrose had been appointed Commander-in-Chief of all Royalist forces that could be raised on the continent and Lieutenant Governor of Scotland.[34] Montrose prepared for an attempt on Scotland which he had been led to believe had the total support of the king. Charles maintained a correspondence assuring him that, despite rumours to the contrary, the Marquis had to press on with his plans. The Danes appeared keen to support these military endeavours. Rumours reached Britain that a Danish naval fleet had been assembled in the Sound specifically to intercept any English ships leaving the Baltic due to their universal hatred of that nation.[35]

Like other monarchies, the Danish royal house wished to see Charles re-instated in his kingdoms, especially as he was a cousin of Frederik III. Since Montrose carried credentials from Charles II, the Danes had every reason to support him. Korfitz Ulfeldt, a brother-in-law of Frederik, arrived in The Hague as the Danish ambassador extraordinary to the United Provinces. He had left Denmark before the news of the execution of Charles I and on a technicality he therefore had no authority to negotiate with Charles II directly. However, as a supporter of the Stuart cause, Ulfeldt met frequently with Charles at the Court of Elizabeth Stuart in The Hague. While Montrose remained in the city he managed to ingratiate himself with Ulfeldt who daily encouraged the military preparations in the name of his king. Ulfeldt informed Montrose that he would be warmly received in Denmark and would be able to obtain arms and ammunition there for his mission against Scotland. The Danish ambassador also suggested that should Charles write to Frederik asking for these commodities, he would receive them instantly. This must have been done since Ulfeldt received orders to advance money directly to Charles from Frederik soon after. Perhaps owing to the friendship which had developed between them, the Dane did not do this. Instead he asked Montrose to get a letter from Charles II authorising receipt of the money which he

---

17/27 July 1648; Morland-Simpson, 'Civil War Papers 1643-1650', 168-169. Two letters survive from Cochrane to Duke James of Courland dated in Copenhagen in November 1648.

[33] *HMC, Pepys Manuscript*, 249, Charles II to Frederik III, February 1649.

[34] James Graham, *Declaration of his Excellency James Marqves of Montrose* (Gothenburg, 1649); DRA, TKUA, England, A I. Charles II to Frederik III, 20/30 January 1649/50; *The Deeds of Montrose*, 250; Maclean, 'Montrose's preparations', 10.

[35] TT 87 E.563 (4). *A declaration of the parliament of Scotland [...] AND the king of Denmark's sending forth a new Fleet to fall upon the English Ships* (London, 1649).

then handed over to the Marquis.[36] Ulfeldt gave over about £5,400 (24,000 *rigsdaler*) from the royal Danish purse and a further sum from his own resources amounting to some 18,700 *rigsdaler*. Montrose also gave the Danish Chancellor a receipt in July for the delivery of a quantity of arms which included 1,500 each of muskets, swords, pikes and cutlasses, 26 cannon and significant quantity of ammunition and powder.[37]

Not content with these resources, Montrose asked Charles II for accreditation to visit several German princes from whom he felt he could raise money. Charles agreed and Montrose sent several Scottish officers into Germany with orders to raise troops and assemble them in Hamburg. Even anti-Stuart observers believed that in Germany and Scandinavia Montrose held more sway than the Argyll faction. One historian, William Parker, has described the Cavalier party as 'distressingly influential on the Continent'.[38] Montrose's popularity sprang from several sources. The remarkable series of military victories he had achieved with Alasdair MacColla in the mid-1640s earned him a reputation abroad as an able commander. Lord Napier told his wife that Montrose was held in 'huge esteem' and indeed in France and throughout the *Reich* the Marquis was offered many prominent military positions.[39] Montrose also had an advantage in having many of his followers, or at least other monarchists, entrenched in the military and civic structures of the Scandinavian countries. Since the Scottish Estates had defeated Montrose in 1645, their supporters had no call to go into exile. Influential Royalist exiles could therefore spread the Montrosian message with little fear of contradiction by supporters of the Estates. Even before the execution of Charles I, Montrose had conducted what amounted to a personal Royalist embassy through Germany, Poland, Scandinavia and the Low Countries. By the time of the regicide of Charles I, he had ensured he was well placed to influence continental leaders in the direction of the Stuart Royalist cause.

Well aware of his popularity, Montrose travelled into Denmark-

---

[36]   Clarendon, *History of the Rebellion*, V, 41-43; *The Deeds of Montrose*, 244-245 and 260.

[37]   E. J. Cowan, *Montrose, For Covenant and King* (Edinburgh, 1995), 273. The 24,000 *rigsdaler* given over by Ulfeldt was still being pursued by the king of Denmark in 1654. See DRA, TKUA England C 132. Frederik III to Simon de Petkum, 14 July 1654. The 18,700 *rigsdaler* was persued in England by Ulfeldt's wife in 1663. See H. L. Schoolcraft, 'England and Denmark, 1660-1667' in *The English Historical Review*, XXV (1910), 458.

[38]   Parker, *Milton*, 368; Gardiner, *Charles II and Scotland*, 29-31. Letter from Rollen, 6/16 March 1649/50

[39]   Cowan, *Montrose*, 258-259.

Norway and Sweden to liase with the kings of those countries and Scottish officers who held commands and/or estates in those places. Indeed, before he left he received a letter from Charles II ordering him to Denmark to prosecute his attempt on Scotland from there.[40] Sir John Cochrane supported the Royalist mission after Charles II had appointed him as ambassador to Denmark-Norway, Poland, Courland and Danzig and he immediately set to work gathering munitions and ships. Colonel John Henderson travelled into Germany with orders to raise arms and support from various German cities.[41] Charles also sent the two Scottish generals, Sir James King and Sir Patrick Ruthven, to Queen Christina in Sweden.[42]

After leaving The Hague, Montrose moved on to Hamburg where he met up with Colonel Cochrane. He had arrived there in June and remained there until September trying to raise money and settle a dispute which had arisen between loyalist and rebel Stuart subjects in that city. Cochrane found his task in Hamburg hampered by influential members of the English Company there. He therefore sent Colonel Henderson to Frederik III to request his assistance by way of a letter of recommendation from the Danish king to the Hamburg senate.[43] From Hamburg, Cochrane launched his fund raising expedition to the Eastern Baltic where he instantly raised 3,000 *rigsdaler* from the Scots in Danzig to provide for his northern embassy.[44] Though also received well in Poland-Lithuania proper, John II Casimir Vasa could only provide him with a small amount of money. The Scottish community, however, apparently furnished Cochrane with the equivalent of £10,000.[45] James Duke of Courland also provided him with six large ships full of corn and a variety of other supplies as requested the previous year.[46]

[40]   Clarendon, *History of the Rebellion*, V, 42.
[41]   *HMC, Pepys Manuscript*, 230 and 257. Memorandum of Dispatches for the marquis of Montrose, May 1649, Prince of Wales to Duke of Courland, 30 September/10 October 1648 and 246, notes by Robert Long; Morland-Simpson, 'Civil War Papers 1643-1650', 169. Cochrane to Duke James of Courland, 21 February 1649. Cochrane here asks for 300 lasts of lead; *CSPV*, XXVIII, 203. Niccolo Sagredo, Venetian Ambassador in Germany, 26 November 1649.
[42]   SRA, Anglica 517. Charles II to Queen Christina, 28 May 1649; TT E.549 (22), *Declaration of the Committee of Estates of the Parliament of Scotland in vindication of their proceedings from the aspersions of a scandelous pamphlet published by that excommunicate traytor James Grahame* (Edinburgh, January 1650); *Charles II and Scotland*, 38-39. Warrant to Sir Edward Nicholas from Charles II, March 19/29 1649/50; Abbott, *Oliver Cromwell*, II, 254; Grosjean, 'Scots and the Swedish State', 205-237.
[43]   DRA, TKUA A II 16. Colonel Cochrane to Frederik III, 28 July 1649.
[44]   *Charles II and Scotland*, 5. A letter from Bremen 24 January/3 February 1649/50.
[45]   S. Seliga and L. Koczy, *Scotland and Poland; a chapter in forgotten history* (Glasgow, 1969), 8.
[46]   *HMC, Pepys Manuscript*, 230. Prince of Wales to Duke James of Courland, 30

Montrose moved his base to Denmark where he was joined by Captain John Hall of Leith. Hall had newly defected with his frigate and cargo of arms from the Covenanters along with Captain John Anstruther with a small 10-gun warship. Montrose spent October and November recruiting soldiers and arranging audiences with Frederik III, the Danish Council of Nobles and the Duke of Holstein.[47] Montrose wrote to the Danish king assuring him that his support for his cousin, Charles II, was invaluable.[48] In November, Sir James Turner reached Hamburg where he found a number of Scottish gentlemen attending Montrose and awaiting the expedition to Scotland.[49] Hall and Anstruther left Denmark with over 200 soldiers, mostly Danes, and sailed to Sweden. There they were joined by some 800 Germans and Danes who had arrived on the several Amsterdam based ships supplied by the Duke of Holstein.[50]

The Danish-Norwegian involvement with the Montrosian scheme did not end there. The Swedes did not wish to be seen to help the Royalists as they hoped to keep their options open with Republican England. They therefore ordered the soldiers to leave Swedish territory which they did by sailing down the river Göta a few miles to Marstrand, just inside Denmark-Norway. Controversially though, Queen Christina had agreed to release a considerable store of arms and ammunition for Stuart service including 6,000 muskets, 5,000 pikes, 3,000 bandoleers, 4,000 infantry swords, 50 drums, 1,800 pistols, 600 cavalry swords and 2,000 cavalry harnesses. The State Marshall noted that 12 cannon could be provided to General Patrick Ruthven who had also been successfully collecting arms for the Duke of Ormond in Sweden. Eventually the Swedish government sold James King the frigate *Harderinne*.[51] The Swedish frigate with two

September/10 October 1648. Charles here requesting ships and introducing Cochrane; Morland-Simpson, 'Civil War Papers 1643-1650', 197-198. Charles II to Duke James of Courland, 2 April 1650; Charles here acknowledges gratitude to the Duke for supplying the ships to Cochrane who, he says has appointed Colonel John Ogilvy to receive them. The accusations that Cochrane later acted dishonestly are, therefore, somewhat surprising and add to the idea that Charles II spread such rumours in order to distance himself from the Montrosians after he had completed his negotiations with the Covenanters. After all, if he could wash his hands of Cochrane, he could deny responsibility for the debts built up in his name; *The Deeds of Montrose*, 258.

[47] *The Deeds of Montrose*, 260; Maclean, 'Montrose's preparations', 14-15.

[48] *The Deeds of Montrose*, 508-509. Montrose to Frederik III, 19 October 1649.

[49] Sir James Turner, *Memoirs of his own Life and Times, 1632-1670* (Edinburgh, 1829), 91.

[50] *The Deeds of Montrose*, 262.

[51] *SRP*, XIII, 43, 31 March and 2 April 1649; Steckzén, *Svenskt och Brittiskt*, 155-7; *HMC, Pepys Manuscript*, 253. Charles II to Duke of Ormond, 25 April/4 May 1649 and 292. Five letters of Patrick Ruthven, 17 March to 7 April 1649; *HMC Report on the manuscripts of the Marquis of Ormond, vol. II* (London, 1899), 93. Robert Long to Ormond, 21 May 1649; See also Grosjean, 'Scots and the Swedish State', 206-211.

months' supplies and 50 more recruits joined Montrose's forces at Marstrand highlighting that the 'expulsion' was just a ruse to deflect attention from Swedish participation.

At this time, Montrose was being entertained by the Danish Viceroy in Norway, Hannibal Sehested, another brother-in-law of Frederik III. Sehested arranged supplies for Montrose through one Ivor Krabbe in Bohus.[52] Krabbe was a business partner of the Scottish trader in Gothenburg John Maclean. Though a major supplier of arms to the Covenanters during the Bishop's Wars, Maclean displayed a strong loyalty to the House of Stuart after the regicide of Charles I. He took a leading role in Montrose's preparations, probably helped by the fact that his eldest son, Colonel Jacob Maclean, had earlier married Colonel Cochrane's only daughter Catherine.[53] Maclean did much to facilitate the cross-border operation. On the 17th of December 1649, he shipped a cargo of arms directly to Scotland with the Gothenburg skipper Hans Mickelson.[54] He also arranged for Royalist soldiers to be picked up in Norway while Montrose travelled overland to Bergen where he stayed with the acting military governor, Colonel Sir Thomas Gray. The Scottish colonel arranged for about 50 soldiers, some Scottish, to join Montrose's expedition and himself went to Scotland as part of the Royalist officer corps.[55]

At the end of December, 200 'Danish' soldiers set off for Orkney under the command of Major David Guthrie hoping to secure a base for a larger landing. They carried with them 12 pieces of artillery and a quantity of arms and ammunition for forces to be levied in Scotland.[56] As Guthrie headed for Scotland, Montrose and other Scots continued to pass between Denmark, Norway and Sweden organising still more support. Cochrane was able to write to Secretary Long in January 1650 that Frederik III 'is ready to contribute all assistance to the Scots' king'.[57] Unfortunately pressing financial considerations led Montrose to order that some of the arms provided by Denmark be sold off to pay his soldiers who were nearly destitute in Bremen.[58] This raised some 3,000 *rigsdaler* which Colonel Taylor distributed to the

---

[52] Maclean, 'Montrose's preparations', 20.
[53] Maclean, 'Montrose's preparations', 10.
[54] Gothenburg Regional Archive manuscript, 'Göteborgs Drätselkammare', I.V.A. no. 1 (819), 1649. This shipment contained 8 cannon, 1,000 cannonballs. 1,536 muskets, 1,510 pikes, 2,550 swords, 200 cavalry swords, 1,040 bandoleers, 36 barrels of shot, 26 ships pounds of match, 24 drums, 2,600 forks, 112 spades, 12 gun carriages and 100 cavalry harnesses.
[55] *The Deeds of Montrose*, 493-4.
[56] *Charles II and Scotland*, 10. Letter from Bremen, 9/19 February 1649/50.
[57] *HMC, Pepys Manuscript*, 288. Cochrane to Long, 13 January 1649/50.
[58] *Charles II and Scotland*, 9. Letter from Bremen, 2/12 February 1649/50.

officers at 10 *rigsdaler* per man to stave off desertions, suggesting about 300 Montrosian soldiers were based in that city. The Royalists were now at the stage of having to turn away offers of help from mercenary officers due to their impoverished condition. This included the approach of Count Woldomar, illegitimate son of Christian IV and half-brother of Frederik III. He had arrived in Breda in April 1650 with many colonels, captains and other officers to offer his services to his cousin, Charles II.[59] Yet by April, it would have been apparent to everyone at the Stuart Court in Breda that Charles had been convinced to abandon Montrose to his fate. Woldomar's plans to visit the British Isles, therefore, had to be postponed.

By the time Montrose sailed for Scotland, Charles II had effectively completed his negotiations with the Covenanters. He issued orders for the halting of the second wave of Montrose's army under command of General King and these men were left stranded in various Baltic ports without shipping.[60] When Montrose's forces (about 1,200 due to the garrison left to secure Orkney for General King's landing) met the Covenanting forces in the north of Scotland they had little chance of success. The advance party of Covenanting horse fell on the Royalist force at Carbisdale so suddenly that they had insufficient time to organise a proper defence. The Orkney men fled instantly but some of the Danes held their ground initially before being broken by the cavalry.[61] In total more than half of Montrose's forces, about 600, were killed and about 400 captured.[62] Montrose was caught soon after the battle and transported to Edinburgh by David Leslie. There, in Scotland's capital city, Montrose was tried and executed. Clarendon claimed in his *History of the Rebellion* that all the Scottish officers taken with Montrose, between 30 and 40, were afterwards executed with the exception of Colonel Whiteford – spared for his assassination of Dr. Dorislaus in The Hague. *The Deeds of Montrose*, however, records only four executions. In fact, most of the officers were simply banished from Scotland or ordered to serve in the Scottish regiments in France. The surviving foreign officers were dismissed and ordered

---

[59]   *Charles II and Scotland*, 51-54. Letter from Breda, 4/14 April 1650.

[60]   This was in contrast to the 'sixty sail of ships with soldiers going for Scotland' reported in London the previous year. See TT 89 E.584 (2), *A great Fight in Ireland [...] with a letter of news concerning Col King and Col Johnston and sixty sail of ships with soldiers going for Scotland* (Criplegate, 1649).

[61]   Abbott, *Oliver Cromwell*, II, 254. Abbott also mentions that Montrose's forces were depleted by 1,000 men who were lost in shipwrecks; D. Stevenson, *Revolution and Counter Revolution in Scotland 1644-1651* (London, 1977), 162.

[62]   *The Deeds of Montrose*, 493-494. Appendix of prisoners taken at Carbisdale; Stevenson *Revolution and Counter Revolution*, 162; Clarendon, *History of the Rebellion*, V, 127.

to return to their own countries. Most of the foreign soldiery were killed during the battle but those that survived were probably released.[63] Remnants of the expeditionary invasion force returned to Norway with Captain Hall and Sir Henry Graham, Montrose's brother. Hall's crew mutinied in Bergen and left the Royalists, including Hall, and returned to join the Covenanters.

The political impact of Montrose's defeat went far beyond the loss of some Scottish Cavalier officers and a few hundred mercenaries. True, Charles had secured the loyalty of the Scottish Estates and the Covenanters in turn had secured the destruction of their most detested enemy – but Charles had also alienated many of his northern European supporters. Richard Bradshaw noted that in Hamburg 'the smart handling of Montrose hath turned the edge of the fury of this people from the English now to the Scots'.[64] The Danish king could surely not have been happy at the sacrifice of his subjects from Denmark and Holstein to satisfy Stuart political duplicity. Heavyweight Danish support from Hannibal Sehested and Korfitz Ulfeldt, both close relatives of the Danish king, had also been lost. Charles's financiers, John Maclean in Sweden and Ivor Krabbe in Denmark-Norway, were unlikely to get involved in another Stuart scheme, having lost so much in this one.

The surviving Cavaliers left behind with the second wave did not forgive the Stuart sacrifice of their friends. John Cochrane abandoned the Stuart cause supposedly taking with him as much as £9,200 of the money raised in Danzig and Poland.[65] He really had little choice for he knew he could not go to Scotland where the Covenanters would kill him. He could not go to England where the Parliamentarians would

[63] *The Deeds of Montrose*, 493-4. Appendix of prisoners taken at Carbisdale; The Danish subjects among the officers taken Rittmaster Wallensius, Ernestus Buerham, Cornet Ralph Marlie, Cornet Henrick Erlach, Cornet Daniel Bennicke, Ensign Adrian Ringwerthe, Ensign Hans Boaz. The majority of these men came from Holstein. Colonel Thomas Gray, on examination by his captors could 'shew that he had beine out of the countrey 34 yeires' and thus avoided serious punishment due to his ignorance of Scottish politics.

[64] *HMC, Sixth Report*, 426. Bradshaw to Fleming, 18 June 1650; Same to Ac'ton, 19 June 1650; Even in Scotland his death was mourned in parts of the country. See for instance Iain Lom's *Cumha Mhontrois* (Lament for Montrose) in A. M. Mackenzie ed, *Oran Iain Luim* (Edinburgh, 1964), 56-58 and notes 257-261. The same poem is called *Oran Cumhaidh air Cor na Rioghachd* (A lament for the state of the country), in C. Ó Baoill ed, *Gair nan Clarsach: The Harper's Cry, An anthology of 17th Century Gaelic Poetry*. Translated by Meg Bateman (Edinburgh, 1994), 132.

[65] Seliga and Kocky, *Scotland and Poland*, 8; *HMC, Sixth Report*, 431. Bradshaw to Frost, 3 September 1650. 'Cockram (it's said) is stolen hence privately with all the money he got in the east parts without paying any debt'. Cochrane also allegedly absconded with at least one of the ships he got from the Duke of Courland. See the *Deeds of Montrose*, 259 which cites an anonymous text called *Montrose Redivivus*.

imprison or kill him.[66] Nor could Cochrane ever again trust that Charles II would not throw him to the wolves at a whim as he had done with Montrose. Colonel John Henderson had expended a lot of energy on the Royalist campaign and had been left alienated from the king. The colonel took his revenge on Charles by turning informant for the Cromwellian government.[67] Other Cavaliers destined to arrive in Scotland with Montrose, like General King, gave up the cause and died in exile in Sweden.

Only a short time after they had aided Montrose in his bid to retake Scotland for the Royalists, two heavyweight Danish diplomats found themselves accused of treason towards Denmark-Norway. Some of Charles II's ministers claimed that Korfitz Ulfeldt had embezzled the money which Frederik III had sent to Charles. Ulfeldt, therefore, found himself in exile with his family in Stockholm where he became friends with the English Republican, Bulstrode Whitelocke.[68] The Danes decided to take up the matter of financial irregularities with the Swedes whom they wished would not show any more favour to the one time Danish Chancellor.[69] In fact, as already discussed, Ulfeldt had not only handed over the Danish Crown money, but contributed much of his own resources to the endeavour.[70] During his stay at the Swedish Court, Ulfeldt confronted the Danish ambassador with the receipts he had received for the money and continued to seek redress for the slander for several years.[71] In 1654, Ulfeldt told Sir William Bellenden, the Scottish Royalist agent who then informed Sir Edward Nicholas, that in order to clear his name he would publish correspondence between the Danish king and the Stuart Court which

---

[66] Balfour Paul, *Scots Peerage*, III, 344. According to this source, Cochrane apparently moved to England in 1653 and lived on until 1657; *HMC, Sixth Report*, 427. Bradshaw to Ac'ton, 19 June 1650. Bradshaw noted that 'Sir John Henderson and some other poor Scots have bills of exchange from their master upon Cockram, but I believe he hath wit enough to keep the whole money to himself; for if neither the Scots nor English suffer him to return, that money will be little enough to maintain his Irish lady and her Hangbyes'.

[67] G. F. Warner ed, *The Nicholas Papers; Correspondence of Sir Edward Nicholas, Secretary of State*, (4 vols., London, 1892-1920), III, 276-277. Ormonde to Nicholas, 26 April 1656.

[68] Spalding, *Bulstrode Whitelocke*, 317. Ulfeldt was married to Frederik's most hated sister, and had other issues with the Danish king, though he does not seem to have mentioned these to Whitelocke.

[69] Spalding, *Bulstrode Whitelocke*, 348. 5 April 1654.

[70] *The Deeds of Montrose*, 260. Here the figure given is about £4,275 where Ulfeldt later claimed himself the amount of his own cash was 12,500 *rigsdaler* (about £2,500). See *The Nicholas Papers*, III, 110-113. Ulfeldt to Nicholas, 5 November 1655.

[71] PRO SP75/16 f. 238 Korfitz Ulfeldt's claim for redress, September 1655; Spalding, *Bulstrode Whitelocke*, 348. 5 April 1654.

would both clear him and damage them.[72] Nicholas believed that such a move would be very prejudicial since he would willingly damage the Stuart cause just to get back at his royal brother-in-law. Ulfeldt himself said he only sought the slandering from the Stuart side to be stopped and, indeed, Nicholas's answer suggests he had a good case against them.[73]

Charles II, Covenanted King of Great Britain

Even before one Scottish episode had ended, another began to unfold on the continent. The Scottish commissioners at Breda negotiated very strict conditions which the Royalist propagandists claimed the Marquis of Argyll thought, or perhaps even hoped, the king would not accept.[74] Charles II had to take the Covenant and banish 'any councillors prejudicial to Presbyterianism and opposed to both the National Covenant and Solemn League and Covenant'.[75] The Scots also insisted that the king had to repudiate treaties with the Duke of Ormond's party and the Irish Catholics although Charles managed to momentarily sidestep this issue.[76] Despite these harsh conditions, Charles really had little option and the Scottish Parliament knew the strength of its position. If he did not establish himself in one of his kingdoms quickly, no foreign state would treat him seriously. Foreign support already came from William II in the United Provinces. This move was backed by the English advisers of Charles II, the Marquis of Newcastle and the Duke of Buckingham, who were both supportive of their king going to Scotland.[77]

In Charles II's own estimation, his return to Scotland would boost his status throughout Europe. Scotland had no force in arms against him and Stuart ambassadors abroad would benefit from being seen as representatives of a king with a kingdom rather than an impoverished itinerant royal.[78] Indeed, this proved to be the case. The Dutch transported Charles past the English Republican navy and convoyed

---

[72] *The Nicholas Papers*, II, 73. Bellenden to Nicholas, 24 June 1654.
[73] *The Nicholas Papers*, III, 110-113. Ulfeldt to Nicholas, 5 November 1655.
[74] Clarendon, *History of the Rebellion*, V, 117-119; *HMC, Pepys Manuscripts*, 250 and 252. Earl of Louden and Marquis of Argyll to Charles II, 2 March 1649; Charles II to Argyll, 18 March 1649 and Louden to Charles II, 24 March 1649; Young, *Scottish Parliament*, 246-258.
[75] Young, *Scottish Parliament*, 224.
[76] *Charles II and Scotland*, 140-142. The Dean of Tuam to Ormonde, 15 October 1650; R. Hutton, *The British Republic, 1649-1660* (London, 1990), 51.
[77] TT E.603 (4) *The great preparation made in Holand, for the King of Scots, going into Scotland. Also the D. of Buckingham, M. Hamilton, and the E. of Newcastle, to be sent embassadors into Germany, Sweden and Denmark; with the large promises of Col. Massey, and Ald. Bunce, to the forsaid King* (London, 1650); Jones, *Royal Politician*, 19.
[78] Clarendon, *History of the Rebellion*, V, 120-121.

him and his supporters to Scotland in three large warships.[79] Between the negotiations at Breda and Charles's departure from the United Provinces, the Covenanting regime issued a new set of conditions. The Scottish Estates now insisted that Charles should immediately take the Covenant and '*in terminis*' break the peace with Ormond and the Irish and agree to impose Presbyterianism into England and Ireland. Charles was so disgusted that he contemplated getting off the ship in Denmark and giving up his designs on Scotland altogether.[80] However, he swallowed this bitter pill and continued on his journey.

When it became clear that Charles had secured Scotland, the Dutch also allowed Scottish merchants in the United Provinces credit in order that they might send him arms and ammunition. After all, Charles only viewed his visit to Scotland as a platform from which he would eventually grasp his other two kingdoms and his situation there seemed to be improving. In Ireland, for instance, Charles's situation seemed to have improved when he heard that the Scots in Ulster had come to terms with the Duke of Ormond.[81] Now Charles granted his cousin, Woldomar, a commission to raise 10,000 men to bring to Britain. He had no money to back this levy, causing immediate problems as Woldomar refused to raise an army without security. Further problems for the king arose when the Scots commissioners told Charles that the Danish count could not bring an army to Scotland since they 'would not impose a yoke upon themselves'.[82] Clearly the Scots did not trust their new king. After what they themselves had been permitted to do to Montrose with royal approval, such suspicions were well founded. Instead the Scots argued that they would assist Charles 'by their own nation' since they expected to find more friends than enemies in England.[83] In the meantime, Woldomar managed to secure permission to raise an army to be brought into England. According to one Cromwellian spy reporting from the Stuart Court, this army was to receive no pay and subsist on free quarter and booty for as long as the expected war in England lasted.[84] This may have only been scare mongering, but such reports stirred up fears in

---

[79] *HMC, Sixth Report*, 427-428. Bradshaw to Ac'ton, 19 June 1650; Same to Strickland, 21 June 1650.

[80] *Charles II and Scotland*, 140-142. The Dean of Tuam to Ormonde, 15 October 1650; Hutton, *The British Republic*, 51.

[81] Clarendon, *History of the Rebellion*, V, 148.

[82] *Charles II and Scotland*, 77-80. Letters from Breda, 26 April/6 May and Paris, 1/11 May 1650.

[83] *Charles II and Scotland*, 80. Letter from Paris, 1/11 May 1650; A. I. Macinnes, 'The Scottish Constitution, 1638-1651. The Rise and Fall of Oligarchic Centralism', in J. Morrill ed, *The National Covenant in its British Context* (Edinburgh, 1990), 127.

[84] *Charles II and Scotland*, 119-120. Letter from The Hague, 6/16 June 1650.

England about the return of the House of Stuart.

Charles II appointed new ambassadors for northern Europe at this time to replace those lost by the Montrosian episode. In The Hague, the Scottish Gael and veteran Royalist soldier, Angus MacDonald of Glengarry (later Lord MacDonnell and Aros), had served as the main ambassador for Charles II since 1649. Given his association with Montrose and MacColla, he had to be replaced by a new agent and thus Henry Lord Percy received his new commission. The Duke of Hamilton was chosen to travel to Sweden while Buckingham assumed responsibility for Germany.[85] The agents of the Scottish Estates asked that these ambassadors only seek money from the various heads of state since they had men enough to form an army. In Sweden however, an extended series of debates took place in the *Riksråd* over what sort of backing Christina should give to the new Scottish-led regime in light of the Breda negotiations.[86]

Across the Scandinavian border, the Marquis of Newcastle took on responsibility for negotiations in Denmark-Norway.[87] His instructions were to collect 160,000 *rigsdaler* that belonged to the English Company and were currently in the possession of the Danish king. Newcastle also had to deliver letters from Charles II to Korfitz Ulfeldt and Hannibal Sehested which were no doubt intended to try to win them back to the Stuart cause. Newcastle also undertook to continue to pay Ulfeldt the pension which Charles I had granted him.[88] In addition to trying to re-ingratiate himself with Ulfeldt and Sehested, Charles also hoped to secure new money from Frederik III. One Cromwellian agent thought that there would be little chance of the Royalists raising any money in Denmark since the Danes themselves were impoverished due to the remaining unpaid debts of Christian IV and Frederik III.[89] However, Frederik did offer some support to the Stuart king. The English ambassador, Richard Bradshaw, complained bitterly that the governor of Glückstadt permitted Royalist privateers to bring in their prizes to his port with the full consent of Frederik which, he argued, was in defiance of article eleven of the English Parliament's

[85] For Macdonald see A. I. Macinnes, 'The First Scottish Tories', in *The Scottish Historical Review*, LXVII, 1; no. 138 (1988), 60; Ó Baoill, *Gair nan Clarsach*, 120; Stevenson, *Highland Warrior*, 258; For the other diplomats see TT E.603 (4) *The great preparation made in Holland*, (1650); *Charles II and Scotland*, 110-115. Letter from The Hague, 20/30 May 1650; Extract from 'Brief relation', 18/28 June 1650.

[86] *Charles II and Scotland*, 110-115. Letter from The Hague, 20/30 May 1650. For a review of the Swedish debates see Grosjean, 'Scots and the Swedish State', 217-223.

[87] TT E.603 (4) *The great preparation made in Holland* (1650).

[88] *Charles II and Scotland*, 123-124. A memorial for the Marquis of Newcastle, June 1650.

[89] *Charles II and Scotland*, 110-115. Letter from The Hague, 20/30 May 1650.

1645 treaty with Denmark-Norway.[90] The English Republicans responded by seizing Danish vessels at Glückstadt which led to an exchange between Bradshaw and Danish agents regarding the whole issue of piracy around the Danish port.[91]

In the midst of such political posturing and military developments, Charles II arrived in Scotland, making the peace between the British kingdoms increasingly fragile. His presence, albeit in Scotland, inevitably served as a destabilising element within England. Despite the abolition of monarchy in that kingdom, some people still argued that the Prince of Wales had succeeded his father legally under English constitutional law. On this point the Royalists had a strong case to argue given that Charles II had been proclaimed king of Great Britain and Ireland in 1649 and his status been confirmed in proclamations by English and Irish Royalists.[92] Obviously the Cromwellian faction did not, and could not, accept these declarations. The solution to them lay in the invasion of Scotland and an attempt to capture or kill the king before he could organise his inevitable invasion of England. In the summer of 1650, the English Rump Parliament launched what Derek Hirst has described as 'a pre-emptive strike against the Scottish kingdom'.[93] Invading Scotland, however, was an act which many people in England felt tested the bounds of legality. They included among their number General Thomas Fairfax, the chosen leader for the campaign.[94] After all, Scotland was a 'free nation, tied to the English only by dynastic accident' and should have been free to go its own way.[95] That was not to be and Cromwell,

---

[90]   *HMC, Sixth Report,* 430. Bradshaw to my Lord President, 3 September 1650. 'that King permits all commissioned captains by the Scotts King to bring in their prizes there to have them adjudged. Of what eveil consequences this may be to the trade of our Company here and the whole Commonwealth, I submit to your Lordship's judgement'; Same to Council of State, 29 October 1650.

[91]   *HMC, Sixth Report,* 434. Bradshaw to Frost, 12 November 1650; Same to Lord President, 26 November 1650; Same to Same 3 December 1650.

[92]   Jones, *Royal Politician,* 13; Morrill 'The Britishness of the English Revolution', 101; See Thomason Tracts 669 f.13 (79); 669 f.13 (82) and E.544 (12).

[93]   Hirst, 'The English Republic', 197 and 200.

[94]   Thomas Fairfax held a Scottish Peerage as Lord Fairfax of Cameron and this may have influenced his desire not to invade Scotland. Other people claim Fairfax simply did not want to fight fellow Presbyterians or had not 'reconciled himself to the abolition of monarchy and did not wish to destroy the last monarchical state in the British Isles'. See Hutton, *The British Republic,* 23; M. Wilding, *Dragon's Teeth, Literature in the English Revolution* (Oxford, 1987), 134-142; J. Morrill, 'Three Kingdoms and one Commonwealth? The enigma of mid-seventeenth century Britain and Ireland', in A. Grant and K. J. Stinger eds, *Uniting the Kingdom? The making of British History* (London, 1995), 185-186; Hirst, 'The English Republic', 197; Clarendon, *History of the Rebellion,* V, 159; Abbott, *Oliver Cromwell,* II, 267.

[95]   Morrill, 'Three Kingdoms and one Commonwealth?', 185.

newly returned from Ireland, led the English army into Scotland. The
Scottish army facing him represented only a fraction of the fighting
capability of the country. The leadership of the Scottish Estates spent
weeks purging the army of all suspected Cavaliers and former
Engagers, as well as the 'ungodly'.[96] By doing so the numbers in the
army fell by as many as 20,000 men, thereby depriving it of many of
Scotland's most experienced soldiers. The Covenanting army gave up
its secure position near Edinburgh only to be defeated by Cromwell
outside Dunbar in September.

Perhaps surprisingly, the Earl of Clarendon recorded that the battle
of Dunbar was the first good fortune for Charles II, since it meant he
would not be the prisoner of the Covenanters for much longer.[97] Such
may have been Clarendon's belief, but it certainly proved not to be the
intent of the Covenanters to release the king from his obligations to
them. On the first day of 1651, Charles II underwent his coronation
ceremony at Scone. A bizarre episode preceded the service where
Charles had to denounce his father's, and grandfather's crimes and his
mother's Papist idolatry. After this he swore, as king of Great Britain
and Ireland, to introduce the Covenants into all his kingdoms. The
result of this Covenanting pre-amble to the coronation was Charles's
enduring hatred for Presbyterians and the majority of Scotsmen whom
he identified with that confession of faith. However, Charles had to
bury such feelings so long as the Scots represented his best hope of
securing his other two kingdoms.

Satirists capitalised on the coronation ceremony, and the image of
Charles II with his nose being held to the grindstone by the Scots
clearly demonstrated one English interpretation of the coronation.[98]
The Royalist view, publicly at least, was somewhat different. A print
appeared which showed the crowning of Charles II by Argyll. In the
foreground an image of the king was shown being dressed for war by
'Ireland' while 'Scotland' handed him a pistol labelled revenge.[99] The
message was obvious. The newly crowned king now sought to build a
truly Royalist army in Scotland (from all his kingdoms) to tackle

[96] John Nicoll, 'A diary of Public Transactions and other occurrences, chiefly in Scotland, from January 1650 to June 1667', in A. Peterkin ed, *Records of the Kirk of Scotland, containing the Acts and proceedings of the General Assemblies from the year 1638 downwards* (Edinburgh, 1843), 612-617.
[97] Clarendon, *History of the Rebellion*, V, 179; Jones, *Royal Politician*, 21; Young, *Scottish Parliament*, 258.
[98] Philalethes, *'Old Sayings and Predictions Verified'*.
[99] British Museum, Huych Allaerdt, *Crowning of Charles II at Scone, 1st January 1651*. Reproduced in Maclean, *A Concise History of Scotland*, 131.

Cromwell.[100] This time the army would be commanded by Charles himself. Scottish Royalists and former Engagers, including General Middleton, were to be drawn out of the Highlands and the burghs north of the Forth.[101] But many Presbyterians suspected Charles's true intentions regarding the Covenant. They were horrified by the perceptible return of power towards the Engager party through the gradual relaxation of the Act of Classes. The rescinding of this Act, in the summer of 1651, saw non-Covenanters allowed into civil office and a greater nation-wide representation in the national army.

Among the rehabilitated army were included such zealous Montrosians as Angus MacDonald of Glengarry. Because of the participation of him and men of similar politics in the new army, many ardent Scottish Covenanters slipped into a state of neutrality.[102] To such individuals, even a Protestant dictator like Cromwell could easily be construed as the lesser of two evils over the perceived 'pro-Papists' of Charles II. More importantly, however, Scotland found itself to be 'a victim of military and financial, if not ideological, exhaustion'.[103] After a stand off of several months in Scotland, the new army of the 'Patriotic Accommodation' crossed into England to avoid being trapped in Scotland. On entering England, Charles was re-confirmed as king of England and Ireland by a proclamation read aloud near Carlisle.[104] Unfortunately for Charles his Irish supporters were kept occupied and significant English Royalist support failed to materialise. The king's army was defeated at Worcester through the superior number and motivation of Cromwell's forces.[105] With no army left in Scotland, and no faction now strong enough to form one, Cromwell set about his incorporative union of the British kingdoms. Despite a huge effort to capture him, Charles II escaped from Worcester, a feat which the king himself attributed to 'a firme argument of God's mercy and future protection of us'.[106]

---

[100] Jones, *Royal Politician*, 22. For one Gaelic reaction to the coronation of Charles II see Iain Lom's *Crunadh an Dara Righ Teàrlach* in Mackenzie, *Oran Iain Luim*, 76-80 and notes 267-268.

[101] Clarendon, *History of the Rebellion*, V, 186.

[102] Jones, *Royal Politician*, 22-23. For MacDonald see D. J. Macdonald, *Clan Donald* (Lothian, 1978), 347-349; Stevenson, *Highland Warrior*, 273-277.

[103] Macinnes, 'The Scottish Constitution 1638-1651', 128.

[104] Turner, *Memoirs*, 94.

[105] Turner, *Memoirs*, 95; PRO SP75/16 ff. 218-220. Charles II to Frederik III of Denmark-Norway. and Queen Christina of Sweden, 20/30 August 1652; Hutton, *The British Republic*, 53-54.

[106] PRO SP75/16 ff. 218-220. Charles II to Frederik III of Denmark-Norway and Queen Christina of Sweden, 20/30 August 1652.

Though Charles believed he still had the support of God, he had certainly squandered support elsewhere. The execution of Charles I gifted British Royalists with a golden opportunity to pursue their propaganda message vigorously throughout Europe. The majority of governments were receptive to the idea that the heinous crime of regicide required punishment. In Scandinavia in particular their cause had been aided by a corps of Scottish Cavaliers who exercised considerable influence in those militarily and economically vital kingdoms. The northern potentates were quick to supply money, arms, men and ships to the Stuart cause. Charles II had won a significant victory by winning back Denmark-Norway as an ally and finding a friend in Sweden for the first time. However, by sacrificing the Marquis of Montrose in order to be enthroned by the Scottish Estates, Charles II wasted his newly won resources and allies. While Sweden had indeed aided negotiations with the Scottish Estates, few expected Charles to be so callous with the lives of Montrose and his followers. The Scottish Estates subsequently forbade Charles to bring Swedish or Danish troops to Scotland even if they supplied them free of charge. As though the elimination of Montrose and his supporters were not enough for him, Charles also relished the destruction of the Scottish Covenanting army at Dunbar, alienating a second group of Scots. Moreover, he then marched his largely Scottish army of 'Patriotic Accommodation' to their demise in England then left the survivors to their fate. In short he had alienated or lost many of the important elements of the Scottish political nation. Perhaps more significantly Charles II lost the important influence of the Scottish exiles in Sweden and Denmark-Norway. Thereafter these men appear to have let the English Parliamentarians press their cause unopposed. The Royalists had lost the propaganda initiative and, of the major potentates of Europe, only the Tsar of Russia remained loyal to their cause. With Scotland occupied, Ireland crushed and England firmly under Parliamentary control, the support of the Tsar was hardly enough to ensure a Stuart comeback in any of kingdoms of the British Isles.

CHAPTER SEVEN

The 'Englishing' of Britain and the demise of the Stuart-Oldenburg alliance

Charles II recognised very quickly that it would be better for him in the long run to be restored by his own subjects rather than to be installed by a foreign power.[1] Despite this he hoped to gain the neutral benevolence, if not actual material support, of the royal houses in Denmark-Norway, Sweden and across Europe. Charles filled his letters to them with extremely emotive language. He appealed to Frederik III to unite with him to aid his subjects the greatest number of whom, he claimed, groaned under the intolerable yoke of the traitors, in opposition to tyranny.[2] While asking for neither arms nor money, it was clear that Charles sought to dissuade Frederik from harbouring agents of the Commonwealth or legitimising that regime with any form of official recognition.[3] Further to his continental and Scandinavian letters, Charles also opened up a correspondence with committed Royalists and potential converts to the cause.

In Scotland there was a small, but significant, military resistance to the Cromwellian occupation orchestrated as early as 1652 by Angus MacDonald of Glengarry and formally led after 1653 by William Cunningham, 9th Earl of Glencairn. The guerrilla war was largely fought within the Highlands and Northeast of Scotland, but gained sufficient momentum to persuade the exiled Royalist leadership to contemplate another attempt on the three kingdoms from a Scottish base.[4] Reports arrived at the exiled Stuart Court that in Scotland the king's party grew stronger by the day. General John Middleton, captured after Worcester, managed to escape from the Tower of London and arrived on the continent to pledge his continued support for the king. Sir Edward Nicholas informed Lord Wentworth that there were in fact 13 Scottish Earls and Barons declared for the king who could field about 7,000 men whenever they chose.[5] There was of course the problem of arming them

---

[1] Jones, *Royal Politician*, 29.

[2] DRA, TKUA England A1. Charles II to Frederik III, February 1653.

[3] PRO SP75/16 ff. 218-220. Charles II to Frederik III of Denmark-Norway and Queen Christina of Sweden, 20/30 August 1652.

[4] Macdonald, *Clan Donald*, 347-348; A. I. Macinnes, *Clanship, Commerce and the House of Stuart, 1603-1788* (Edinburgh, 1996), 110.

[5] *The Nicholas Papers*, II, 15. Sir Edward Nicholas to Thomas, 5th Baron Wentworth, 18/28 July 1653. Nicholas names the Marquis of Huntly, The Marquis Seaforth, Lord Lorn, 'old' Lord Chancellor Louden, Alexander Lindsay, 2nd Lord Balcarres and John Murray, 2nd Earl

all. Charles signed over control of his Scottish affairs to General Middleton who superseded Glencairn as leader of the resistance movement in Scotland. Charles encouraged all his Scottish subjects living under foreign princes to assist Middleton with loans of arms, ammunition and money 'whereby we may be enabled to free their country from the servitude and dishonour it suffers under'.[6]

Soldiers for the Royalist invasion were to be provided by the Count of Waldeck, who was prepared to allow Middleton to secretly levy 1,500 soldiers to be used to secure a port near Edinburgh. The soldiers were to be recruited as if they were going into the service of the king of Denmark. The Count also suggested that to cover the embarkation it should be publicly believed that the troops were going to leave Glückstadt as if *en route* to Norway. By doing so the English resident in Hamburg would not become suspicious and summon a fleet to the Elbe to prevent the departure of the expedition. The soldiers raised by Waldeck were to assemble in Glückstadt but only under a strict set of guarantees. Amongst other things, Waldeck insisted that on arrival in Glückstadt the soldiers were to be paid for either by Charles II or Frederik III and not cost him any further expense. He wanted assurances from the king of Denmark that there would be ships to transport the men to Scotland. He also told Middleton that he needed assurances that the men would be suitably armed to enter and maintain their positions. Waldeck also wanted to be assured that this soldiers should have a place to which they could retreat should things go wrong, perhaps reflecting on the fate of Montrose's expedition. He also wanted 7-8,000 *rigsdaler* to offset expenses and pay the officers danger money for the risks they took *en route* to Scotland.[7] Neither Frederik or Charles could provide the guarantees required by Waldeck and the mercenary enterprise was abandoned.

This setback did not prevent Royalist preparations for an attempt on Scotland. Charles II sent Thomas 5th Baron Wentworth, as his ambassador to Denmark-Norway in June 1653 with instructions to inform the Danes that General Middleton was raising new forces and to ask if Frederik III would help with these preparations. Specifically, Charles wanted Frederik to open up his ports to Royalist vessels and

of Athole.
[6] Turner, *Memoirs*, 105; C. H. Firth ed, *Scotland and the Commonwealth; letters and papers relating to the military government of Scotland from August 1651 to December 1653* (Edinburgh, 1895), 52. Charles II's instructions to General Middleton, 9/19 August 1652.
[7] *Scotland and the Commonwealth*, 123-124. The Count of Waldeck to Middleton, 27 April 1653.

perhaps even loan some ships for the transportation of soldiers to Scotland under the Stuart standard.[8] Wentworth also told the Danes that the Dutch had asked the king to move to The Netherlands and also if there was any possibility providing further arms to his Scottish supporters. These requests were repeated elsewhere with some success. Middleton dispatched agents, including Colonel James Turner, through the Low Countries, to the German princes and to the Count of Oldenburg in search of weapons and money.[9] Despite being in negotiation with the English Parliament at the time, the Danes were prepared to facilitate an attempt on Scotland from Danish soil. Charles again wrote to Frederik in August, this time from Paris, to inform him that preparations continued in Scotland to 'wipe out this progeny of parricides' with whatever Danish help was available.[10]

During the autumn of 1653, Middleton sent a small number of arms to Scotland. Backed by letters from Charles II he also conducted negotiations in the United Provinces hoping to acquire a larger consignment and perhaps even some ships.[11] Nicholas correctly foresaw that the Dutch government would be unhappy at such an arrangement while they were still negotiating with the English Commonwealth. Obviously they would see such supplies as jeopardising their chances of a successful outcome with England. However, although the ruling party in Holland was against Middleton, they were out voted by a majority formed from the other states of the United Provinces. The only thing that prevented him from collecting as many arms as he desired lay in the shortage of cash or credit. Charles had succeeded in securing 200,000 *rigsdaler*, from the Emperor and the princes of Germany of which a portion was destined to support the armed attempt.[12]

By December, Middleton prepared to send 1,500 arms and 40 barrels of powder back to Scotland.[13] His plans to front an armed insurrection

[8]   DRA, TKUA England AI, Charles II to Frederik III, 7 February 1653; *Scotland and the Commonwealth*, 109-110. Charles II to Lt. General Middleton, 5/15 April 1653; C. Rise Hansen ed, *Aktstykker og Oplysninger til Rigsrådets og Stænderødernes Historie i Frederik III's Tid, 1653* (Copenhagen, 1975), 633 and 766-7, no. 615. 'Den skotske konges udsending Thomas Wentworths forslag om hjælp til kong Karl II, refereret i rigsrådsmødet 27 juni 1653'.
[9]   Turner, *Memoirs*, 107; *Scotland and the Commonwealth*, 54-55. Middleton to the Count of Oldenburg, 16/26 October 1652.
[10] DRA, TKUA England AI, Charles II to Frederik III, 8 August 1653.
[11] *The Nicholas Papers*, II, 21-22. Nicholas to Wentworth, 5/15 September 1653; Israel, *The Dutch Republic*, 720.
[12] *The Nicholas Papers*, II, 23-26. Nicholas to Wentworth, 10 November (ns) 1653 and Nicholas to Hyde, 17/27 November 1653.
[13] *The Nicholas Papers*, II, 32 and 39-42. Nicholas to Hyde, 8/18 December 1653; Lord Hatton to Nicholas 2 January 1654.

were given a boost when Charles II resolved to leave France and join the army in person. Charles's decision to do so may well have been influenced by the rumours circulating that Cromwell was on the verge of assuming a sovereign title.[14] Indeed, after Cromwell had been installed as Lord Protector, Nicholas declared that 'I assure you it seems to me to be the saddest change that could be to have that Bloody Rebel so enthroned'.[15] Charles was also further encouraged to go to Scotland through a direct invitation from Angus MacDonald of Glengarry.[16] MacDonald suggested that the low morale in the army, caused by Middleton's arrival in Scotland with so few officers and a small quantity of arms and ammunition, could be raised by the king's presence. Low morale was not the only problem for the army however. Tensions surfaced almost immediately within the Scottish guerrilla movement as Middleton and Glencairn fell out over the appointment of Sir George Monro as second in command rather than Glengairn. Disputes over rank and station aside, the commanders could not agree upon a strategy and were hopelessly under-resourced. Royalist agents implored Charles not to go to Scotland unless the situation improved dramatically.[17] In the end the king wisely opted to remain on the continent.

The insurrection went ahead without the royal presence and Middleton managed to keep a military presence in Scotland for almost a year but once the Highland chiefs and landed gentry began to negotiate separately for peace between January and May 1655, the venture was bound to fail. The lack of co-ordination in Scotland was not helped by a lack of any serious help from Royalists in England or Ireland. That, coupled with the reasonable terms for the cessation of hostilities offered by General George Monck, English Commander-in-Chief in Scotland, brought the revolt to a close with MacDonald of Glengarry being the last to submit.[18]

---

[14] *The Nicholas Papers*, II, 32. Nicholas to Hyde, 8/18 December 1653. Nicholas noted the serious implications of such a move by the Cromwell. He wrote 'I assure you I do with you apprehend nothing more prejudicial or pernicious to His Majesty's interest than that Cromwell should by any title take on himself (as is evident in his design) the sovereign power in England; which tho' some here (wiser than I am) make light of, I very much fear, as affairs now stand at home and abroad, may meet with in England and procure from foreign princes (who are not yet sensible how much they are concerned in this prodigious usurpation in England) too great a compliance, unless some strange judgement fall on him for his so proud an arrogancy'.

[15] *The Nicholas Papers*, II, 42. Nicholas to Hyde, 8 January 1654.

[16] *The Nicholas Papers*, II, 23-24. Nicholas to Wentworth, 10 November (ns) 1653. The letter from Glengarry to Charles II, 5 June 1654, is printed in full in Macdonald, *Clan Donald*, 348.

[17] Turner, *Memoirs*, 109-110; *The Nicholas Papers*, II, 86-87. J. Jane to Nicholas, 24 September 1654; Clarendon, *History of the Rebellion*, V, 343-344; K. Brown, *Kingdom or Province? Scotland and the Regal Union, 1603-1715* (London, 1992), 136-137.

[18] The terms for the laying down of arms by the Royalists included a guarantee of not being

By allowing surrendering Royalist officers the opportunity to levy troops for foreign service, General Monk believed he could prevent further clandestine operations against his forces (and the pillage of the countryside) without risking more English lives.[19] The scheme did not always work out exactly as planned for the Cromwellians. With permission from Cromwell, Colonel Thomas Lyon raised a regiment of 2,000 men for service in France which he immediately proposed to put at the service of Charles II.[20] Luckily for Cromwell, Charles could not afford to keep these men in service himself and so they remained in France awaiting the opportunity to return home.

At this time Charles again looked to his disparate factions both within his kingdoms and in exile which he hoped to bring together to secure his restoration. There were hopes that Mr Mowbray, a kinsman of the Scottish Imperialist Count Walter Leslie, would be able to secure a reconciliation between the Presbyterian faction and the other groups that supported the king. Mowbray kept up a correspondence with the Catholic priest Father John Wilfourde at Rome in the hope of facilitating some form of co-operation.[21] Charles II also undertook negotiations with leaders of the disaffected Leveller faction in England. Colonel Robert Phelips, one of the men accredited with the escape of Charles II after Worcester, wrote to Nicholas to inform him that he had established contact with 'the most eminent Leveller' Colonel Edward Sexby. He too had escaped to the continent and allowed Phelips access to letters which allegedly showed the defection of some of Cromwell's own party to the Levellers.[22] Sexby assured Phelipps that should the Levellers gain the

transported to the colonies and the release of those already taken; Officers were to keep their swords and horses. Soldiers could sell their horses. Passes would be issued for soldiers to return to their homes or travel overseas. Many senior officers would be allowed to levy regiments for foreign service so long as the nation in question was in amity with the Commonwealth. See C. H. Firth, *Scotland and the Protectorate; letters and papers relating to the military government of Scotland from January 1654 to June 1659* (Edinburgh, 1899), 154-293; Macdonald, *Clan Donald*, 349; Brown, *Kingdom or Province*, 137; D. Stevenson, 'Cromwell, Scotland and Ireland', in J. Morrill ed, *Oliver Cromwell and the English Revolution* (London, 1990), 169; Macinnes, *Clanship, Commerce and the House of Stuart*, 111-114.

[19] *Scotland and the Protectorate*, 154. Monck to Cromwell, 17 August 1654. Contempt for Middleton after the rising failed can be found in the poem *An Cobhernandori*. See A. I. Macinnes, 'The First Scottish Tories', in *The Scottish Historical Review*, LXVII, 1; no. 138 (1988), 66; C Ó Baoill ed, *Gair nan Clarsach: The Harper's Cry, An anthology of 17th Century Gaelic Poetry*. Translated by Meg Bateman (Edinburgh, 1994), 120.

[20] *Scotland and the Protectorate*, 244-245. Colonel Thomas Lyon to Charles II, 29 January/8 February 1654/55.

[21] *The Nicholas Papers*, III, 50-55. Langdale to Nicholas, 20 September 1655.

[22] *The Nicholas Papers*, II, 299. Colonel Robert Phelips to Nicholas, 21 July 1655; Jones, *Royal Politician*, 31. Colonel Robert Phelips was the second son of Sir Robert Phelips, Knt., of Montacue. He was a gentleman of the bedchamber to the Duke of Gloucester, and after the

upper hand they would do their best for the king's party.

By 1655, Charles undertook negotiations with the Spanish who had become disenchanted with the Cromwellian regime and with whom the Republicans, correctly, soon expected to be at war.[23] During a meeting in The Hague in August, the Spanish ambassador was asked by Sir Robert Stone, a covert Cromwellian agent, if Spain was for Cromwell or Charles II. Stone pointed out that the king of Spain had been the first to recognise Cromwell, to which the reply came that 'we have payed for it'.[24] There followed a round of toasts which the company, including Stone, joined in. There were hopes among the Royalists by December that Spain might join with the Emperor and Denmark-Norway in supporting Charles II's cause.[25] Once more Charles looked for support far and wide, and as always the Court of Frederik III was seen as potential ally. Colonel Turner moved his base to Copenhagen from where he sent weekly reports to Chancellor Hyde, the future Earl of Clarendon, relating to Denmark-Norway. To bolster Stuart diplomacy in the region, Charles sent Major-General Montgomerie to Frederik in 1657 armed with letters of accreditation from the Stuart king and his aunt, Elizabeth of Bohemia.[26]

Charles had also opened talks in Brussels which led to a treaty being signed on 12 April 1656, though many Royalists, like Sir Edward Nicholas, felt the Spanish were too reticent with their promises and actions.[27] Charles, however, established a government in exile in the Spanish Netherlands. In addition, he hoped to win Spanish support for a co-ordinated uprising in England backed by the landing of Spanish troops.[28] Charles had been promised aid from the Spaniards and Austrians, which included the right to establish an army in the Spanish Netherlands. This army contained a Scottish regiment under General Middleton, an Irish regiment commanded by the Duke of Ormonde and an English regiment under the command of Lord Wilmot.[29] The force was to be bolstered with two further regiments under the Duke of York and 6,000 Spanish veterans were to be 'loaned' for any campaign. In

restoration Groom of the Bedchamber to the King and MP for Stockbridge and Andover. *The Nicholas Papers*, II, 296, footnote.

[23] *HMC, Sixth Report*, 439, Waynwright to Bradshaw, 5 October 1655; Hutton, *The British Republic*, 60 and 110.

[24] *The Nicholas Papers*, III, 34-36. Jane to Nicholas, 24 August 1655.

[25] *The Nicholas Papers*, III, 217. Earl of Norwich to Nicholas, 21 December 1655.

[26] Turner, *Memoirs*, 122 and 118-120.

[27] *The Nicholas Papers*, III, 270-271. Nicholas to Thomas Ross, 19/29 February 1655/56; Ormonde to Nicholas, 27 March 1656.

[28] Turner, *Memoirs*, 118-120; Hutton, *The British Republic*, 110.

[29] Turner, *Memoirs*, 120.

return, Charles promised that on his restoration he would help Spain retake Portugal and cede the West Indies and all Commonwealth conquests to the Spanish.[30] One of the first objectives for the Royalists had to be the securing of an appropriate port to land the troops. However, the Royalists in England remained as uncoordinated as ever and Cromwellian agents continued to monitor Royalist plans closely.

By September 1656 rumours were circulating in England of 'the King of Scotts in Flanders making preparations for some of these nations'.[31] Lord Cranston noted in 1657 that the people of Danzig continued to provide money, men and assistance to General Middleton for the Stuart arrangements.[32] Oliver Cromwell also knew of the Stuart intention to launch an invasion on the English coast. In his speech to Parliament on 4 February 1658, Cromwell noted 'that the King of Scots hath an army at the waterside [...] ready to be shipped for England'.[33] Plans to execute an invasion from Ostende were scuppered when the English navy blockaded the port. The French also applied enough military pressure on the Spanish to make them rethink their involvement in any Stuart invasion, at least for the foreseeable future. Charles II grew tired of Spanish inaction and in July 1659 he resolved to join Booth's uprising in Cheshire. Fortunately for Charles, he heard the news of Booth's defeat just as he was due to embark. He quickly changed his plans and set out for the Pyrenees in an attempt to secure a place for Stuart Royalism in the ongoing Franco-Spanish negotiations, albeit with minimal success. Indeed most observers of Charles II's manoeuvres during the second period in exile argue that Charles had used up all his options.[34] His English Royalists had failed to stage an uprising that threatened the Republican regime; Scottish and Irish Royalists had been comprehensively defeated; no major military aid had materialised from Spain or France (and that which had come from Denmark-Norway had been squandered). The small army in exile ran out of resources. The troops dispersed and variously found service throughout the Habsburg Empire and Scandinavia and thus ended Royalist hopes of seizing power back in the British Isles by force.[35]

[30] Jones, *Royal Politician*, 27.
[31] *HMC, Sixth Report*, 440, Waynwright to Bradshaw, 26 September 1656.
[32] *Scotland and the Protectorate*, 353. Lord Cranston to Monck, 8 April 1657.
[33] Abbott, *Oliver Cromwell*, IV, 728-732; *HMC, Sixth Report*, 443, Waynwright to Bradshaw, 12 March 1657/58.
[34] Jones, *Royal Politician*, 33-35; Hutton, *The British Republic*, 130.
[35] Turner, *Memoirs*, 121.

The Danes, the Dutch and Oliver Cromwell

In late 1651, possibly due to the defeat of the Stuart forces at Worcester, Frederik III made positive overtures towards the English Republic. After all, Frederik had to place the economic interest of his dominions over the well-being of his fugitive cousin, Charles II. It was decided in the *Rigsråd* to follow the Dutch example and recognise England as a 'free republic' and to send an embassy to London to secure friendly relations.[36] The Danish envoy, Henrik Villumsen Rosenvinge, was ordered to find out what the English plans were for future relations with the Dutch and Sweden. As Rosenvinge travelled to England, Richard Bradshaw made his way to Denmark – though apparently Frederik III put his feasting before his desire to see the Republican envoy.[37]

The death of William II of Orange in the United Provinces in October 1650 saw the harder line Republicans there take power.[38] The new Dutch leadership valued the economic possibilities of the Commonwealth and quickly thereafter recognised the English Republic. In response a large English embassy under Oliver St. John and Walter Strickland travelled to The Hague to form an alliance. St. John suggested a union between the two republics that would have seen the Commonwealth of England and Ireland combine with the United Provinces to form a single commercial and diplomatic unit.[39] The Dutch rejected this proposal, largely out of the strength of anti-English feeling amongst the populace, but also since St. John demanded an agreement for mutual aid against the enemies of either republic. Such an arrangement would, anyway have been incompatible with the treaty of confederation, *Forbunds og Redemtionstraktaten,* agreed upon between the Danes and the Dutch in September 1649.[40]

Oliver St. John had been very bitter at the rejection of his overtures for unification with the United Provinces, and subsequently introduced the provocative Navigation Act in the English Parliament in August 1651. When this became law in October, England and the United Provinces seemed destined to go to war.[41] In May 1652 a fleet under Admiral

---

[36] Abbott, *Oliver Cromwell*, II, 489 and 524; *Danmark-Norges Traktater*, V, 136.

[37] *Danmark-Norges Traktater*, V, 136; *HMC, Sixth Report*, 436. Waynwright to Bradshaw, 14 January 1652.

[38] Howatt, *Stuart and Cromwellian Foreign Policy*, 70.

[39] Jones, *Royal Politician*, 22; Howatt, *Stuart and Cromwellian Foreign Policy*, 70; Hutton, *The British Republic*, 55.

[40] *Danmark-Norges Traktater*, V, 16 and 626-650; Abbott, *Oliver Cromwell*, II, 419-420. J. A. Fridericia, *Adelsvældens Sidste Dage. Danmarks Historie fra Christian IV's død til enevældens indførelse 1648-1660* (Copenhagen, 1894), 114.

[41] Fridericia, *Adelsvældens Sidste Dage*, 208; Abbott, *Oliver Cromwell*, II, 485 and 489; Hutton, *The British Republic*, 55.

Martin Tromp was sent to protect the Dutch merchant ships and there was a serious encounter with the English under Admiral Blake ostensibly over a breach of nautical etiquette. A Dutch envoy was sent to the English Parliament but could not prevent England declaring war on the United Provinces.[42] The Dutch resident in Elsinore pointed out to Frederik III that should the Dutch succumb to England then his kingdoms would be next in line for attack, particularly because of the blood ties between the British and Danish royal houses. A further Dutch envoy was sent to ask for 15 warships on loan from Denmark, or even permission to rent them for two months.[43] As a result of these approaches, the Danes increased their naval activity in the Sound. Some 21 English merchant ships in Elsinore, awaiting convoy to England, were warned to return to Copenhagen or face attack by the Dutch.[44] Under the guise of protecting the English, the Danes were effectively taking them hostage. Eighteen ships returned to Copenhagen, and the other three were taken by the Dutch.[45]

In mid-April 1652 the English Parliament replied favourably to Frederik III's overtures for a renewed confederation.[46] This came as a direct result of the Danish blockade of their ships and Dutch privateering in the Sound. The Danish agents, Reedtz and Rosencrantz, were to draft a treaty which would give both countries' subjects freedom of trade as long as existing tolls and laws were abided by. Frederik also wished to take any opportunity provided to remind Cromwell, in his capacity as head of the Commonwealth of England, Ireland and now also Scotland, that Denmark-Norway retained an inherited right to the Orkney and Shetland islands.[47] The agents had an audience with the Westminster Parliament in May, followed by a conference with the State Council in June. The negotiations appeared to be going well and the agreement of a renewed confederation between England and Denmark-Norway looked imminent by September. Unfortunately for Frederik III, the meetings of

---

[42] *Danmark-Norges Traktater*, V, 17; Howatt, *Stuart and Cromwellian Foreign Policy*, 71-72; Abbott, *Oliver Cromwell*, II, 541-571; Hutton, *The British Republic*, 55.

[43] *Danmark-Norges Traktater*, V, 18; Abbott, *Oliver Cromwell*, II, 555.

[44] DRA, TKUA England A II 16. 'Information regarding Anthony Knipp, an Englishman, Chief of Customs in Norway and Favourite of the King of Denmark, from the Eastlands Merchants, 21 October 1652'.

[45] Fridericia, *Adelsvældens Sidste Dage*, 210-211; *Danmark-Norges Traktater*, V, 19; *HMC, Sixth Report*, 436, Waynwright to Bradshaw, 28 January 1652. Waynwright described the seizing of the English ships as 'the stingking'st action that ever prince did show, and cannot be forgot'.

[46] DRA, TKUA A 1, English Parliament to Frederik III, 13 April 1652. A printed version can be found in Patterson, *Milton State Papers*, 66-69.

[47] Fridericia, *Adelsvældens Sidste Dage*, 210; *Danmark-Norges Traktater*, V, 136-7.

his ambassadors with the English coincided with the first hostilities between the Dutch and the Commonwealth which brought Denmark-Norway into the war on the Dutch side under the terms of the 1649 alliance.[48]

Charles II saw an advantage in the Anglo-Dutch hostility and strongly urged Frederik III to support the United Provinces in their war against the English 'rebels'.[49] Charles pressed the notion of a three way alliance of Denmark-Norway, the United Provinces and the exiled Royalists, offering his fleet under Prince Rupert and Royalist privateers as his commitment to the war.[50] Charles also, apparently, offered the Dutch the Orkney Isles and the Isles of Scilly in return for money and military support.[51] The offer was rejected by the Dutch and was anyway quite a desperate move by Charles given the ongoing Danish claims to the Orkneys.

In response to Danish interference with Commonwealth shipping, and strong protests from the English merchants in Copenhagen, an English war fleet of 18 ships anchored off Elsinore in late September 1652. The next day two state councillors were sent to negotiate with the English admiral, Captain Ball. They complained at the fleet's unannounced arrival, particularly as Frederik III presently had envoys in England and was, in their diplomatic words, 'so generously protecting' the English merchant ships in Copenhagen from Dutch attack.[52] Captain Ball produced instructions to retrieve the English merchant ships and convoy them back to England. The Dutch agent successfully encouraged the Danes to refuse the English admiral's passage to Copenhagen to present his papers to Frederik III. The Danes rejected Captain Ball's instructions saying that it could lead to open war 'right in front of the king's windows' at Elsinore.[53] The English merchant ships were guaranteed 'continued safety' in Copenhagen, and Captain Ball returned to England without them. As a result, the English Parliament issued orders on 17 October to seize all Danish and Norwegian ships on the Thames. This caused an immediate protest from the Danish envoy, Rosenvinge, who

---

[48] DRA, TKUA England A II 16, f.5. Council of State's answer to the Danish Ambassador, 14 September 1652; *Danmark-Norges Traktater*, V, 138-142.

[49] PRO SP75/16 ff. 218-220. Charles II to Frederik III of Denmark-Norway and Queen Christina of Sweden, 20/30 August 1652.

[50] DRA, TKUA England A1. Charles II to Frederik III, February 1653; Jones, *Royal Politician*, 26.

[51] Jones, *Royal Politician*, 26.

[52] DRA, TKUA England A II 16. A narrative of the matter of fact concerning the detention of the English merchant ships in Copenhagen by command of the King of Denmark, 1652; Fridericia, *Adelsvældens Sidste Dage*, 211; *Danmark-Norges Traktater*, V, 21-22.

[53] Fridericia, *Adelsvældens Sidste Dage*, 211; *Danmark-Norges Traktater*, V, 21-22.

wrote to the English Council of State the very next day to complain.[54]
The Danish ambassador suggested that the English should not act so
rashly since the full reason for the hindrance of the English ships in the
Sound had not yet been established. This stalling did not impress the
English who asked the Danish envoys for an explanation of what had
happened to Captain Ball's mission. These agents of course knew
nothing about these events and opted to return to Denmark for
instructions. The English resident in Hamburg, Richard Bradshaw,
travelled to Copenhagen in late December 1652 to demand the restitution
of the arrested ships. He argued that since the Danish ambassadors 'were
in actuall treaty of confederation' with the Commonwealth, the refusal to
allow the ships home was a remarkable decision. The Commonwealth
also demanded the return of the cannon which had been stripped by the
Danes from the English Republican ship, *Antelope*, which had been
wrecked on Jutland. The Danes kept demanding satisfaction for the
infraction against the Danish king's sovereignty by Captain Ball and his
fleet the previous September.[55]

As the Anglo-Danish negotiations continued, the Danes concluded a
new treaty with the Estates-General of the United Provinces in February
which was ratified by the Dutch in May 1653.[56] This realignment of the
Danes and the Dutch received a cool response from the exiled Royalists.
Sir Edward Nicholas informed Sir Edward Hyde of the new alliance
noting that the king of Denmark-Norway would, in future, follow the
lead of the United Provinces since his business had now become so
closely connected with that state.[57] According to Nicholas, this new
alliance signalled the end of any concern that Frederik III had for the
Stuart cause. In June, after bitter naval exchanges, the Dutch wanted to
send envoys to England to settle a peace agreement with the
Commonwealth. Frederik asked that the Danes' interests be safeguarded
by these Dutch envoys. Nicholas felt concerned by this and again warned
that if the Dutch were successful in making a peace with the 'English
rebels' the Danes would not even do anything privately to support
Charles II, let alone publicly.[58]

---

[54] *Danmark-Norges Traktater*, V, 23-24 and 142-143; PRO SP75/16 ff. 218-220. Eric
       Rosenvinge and R. Reed to the Council of State, 18 October 1652.
[55] DRA, TKUA England A II 16. Council of the Commonwealth to the *Rigsråd*, 9 November
       1652. An almost identical letter of the same date is printed in Patterson, *Milton State Papers*,
       102-103; *Danmark-Norges Traktater*, V, 25.
[56] *Danmark-Norges Traktater*, V, 28-38. 'Alliancetraktat mellem Danmark-Norge og
       Generalstaterne, 8/18 February 1653'; Israel, *The Dutch Republic*, 721.
[57] *The Nicholas Papers*, II, 9-10. Nicholas to Hyde, 1 May 1653.
[58] *The Nicholas Papers*, II, 16. Nicholas to Hyde, 21/31 July 1653.

Frederik III decided to enquire if a Danish envoy would be welcome in England to join the negotiations then ongoing between the Dutch and English. Indeed, he ordered the Duke of Holstein's agent, Paul Wurtz, to offer the Commonwealth peace and friendship and declared Denmark-Norway and all her dominions to be neutral if that was agreeable to the English.[59] This overture went unnoticed by the Royalists and anyway Nicholas doubted that the Danes would actually do such a thing since their relationship with the Commonwealth appeared to be deteriorating at the time.[60] Indeed, the Royalists believed that Frederik III had recommended to the Dutch ambassador in Copenhagen that the United Provinces should also begin to help Charles II again. So optimistic had Nicholas become that he declared 'I hope, this being the first king that hath done himself the honour to recommend His Majesty's cause to these States, that other princes will for their own honour and interest of monarchy follow so princely and pious an example'.[61] Unfortunately for Charles, the returning Dutch ambassador confirmed the renewed Anglo-Danish overtures for peace. He related Frederik III's demands to be included in the peace negotiations in England. Frederik also employed commercial pressure to ensure he would be included in the talks. In early February 1653, the Danish king had ordered the English ships in Copenhagen to be unloaded and their cargoes stored in warehouses to prevent the ruining of the goods.[62]

The following October, the English merchants drafted a petition to Oliver Cromwell which noted the 'extraordinary damage' done to the petitioners by the king of Denmark. But the petition included a plea for Denmark-Norway to be included in the Anglo-Dutch treaty negotiations suggesting that Frederik had placed pressure on them to do so. After all, his need for peace had become more pressing with rumours that Sweden and England were contemplating the conquest of the main Danish island of Zealand to gain control of the Sound.[63] The Dutch decision to uphold Frederik's requests in London almost ruined the peace talks and the ambassadors had to leave England in January 1654 without achieving anything. Cromwell did not initially accept the inclusion of Denmark-Norway in the peace talks. He later changed his mind as he could use this opportunity for communication with the Dutch as a pretext for

[59]   PRO SP75/16 f.223. Paul Wurtz to the Council of State, 24 August 1653.
[60]   *The Nicholas Papers*, II, 23-24. Nicholas to Hyde 6/16 October 1653.
[61]   *The Nicholas Papers*, II, 23-24. Nicholas to Hyde 6/16 October 1653.
[62]   *Danmark-Norges Traktater*, V, 27 and 143.
[63]   PRO SP75/16 f. 233. Letter of Petition to Oliver Cromwell Lord Protector of the Commonwealth of England, Scotland and Ireland, 28 December 1653; *The Nicholas Papers*, II, 30. Nicholas to Hyde, 4 December (ns) 1653; *Danmark-Norges Traktater*, V, 143-144.

holding secret negotiations.[64] Unaware that they were being used as a cover for a secret Anglo-Dutch agenda, the Danes were very keen to be part of these new negotiations. Frederik sent Henrik Rosenvinge to The Hague in late January 1654 to take part in the talks with England, but also to see if the Danish subjects whose ships had been seized on the Thames could also be compensated.[65]

But even as Frederik III negotiated with Cromwell, Dutch agents warned of an English plan to send a fleet against Denmark-Norway and to occupy the Sound.[66] This scheme had been hatched by the Danish exile, Korfitz Ulfeldt. The former Danish councillor contemplated ways to hurt the Danish government and Stuart exiles who he believed had slandered him. He absolutely astounded Bulstrode Whitelocke by describing in detail the best way for the English to capture the Danish cities of Elsinore and Copenhagen. He argued that he believed that the government of his wife's brother had become tyrannical and that Denmark-Norway needed to be released from it. Queen Christina seemed to support this plan and told Whitelocke that, on the fall of Zealand, he could become commander of all English and Swedish forces on the island.[67] Given the Swedish fear of Dutch reaction to an invasion of Denmark-Norway, the looming peace between the Dutch and the English and uncertainty over Queen Christina's future, the invasion plans were shelved. Due to Ulfeldt's bitterness, however, he also informed the Cromwellians that a clause in the treaties between James VI and Christian IV meant that on their deaths the Copenhagen government could buy the Orkney Islands for £13,000. Ulfeldt suggested that a clause should be inserted in the Anglo-Dutch treaty negotiations repudiating Denmark's claim, therefore securing the islands for the Commonwealth, though this did not come about.[68] Henrik Rosenvinge had asked the Dutch agents in England to negotiate on behalf of Frederik III and they officially worked towards settling the amount of Danish compensation to be paid for seized English goods. Simultaneously they undertook secret talks designed at keeping the House of Orange out of the Dutch government. A peace between the Protectorate and the United

---

[64] *Danmark-Norges Traktater*, V, 144-146.

[65] DRA, TKUA England A I. Frederik III to Oliver Cromwell, 4 February 1654; Abbott, *Oliver Cromwell*, II, 182. Abbott related that Frederik III hastened to send his envoy believing that the compensation of the English ships was the main concern and that the Danes hoped that this would be the only compensation Cromwell would want for peace.

[66] Fridericia, *Adelsvældens Sidste Dage*, 213-214; Abbott, *Oliver Cromwell*, II, 224 and 287.

[67] Spalding, *Bulstrode Whitelocke*, 328 and 348, 21 January 1653/54 and 5 April 1654.

[68] Spalding, *Bulstrode Whitelocke*, 352. footnote. The supply of such information to the enemies of Denmark later led to Ulfeldt's conviction for treason, though he escaped Denmark and died in exile.

Provinces was secured by the Treaty of London in April. These proceedings also led to the May 1654 Act of Exclusion, virtually dictated by Cromwell.[69] This Act outlawed the House of Orange from taking power in the United Provinces and ensured that Charles II received no official support from that quarter. Further, the new agreements meant the expulsion of all remaining Stuart Royalists from the United Provinces.[70]

The Dutch were not only taking a hand in Stuart affairs, but they now interceded for, and directed Danish-Norwegian diplomacy as well.[71] The Dutch had decided that their agents in England would be authorised to sign an agreement with Cromwell about the compensations required from Denmark-Norway which the Dutch would then pay.[72] Thus, Danish international diplomacy had been undertaken by the Dutch and delivered to the Danes as a *fait accompli*. Rosenvinge travelled to England in April but only got an audience with Cromwell after the Anglo-Dutch treaty had already been signed.[73] The Danes were extremely upset to learn of the agreement undertaken without their approval but there was not really anything to be done about it. In the same month Cromwell sent John Edwards and Michael Evans to Copenhagen to take the remaining English ships and goods back to England under article 28 of the Anglo-Dutch agreement. They also sought compensation of 20,000 *rigsdaler* for the cargo that Frederik had sold and added that both points should be complied within six days.[74] The requests made in Copenhagen by the English were reinforced in London in the answer given to Rosenvinge.[75] The Danish king would not agree to this until his own demands regarding the Danish ships on the Thames were met. In any case, Frederik III could only return 18 ships and 1 cargo load of goods. The rest had been sold despite Rosenvinge's assurances that there would be full compliance to the Dutch terms from the Danes.[76] Negotiations dragged on in Denmark until September. However, with the Dutch already signed up to their own treaty, Denmark-Norway could not really hope to secure much better terms than those on offer. The Danes signed in mid-September, Frederik ratified it in October 1654 and Cromwell

---

[69]   Abbott, *Oliver Cromwell*, II, 300; *HMC, Sixth Report,* 437, James Waynwright to Richard Bradshaw, 7, 21 and 28 April 1654; Hutton, *The British Republic*, 108.

[70]   Howatt, *Stuart and Cromwellian Foreign Policy*, 75; Jones, *Royal Politician*, 26; Hutton, *The British Republic*, 55.

[71]   Abbott, *Oliver Cromwell*, III, 300.

[72]   *Danmark-Norges Traktater*, V, 145-146.

[73]   Abbott, *Oliver Cromwell*, III, 287.

[74]   DRA, TKUA England A II 16. Michael Evans and John Edwards to Frederik III, 2 June 1654.

[75]   DRA, TKUA England A II 16. N. Fiennes and W. Strickland to Rosenvinge, 7 June 1654.

[76]   *Danmark-Norges Traktater*, V, 151; Abbott, *Oliver Cromwell*, III, 263 and 304.

himself towards the end of February 1655.[77]

The Protectorate and the Northern Wars 1657-1660

Despite the 1654 treaty, Cromwell did not consider Denmark-Norway to be important in terms of his foreign policy.[78] Within months of ratifying the new treaty, he threatened to issue letters of reprisal against Frederik III for a private debt owed by the late Christian IV to one deceased Peter Rychaut.[79] He further insisted that Frederik pay compensation for the English ships arrested in the Sound in 1645 and intervene in several other cases raised by English merchants.[80] Cromwell knew that Frederik was not in a strong position to resist such threats and that the new treaty had only been a matter of convenience for both parties. Indeed, the new 'Protector' proved repeatedly that he believed Sweden to be a far more important nation to him as the Baltic region once more erupted into war. None-the-less, Frederik continued to stall payment. While he may have believed he had scored a point off Cromwell on this subject, he did himself no favours which he found to his cost when hostilities broke out between Denmark-Norway and Sweden in 1657.

The 1657 war had, at least from a Danish-Norwegian perspective, been coming since the opening of the Polish-Swedish war of 1655.[81] The Danes launched a pre-emptive strike and attacked the Swedes, catching them off guard when they were embroiled in their Polish campaign. Frederik III believed that since the Swedish king and his army were physically in Poland-Lithuania, there was little they could do to prevent complete Danish success. The object of the war was primarily to reverse the losses suffered during the Torstensson War of 1643-1645.[82] The Danes had, however, removed one of their potential allies by their pre-emptive strike. By initiating hostilities, the Danish defence treaty with the Dutch was invalidated although other sources of support for the Danes, albeit limited initially, came from the Russians, Brandenburgers

---

[77] *Danmark-Norges Traktater*, V, 152-159. 'Traktat mellem Oliver Cromwell, Protector af England, og Kong Frederik III af Danmark-Norge', 15 September 1654. See also Frederik's views on the treaty in Patterson, *Milton State Papers*, 497-498. Frederik III to Oliver Cromwell, 16 February 1656.

[78] *HMC, Sixth Report*, 440, James Waynwright to Richard Bradshaw, 9 May 1656.

[79] PRO SP75/16 f.236. Oliver Cromwell to Frederik III, 30 April 1655.

[80] DRA, TKUA England A I, Cromwell to Frederik III, 23 and 28 November 1655; Patterson, *Milton State Papers*, 206-211. Oliver Cromwell to Frederik III, February 1656.

[81] Fridericia, *Adelsvældens Sidste Dage*, 265-476. A Swedish perspective is given in G. Landberg, *Den Svenska Utrikes Politikens Historia* (Stockholm, 1952), vol. 1: 3, 101-122; Lind, *Hæren og Magten*, 92.

[82] Lisk, *The Struggle for Supremacy in the Baltic*, 99-100. The provinces in question being Gotland, Herjeland, Jemtland and occupied Halland.

and the Poles.[83] Austria too promised qualified support if the Danes went to war. Unfortunately for Frederik, by a series of well recorded diplomatic negotiations and military skill, Karl X managed to disengage his army from his war in Poland-Lithuania. He then marched his forces overland, avoiding any conflict from the Duke of Holstein while also receiving aid from Hamburg, a constant thorn in the side of Danish monarchs. Karl X invaded Denmark-Norway from the south of Jutland and the Danes had to scramble to find support for their cause. In desperation, Oliver Cromwell was approached to act as a middleman in the conflict.

It was in the interest of British trade for the war to stop so that commerce could continue through the Sound. But the path to reconciliation did not take the route the Danes expected. Far from acting as an arbitrator of peace, Cromwell promised the Swedes 1,400 men (some reports even said 6,000 men) to help subjugate Jutland for Karl X. By December, about 700 of these English troops had already arrived, with the remainder expected presently.[84] The Danes were caught by surprise at the speed of the Swedish advance and their army withdrew from Jutland to Fredricksodde. The Poles and the Brandenburgers quickly made alliances with the Danes and it looked like the Swedish army might be cut off in Jutland. The triple alliance was defeated by the freak weather conditions which froze the Little and Great Belts. Not only did the freezing of the sea prevent the Swedes from being cornered in Jutland as suspected, but the ice also prevented the Danish-Norwegian navy from being used to hinder the Swedes' advance. This allowed the Swedish army to walk from Jutland to the island of Fyn then over to Taasinge, Langeland, Laaland and Falster to Zealand.

In August 1657, Oliver Cromwell sent Philip Meadowes to Frederik III and William Jephson to Karl X to offer mediation between Denmark-Norway and Sweden.[85] Cromwell stressed that this could only be done so long as Frederik did not associate with the Spanish, Austrians or Hungarians or any other state which might render a peace with Sweden more difficult – and whom Cromwell directly blamed for the war.[86] In

---

[83] Turner, *Memoirs*, 124.

[84] For the Republican support to the Swedes see *HMC, Sixth Report*, 436, Waynwright to Bradshaw, 22 May 1657; *The Nicholas Papers*, IV, 21. Sir Henry de Vic to Sir Nicholas, 2 December 1657; Howatt, *Stuart and Cromwellian Foreign Policy*, 80. Howatt argues that these men were volunteers which he allowed Karl X to raise in return for trading concessions in Swedish dominated trading ports.

[85] T. Venning, *Cromwellian Foreign Policy* (Hampshire and London, 1995), 207-212.

[86] PRO SP75/16 ff. 241-245. Instructions unto Philip Meadowe upon his repair to the King of Denmark, August 1657; DRA, TKUA, England, A I. Oliver Cromwell to Frederik III, 20 August 1657. Cromwell's attachment of blame to Frederik's Catholic allies can be found in

other words, Frederik had to abandon his allies and submit himself to the arbitration of the leader of a state which had provided troops to his enemies. Both Denmark-Norway and Sweden supplied written declarations allowing for Cromwellian mediation in the conflict.[87] Cromwell's proposals to Frederik III, Karl X and the various German princes were plainly intended to prevent the Spanish or Imperialists from gaining an alliance with either Scandinavian kingdom and thus disrupting trade between the Protectorate and the Baltic.[88] With Copenhagen at the mercy of Karl X, the Danes sued for peace resulting in the Treaty of Roskilde in February 1658. This settlement meant that the Danes had to cede the regions of Skåne, Blekinge and Halland to the Swedes while the Norwegians had to give up Trondheim and Bohus. In May 1658, Philip Meadowes added his name to the *coup de grâce* as a signatory to the document of cession whereby Frederik III, under pressure from the Swedes, ceded Schleswig and all accompanying responsibilities over to the cousin of the Danish king, Frederik, Duke of Holstein.[89]

Despite the new peace agreement, problems quickly developed between the two Scandinavian monarchs. Karl X wanted the Sound closed to foreign warships which Frederik III was not keen on, but in little condition to refuse. Meadowes, however, managed to intervene to ensure that the Swedes moderated this clause.[90] Yet, despite Frederik striving for an accommodation with Karl X, the Swedish king attacked the Danes and the second war began. In the renewed conflict the Frederik III, no longer the aggressor, received support from the Dutch while the English Protectorate assumed a position somewhat removed from their former Swedish allies.[91] These two powers decided to use force to get a treaty, though Karl X remained defiant. In 1658, Protectorate forces under Sir George Ayscue left England with four merchant ships and an English fleet under Admiral Montegue destined for the Sound. Their intention was to find a peaceful settlement to the conflict between the Danes and the Swedes. They were also to hinder the transportation of German reinforcements trying to get through to break

Patterson, *Milton State Papers*, 346-349 and 390-391. Oliver Cromwell to Karl X, 30 March and 4 June 1658.

[87] DRA, TKUA, England, A II 16. Both declarations are kept together in the Copenhagen archive.

[88] Abbott, *Oliver Cromwell*, IV, 605-606.

[89] PRO SP75/16 f. 245. Cession of Holstein by Frederik III, 29 May 1658; *Danmark-Norges Traktater*, V, 218-243; Lisk, *The Struggle for Supremacy*, 100.

[90] Venning, *Cromwellian Foreign Policy*, 213.

[91] Israel, *The Dutch Republic*, 736.

the siege of Copenhagen.[92] Peace, again it seems, had to be imposed rather than negotiated.

Rumours began circulating in 1659 that the English fleet did not wish to prejudice the king of Denmark's interest; indeed the English fleet were widely believed to have refused Karl X's orders to blockade Copenhagen.[93] Their actions were supported by the English Parliament which, freed from Richard Cromwell's Protectorate regime, appeared to be taking a pro-Danish stance in the war.[94] Frederik III therefore encouraged Rosenvinge, once more in London, to point out that the current negotiations for peace contravened the 1654 treaty between the Protectorate and Denmark-Norway. The Danes played on the aspects of the negotiations which they knew gave the English scope for concern. If the Danes could not retain the means to defend themselves against future Swedish aggression or became subject to Swedish power, then Britain's interests in the Baltic would be jeopardised.[95] Despite the intention of the English Parliament to aid Frederik III, the northern conflict eventually resolved itself with the death of Karl X in February 1660 which removed the main obstacle to peace. There soon followed the three treaties of Olive, Copenhagen and Kardis which settled Swedish differences with her Baltic neighbours and temporarily calmed the troubles in the Baltic region.[96] Yet even before any of these treaties were concluded, Charles II had arrived in Britain to reclaim his three kingdoms.

The failure of Royalist uprisings to topple Oliver Cromwell's government throughout the 1650s proved to be symptomatic of the dictator's great power. Peace and trade agreements between the Protectorate and the United Provinces, Sweden and Denmark-Norway in 1654 were indicative that his strength had been recognised abroad. Portugal too had been brought to peace at a heavy price and France

---

[92] *The Nicholas Papers*, IV, 88-91. 'A Giles' to Nicholas, 1/11 April 1659; Richard Cromwell anounced the departure of his forces to Karl X in a letter dated 13 October 1638. The letter can be found in Patterson, *Milton State Papers*, 407-409; R. C. Anderson, 'English Officers in Sweden' in *Mariner's Mirror*, XII, (1926), 458.

[93] *The Nicholas Papers*, IV, 118-120. Sir Alexander Hume to Nicholas, 6 May 1659 (ns).

[94] Patterson, *Milton State Papers*, 432-433. William Lenthal [Speaker of the Parliament] to Frederik III, 15 May 1659.

[95] PRO SP75/16 ff. 256 and 259. Rosenvinge to the Council of State, July 1659.

[96] Danish-Swedish hostilities were ended by the treaty of Copenhagen on 27 May 1660. The Peace of Olivia between Sweden and Poland-Lithuania in 1660 ended the feud between the contesting branches of the Vasa dynasty when John Casimir gave up all claims to the throne of Sweden. The Swedish-Russian peace was settled at Kardis in Estonia in 1661. See A. Kan, *Sverige och Ryssland ett 1200-Årigt Förhållande* (Stockholm, 1996), 70-73; Lisk, *The Struggle for Supremacy*, 102-104.

began her own negotiations with the Protectorate. For British Royalists, 1654 marked their lowest ebb in the struggle to retain international allies. Only the instability of the Protectorate in the period following Oliver Cromwell's death altered the political situation for the three kingdoms. The contesting political and military factions of England revealed themselves, as they all sought to secure positions of advantage. Richard Cromwell was soon deposed and civil war once more loomed in England. As a counter-revolutionary, Charles II had failed to win back his kingdoms. Yet by carefully managing his image abroad, he could be presented to the three kingdoms as one of the few men that could govern by constitutional and. legal methods. Charles promised to unite his former kingdoms by agreeing to pardon everybody with the exception of the regicides, and the Stuart Restoration was secured.[97] The king arrived at Dover in late May 1660 having been restored without any significant help from a foreign power other than being allowed to remain in various countries for limited periods of time.[98]

Only the month after Charles II returned to London, Frederik III sent Henrik Villumsen Rosenvinge to him to safeguard Danish and Norwegian interests in Britain.[99] The Dane delivered a letter in which Frederik announced the imminent arrival of a full embassy to congratulate Charles on his restitution which apparently pleased the king. Another envoy from Copenhagen, Frederik Ahlefeldt, was authorised to sign an interim alliance agreement in June and in early July he was instructed to seek a private audience with Great Britain. During this meeting Ahlefeldt specifically intended to propose a defensive alliance based on the 1621 agreement between King James and Christian IV. The audience took place at the end of August and Charles agreed to a new alliance, but on his terms. Ironically, he used the Cromwelliam alliance from 1654 rather than his grandfather's one as the template for the renewed Stuart-Oldenburg alliance. In a move typical of Stuart-Oldenburg relations he opportunistically exploited the advantageous conditions won by his erstwhile enemy, Oliver Cromwell to make some gains with his kinsman Frederik. This treaty was finally signed in February and ratified by Charles in May 1661, the first of the restored

---

[97] Jones, *Royal Politician*, 32. The news of return of the Stuart dynasty to Britain was received in a variety of ways. Sir Thomas Urquhart of Cromarty, an exiled survivor from Worcester, is alleged to have died in a bought of hysterical laughter when he heard the news of Charles II's Restoration. See T. Royle, *The Macmillan Companion to Scottish Literature* (London, 1983), 306-307.

[98] Howatt, *Stuart and Cromwellian Foreign Policy*, 95.

[99] For more on the period from 1660 until the Stuart-Oldenburg treaty of 1667 see Schoolcraft, 'England and Denmark, 1660-1667', 457-479.

monarchy with any foreign state.[100] However Charles viewed the Danes with suspicion since, in his eyes, his cousin had let him down while the Stuart Court had been exiled. Any denial of that by Frederik III could be challenged by the words of Rosenvinge from the previous year. The Danish ambassador he had spoken of the great friendship with the Protectorate which he believed to be so good that 'we cannot doubt but that there was something of divine providence co-operating, so we may rest confident of its future success'.[101]

Crown Prince Christian of Denmark-Norway arrived in London in 1662 to re-strengthen familial ties with the House of Stuart. His visit was followed by that of Leonora Christina who hoped to collect money owed to her husband, Korfitz Ulfeldt, by Charles II. Despite an initial warm reception she ended up being arrested at Dover after a request by Frederik III.[102] The visit by the Crown Prince and co-operation in the arrest of Leonora Christina may have lulled Charles into believing Stuart-Oldenburg relations were truly improving. However, a series of unratified trade and diplomatic agreements between Copenhagen and London highlighted deteriorating relations over the next few · years. Charles II expected that Frederik would join in an offensive alliance against the Dutch, but in this he was sorely disappointed.[103] Instead, Frederik renewed his existing alliance with the Dutch Republic which more or less coincided with a British declaration of hostilities directed to the Dutch fleet in Norway in July 1665.[104] These developments led Charles into a war with Frederik, albeit as a side show to the Second Anglo-Dutch War (1664-1667). The Stuart-Oldenburg part of the conflict centred on Bergen and the Sound with the Danish-Norwegian fleet effectively blocking their waters to English shipping throughout 1666. The Danish conflict was brought to a close at the same time as the Dutch war by the treaty of Breda in July 1667, although rumours of further actions against the Danes persisted thereafter.[105] These did not

---

[100] *Danmark-Norges Traktater*, V, 389-410. 'Alliance og Handelstraktat mellem Danmark-Norge og Storbritannien', 13 February 1661; Schoolcraft, 'England and Denmark, 1660-1667', 457.

[101] PRO SP75/16 ff. 256-259 and f. 271. Rosenvinge to the Council of State, July 1659 and to the English Parliament, 13 July 1659.

[102] Schoolcraft, 'England and Denmark, 1660-1667', 458.

[103] The unratified treaties can be found in *Danmark-Norges Traktater*, VI, 38-51 and 53-58; See also Schoolcraft, 'England and Denmark, 1660-1667', 461.

[104] *Danmark-Norges Traktater*, VI, 58-60. 'Den Engelske Gesandt Gilbert Talbots Deklaration angaaende det paatænkte Angreb paa den nederlandske Handelsflaade i Bergens Havn, 22 Juli 1665'; For more on the Dutch-Danish treaty see Israel, *The Dutch Republic*, 771-773.

[105] *Danmark-Norges Traktater*, VI, 212. 'Fredstraktat mellem Danmark-Norge og Storbritannien, 21/31 Juli 1667'; A. Bryant, *The letters of King Charles II* (New York, 1968 reprint), 221. Charles II to Madame, 14 June 1668; For the failure of English policy see

happen. None-the-less there had been a war between two former allies that radically altered the British relationship with Denmark-Norway from where it had stood in the reign of King James.

It was not just the external politics of the House of Stuart that had changed. The first decade of the reign of Charles II also witnessed a massive realignment between the House of Stuart and the various nations and factions of the British Isles. The executing of Argyll, the reintroduction of Episcopacy and the hounding of Presbyterians exacerbated this in Scotland after 1660. Thus Charles proved that he cared little for the majority of the Scottish population whom he drove into a hostile anti-Stuart posture. Those men who worked for the new Anglo-British incarnation of the Stuart polity during the reign of Charles II normally represented the English rather than the Scottish interest. From that juncture onwards it becomes anomalous to consider a positive political connection binding the Scots and the House of Stuart, let alone a Stuart driven relationship between Scotland and Denmark-Norway. Since the end of the Solemn League and Covenant, the English had dominated British foreign politics. That did not change after the Restoration and from 1660 onwards, those Scots that were to be found in Denmark-Norway were usually working for themselves rather than any national Scottish *or* British interest.

Schoolcraft, 'England and Denmark, 1660-1667', 478-479.

CHAPTER EIGHT

Military Service I:
The promotion of Scots into the
Danish-Norwegian military establishment

Between 1589 and 1660, the military presence of Britons or Irishmen in the Danish-Norwegian armed forces was always dominated by Scots. Indeed, apart from a few occasions, English, Irish and Welsh participation was so statistically irrelevant in the reign of Christian IV that in military terms this aspect of the Stuart-Oldenburg alliance remained a firmly Scottish concern. That said, it would be impossible to understand the role of Scots in this capacity without some background analysis of Scottish and military migrations elsewhere. Scottish soldiers who served abroad at the opening of the seventeenth century represented the continuation of a tradition of military migration dating back to the middle ages. Since the 15th century, the *Garde Ecossais* served as the personal bodyguard of the king of France.[1] By the seventeenth century, however, there were few actual Scots in the *Garde* although Frenchmen of Scottish ancestry continued to serve until the end of the century. Throughout that period, Scotsmen were more likely to appear in countries more politically or theologically aligned with their own, particularly the Dutch and Scandinavian armies. In 1572, the Scottish Privy Council issued a proclamation calling on able-bodied Scotsmen to fight in The Netherlands. Over the next eight years, some 3,000 Scots were levied for service in the Low Countries to assist in the fight against Catholic Spain. Thereafter, in 1586, a permanent 'British' brigade consisting of three English and three Scottish regiments was formed as part of a multiple alliance between England, the Scots and the Dutch with Robert Dudley, the Earl of Leicester, at its head.[2] By the time the British-Dutch Brigade became established, however, Scots had also become regular members of the Scandinavian armies.

---

[1]   W. Forbes-Leith, *The Scots Men-at-Arms and Life Guards in France, 1458-1830* (2 vols., Edinburgh, 1882).

[2]   Anon., *An Historical Account of the British Regiments Employed since the Reign of Queen Elizabeth and King James I in the Formation and Defence of the Dutch Republic* (London, 1794); J. Ferguson ed, *Papers illustrating the history of the Scots Brigade in the Service of the United Netherlands, 1572-1772* (3 vols, Edinburgh, 1899); G. Parker, *The Dutch Revolt* (London, 1990), 148; Israel, *The Dutch Republic*, 220-229; J. P. Puype, 'Victory at Nieuwpoort, 2 July 1600' in M. van der Hoeven ed, *Exercise of Arms; Warfare in The Netherlands, 1568-1648* (Leiden, 1997), 70.

During 1573, officers such as Archibald Ruthven recruited regular companies of Scots for Sweden.[3] Scottish enlistment continued and by 1593 there were three independent troops of Scottish cavalry in Swedish service commanded by Henry Lyell, William Ruthven and Abraham Young.[4] Across the Scandinavian frontier from Sweden, Danish records show that Scottish officers and soldiers were stationed in both Jutland and Fyn by 1570.[5] These soldiers had a good reputation and soon after Christian IV attained his majority, Colonel William Stewart left Denmark for Scotland with orders from Christian IV to raise between 3-5,000 Scottish troops for service against the Swedes.[6] It is not clear how many of these soldiers arrived, but throughout the seventeenth century Scottish soldiers were found all over the Danish-Norwegian kingdoms. By the middle of the century, in Russia, Poland, Scandinavia, France and the United Provinces, Scots were either found in significant numbers and/or positions of prominence.[7]

Officers, Governors and Ennoblement

The numbers of Scots arriving in particular times of crisis for Denmark-Norway (usually war with Sweden), were added to by a small but important number of men in Christian's officer corps. King James and Christian IV used their powers of patronage to place these men into advantageous positions within the military elite. This route into the Danish armed forces led to some 15 Scottish gentlemen arriving in Denmark-Norway between 1589-1624. Of these the majority, all but four, were above the rank of captain. This might not seem significant until it is considered that during the same period only one English officer found a post, suggesting preferential treatment for the Scots even after the Union of Crowns in 1603. None-the-less, at least one Irish officer, Captain John Perkins, also found employment in Christian's army during this period and received a good recommendation from Christian IV for his valour. The service of any of these officers in Denmark has seldom been recognised. Indeed, the appearance of Lieutenant Colonel Patrick Cockburn and

---

[3]   Grosjean, 'Scots and the Swedish State', 50-54.

[4]   Berg and Lagercranz, *Scots in Sweden*, 14; Grosjean, 'Scots and the Swedish State', 53.

[5]   DRA, Militærregnskaber Folioreg 266, ff.16-19. Register of pay for seven Scottish captains and their soldiers, in money and clothes, 15 July 1570 to 14 March 1571.

[6]   *CSP*, XIII, 901, 22 November 1601 and 1004-1008, 20 June 1602. Letters from George Nicolson to Sir Robert Cecil.

[7]   According to J. A. Fallon, 'Scottish Mercenaries in the service of Denmark and Sweden 1626-1632' (unpublished PhD thesis, University of Glasgow, 1972), 34, some 58,880 Scots were levied in first part of the seventeenth century. This misses out the 300 raised for Poland in 1621 and some 1,000 who we know served under Seton in the Palatinate in 1620.

Captain Thomas Home in 1626 have previously been presented as the first British officer enlistment into Christian's army in the seventeenth century.[8]

Not only did these men do well in their military careers, but often they found themselves gaining serious advantages in Danish civic society. One manifestation of this can be seen through the raising of Scotsmen into the Danish-Norwegian nobility. Alexander Durham, Andrew Mowatt, John Cunningham, Axel Mowatt, Andrew Sinclair, Christian Sinclair and Patrick Dunbar all found their way into the Danish nobility, albeit through marriage. However, with the exception of Christian MacAlpine in 1580, all Scots were ennobled after the dynastic union of 1589 and within the reign of Christian IV.[9] Indeed, no other British Isles subjects are known to have been elevated in this way until the Englishman, Christopher de Watkinson, in 1724. Most of the Scottish ennoblements were of men who achieved their successful careers through the patronage of King James, two of them in the army and four of them in the navy.

Perhaps surprisingly, the enlistment of Scottish officers did not rise dramatically during the Kalmar War between Denmark-Norway and Sweden (1611-1613). Most Scots who took part in that war actually did so for Denmark-Norway's enemy Sweden, having been enlisted by warrants issued before the war broke out.[10] Although King James did not prevent individuals already serving the Swedes from taking part, he outlawed a particular group of soldiers who sailed from Caithness for Sweden and were massacred *en route* in Norway. The soldiers had been ordered not to leave Scotland since they were specifically going to join the Swedish army to fight against Christian IV. The incident was investigated but there was little perceivable rift in relations between the two monarchs. This was in part due to James's apparent disapproval of the expedition and the various actions of the Scottish Privy Council forbidding the levy and denouncing the leader, Colonel Andrew Ramsay as a rebel.[11]

---

[8] See for example Fallon, 'Scottish Mercenaries', 196. For Perkins see *CSPI*, 1615-1625, 551. List of Irish soldiers with their services and qualifications enumerated, December 1624.

[9] See A. Thiset and P. L. Wittrup eds, *Nyt Dansk Adelslexicon. Fortegnelse over Dansk Adel i Fortid og Nutid* (Copenhagen, 1904) passim; H. C. Wolter, *Adel og Embede: Embedsfordeling og karriermobilitet hos den Dansk-Norske Adel 1588-1660* (Copenhagen, 1982), 87-103. A. Fabritius, *Danmarks Riges Adel* (Copenhagen, 1946), 136-145.

[10] PRO SP95/1, ff.170 and 187. Spens to the Earl of Salisbury, 30 September and 8 November 1610; SRA, Anglica 4, f.5. Karl IX to Spens, 24 January 1611; SRA, Anglica 5. Duke Johan of Ostergotland to Spens, 13 September 1611.

[11] T. Mitchell, *History of the Scottish expedition to Norway in 1612* (London, 1886); *RPCS*, IX, 1610-1613, 430-434.

The intention of the king of Denmark had been to raise as many as 8,000 British subjects for his army and in March 1612, some 4-6,000 troops were reported to be mustering for his service under Lords Willoughby and Dingwall. Thomas Riis suggests that number engaged in total from the British Isles amounted to less than 4,000 and that of these some 600 were Scots.[12] Even once in Danish service, the British troops arrived too late to take part in the fighting and appear not to have been incorporated into the Danish-Norwegian army but instead most of them were disbanded soon after. While numerous contemporary sources can be found suggesting the English were good soldiers, this appraisal was apparently far from universal, particularly in Denmark-Norway. The English in service under Christian IV were certainly viewed as less committed than the Scots and the king did not hesitate to voice his disillusionment on several occasions.[13]

Despite the Norwegian incident and low numbers of Scottish recruits compared to the English, Christian continued to promote the Scots in his service. One contemporary report by the Venetian, Antonio Foscarini, claimed that the Dane placed all the cities and fortresses he had taken from the Swedes into the hands of German or Scottish governors, apparently trusting none of his own subjects as much as he did them.[14] Foscarini's assertions for the captured Swedish towns does not appear to stand scrutiny as the occupied Swedish city of Älvsborg had Jørgen Lunge installed as governor in 1612. There were, however, reasonable foundations for his belief. One Scottish contemporary, Thomas Urquhart of Cromarty, suggest that Christian IV employed as many as 10 Scottish governors in similar capacities throughout his reign and there were a couple of appointments that Foscarini may have been aware of.[15] The Kalmar War certainly brought a new phase in the career of Andrew Sinclair. He had never held a military command before the outbreak of the war. His status as a Danish nobleman meant that he was expected to

---

[12]   *CSPV*, XII, 239-240, 252 and 298. Antonio Foscarini, November 1611-March 1612. Specifically, letter nos. 316, 342, 355, 372, 373, 387, 446, 452, 583 and 789; *CSPD*, 1611-1618, 124. Chamberlain to Carlton, 25 March 1612; Riis, *Should Auld Acquaintance*, I, 95-96.

[13]   Although Antonio Foscarini states in his 'Relation of England' that 'The English, Scots and Irish are all fond of war and make good soldiers', the same report records Christian IV's disillusionment with the English in his service c.1618. See *CSPV*, XV, 1617-1619, 387 and 397. Christian IV's disillusionment in the 1620s is recorded in *KCFB*, II, 230-233. Christian IV to Frederik Gunther, 3 December 1629.

[14]   *CSPV*, XII, 1610-1613, 239-340. Antonio Foscarini, 20 November 1611.

[15]   Thomas Urquhart of Cromarty wrote that there were 'besides ten governors at least, all Scots, intrusted with the charge of the most especial strengths and holds of importance, that were within the confines of the Danish authority'. See S. D. Stirling ed, *The Works of Sir Thomas Urquhart of Cromarty, Knight* (Edinburgh, 1834), 215.

participate and so, despite his high civic rank, Sinclair joined the army with the rank of captain.[16] He displayed the leadership qualities for which his courtly, civic and diplomatic service had groomed him. He participated in the attack on the city of Kalmar with a large Danish force. After a long siege, the garrison capitulated and Sinclair became the governor of both the city and region of Kalmar.[17] This was a premier appointment indeed by Christian IV. Elsewhere, Scotsmen also featured as a part of Christian IV's ongoing occupation and defence strategy. In Finmark, the region felt to be most at threat from Swedish attack, Christian sent the Scot, Tamis Cunningham, as commandant to the royal fortifications in Altafjord to prevent the area from falling to the Swedes.[18] He took with him a fellow Scot to act as his second in command, Captain John Robertson. Tamis Cunningham retained military command of the region throughout the war and for several years after.

In terms of foreigners serving in the Danish-Norwegian army, Scottish officers like Cunningham and Robertson were numerically second only to the combined numbers of men from the various German states. Thanks to Dr Gunner Lind's database of Danish officers, it is possible to extrapolate comparative statistics for the various nationalities that served in Denmark-Norway from 1614 to 1661.[19] In the years between 1614 and 1625 specifically, nine Scottish army officers served Christian IV, which represented 3% [9/272] of the total.[20] While that number is small, it is still greater than, say, the Dutch total of 1% [2/272]. Perhaps even more remarkable is that the Norwegians only formed a fraction of the total, having only two officers which, like the Dutch, equates to a fifth of the number of Scots. The largest number of foreigners in the Danish army at this period were soldiers from the various German states with 18% [49/272] of the total officer corps. This number is greater than that provided by Christian's own duchies of Schleswig-Holstein, which contributed 10% [27/272] of the officers. The Danes themselves

[16] Lind, *Danish Data Archive 1573*; J. C. W. Hirsch and K. Hirsch, eds, 'Fortegnelse over Dansk og Norske officerer med flere fra 1648 til 1814' (12 vols. Copenhagen, manuscript compiled 1888-1907), vol 10, 4; *DBL*, 1933-44, vol 3, 399-400; Riis, *Should Auld Acquaintance*, II, 74.

[17] *DBL*, 1933-44, vol 3, 399-400.

[18] O. Solberg, *Finnmark Omkring 1700, Tredie Bind: Lilienskiolds Speculum Boreale* (Oslo, 1945), II, 61; J. P. Nielsen, *Altas Historie: De glemte århundrene 1520-1826* (Alta, 1990), I, 102.

[19] G. Lind, *Danish Data Archive 1573* (Copenhagen, 1995).

[20] Wherever a percentage is shown in this study, it will have been rounded off to the nearest whole number. The specific number of individuals concerned and the total number of individuals involved are given in brackets. In this case the total was 3.86%, rounded up to 4%. The numbers in brackets represent 9 individuals out of 272 expressed as [9/272].

contributed just over half the officers in their army with 52% [142/272] of the total officer corps (Fig. 2).

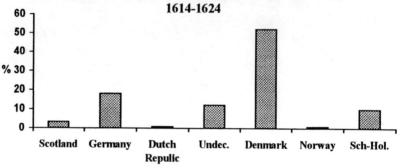

Fig. 2
Nationality of Officers in Danish-Norwegian Service 1614-1624

Place of Origin

(Source: *SSNE* and *DDA 1573* databases)

Fig. 3
Nationality of Foreign Officers in Danish-Norwegian Service 1614-1624

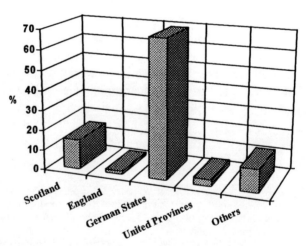

Place of Origin

(Source: *SSNE* and *DDA 1573* databases)

Perhaps a more valuable way of interpreting these figures is to subtract the data relating to Denmark, Norway and Schleswig-Holstein to focus specifically on foreign participation (Fig. 3). The percentage of Scots equates to 15% [9/61], the Dutch to 3% [2/61] and the 'unknown origin' and English to just over 1% [1/61] each. Given that the Germans came from a variety of states, Scotland was probably the largest single source of foreign officers in the Danish-Norwegian army in this period.

Many of the Scots, like captains Cunningham and Robertson in Alta, were important because they undertook both military and naval duties. Indeed, their nautical service came as a result of another form of patronage network operating between Christian IV and James VI. Between 1589 and 1624, more Scottish officers were actually appointed to the Danish-Norwegian navy than to the army.

Britons in the Danish-Norwegian Navy

While there have been several studies of British military involvement in Denmark-Norway, investigations into the presence of Britons and Irishmen in the Danish-Norwegian navy are minimal, and those that have been undertaken seldom reflect the extent of the influence some Stuart subjects exerted in that service.[21] This is actually quite remarkable since both the Stuart and Oldenburg states relied on the sea for their very existence, not only in terms of defence, but more importantly for trade. An exchange of naval technology would seem like an obvious consequence of a relationship between sea-faring nations, especially where the very waters they sailed on formed the only border between them.

The Danish-Norwegian navy sought to present itself as a significant naval power as it entered the seventeenth century. The Danish king specifically laid claim to *Dominium Maris Septentrionalis*, or the domination of the Northern Seas and *Dominum Fluminis*, domination of the Elbe river. He also confirmed his right to the Baltic with the publication of *Mare Clausum* in 1638.[22] Spurred on by such declarations, the Danish-Norwegian navy grew considerably throughout the reign of

---

[21] Fallon, 'Scottish Mercenaries', 241. Riis, *Should Auld Acquaintance*, I, 105-109. One exception that does attempt a meaningful comparative of the Scandinavian navies is A. Grosjean, 'Scottish-Scandinavian naval links in the seventeenth century; a case study from the Scotland, Scandinavia and Northern Europe 1580-1707 database', in *Northern Studies*, no. 32 (1997).

[22] J. Lisk, *The Struggle for Supremacy in the Baltic* (London, 1967), 30-38; M. Bellamy, 'Danish Naval Administration and Shipbuilding in the reign of Christian IV, 1596-1648' (unpublished PhD thesis, University of Glasgow, 1997), 15-39; P. D. Lockhart, *Denmark and the Thirty Years' War, 1614-1648; King Christian IV and the decline of the Oldenburg State* (Selinsgrove, 1996), 250.

Christian IV. He financed his fleet by the Sound Tolls and could therefore afford to bring in foreign shipwrights 'to build for him warships of the most modern design'.[23] Among these men were many notable Britons.

Throughout the 1580s and 1590s, the Englishmen Hugo Bedow and Hans Madsen produced a number of military vessels for the king in the style of English warships.[24] Christian IV also delighted in the design of Scottish ships and employed several Scottish shipwrights directly into his naval service.[25] One of these men, Robert Peterson, entered Danish-Norwegian service in 1596 with a commission to build three or four ships for the royal fleet. Eight years later he was appointed as Royal Shipbuilder to Christian IV. Peterson made a significant contribution to the Danish-Norwegian fleet when he built the 44-gun *Victor* which became Christian IV's flagship in 1599.[26] While this ship was still being built, another Scot, David Balfour, also entered Danish service as a shipbuilder, and served between 1597-1634.[27] A third Scottish shipwright, Daniel Sinclair also served between 1614-1636, though some reports suggest he may have been employed as early as 1601 or 1602. He was probably born in Norway but was certainly regarded as a Scot by his fellow countrymen as Robert Monro makes clear in his memoirs.[28] These three men together established something of a 'Scottish Period' in Danish naval design. Indeed, the contribution of Balfour and Sinclair as two of the three royal shipbuilders during *Kejserkrig* in particular is incalculable.[29] Certainly some of the prime ships of the fleet were built by these men including *Hummeren* (Balfour), *Den Røde Løve* and *Store Sophia* (both Sinclair). *Store Sophia* was the largest ship in the fleet during *Kejserkrig*, with 54 guns. Launched in 1627, she arrived in time to

[23] M. Roberts, *A history of Sweden 1611-1632* (2 vols, London 1958), II, 273.

[24] Bellamy, 'Danish Naval Administration', 312.

[25] Espelland, *Skottene i Hordaland og Rogaland*, 50-51 and 66.

[26] Espelland, *Skottene i Hordaland og Rogaland*, 50; Riis, *Should Auld Acquaintance*, II, 72; N. M. Probst, *Den Danske Flådes Historie, 1588-1660; Christian 4.s Flåde* (Copenhagen, 1996), 49 and 62; Bellamy, Danish Naval Administration, 315-316; *SSNE* no. 1565.

[27] *SSNE* no. 1474; Bellamy, 'Danish Naval Administration', 318-341; Probst, *Den Danske Flådes Historie*, 36, 40-51, 62-68, 128, 162.

[28] In the description of Laaland in November 1627, Robert Monro mentioned that the island 'is plentiful of wood for building of ships, where his majesty every yeare hath some builded by his owne master builder, a worthy gentleman begotten of Scots ancestors, called Mr. Sinclaire, who speaks the Scottish tongue, and is very courteous to all his countrymen which come thither'. R. Monro, *Monro His Expedition with a worthy Scots regiment (called Mac-Keyes regiment)* (London, 1637), I, 42. See also Riis, *Should Auld Acquaintance*, I, 108. Riis notes that in a move typical of the Scots in Scandinavia he married David Balfour's step-daughter; Probst, *Den Danske Flådes Historie*, 130, 155, 181, 187; Bellamy, 'Danish Naval Administration', 342-354; *SSNE* no. 1560.

[29] Tandrup, *Svensk Agent ved Sundet*, 525-6. The third master shipbuilder was the Dutchman, Peter Michaelsen.

be a valuable deterrent to Imperial designs on the Danish archipelago.[30] Both Sinclair and Balfour were gone from Danish-Norwegian service by the mid-1630s. When Christian asked his nephew for a replacement master shipbuilder in 1641, Charles I found himself in no position to send Scots due to his ongoing conflict with the Covenanters. He therefore sent the Englishman, James Rubbins, whom Christian IV made Royal Shipbuilder and effectively ended the 'Scottish Period' of influence in Danish naval design.[31] Rubbins produced at least three warships throughout the 1640s which were all sent to Norway to be put at the disposal of Hannibal Sehested.

At the start of the seventeenth century, some Scottish shipwrights also worked in Norway, but on a private basis. William Duncan and Jacob Clerck both built ships there to the annoyance of Christian who had the vessels confiscated in 1604 and 1605.[32] The decision to relieve Clerck of his ships possibly rebounded badly for Christian IV. A Jacob Richard Clerck, almost certainly the same man, arrived in Swedish service as master of shipbuilding in 1606.[33] Not only did that man become *Holmamiral* of the Swedish navy (1619-1625), he took his brother Johan with him and he too became *Holmamiral* (1625-1644). The brothers started a dynasty of Swedish admirals which Christian IV had to contend with for the duration of his reign.[34]

In addition to shipbuilding, official or otherwise, many Scots became involved in Denmark-Norway through the route of privateering. An early mention of such activity revolves around Robert Stewart who was commanded by Frederick II of Denmark to apprehend the privateer John Clerk in Shetland in 1580. This determination on the part of the Danish king to catch Clerk would imply that he and/or other Scots privateers were making an impact on the North Sea.[35] By commissioning another Scot to catch Clerk, the Danish king confirmed a certain acceptance of Scottish privateering on behalf of the Danish-Norwegian fleet. As one

---

[30] Tandrup, *Svensk Agent ved Sundet*, 525-6. Polisensky, *The Thirty Years' War*, 173; Munck, *Seventeenth Century Europe*, 14; Parker, *The Thirty Years War*, 71 and 95.

[31] See *KCFB*, VIII, 183-184, Christian IV to Korfits Ulfeldt, 8 June 1642; J. T. Lauridsen, 'Skibsbyggeri for den Danske Krone i Neustadt i 1640'rne' in *Særtryk af Handels- og Søfartsmuseets Årbog* (1982), 79; Bellamy, 'Danish Naval Administration', 369-373. Rubbins is variously also called Robbins and Rubbens.

[32] DRA, TKUA England A 1, 2. James VI to Christian IV, 4 April 1606; *The Letters of King James*, 75; *Norske Rigs Registranter*, IV, 79. Christian IV to Laurits Krus, 24 July 1604 and 123. Christian IV to Styring Boel, 3 August 1605; Duncan, *SSNE* no. 1134; *SSNE* no. 4137.

[33] *SAÄ*, II, 23.

[34] Grosjean, 'Scottish-Scandinavian naval links', 115-119.

[35] Grosjean, 'Scottish-Scandinavian naval links', 111.

Danish historian noted 'privateers acting with the state's blessing became an important element in the prosecution of economic warfare'.[36] The expertise displayed by the privateers was put to good use within the Danish-Norwegian navy proper and many Scots joined the regular navy. King James was keen to help his brother-in-law develop his navy, and as well as sending shipwrights, James recommended naval officers into his brother's service. Bearing in mind that there were 15 Scottish officers appointed by Christian IV into the Danish-Norwegian army, it is worthy of note to realise that at least 16 Scottish officers also joined his navy during his reign. A further seven enlisted between 1625 and 1629.[37]

Four of these Scots sailors held the position of 'admiral'. Martin Bellamy has established that an admiral in the Danish-Norwegian navy was not a fixed rank, but a ship's captain in charge of a squadron of ships who retained the rank of captain.[38] However, some captains commanded larger squadrons more consistently and have familiarly become known by the title of admiral. The first of the Scots of importance was Alexander Durham who arrived in Danish service in 1569.[39] After serving as a captain from 1573, Durham commanded the entire Baltic fleet as its admiral between 1578-86 and the North Sea fleet from 1587-99 in the same capacity.[40] Durham was joined in naval service by Andrew Mowatt who, like the Clercks in Sweden, started something of a naval dynasty in Norway with many of his sons and grandchildren becoming senior naval officers.[41]

The longest serving admiral, John Cunningham, was recommended by James VI for Danish service in 1603 and appointed a naval captain in the Danish-Norwegian fleet.[42] Cunningham's main role initially centred on the

[36] L. Jespersen, 'The machtstaat in seventeenth century Denmark', in *Scandinavian Journal of History*, 10, no. 4 (1985), 274.
[37] Topsøe Jensen and Marquard, *Officerer i den danske-norske søetat*, I, passim. Anton Espelland lists a number of foreign, probably Scottish, officers in the Danish-Norwegian navy but has not given sources for their Scottish origins. These men include Kato Gertsen, Thomas Normand de la Nancte and Jørgen Hjelt. See Espelland, *Skottene i Hordaland og Rogaland*, 34.
[38] Bellamy, 'Danish Naval Administration', 283.
[39] *SSNE* no. 279.
[40] Riis, *Should Auld Acquaintance*, 2, 87; A. Thiset and P. L. Wittrup eds, *Nyt Dansk Adelslexicon: Fortegnelse over Dansk Adel i Fortid og Nu* (Copenhagen, 1904), 70; Espelland, *Skottene i Hordaland og Rogaland*, 19; Probst, *Den Danske Flådes Historie*, 80, 81 and 87.
[41] F. J. Grant, *The County Families of the Shetland Islands* (Lerwick, 1893), 179-181; A. M. Wiesener, 'Axel Movat og hans slegt', in *Bergens Historiske Forening Skrifter*, no. 36 (Bergen, 1930), 95-98; *SSNE* no. 3837.
[42] Espelland, *Skottene i Hordaland og Rogaland*, 19-20; *Dansk Biografisk Leksikon* (16 vols, 1979-1984, 3rd edition), IV, 121; Probst, *Den Danske Flådes Historie*, 94-140, 102-103, 138-140; *SSNE* no. 1497.

field of naval exploration. He held several commands during his 'voyages of inspection' especially in the western and northern seas between 1605-18. Cunningham became the governor of Vardøhus and Finmark in 1619, which was surely a mark of complete trust, given the region's significance during the recent Kalmar war with Sweden.[43] As noted in chapter one, this promotion also meant that Cunningham had responsibility for policing the tolls to be paid by traders entering or leaving Archangel in Russia, who had to sail past his base at Vardø. In 1632, John Cunningham suggested the radical notion that the inhabitants of Finmark should pay taxes instead of furnishing boatswains in order to avoid a shortage of manpower in the locality. The suggestion was accepted by the Danish-Norwegian authorities and allowed both the retention of the local population and the development of a more professional navy. This was not the first time that innovations suggested by Scots had been implemented. They had also pointed out shortcomings in the naval arsenal in 1625 after which their recommendations were taken seriously and acted upon.[44]

Axel Mowatt was the son of Andrew Mowatt, mentioned above, and retained strong Scottish connections despite being born in Norway. For instance, Axel's elder half-brother, John Mowatt of Hugoland in Shetland, maintained contact with his younger sibling allowing a direct Scottish link for Axel.[45] One of Axel's sisters, Ursula, married Andrew Bruce, Laird of Mouns, also in Shetland, while his other sister, Karen, lived in Scotland for eighteen years with her husband Eric Orning. Karen was also born in Norway but her father ensured she received her education from a Scottish governess. Even before she moved to Scotland, Karen could apparently write better Scots than Norwegian indicating the degree of identification the family retained with their father's native land.[46] Certainly Axel also had friends as well as family in Scotland. During his several voyages to Scotland in the 1650s, Christoffer Orning always carried with him greetings to and from Axel Mowatt's good friends in Scotland.[47]

Christian IV referred to Axel as 'the young Movat' and he was noted as a ship's captain in 1628. Mowatt first saw action for Denmark-Norway when he served under Henrik Vind's command against

[43] C. C. A. Lange et al eds, *Norske Rigs-Registranter Tildeels i Uddrag* (12 vols, Christiana, 1861-1891), V, 12-14; R. Fladby, *Hvordan Nord-Norge ble styrt: NordNorske administrasjonshistorie fra 1530-åra til 1660* (Tromsø, 1978), 65.

[44] Riis, *Should Auld Acquaintance*, I, 58 and 108.

[45] Grant, *The County Families of the Shetland Islands*, 180; SSNE no. 1817.

[46] Wiesener, 'Axel Movat og hans slegt', 93.

[47] A. Næss, 'Skottehandelen på Sunnhordland', in *Sunnhordland Tidsskrift*, VII (1920), 43; Wiesener, 'Axel Movat og hans slegt', 103. I would like to thank Nina Østby Petersen for the 'Næss' reference.

Hamburg's fleet. By 1631 he was admiral of all the ships in the seas between Iceland, Faeroes and Norway and in 1632-33 he personally commanded the ships in the Norwegian Sea.[48] In autumn 1633 and spring 1634, Mowatt was moved from his northern command to act as the senior admiral in and around the river Elbe. By the Bishops' Wars of 1639-1640, Mowatt had been appointed by Christian IV to act as senior admiral over the entire Norwegian navy. Axel Mowatt's brother, Christopher, also made a successful career for himself in the navy.[49] He enlisted in 1625 and commanded *Merkatten*, one of the two ships that patrolled the Danish 'Great' and 'Little' Belts against naval forces working for Christian's enemies.[50] By 1628, Christoffer Mowatt acted as a vice-admiral and captain of the 54 gun *Spes*.[51] He continued to serve the Danish Crown well into the 1640s and was briefly joined in service by his half brother, Andrew Mowatt, who acted as a ship's lieutenant between 1629 and 1631.[52]

Fallon asserts in his thesis that by 1628 the valuable period of Scottish military involvement in Denmark-Norway was over.[53] Given the Scottish input in the navy, that view should be revised. This was the very time that the Empire was contemplating ways to develop its navy, which would have presented Denmark-Norway with her greatest threat. Charles I intended more British assistance in the form of a naval squadron of five ships under Admiral Sir John Pennington to counter the Imperial threat. His ships, the *Red Lion*, the *Adventure* and three 'whelps' never reached the Elbe in time to contribute to the war effort and thus left the Danish fleet on its own.[54] Despite this setback, Christian's navy fulfilled its function quite effectively during this period. The most significant military successes throughout *Kejserkrig* must include the defence of the Danish archipelago in 1628-1629, and that was accomplished because of the navy. During this time, Scots were drafted into Danish-Norwegian naval service in one of the very last offensive actions attempted during the war.

---

[48]   Wiesener, 'Axel Movat og hans slegt', 97; Probst, *Den Danske Flådes Historie*, 198-226.

[49]   Probst, *Den Danske Flådes Historie*, 166-168 and 177; *SSNE* no. 1375.

[50]   Polisensky, *The Thirty Years' War*, 173; See also Tandrup, *Svensk Agent ved Sundet*, 541-546. Anders Svensson to Gustav II Adolph and Axel Oxenstierna, 23 February 1625. Surprisingly there were only ten Danish-Norwegian vessels listed as 'on patrol' at this point. Two in the Wesser, four in the Elbe and North Sea, two in the Belt and two others, presumably roving. The rest of the flet must stil have been in their winter anchorage. See also Espelland, *Skottene i Hordaland og Rogaland*, 58.

[51]   *KCFB*, VII, 45. List of Warships and officers, March-April, 1628.

[52]   Wiesener, 'Axel Movat og hans slegt', 92; Andrew's two brothers Jacob and Henrik also joined the navy although the exact capacity in which they served remains unclear.

[53]   Fallon, 'Scottish Mercenaries', 240.

[54]   *CSPV*, XXII, 1629-1632, 103-105; *CSPD*, IX, 1628, 556, 572, and 180.

Scottish companies under captains Forbes and Stewart were drafted into the fleet to serve as marines to take part in an assault on Holstein but the mission was halted by the negotiations at Lübeck.[55]

The Scottish presence at the highest operational level continued into the 1630-40s. As noted in chapter four, Captain Alexander Arrat on the 28 gun *Merkatten* and Albert Jack in command of the 26 gun *Gabriell* were both significant naval commanders in positions of authority.[56] When Colonel Alexander Seaton, an army colonel, accepted the position as admiral of a Danish naval squadron of eight ships in 1645 during the war against the Swedes, he represented the last senior British appointment into Christian IV's navy.[57] The Danish king did try to recruit other Scots, particularly one wolf-pack of Scottish privateers who had been observed operating in and around the Sound in 1645, but ultimately the hayday of the British in the Danish-Norwegian navy were numbered.[58]

At all times during the reign of Christian IV there was an overwhelming presence of Scots and little evidence of significant English or Irish enlistment in the Danish-Norwegian navy. Indeed, during the entire period between 1589 and 1660 there appear to be only six Englishmen who joined that navy as officers or shipwrights. The good work of the English shipbuilders has already been mentioned above. Of the operational commanders, the most significant Englishman was Captain James Hall from Hull. He famously undertook the naval exploration of Greenland as a subordinate of John Cunningham in 1605 after being recommended to Danish service by King James.[59] He appears to have been in and out of Christian's service and eventually ended his days as a private explorer working for an English consortium. A less savoury individual appears to have been Captain Marcus White. His fourteen years of service ended rather ingloriously on the gallows after he deserted with two Danish frigates to the Swedes during the Torstensson campaign in 1644.[60] As far as the records have so far revealed, only one Irish officer took up naval service for the Danes. Hugh Duncan enlisted in

[55] Monro, *His Expedition*, I, 85.
[56] *KCFB*, IV, 334. List of Warships and Crews, 7 May 1640; Riis, *Should Auld Acquaintance*, 225; Arrat, *SSNE* no. 990; Jack, *SSNE* no. 1109; Probst, *Den Danske Flådes Historie*, 220.
[57] Espelland, *Skottene i Hordaland og Rogaland*, 34; *SSNE* no. 91.
[58] *Kancelliets Brevbøger, 1644-1645*, 320. Missive to Falke Lycke and Gabriel Ackeleye, 20 May 1645.
[59] *DBL*, V, 497; *SSNE* no. 1316. Another English officer called Hans Kansler gets the briefest mention in Espelland, *Skottene i Hordaland og Rogaland*, 34.
[60] *KCFB*, IV, 336 footnote; 'Meritförteckningar. Svenska Sjöofficerare, II, 'Biografiska anteckningar om officerare vid örlogsflottan 1600-1699' (Stockholm, 1971 manuscript in Svenska Krigsarkivet), 412.

1651 and served until 1675, but reflecting on his name it would be interesting to establish whether he considered himself as Irish, Scottish or British.

Throughout the reign of King James, his British and Irish subjects could be found in a variety of military service outwith the British Isles and, as discussed above, this usually resulted as part of Stuart alliances with foreign powers. Bearing that in mind, it would have been surprising if numbers of Britons were not found in the service of Christian IV. What is astonishing is the degree to which the English failed to break into the Danish-Norwegian officer elite, especially during the Kalmar War when the numbers of Englishmen in Danish service outnumbered the Scots by six to one. This can only reflect one of two things: the desire of either James and Christian to keep that particular form of service for the Scots, or a lack of appetite by the English to participate in the Stuart-Oldenburg alliance. Whichever is the case, a small number of Scottish soldiers did very well out of the alliance indeed.

The apparent preferential enlistment of Scottish officers into Christian's navy followed a similar pattern to that of his army. Fairly equal numbers joined both services and recruitment remained a Scottish rather than British affair. As the following chapter reveals in more detail, Scottish naval officers never achieved the numbers that their counterparts in the army did in the Carolinian period. This can, in part, be explained by the comparative size of the navy in relation to the army and the role of the two services during Christian's various wars. It is also compensated for by the positions of seniority that the Scots reached and the duration of time the naval officers spent in service. In discussing foreign enlistment into the Danish-Norwegian navy, Martin Bellamy concluded that 'only a few skilled English and Dutch officers were hired by Christian IV, but they had little real impact on the navy as a whole'.[61] However, apart from the shipbuilders, Bellamy does not discuss the Scots in Christian's navy. Given the evaluation of the numbers and status of British and Irish officers noted above, this conclusion must surely be revised. Between 1580 and 1660 Scotland produced at least 35 senior naval personnel for the Danish-Norwegian navy. This far exceeds the quantity of English or Irish officers over the same period which numbered no more than six or seven combined. Twelve of these Scotsmen served during *Kejserkrig*, ten

---

[61]   Bellamy, 'Danish Naval Administration', 304.

as fleet officers and two as master shipbuilders. During the same period, Scottish captains and marines could be found on board many Danish-Norwegian ships. Through John Cunningham, Axel and Christoffer Mowatt the senior captains Arratt and Jack, the Scots could claim a strong degree of influence over the operational command of the navy of Christian IV. As discussed in chapter four, that fact carried serious potential implications for the traffic of weapons and officers from the continent to Scotland during the Bishops' Wars. The trend continued into the 1640s when at least 11 Scottish officers served in Christian IV's navy during the Torstensson War (1643-1645), including Colonel Seaton in his capacity as admiral.[62] It was only in the reign of Frederik III that there was a significant decline in numbers. No new recruitment took place to fill the positions left by the death or retirement of the Scottish officers and their presence thereafter dwindled to only three naval commanders by the Swedish wars in the later 1650s.

The naval and army officers who were placed by patronage during the reign of James VI & I had a much higher prospect of advancement after they left military service than those men who arrived at any other time. Of the 30 Scots placed in this period, five became Danish-Norwegian noblemen. A further three, Alexander Durham, Andrew Sinclair and John Cunningham all reached the position of *lensman*, or regional governor, for the Danish-Norwegian government, while Sinclair also joined the *Rigsråd*. Such advancement of Scots or other Britons was never to be achieved again in Danish-Norwegian society. This was despite the fact that the following years would see a massive influx of highly skilled and motivated military personnel from the British Isles.

---

[62]   Axel Mowatt's son, also called Axel, joined the navy as an officer on his father's ship in 1640. Being a second generation Scot, he has not been included in the above statistic. In 1643, young Axel Mowatt was killed in a duel by a fellow officer, Lauritz Galtung. He had to flee Denmark-Norway, but later returned to become an admiral himself. Wiesener, 'Axel Movat og hans slegt', 105.

CHAPTER NINE

Military Service II: *'Kejserkrig'* 1625-1629

Undoubtedly the greatest British military migration to Denmark-Norway in the seventeenth century occurred during *Kejserkrig*, or the Danish period of the Thirty Years' War.[1] The recruitment of Scottish soldiers through the Stuart-Oldenburg alliance of 1589 had provided Christian IV with a body of veteran officers and men on which he knew he could rely. To this select band were soon added thousands of Scottish and English soldiers who brought with them a variety of skills. Many of these men had experienced campaigns against the forces of the Catholic League and their recruitment was intended to bolster the Danish army in Holstein which, in 1625, stood at around 12,000 infantry and 4,000 cavalry.[2] In addition to this multitude, new units were formed throughout the summer and autumn of that year. Responsibility for mustering this army was given to Christian in his capacity as leader of the Lower Saxon Circle. For their part, the members of the Circle would finance the army while some of its members were expected to provide small auxiliary forces outwith direct Danish command. Theoretically, by the end of 1625, the Danish king should have had 37,000 men under arms. A contemporary diplomatic report by the Swedish resident in Denmark, Anders Svensson, put the number at closer to 26,000 while Danish historians have estimated the size of the army by the end of the year as between 18-20,000 men.[3] This force was supplemented by the independent army of Count Mansfeld which stood at over 8,000, and included up to 6,000 Scots and English survivors of the '1624' levy. Again, some historians favour a much lower number and calculate that Mansfield's army only contained 4,000 men at most, although that does put their figures into conflict with the more contemporary source.[4] Whichever is the correct number for 1625, Mansfeld augmented his military strength through local conscription and 'borrowing' regiments, increasing his forces to

---

[1]   For more on the war itself, see R. Asch, *The Thirty Years War The Holy Roman Empire and Europe, 1618-1648* (Basingstoke, 1996); G. Parker et al., *The Thirty Years' War* (London, 1997); J. V. Polisensky, *The Thirty Years' War* (London, 1971); S. Murdoch ed, *Scotland and the Thirty Years' War, 1618-1648* (Leiden, 2001).

[2]   G. Lind, *Hæren og Magten i Danmark* (Odense, 1994), 52-59.

[3]   Tandrup, *Svensk agent ved Sundet*, 546-547. Anders Svensson to Axel Oxenstierna/ Gustav II Adolf, 24 July 1625; Lind, *Hæren og Magten*, 53; E. Ladewig Petersen, 'The Danish Intermezzo' in Parker, *The Thirty Years' War*, 67.

[4]   Tandrup, *Svensk agent ved Sundet*, 546-547. Anders Svensson to Axel Oxenstierna/ Gustav II Adolf, 14 March 1625; Lind, *Hæren og Magten*, 53.

between 12-14,000 men by the following year. This army was defeated on the Elbe by Wallenstein in April at Dessau Bridge with the loss of 4,000 men. Thereafter Mansfeld's forces moved south to link up with the Transylvanian prince, Bethlen Gabor. After the Peace of Pressburg in December 1626, Gabor came to terms with Ferdinand II and the remnants of Mansfeld's army were disbanded.[5] Some of the British survivors would later re-appear in the armies of Christian IV and Gustav II Adolf of Sweden, but they had ceased to serve as an independent fighting unit in the meantime.

Christian IV's own army also grew at the start of 1626, reaching somewhere in the region of 30-50,000 men depending on the sources consulted. Obviously those forces were spread over a large multiple kingdom. Fear of attack by Sweden kept many soldiers in Norway and so the army that took part in the battle of Lutter-am-Barenberg on 27 August 1626 was probably in the region of 20-30,000 men. This force was reduced by as much as 10,000 in the course of the battle. Despite this setback the Danes kept recruiting and during the winter and spring of 1627 warrants for between 25-30,000 more men were served.

Determining the numbers of soldiers in Danish-Norwegian service is a difficult task, compounded by the cessation of hostilities during winter periods. Numbers that are given in various sources sometimes vary by up to 10,000, which was the total size of some of the participating armies. Christian IV himself believed the number of soldiers in Silesia to be 20,000 strong after a large exchange of prisoners in spring 1627, though no figure is given by the king for troops in Denmark-Norway proper.[6] Gunner Lind suggests that after 1627 the Danish armies were reduced to remnants with perhaps only 11,000 troops on the Elbe and a further 8,000 in Denmark.

Britain and 'Kejserkrig'

A major component of the new Danish-Norwegian army was to be the 7,000 troops from Britain to be mustered under the terms of The Hague agreement. The first English company of 500 men arrived 3 days before the battle of Lutter, and they were too late to take part. However, by March 1627, larger English regiments arrived, albeit still under-strength. Indeed, of the 6,000 Englishmen promised by Charles at the start of 1627, less than 3,000 made it to Danish territory by March and Christian IV noted their arrival with contempt.[7] Despite the numbers rising to

---

[5] Ward et al. eds, *The Cambridge Modern History*, IV, 98; Ladewig Petersen, 'The Danish Intermezzo', 70.
[6] *KCFB*, II, 73. Christian IV to Christian Friis, 23 April 1627.
[7] *KCFB*, II, 65. Christian IV to Christian Friis, 27 March 1627.

almost 5,000 by April, Christian became incensed by the low turnout and
declared that 'they are so few they are almost unprofitable' and argued
that he had to reconsider his military strategy as a consequence.[8] James
Fallon estimates that the English lost nearly 1,000 men in 3 months, a
decrease from 4,707 to 3,766 and this further displeased Christian.[9]
Christian was particularly enraged when Morgan surrendered the
garrison and town of Stade to General Tilly in 1628 and promised to take
no further part in the war for six months!

The English force did not form part of the Danish army proper and
only General Morgan himself received a Danish royal appointment. The
rest of the officers and men did not swear fealty to Christian IV and were
mustered and paid by their own commissioners.[10] The service of these
men, as noted in chapter three, proved a pivotal issue on which the
Stuart-Oldenburg alliance nearly faltered. However, the perception of
military aid from Britain and the actual support provided seldom tie up
in historical writings. For instance, Sir Charles Morgan's expedition to
Germany in 1627-1629 has been described as 'the only military
assistance given to Christian by his nephew Charles I [and] the king of
Denmark's military situation demanded more than the army of under
5,000 men which Morgan commanded'.[11] This statement simply
misrepresents the facts. Although the English regiments never lived up to
the expectations placed on them by Christian IV they only formed a
limited portion of the British forces sent to aid Denmark-Norway.

For a start, Morgan himself was Welsh and undoubtedly many other
Welsh soldiers in his army are usually counted amongst the English
volunteers. The identification of the General as Welsh, not English, is
not simply a piece of twenty first century pedantry, but reflects an
awareness of nationality found in contemporary sources. For instance,
when another Welsh officer, Captain Francis Trafford, joined a Scottish
regiment with a company of his countrymen in 1629, their nationality
was felt important enough to be recorded by Robert Monro.[12] Colonel
Monro also made it clear that he wished the war for the Palatinate to be

8   PRO SP75/8, f.72. Defects of Regiments sent to Denmark, 4 April 1627. This source
     gives the number arriving from England as 4,693; Other sources give the number as
     4,913. See Beller, 'The Military Expedition of Sir Charles Morgan', 530; PRO SP75/8,
     f.75. Christian IV to Charles I, 29 April 1627.
9   Fallon, 'Scottish Mercenaries', 210.
10   PRO SP75/8, f.61. The King of Denmark's Army, March 1627; Lind, *Hæren og Magten*,
     54.
11   E. A. Beller, 'Recent Studies on the Thirty Years' War', in *Journal of Modern History*,
     (1931), 3, no. 1, 74; E. A. Beller, 'The Military Expedition of Sir Charles Morgan to
     Germany, 1627-9', in *English Historical Review*, XLIII (1928), 539.
12   The nationality of Trafford and his company were recorded in R. Monro, *His Expedition
     with the worthy Scots Regiment called Mac-Keyes* (London, 1637), I, 82.

undertaken by soldiers from Britain *and* Ireland.[13] There were probably several hundred soldiers from Ireland mixed throughout the British regiments, but their names often make them hard to separate from the Scots. Sir George Hamilton, complained bitterly on behalf his fellow Catholics in the north of Ireland at the removal of 'their idle swordsmen' leaving for Danish service. There they joined Protestants from the same region. A letter from John Hamilton of Bangor makes it quite clear that he and other officers from Ulster were serving within Scottish units in the Danish army in 1627.[14] Sir Alexander Hamilton, apparent of Innerwick, certainly raised another 500 men in Ireland throughout 1628 and these men were destined for service in the Earl of Nithsdale's Scottish regiment.[15] These examples of soldiers from Ireland serving in Denmark also highlight part of the problem of distinguishing Irish and Scots in Christian's army. Various branches of the Hamilton family form both sides of the Irish Sea were involved in raising or blocking the levies, yet they shared the same name. Many non-Gaelic soldiers from Ireland were also as likely to have called themselves Scottish or British as Irish, while Scottish Gaels were equally as happy to have refer to themselves as Irish or Scots. Indeed this latter case has led to the erroneous identification of Scots from Mackay's regiment on the famous 'Stettin Woodcut' of 1630 as Irishmen.[16] Such confusion aside, there is plenty of evidence to show that Scottish troops provided by far and away the largest fighting force from the British Isles to Christian IV.

By January 1626, John Chamberlain reported that the Court in London had 'great store' of Scots offering up to 5,000 men for the Palatine cause. These men desired royal permission to raise the soldiers, but wished to retain the right to pay and dispose of them themselves.[17] The desire to assemble a separate army to that of England probably resulted from the shambolic efforts of the English recruiters to supply their troops in the 1624 'Mansfeld' levy. In any case, news of the Scottish offer reached Christian IV and in November he made a direct request to Charles I to raise two regiments of Scottish soldiers in addition to the contingent due

---

[13] Monro, *His Expedition*, I, 5 and 38.
[14] *CSPI*, 1625-1632, 227. Lord Deputy to Conway, 29 April 1627; Jhone Hammyltone to Archibald Edmonstone, 25 December 1627, reproduced in *Ullans*, no. 5 (1997), 51-52. He is perhaps the same man as Captain John Hamilton reported dead to officials in Ireland in 1629. See *APC, July 1628-April 1629*, 24. 22 May 1629.
[15] *RPCS*, second series, II, xiii, 241, 316 and 335-336. Alexander Hamilton to Scottish Privy Council, 26 February-19 June 1628; *CSPI*, 1625-1632, 345. Charles I to Lord Deputy, May 1628. Pass allowing 200 men raised by Captain Stewart for Christian IV to pass freely from Irish ports. It is not clear if these were part of Hamilton's levy or in addition to it.
[16] J. R. Paas, *The German Political Broadsheet 1600 – 1700*, 5 (Wiesbaden: 1996) 101.
[17] Thomson, *The Chamberlain Letters*, 356-357. Chamberlain to Dudley Carleton, 19 January 1626.

to arrive with Morgan.[18] Two weeks later, Christian wrote to Charles in regard to a request put to him by James Sinclair of Murckle, who had offered to raise 3,000 Scots if Charles I would allow it.[19] By March 1627, patents had been issued for the raising of 9,000 Scots to be formed in three regiments, one under Robert Maxwell Earl of Nithsdale, one under Alexander Lindsay Lord Spynie and one to be commanded by James Sinclair Baron Murckle.[20] These troops were to be in addition to the 3,000 Scots already mustered by Donald Mackay who had been intended for Mansfeld's army but were diverted into Danish service.[21] Even if the low figure of 4,900 Englishmen is added to Mackay's 3,000 Scots, Christian still had 8,000 Britons in his army by April 1627, exceeding the British commitment given in The Hague. At least 3,000 of the Nithsdale, Spynie and Murckle levies had also arrived by October 1627 to supplement Morgan and Mackay's troops, bringing the total of Britons who had been sent to Christian's army to almost 11,000 men by that date.[22] These numbers were reduced by disease and battlefield casualties, but Charles I had easily ensured the provision of more men that he had been required to by the agreements of 1625. Lind has calculated that by spring of 1628 the entire Danish-Norwegian strength stood at 10,000 royal Danish troops supplemented by 8,000 loyal to Charles I, which by that time would have been split between about 3,000 Englishmen and 5,000 Scots.[23] These were joined throughout 1628 by numerous Scottish, Welsh and Irish companies brought over to replace the casualties of war, while Morgan tried to build a new army of 2,000 men in the United Provinces which he hoped to have ready for Danish service by November.[24]

Given the conflicting information regarding the size and distribution of the Danish army, the exact numerical contribution of the Scots is quite hard to ascertain. Some scholars have argued that probably no more than 10,000 of the 13,700 actually served, but do not give reasons for their

[18] PRO SP75/7, f.228. Anstruther to Charles I, 2 November 1626; PRO SP75/7, f.230. Anstruther to Conway, 2 November 1626.
[19] PRO SP75/7, f.235. Christian IV to Charles I, 17 November 1626; *SSNE* no. 538.
[20] PRO SP75/8, f.42. Anstruther to Buckingham, 9 March 1627; *RPCS*, second series, I. Nithsdale's levy, 531 and 565, Spynie's levy, 556 and 565 and Sinclair's levy, 563-565; Nithsdale's recommendation to Christian IV from Charles I can be found in DRA, TKUA England A I 3. Charles I to Christian IV, 8 February 1627; For Alexander Lindsay see *SSNE* no. 177
[21] DRA, TKUA England, A I 3. Charles I to Christian IV, 20 July 1626; *RPCS*, second series, I, 244.
[22] PRO SP75/8, f.353. Anstruther to Secretary of State, 14 October 1627.
[23] See Lind, *Hæren og Magten*, 54 and 58; Fallon, 'Scottish Mercenaries', 200.
[24] Monro, *His Expedition*, I, 80-82; *RPCS*, second series, II, 241, 316 and 335-336; *APC*, *June 1628-April 1629*, 211, 248 and passim.

estimate.[25] Adding the hundreds, if not thousands of Scots scattered throughout English, Dutch and Mansfeld's regiments, the figure could conceivably have been exceeded if patterns of recruitment proven to have happened elsewhere also applied to Denmark-Norway.[26] After all, entire regiments, such as that of Colonel Seton's in Bohemian service in 1620, are not mentioned in the *Register of the Privy Council of Scotland*, yet we know they were in service. As noted in chapter two, Sir Andrew Gray left Scotland in 1620 with 500 soldiers over the limit allowed by his warrant and this was not an isolated case. Scottish recruiters in Sweden could still fill their quota with ease after 1629. James Spens went over his levy by 70 men and told Gustav II Adolph that he could raise 10,000 soldiers for Swedish service immediately in Britain at that time.[27] There does not, therefore, appear to have been a lack of manpower in Scotland even after the French, Spanish and Danish campaigns of the late 1620s. In addition to the 'sanctioned levies' in Scotland, Robert Frost has highlighted that units of as many as 900 Scots could be mustered from the Scottish diaspora in Poland at any time, as per their levy in 1621.[28] But the Poles were not the only people to rely on this source and Alexia Grosjean has noted that the Swedes, for instance, sent Captain Thomas Hume to recruit 200 Scots from Scottish community in Poland in 1632.[29] Thomas Riis has also noted that many members of the Scottish communities throughout Denmark and Norway were expected to serve in some military capacity throughout the war and it is unlikely that Scottish citizens did not take their turn in defending Danish towns as the Habsburg forces advanced into Denmark.[30] Individual Scots on the continent also sought out Scottish, or Scottish led units as a way out of any financial or personal difficulties. Andrew Melvill, for example, managed to escape dire situations twice through this method, once in the Spanish Netherlands in 1648 and again in

---

[25] Fallon, 'Scottish Mercenaries', 246.

[26] Even some of Morgan's high ranking officers were Scots, such as Sir Archibald Douglas who took a regiment of 1,150 London Foot out to Denmark in the summer of 1627. See *APC, January to August 1627*, 145. 20 March 1627; Ibid., *September 1627-June 1628*, 237. 14 January 1627/1628.

[27] He also told the Swedish king that if Britons were not received in a kindly manner the same fate would befall him 'as befell the King of Denmark following unsavoury reports: even if his realm were in the greatest danger not even a dwarf from this kingdom would engage in his service'. See DCJS, 408; SRA, Anglica 3, f.103. Spens to Gustav II Adolf, 12 July 1629.

[28] R. I. Frost, 'Scottish Soldiers, Poland-Lithuania and the Thirty Years' War' in S. Murdoch ed, *Scotland and the Thirty Years' War, 1618-1648* (forthcoming, Leiden, 2001).

[29] *RAOSB*, VII, 16 June 1632, 418-420. I would like to thank Alexia Grosjean for providing me with this very useful reference.

[30] Riis, *Should Auld Acquaintance*, II, passim.

Germany in 1652.[31] In other words, regardless of whether or not the number of soldiers reached the numbers suggested by the Scottish Privy Council warrants, evidence exists proving that enlistments often occurred in such a way that they were not officially recorded in Scotland. Many other individuals were also undoubtedly absorbed into Danish, Norwegian and German units from other locations on the continent.

A Question of Motivation and Loyalty

Having established that there were probably twice as many Scots as Englishmen in Danish-Norwegian service, some thought should be given as to why they might be so keen to enlist compared to their fellow Stuart subjects. The majority of historical commentary on military involvement misrepresents the variety of motivations that led to overseas service under foreign powers. James Fallon attributed mercenary motives to the Scots in Danish-Norwegian service, arguing that they fought for money, and not loyalty to the Stuart or Danish Crown. Yet to back his argument Fallon cited General Morgan's description of his English troops and did not produce any Scottish examples. Both Colonel Monro and subsequent historians noted that the Scottish regiment of Donald Mackay fought initially in return for bread and lodgings, while Morgan's troops fought for money, surely evidence that their motives were poles apart.[32] While the contrasting nature of British service may have been lost on the Scandinavian historical world, the difference has been noted in a different context. Certainly Danish historians make the distinction between the 'British' troops who served in Denmark-Norway after 1625 and soldiers of other nationalities. Britons are called *hjælptropper* (help troops) as an indication of their status as people from an allied country. Individuals from other countries are usually called *lejetropper* (literally 'rented' troops), especially soldiers from Germany.[33] Throughout the reign of Gustav II Adolf, the Swedes too made this distinction. The Scots in particular are never referred to as *legotrupper* as they had been the century before (and as the Germans continued to be during the

---

[31]   T. Ameer-Ali ed, *Memoirs of Sir Andrew Melvill* (London, 1918), 90-91 and 158.

[32]   Monro felt compelled to make the point twice. See Monro, *His Expedition*, I, 5 and 7; J. Mackay, 'Mackay's Regiment' in *Transactions of the Gaelic Society of Inverness*, VIII, (1878-1879), 135; E. A. Beller, 'The Military Expedition of Sir Charles Morgan to Germany, 1627-1629' in *The English Historical Review*, XLIII (1928), 531; Fallon, 'Scottish Mercenaries', 61-62.

[33]   *KCFB*, II, 44, notes to the letters from Christian IV to Charles I, 25 October 1626 and 230-233, Christian IV to Frederick Gunther, 3 December 1629; Tandrup, *Svensk agent ved Sundet*. In the notes on 527-528, Tandrup relates information regarding 'troppehjælp' from England *(sic)*, while in talking about Mansfeld and Christian of Halberstadt the wording is of the two 'lejetropførere' or mercenary leaders and their men. See 546-547

seventeenth century) but are considered an important allied nation.[34]

Other reasons for service in the anti-Habsburg armies abound, but are seldom considered in any detail. Undoubtedly many Scots sympathised with the distressed Protestants in Germany and the Scottish Kirk felt that Scottish Calvinists had a special role to play in the protection of their fellow Protestants in Europe. Indeed, in July 1627, a fast was ordered to show solidarity with 'the distress and cruel persecution of the members of the reformed Church of Bohemia'.[35] Of course, some Scottish Catholics joined the Habsburg armies during this period, but in comparison to the numbers of Scots on the anti-Habsburg side, their numbers were small, or at least Colonel Robert Monro noted as much in his diary.[36] What is revealing is the number of leading Scottish Catholics, such as Colonel Sir Andrew Gray, General Robert Maxwell Earl of Nithsdale, Lt. Colonel John Henderson and Colonel Sir John Hepburn who were found in 'Protestant' armies in the Thirty Years' War.[37]

There has to be an explanation as to why Scottish (and Irish) Catholics would join an army ostensibly fighting for the 'Protestant Cause'. This is best achieved by looking at the war from a perspective other than that of religious division. The Stuarts were in the remarkable position of being the monarchs of three kingdoms in each of which a different confession of faith prevailed. As far as the Scots Calvinists were concerned, the king's personal confession of faith was his own business so long as he left the Kirk in Scotland to its own devices. Importantly, to the Irish learned class the fact that the king was, in their eyes, a heretic appears to have been of little consequence. James's mother had been a Catholic and it was hoped, therefore, that he would be more tolerant of their faith than previous English monarchs had been. This was of course in addition to

[34] *Konung Gustaf den förstes Registratur,* Handlingar Rörande Sveriges Historia, första serien (29 vols, Stockholm, 1861-1916), XXVI, 442. Gustav Vasa till Egon Dodis och Michael Lermont i Edinburg angående deras erbjudande af skotska legotrupper i kriget mot ryssarne, 15 August 1556; SRA, Anglica 3, f.87. James Spens to Gustav II Adolf, 24 April 1627. Spens calls them simply 'voluntariourum militum'. The Riksråd treated Scotland as an independent allied nation. See Grosjean, 'Scots and the Swedish State', particularly 157-161 and 166-173.
[35] 'Proceedings of the Commissioners of the Kirk at a meeting held in Edinburgh in July 1627', in *Bannatyne Miscellany,* III (Bannatyne Club, Edinburgh, n.d.), 222-223.
[36] Monro, *His Expedition,* II, 75; *SSNE* no. 94.
[37] Nithsdale's Catholicism featured in Charles's correspondence to Denmark. DRA, TKUA England A 1 3. Charles I to Christian IV, 8 February 1627. C. Rogers ed, *The Earl of Stirling's Register of Royal Letters* (Edinburgh, 1885), 130. Charles I to Sir Robert Anstruther, 8th February 1627. Charles I told Christian IV about Nithsdale's Catholicism and instructed Anstruther to vouch for Nithsdale's loyalty; 'Although he is addicted to the Romish religion, yit in regard of the proof we have had of his sufficiencie and affection to our service, yow shall answer for his fidelitie in our name'. For Hepburn see *SSNE* no. 260, Nithsdale, *SSNE* no. 531 and Gray, *SSNE* no. 378.

the fact that the Irish viewed the Stuarts as sharing the same origins in Silesia and, indeed, as descendants of Irish kings. To bolster a positive attitude to the Stuarts even further, the Jesuits Bellarmine and Suarez argued that 'as temporal and spiritual authority were to be clearly distinguished it was possible for a Catholic people to give allegiance at least in temporalibus to a "heretical" Prince'.[38] Their doctrine was accepted at the clerical synods of Drogheda and Kilkenny in 1614, Armagh in 1618 and Cashel in 1624. It is very likely that Scottish Catholics would have been aware of these teachings and they may have had a bearing on their loyalty to King James and his family.

An assault by forces of Ferdinand II on Bohemia in 1619 was seen in Scotland as more than an attack on European Protestantism; it was also taken as a direct act of aggression against the House of Stuart. Colonels Gray and Hepburn, and other loyal Roman Catholics, had at least two valid reasons to return to Bohemia, regardless of their religious affiliations: defence of Queen Elizabeth and her family in particular and upholding the honour of the House of Stuart in general. Robert Monro spoke of fighting a good cause against the enemy of the daughter of his king, the queen of Bohemia, and ascribed similar motives to Colonel Donald Mackay.[39] The Colonel himself related to a friend that he was no true soldier of fortune but served abroad because of his loyalty and affection for King Charles.[40] Another Scottish soldier, Thomas Kellie, published a military manual after service in Christian IV's army in which he exhorted others to join the fight for Elizabeth of Bohemia 'the Jewell of Europe'. This name found favour among the Scots and Monro adopted the same title for her in his memoirs.[41] Some Scots serving in Imperial service even left to serve in the 'Protestant' armies. Sir Henry Bruce, Imperial Governor of Mikulor, relinquished that position to raise a regiment for Elizabeth Stuart whom he declared 'he no longer wished to fight'.[42] Both primary and secondary sources cite the cause of

---

[38] See B. Ó. Buachalla, *Aisling Ghear; Na Stiubhartaigh agus an t-aos léinn* (Dublin, 1996), 47; Ó Buachalla, 'James our true king', 10-11.

[39] Monro, *His expedition*, I, 21. He noted 'fighting in a good cause against the enemies of the daughter of our king, the Queen of Bohemia, for whose sake, our Majestie and royal master did undertake the warres, and for her sake, we resolved to have followed such a courageous leader'; *SSNE* no. 93.

[40] Mackay quoted in R. Mackay, *The house and clan of Mackay* (Edinburgh, 1829), 272; Monro, *His expedition*, I, 21. Grant, *Memoirs of Sir John Hepburn*, 12; J. H. Burton, *The Scot Abroad* (Edinburgh, 1864), 315; T. Fischer in *The Scots in Germany*, 73.

[41] T. Kellie, *Pallas Armata or Militarie Instructions for the Learned* (Edinburgh, 1627), 2a; Monro, *His Expedition*, I, 37.

[42] J. V. Polisensky, *Tragic Triangle* (Prague, 1991), 181. See also Ferguson, *The Scots Brigade in Holland*, 224. Footnote 1 reproduces a letter from Carlton to Secretary Naughton, 15 April 1620, which notes that Bruce left the Emperor's service since he would not bear arms against 'his Majesty's son-in-law'.

Elizabeth Stuart above all others as the reason why the majority of the Scottish officers volunteered. They also show that even among the non-commissioned officers and privates there were high numbers of gentlemen's sons.[43]

The fact that Elizabeth Stuart was regarded as a Scottish princess from the Scottish royal house was not lost on the Scottish Parliament, the Kirk or military recruiters. The young queen of Bohemia had many Scots in her household and not least of these was Colonel Sir Andrew Gray, her quartermaster since 1613. Colonel Gray recruited thousands of soldiers in Scotland, but it has been a feature of historical assessments to imply that many of these soldiers were the unworthies of society. Scrutiny of the *Register of the Privy Council of Scotland* show that missives were indeed sent out to various Scottish burghs regarding the enlistment of beggars and masterless vagabonds who might have been 'in danger of punishment of death' to enlist and escape punishment. These missives give credence to the belief that many of the soldiers were criminals or members of the 'redundant population'.[44] This perception is contradicted in the writings of several contemporary commentators of Scottish military personnel in Europe. The Venetian ambassador concluded, for instance, that Andrew Gray's Regiment 'included a larger number of Scots than English and of better quality, owing to the efforts of that Colonel to show more honour to those of his own nation'.[45] The numbers of beggars and bandits, therefore, must have been low in this case. Some of the enlisted Scots were undoubtedly 'local troublemakers whom the magistrates allowed to be kidnapped, and not a few were outlaws'.[46] The majority, however, were as likely to have been volunteers of good social standing as criminals. Indeed at most, if the Scottish Privy Council records are to be believed, the iniquitous element amounted to only several hundred out of tens of thousands of men who served during the course of the Thirty Years' War. Some gentlemen, like Sir Thomas Kellie noted above, even left Scotland with only their personal servants in attendance to join the anti-Habsburg armies as private soldiers. As Charles I said of him, Kellie 'out of the affection he caryes to our service, is to goe and serve a voluntarie soldiour in the King of Denmark, his army, upon his own charges', though it seems he eventually gained a company and doubled as a Stuart agent there.[47]

---

43   Grant, *Memoirs of Sir John Hepburn*, 12; Burton, *The Scot Abroad*, 315; Fischer, *The Scots in Germany*, 73; Mackay, *An Old Scots Brigade*, 6.
44   *RPCS*, XII, 1619-1622, 259-261 and *RPCS*, second series, vols. I-III passim; Fallon, 'Scottish Mercenaries', 77.
45   *CSPV*, XVI, 1619-1621, 326-7. Girolamo Lando, 9 July 1620.
46   Parker, *The Thirty Years' War*, 173.
47   See 'A Licence to Travell' issued by Charles I to Mr Thomas Kellie July 1626. *Earl of*

Given the information published to date on British military service in Denmark-Norway, it would seem that historians have failed to grasp the significance of the role of Stuart subjects during *Kejserkrig*. Indeed, outwith Morgan's or Mackay's regiments, there is really little secondary material available. Part of the reason for this, at least in Mackay's case, is the existence of the campaign memoirs of Major Robert Monro which has captured the attention of Scottish scholars for years. This work traces the fortunes of Mackay's regiment from its arrival in Danish service to its departure from Swedish service.[48] To compound the magnetic effect of Monro's *Expedition*, there are the many other works that draw from it.[49] The availability of information on the regiment means that Mackay's has traditionally been taken to be the most important military assistance that the Scots gave to Denmark-Norway during the course of the war. Certainly the regiment took part in several actions which must be briefly highlighted in order to demonstrate not only how many, but in what way Scottish soldiers conducted themselves during the *Kejserkrig* campaigns. Though this was normally positive, there could be moments where the Scots behaved in ways that were beyond the ken of the Stuart and Oldenburg kings.

Almost immediately on the arrival of the Scottish regiments in Danish territory, a crisis arose over which flag they would fight under. This situation is said to have 'rankled the breast' of Christian IV who could not understand the problem of fighting under Danish colours. One German historian observed that 'when the king of Denmark at first refused to let them retain their silk flag with the cross of St. Andrew on it, they all threatened instant departure'.[50] The incident was recorded by Robert Monro:

> His majesty [of Denmark] would have the officers to carry the Dane's crosse, which the officers refusing, they were summoned to compeare before his majestie at Raynesberge to know the reasons of their

    Stirling's Register of Royal Letters, 60. This is the author of *Pallas Armata* (Edinburgh, 1627); See also *APC, January-August 1627*, 53. Pass for Kellie to go to Denmark on business of Charles I, 8 February 1626/27; *APC, September 1627-June 1628*, 49. Pass for Kellie to return to his company in Denmark, 25 September 1627.

[48] Monro, *His Expedition*. For an excellent new edition of this work see W. S. Brockington, jnr., ed, *Monro, His Expedition with the Worthy Scots Regiment called Mac-Keys* (Westport and London, 1999). See also the German language edition by H. Mahr ed, *Oberst Robert Monro. Kriegserlebnisse eines schottischen Söldnerführers in Deutschland 1626 - 1633* (Neustadt an der Aisch, 1995).

[49] R. Mackay, *The house and clan of Mackay* (Edinburgh, 1829); J. Mackay, 'Mackay's Regiment', in *Transactions of the Gaelic Society of Inverness*, VIII, (1878-79); J. Mackay, *An Old Scots Brigade* (Edinburgh, 1885); I. Grimble, *The Chief of Mackay* (London, 1965).

[50] Fischer, *The Scots in Germany*, 75,

refusals; at the meeting none would adventure, fearing his majestie's indignation, to gainestand openly his Majestie's will, being then his Majestie's sworne servants; and for the eschewing of greater inconvenience the officers desired so much time of his Majesty as to send Captain Robert Ennis into England to know his majestie of Great Britaine's will, whether or no they might carrie without reproach the Dane's Crosse in Scottish colours.[51]

This incident illustrates that loyalty to their country and king was strong on the part of many Scottish soldiers. On the whole they were not willing simply to fight under anyone's banner without thought for, or indeed sometimes consultation with their own monarch. In their own way, these officers had shown they were not the sort of malleable mercenaries Christian was recruiting elsewhere.

The determination and loyalty of the Scots set them apart from the other nationalities engaged in the Danish-Norwegian army. During July 1627, four companies of Mackay's regiment were stationed at Boitzenburg, defending a strategic Elbe crossing, under the command of Major Dunbar.[52] John de Tsercua, Count of Tilly, whose men numbered some 10,000, immediately put Dunbar, with a garrison of only 800 men, under siege. Despite running out of ammunition at one point, the Scots losses at the end of the engagement were minimal, while Tilly's are reckoned at between 1-2,000. The Imperialists crossed the Elbe further up-river where they surprised the German guards and crossed with relative ease. Boitzenburg demonstrated the fighting quality of the Scots who had also gained the respect of the gentry and nobility of Germany in the process. The Dukes of Mecklenburg and Weimar visited the unit personally to congratulate them while General Morgan commented 'I heare they did very well'.[53]

Within weeks, Major Dunbar took command of the late Field Marshal Gert Rantzau's castle of Breitenburg.[54] Rantzau has been described as the Danish realm's greatest magnate and had been responsible for the raising of the Holstein army.[55] Before his death he had been Field Marshal of all

---

[51] Monro, *His Expedition*, I, 2. Charles I eventually gave the Scots the choice of two colours. One had a *Dannebrog* with a Saltire in the corner, the other had a Saltire with a *Dannebrog* in the corner. The comment was added that they could choose which one they wanted, but they had to choose one in order to get the King of Denmark's pay. See PRO SP75/8, f.61. The state of the King of Denmark's army, March 1627.

[52] *SSNE* no. 129.

[53] Monro, *His Expedition*, I, 10-12; PRO SP 75/8, f.252. General Morgan to Secretary of State, 6 August 1627.

[54] Monro, *His Expedition*, I, 38.

[55] Lind, *Hæren og Magten*, 33.

Danish forces, second only in command to the king himself.[56] Given that fact one might ask why there had not been a strong Holstein garrison placed in command of the castle. After all, inside there were many of the local civilian population seeking shelter from the encroaching army of Count Tilly.[57] Dunbar's total garrison only amounted to some 400 men, yet they held out despite offers of terms. Tilly conducted a seven day siege before the walls were breached and the majority of the defenders and civilians killed.[58] Despite the slaughter of the garrison, Tilly had again suffered heavily from the ferocity of their defence, this time losing 1,000 men while taking possession of the castle. During the two conflicts Dunbar's companies had reduced Tilly's army from 10,000 to 7,000 men before their own demise. This works out as a 'kill ratio' of almost four to one, a fact not lost on the Imperialists, the Danes and certainly not the Scots.

Another hard fought action took place at the pass of Oldenburg in 1627. During the battle, Mackay's regiment held the pass for nine hours while their comrades from Holstein and Germany retired in disorder. The military council decided that Tilly's force was too great and that the army should retire to Heilingenhavn and sail for Denmark. At Heilingenhavn the German cavalry in Danish service crowded the pier and Sir Donald Mackay ordered his pikemen to clear them before pressing ships to evacuate the regiment. Of the whole of the Duke of Weimar's army, only Mackay's regiment escaped. Monro described watching 36 German cornets of horse and five entire German regiments surrender without firing a shot, and in fact afterwards they switched sides and joined the Imperialist army.[59] This action led inevitably to the occupation of Holstein and Jutland and indeed the heart of Denmark itself was threatened. The situation was only saved due to the Danish-Norwegian superiority in naval strength and the tenacity of the remaining troops on the Danish archipelago. Christian IV was particularly impressed with the Scottish troops and, according to Monro, he favoured Scottish troops above any other nationality, even Danes.[60] Christian wrote to Charles I praising them and adding that 'these soldiours of the Scottish nation whom wee have employed, have served us so faithfully, that if wee could obtaine more from your majestie, we would most willingly accept them'.[61] In recognition of Mackay's service,

[56]   Lind, *Hæren og Magten*, 291 and 296.
[57]   Monro, *His Expedition*, I, 12 and 35.
[58]   Monro, *His Expedition*, I, 38-39.
[59]   Monro, *His Expedition*, I, 26-28.
[60]   Monro, *His Expedition*, I, 81.
[61]   PRO SP75/8, f.365. Christian IV to Charles I, 18 October 1627. In the same letter Christian requested permission to levy another 1,000 men.

Christian IV arranged for Mackay's sons to attend the academy of Sorø at his own expense.[62]

Elsewhere in the Danish army, Scots were being rewarded for their service in other ways. In December 1627, Christian IV named three new 'General Commissioners' for the regions of Skåne, Halland and Blekinge. Alexander Lindsay Lord Spynie had the honour of being appointed to that position in Skåne.[63] In addition to assuming overall command of the garrisons in their regions, they were also responsible for the defence of the countryside surrounding them. Good relations were also to be maintained between the soldiers and civilians. To ensure the preservation of discipline Courts of Justice, war trials and executions arising from them were to be held on a weekly basis. We know from other royal missives that Scottish regiments comprised the majority of Spynie's garrisons, but that he also had 250 Danish soldiers under his command in 1628 as replacements for his casualties. These, the king insisted, were to be accommodated as comfortably as the Scots![64]

Stralsund and Beyond

After the loss of Holstein and Jutland, Christian IV's military operations were little more than a series of defensive actions within Danish sovereign territory. That was, of course, with the exception of Stralsund where the Scots were to play a decisive role. The Danes were also bolstered by military support from Sweden. The Swedes could see that an invasion of Denmark would give the Empire a powerful position on the Baltic coast, greatly increasing Imperial influence in the region and threatening Sweden itself. Gustav II Adolf was prepared to set his differences with Christian IV (who as recently as 1624 was still contemplating a war to dominate Sweden) temporarily to one side to face the common enemy. Swedish forces had already captured the port of Pillau in East Prussia in 1626. In 1628, they engaged the forces of the Empire directly for the first time at Stralsund and set the scene for a new aggressive role for Sweden in northern European politics.

Stralsund was of great strategic importance to all the combatant

---

62   *HMC, Sixth Report* (London, 1877), 685. John Mackay to Sir Robert Farquhar, 6 October 1628. John Mackay wrote that 'hauing at last obtained of the King of Denmarks Majestie to giue us frie intertinament, hes Majestie hes dereckted us to an Universitie called Soare, quhilk is eight Dutch myle laying from this toune [Copenhagen], and there we three geat frie meat and chamer, our father furnishing the rest off our necessaries'.

63   E. Marquard ed, *Kancelliets Brevbøger Vedrørende Danmarks Indre Forhold i Uddrag 1627-1629* (Copenhagen, 1929), 259. Letter of Appointment, 1 December 1627; Ibid., 435, Missive til Kommissarierne i Skaane, 26 May 1628.

64   *Kancelliets Brevbøger 1627-1629*, 406. Missive, 1 May 1628; Monro, *His Expedition*, I, 78.

nations and Gustav II Adolf agreed to support the Danish-Norwegian fleet with the Swedish one and also to add troops to the Stralsund garrison.[65] The incumbent soldiers were drawn from Mackay's regiment who had arrived in May 1628. Towards the end of June the Swedish king allowed volunteers from his army to join them once it became clear they were in difficulty. The first to arrive were a largely Scottish company led by Colonel Fretz, Lt. Colonel Macdougall, Major Semple and 80 musketeers.[66] They engaged straight away and Semple was killed almost immediately on arrival. During the Stralsund campaign, Colonel Alexander Seaton took over as temporary Governor of Stralsund and acting commander of Mackay's regiment. The official Governor, Colonel Holke absented himself on several occasions during the siege leading Monro to conclude that he was not up to the task in hand. Monro particularly took delight in recording an incident during a foray when a Scottish lieutenant called Lumsdell noted the speed at which Holcke retreated from his enemy. Lumsdell called out an invitation to the German to stay for a while to see how well the Scots could fight, but as Monro noted, Holcke knew he was being baited and left the field.[67]

Whether the sniping at Holcke was justified or not, the battle for Stralsund was bitterly contested. The Scots managed to force a treaty until more Scottish and Danish reinforcements recruited by Lord Spynie arrived. Alexander Leslie, the future Earl of Leven, soon after landed his Scottish forces from Sweden and took over as Governor from Seaton, after which the defence of the island became the responsibility of Gustav II Adolf. In the meantime, Mackay's regiment had lost several hundred men and Spynie's regiment had been reduced to remnants.[68] Whether in the service of Denmark-Norway or Sweden, the defence of Stralsund was undoubtedly a Scottish military affair.

After Stralsund, Christian IV decided to raise another army during the winter of 1628-1629 for a further campaign against the Habsburg forces on Danish territory. While plans for this army were being discussed, talks were also held at Lübeck to arrange the peace. In April 1629, Mackay's regiment, including remnants of Spynie's contingent, received orders to leave their quarters and assemble at Enge, as renewed hostilities seemed imminent. Despite the military arrangements, the Treaty of Lübeck followed within days. When Denmark-Norway

---

[65]   Monro, *His Expedition*, I, 64-79; Mackay, *An Old Scots Brigade*, 60-80; Grosjean, 'Scots and the Swedish State', 78-80.
[66]   Monro, *His Expedition*, I, 69.
[67]   For Seaton see Monro, *His Expedition*, I, 75; *SSNE* no. 91. For Monro on Holcke see ibid., I, 64-65, 74-75 and 79.
[68]   Monro, *His Expedition*, 74-79; For Leslie see *SSNE* no. 1.

withdrew from the war most Scottish troops in Christian's service were ordered to Fyn to settle their financial and contractual arrangements with the Danish Chancellor.[69] Christian IV ordered that the Scottish officers were to be quartered at Elsinore until shipping could be arranged to take them home to Scotland although over 1,300 Scottish soldiers still remained in Danish service.[70] This left the Swedes on their own in the Baltic theatre to face the forces of Ferdinand II. The first major phase of Scottish military involvement with Denmark-Norway had ended. Mackay's regiment, joined by remnants of other regiments, did not retire from military service, but transferred directly to that of Sweden.[71] Gustav II Adolf's warrant to them is dated 17 June 1629, showing that they were preparing to leave even before they had settled with the Danish Chancellor.[72] Some of the veterans, such as Alexander Crawford and Eremii Garten ventured farther afield and arrived in Muscovy bearing testimonials of service from Christian IV.[73] Lord Reay himself decided to move his entire family over to Denmark while he prepared to join his regiment in the Swedish campaign.[74]

The Officer Corps 1625-1629

At the outset of the war, the Danish-Norwegian armed forces contained only 153 officers. Between 1625 and 1629 some 1,200 new officers enlisted into Christian's army.[75] By the end of the war the total number who served above the rank of NCO amounted to about 1,380 individuals. The highest number in service at any given point was reached in the summer of 1627 with a total officer corps of about 660 men. From the early part of 1628 that number fell to around 380 individuals. The total did not exceed this amount again during the course of the war. The majority of the new men were foreigners who, by the end of the war, made up some 66% of the officer elite. In order to understand the significance of the Scottish contribution it is important to consider the information relating to all the foreign officers in the army.

Officer enlistment and service for the war against the Empire is

---

[69] *Kancelliets Brevbøger 1627-1629*, 727. Missives to Niels Krag, 28 June 1629; Fallon 'Scottish Mercenaries', 241-243.

[70] *Kancelliets Brevbøger 1627-1629*, 727. Missives to Niels Krag, 28 June 1629; Monro, *His Expedition*, I, 85.

[71] For Scottish service in Sweden 1630-1648, see Grosjean, 'Scots and the Swedish State', 80-106.

[72] Mackay, *An Old Scots Brigade*, 83-86.

[73] P. Dukes, 'The First Scottish Soldiers in Russia', in G Simpson ed, *The Scottish Soldier Abroad 1247-1967*. (Edinburgh, 1992), 49; *SSNE* no. 126.

[74] *APC, May 1629-May 1630*, 47. 12 June 1629. Pass for Lord Reay to return to Denmark with his mother, wife, maid, nurse, children, servants and whole retinue with baggage.

[75] Lind, *Hæren og Magten*, 161.

presented in Fig. 4. The first column for each country shows the percentage the officers of a given country formed of the Danish army on the eve of the conflict, specifically the 31st December 1624. This set of information shows that Danes formed just over half of their own officer corps at this date, 50% [77/153]. The next most important named national group were the Germans with 14% [21/153] and the officers from Schleswig-Holstein who contributed 12% [19/153]. Apart from those of undecided origin, the only other group of officers to register above 1% at this juncture were the Scots with 4% [6/153]. This was more than the Dutch and, very surprisingly, the Norwegians.

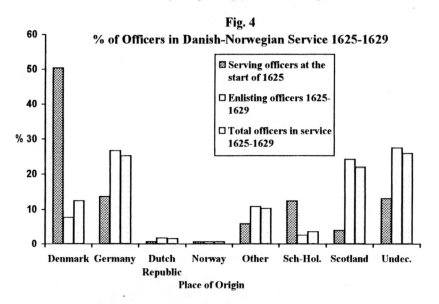

Fig. 4

% of Officers in Danish-Norwegian Service 1625-1629

(Source: *SSNE* and *DDA 1573* databases)

The second column given for each country in Fig. 4 shows the percentage of officers who enlisted into the Danish army between 1625 and 1629. Obviously this means that several individuals are included in the calculation for wartime enlistment who actually joined before the start of hostilities. However they have deliberately been included on the basis that they enlisted knowing Christian's intention to engage in a war with the Empire. These figures are perhaps the most revealing of the three in this particular group, showing as they do, the numbers of officers from each nation which sought to go to war in the service of Denmark-Norway.

Several statistics make themselves obvious in the second column group. Firstly the percentage of Danish officers in the army drops dramatically. The wartime intake of officers from Denmark only formed 8% [95/1,227] of the total of 1,227 new officers. Their colleagues from Schleswig-Holstein contributed another 2.5% [31/1,227] while almost unbelievably the Norwegians only contributed 0.6% [8/1,227]. This means that in total just under nine out of ten of the officer recruits into the Danish army of known nationality were foreigners from countries outwith the control of Christian IV. Perhaps unsurprisingly the combined German officer group formed a significant proportion of these men, some 27% [327/1,227] and a further 27% were of unknown origin. However, perhaps most surprising is the fact that Scottish officers made up 24% [297/1,227], almost a quarter of the total intake of officers during this period. The next nation to this were the Dutch with slightly less than 2% [21/1,227] and the English, not shown in Fig. 4, with 1% [15/1,227]. The ratio of Scots officers to English was a significant 20:1, while the Scots outnumbered the Danes themselves by 3:1.

When the numbers of 'currently serving' [153] and 'newly recruited' [1,227] officers are tallied together [1,380] the significance of the Scottish enlistment becomes obvious in the third column. The Danes' contribution to the officer corps shrank from just over half at the opening of 1625 to 12% [172/1380] throughout the course of the war. Even when all Christian IV's subjects are added together this percentage only rises to 17% [231/1380]. The proportion of officers from the allied German states rose to 25% [348/1380]. Remarkably, over one in five officers in Christian IV's army came from Scotland, 22% [303/1380]. No other single state reached over 2% of the total. It must also be recalled that the German contribution is a combined total from several of Christian IV's allies. It could be argued therefore that in terms of military leadership in the form of army officers, Scotland was by far the largest single contributing nation to the Protestant cause during the Danish period of the Thirty Years' War, much larger than Denmark itself.

The total contribution of foreign officers, excluding those soldiers of undetermined origin who might have been foreign, amounted to some 57% [793/1380] of the total. The significance of the Scottish proportion of this becomes explicitly clear in Fig. 5 which expresses each country's contribution as a percentage of the total number of foreign officers. The German allies make up the bulk with 44% [348/793]. The Scots come second with 38% [303/793]. The next largest contributors are the United Provinces with 3% [22/793] and the English with 2% [16/793]. The analysis of these figures illuminates many peculiarities and factors worthy of study. One cannot help but wonder at the extraordinarily low numbers of Norwegian officers during this period given that Norway was one of the component kingdoms of the Danish-Norwegian state. Gunner Lind attributes the absence of Norwegians to the Danish king's preference for experienced officers of which Norway, apparently, had few.[76] This statistical analysis of men from the Stuart kingdoms highlights the overwhelming presence of Scots and the shortage of English, Welsh and Irish officers (Fig. 6).

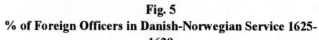

Fig. 5
% of Foreign Officers in Danish-Norwegian Service 1625-1629

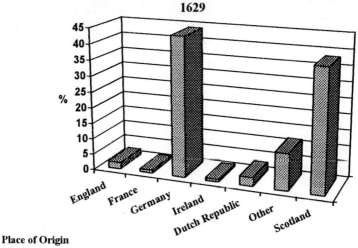

Place of Origin

(Source: *SSNE* and *DDA 1573* databases)

Gunner Lind has vigorously argued that the Danish war of 1625-1629 must be broken into two component parts: the war *against* the Empire from 1625-1627, and the war *for* Denmark 1627-1629. While this may have been of relevance to the way the Danes perceived the war, it is unlikely to have been a factor in influencing the way that the Scottish volunteers viewed the conflict. Despite the fact that almost half of the Scottish officers enlisted in this second phase of the conflict against the Imperial army, their late arrival merely demonstrates the time it took to organise and transport soldiers after permission was granted to levy them. It would be surprising if any evidence existed to suggest that the Scottish officers joined the Danish-Norwegian army for the defence of Denmark or Norway rather than the continuation of the war for queen Elizabeth of Bohemia and her family.

[76] Lind, *Hæren og Magten*, 161.

Fig. 6
Scottish, English and Irish Officers [325 men] in the
Danish-Norwegian Army 1625-1629

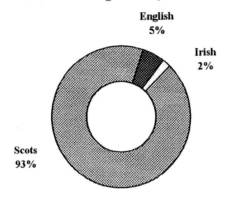

(Source: *SSNE* database)

The breakdown of the Scottish officer contribution to the Danish-Norwegian army from 1625-1629 reveals that the majority of the officers enlisted in the years 1627 [109] and 1628 [125] though with a significant group arriving in 1626 [42]. These enlistments were preceded by four individuals arriving in Denmark in 1624 and five in 1625 (see Fig. 7).[77] These nine officers probably represent the remnant of the troops which had been engaged in the Bohemian campaign and the advance guard of the individuals who decided to enter Danish-Norwegian service when it became clear that that state was going to join the war.

---

[77] In 1624 the following officers enlisted; Captain Magnus Alexander, *SSNE* no. 225; Quartermaster Daniel Berwick, *SSNE* no. 1469; Lieutenant David Falconer, *SSNE* no. 281 and Captain George Gray, *SSNE* no. 98. These men were followed in 1625 by Captain Archibald Carmichael, *SSNE* no. 495; Ensign Patrick Dunbar, later Baron Spannerup, *SSNE* no. 272; Captain Hans Gillis, *SSNE* no. 192; Major Alexander Ramsay, *SSNE* no. 230 and Lt. Colonel David Russel, *SSNE* no. 97.

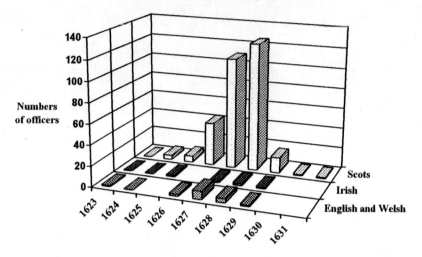

Fig. 7
Enlistment of British Isles Officers in the
Danish-Norwegian Army 1623-1631

(Source: *SSNE* database)

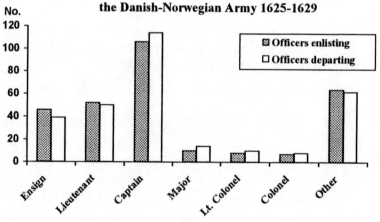

Fig. 8
Rank of Scottish Officers at Enlistment and Departure from
the Danish-Norwegian Army 1625-1629

(Source: *SSNE* database)

Quality and rank of British and Irish officers

Throughout *Kejserkrig*, there appears to have been little change in the rank of English, Welsh and Irish officers in the Danish-Norwegian army. However, there is plenty of statistical data on the Scots. A review of the rank of the Scottish officers in *Kejserkrig* reveals that a very large proportion of the Scots were of the rank of captain or above: 106 captains, 10 majors, 8 lieutenant colonels and seven colonels (see Fig. 8). This is in comparison with some 98 junior officers, 46 ensigns and 52 lieutenants. The category of 'other' contains ranks such as staff officers, chaplains and secretaries, but also 33 field officers of unknown rank. The prevalence of senior officers is perhaps not surprising since many of these men had been in the field in various armies for many years. It can be surmised therefore that the officers were of good quality and experience and made an important contribution to the Danish-Norwegian armed forces.

By contrasting the numbers of each given rank between those on arrival and those on departure it becomes clear that there were not many promotional opportunities for the Scots in Danish-Norwegian service during *Kejserkrig*. A small number of ensigns and lieutenants made the rank of captain, while four officers were promoted to major, three to lieutenant colonel and only one to full colonel. Few of the senior Scottish officers gained promotion beyond the rank of Colonel. The reason for this lack of advancement in military rank can be attributed to several factors. The Danes had a policy of maintaining control of the higher echelons of their armed forces. Lind argues that whenever the indigenous officer corps was stable, the foreign officers simply had to accept their conditions.[78] However, Robert Scott apparently became Master General of all Danish artillery while Nithsdale's appointment as general of Scottish troops would have placed him at the head of an army of between 10,000 - 14,000 men, albeit his appointment was contested by his fellow Scot, Lord Spynie.[79] A source documenting the demotion of Nithsdale has yet to be found, but certainly the Scots did not serve in one body in the war. Some individual commanders took care of their own troops, such as those under Lord Spynie. Other regiments, like Mackay's appear to have fallen mostly under Danish control with some companies joining General Morgan's troops. Morgan was certainly appointed General with

---

[78] Lind, *Hæren og Magten*, 163.

[79] For Nithsdale's appointment as General see PRO SP75/8, f.42. Anstruther to Buckingham, 9 March 1627; PRO SP75/8, f.45. Anstruther to Charles I, 9 March 1627; PRO SP75/8, f.61. The State of the King of Denmark's Army, March 1627. For Spynie contesting this appointment see DRA, TKUA Skotland A II 4 (n.d); For Scott see Riis, *Should Auld Acquaintance*, II, 116; Blom, 'Smaa Bidrag til Artilleriets Historie', 332-44.

responsibility for all English infantry, although Trafford's Welshmen came under Scottish command. Yet according to some sources, all the infantry in the Danish-Norwegian army – indigenous soldiers included – were to be commanded by Morgan, although this certainly did not happen.[80] His status serves to show that promotion was not necessarily attained by ability or loyalty. Unlike General Morgan, the Scottish officers were not renowned for the surrender of their commands.[81] The actions at Boitzenburg, Breitenburg, the Pass of Oldenburg and Stralsund are testament to that.[82]

These actions bring us to what is possibly the main reason that so few promotions took place for Scots in Danish-Norwegian service. The rate of attrition was so high in the Scottish regiments that many of the officers simply did not live long enough to gain promotion. Apart from those who were killed, there were others who returned home through injury. Lind puts the figure of officers who 'disappeared' from the army muster rolls and were replaced by new ones at around 71%.[83] These losses did not necessarily facilitate many promotions in the field since there were fewer and fewer men to command. Many officers therefore found themselves to be 'reformed' in another company to their own. In the 'great reduction' of 1627-1628 cavalry soldiers were moved to the infantry and many officers had to accept a change in status. What this meant in practice was that they retained the right to their rank but often acted in a capacity below it. Indeed many reformed officers fulfilled the role of common soldiers.

Scottish enlistment into the Danish-Norwegian army did not arise as a sudden or surprising development between 1625-1627. Coupled with the investigation of Scottish participation in the Danish army between 1614-1624, previous chapters have shown that the Scots had been mobilising for the Thirty Years' War in large numbers since 1620. Consequently, their arrival in the Danish-Norwegian army after 1625 represented the

[80] PRO SP75/8, f.123. Charles I to Sir Charles Morgan, May 1627; *HMC 4th Report*, 410. 'We understand by or Amr [Ambassador] that or dear uncle the K. of Denmarke hath offered unto you the Generall command of all his infantary'. See also Parker, *The Thirty Years' War*, 178.
[81] *KCFB*, II, 230-233. Christian IV to Frederick Gunther, 3 December 1629. Christian IV expressed his dissatisfaction with both Morgan and the English regiments and told Gunther that Morgan would have to look to Charles for any payment he thought he was owed. There was no such criticism levelled at the Scottish soldiers.
[82] Morgan held the town of Stade, but surrendered it to General Tilly in May 1628. He was released from Danish service and went to The Netherlands. He returned to Glückstadt by the winter of 1628 with a smaller force of 2,000 men.
[83] Lind, *Hæren og Magten*, 163.

continuation of a process started by Colonel Gray five years earlier. The traditional view that Scottish participants in *Kejserkrig* should be considered as mercenaries is over simplistic. Many contemporary Danish observers and modern Scandinavian historians view the Scots as confederates in the anti-Habsburg campaign. That point is reflected in the vocabulary used to describe them: allies not hirelings. The Scots in turn demonstrated through the integrity of their actions that they were participating in the conflict for a very different agenda to that of their contemporaries. As one proof of that, deserters from the Scottish regiments could only rarely be counted in numbers above 'tens' at a time. For the English it could often be recorded in hundreds and for the Germans it might even be thousands. This was noted by Christian IV at the time and resulted in repeated praise for Scottish troops, particularly those under Spynie and Mackay.

Numerically too Scotland equalled or surpassed Denmark-Norway's other allies, including England. James Fallon concluded his analysis of Scottish soldiers in the Danish-Norwegian army by saying that there was little doubt 'that numerically the Scottish contribution was considerable'. However, he also placed the most significant role of the Scots as either 'shock troops' or as useful 'in rearguard actions and as reserve troops'.[84] While there is little doubt that the Scots fulfilled these functions well, their part was more fundamental than such categorisations imply. Scotland did not simply provide a source of brawn in the form of foot soldiers. A significant proportion of officers at both junior and senior level left Scotland to serve in Christian IV's army. As Sir Thomas Urquhart of Cromarty went to pains to remind his audience, 'Denmark, in my opinion, cannot goodly forget the magnanimous exploits of Sir Donald Mackie Lord Reay...nor yet of the Colonels of the name of Monro and Henderson, in the service of that king; as likewise of the Colonel Lord Spynay and others'.[85] The comparative contribution of foreign and domestic officers in the Danish-Norwegian army clearly illuminates the importance of the Scottish military elite to Christian IV. Given the analysis above, the long-held belief that the only significant military assistance given to Christian IV from the kingdoms of Charles I arrived in the form of Morgan's army can be dismissed. Indeed Urquhart's interpretation, once more, is probably closer to the truth.

---

[84] Fallon, 'Scottish Mercenaries', 247.
[85] S. D. Stirling ed, *The Works of Sir Thomas Urquhart of Cromarty, Knight* (Edinburgh, 1834), 215.

CHAPTER TEN

Military Service III:
The Danish-Norwegian wars with Sweden
1643-45 and 1657-60

Despite the variety of works that discuss British and Irish enlistment for Denmark-Norway, two significant increases in the officer intake have largely gone unnoticed. Thomas Riis devotes a couple of sentences to the Scottish aspect of these events, but does not develop any argument relating to them, remarking only that Denmark was at war and that some Scots took part.[1] Like the Kalmar War and *Kejserkrig*, these military campaigns were of a particularly Caledonian nature in terms of the officer intake from the British Isles, although in the 1650s the Irish made a statistically significant contribution for the first time.[2] The diplomatic tensions that led to the Torstensson War (1643-1645) have been well documented and described in Scandinavia.[3] Lennart Torstensson, the Swedish commander, attacked Holstein in December 1643 in a pre-emptive strike ordered because the Swedes felt sure Denmark was about to join the war in Germany on the side of the Emperor. The Danes were in significant trouble after Torstensson's invasion for a variety of reasons. Although Denmark-Norway had access to its largest ever peacetime army, the conscripts had been de-mobilised and the permanent recruits were in their winter quarters. Because of this the Danes were unable to assemble their forces and the war developed into a series of sieges at points where garrisons were strong enough to resist attack. Lind describes the situation as one where soldiers were continually transported between the areas of greatest pressure and whichever locations could bring the best results.[4] Because of such manoeuvres, the war was fought on five separate fronts, Norway, Skåne, the Sound, the Little Belt and the Elbe, before a peace was declared in August 1645.

---

[1] Riis, *Should Auld Acquaintance*, I, 94-95 and II, 143-147.
[2] For Irishmen in these wars see J. Jordan, 'Wild Geese in the North, Denmark and Norway', in *An Cosantoir*, xiv, no. 2 (1954) and J. Jordan, 'Wild Geese in the North, Sweden', in *An Cosantoir*, xiv, no. 3 (1954).
[3] For a Danish perspective see Fridericia, *Danmarks Ydre Politiske Historie*, 293-447. A comparative Swedish view is presented in W. Tham, *Den Svenska Utrikes Politikens Historia, 1:2, 1560-1648* (Stockholm, 1960).
[4] Lind, *Hæren og Magten*, 76-77.

Fourteen new companies and fourteen new regiments were established during this war, largely manned by former soldiers. Twenty-two of these units were established within the first six months of the war. These regiments were mainly created out of existing ones and only five regiments were formed from scratch. On paper the army had around 40,000 men at the start of the invasion, though by the autumn of 1644 it had risen by 6,000, distributed in Holstein [3,000], Norway [10,000] and Denmark [33,000]. Lind argues that there were probably many more recruits than these numbers suggest, though the exact number is concealed within the total which does not take casualties into consideration.[5]

The relative poverty of the Danish-Norwegian Crown at the start of the war meant that they were unable to hire foreign regiments. In Norway, foreign officers were recruited to join the Danish forces with a cadre of their own subordinate officers, after which they were supplied with men conscripted locally. This is the area where a concentration of Scottish officers in particular could be found.[6] Many of the foreigners were military entrepreneurs who financed their own companies, though this was not the only means of engaging non-Danish officers. In one instance the entire army of Bremen became part of the Danish army north of the river Elbe.[7] It was during this conflict that, for the first time, the Danish-Norwegian army became thoroughly integrated, as old and new soldiers, foreigners and indigenous men and officers from all social backgrounds became homogenised.

The participation of any British or Irish troops in the Danish-Norwegian service in the 1640s requires explanation, given the relative situations of the Stuart kingdoms. England was in the midst of her civil wars and Charles I could ill afford to let men go to the aid of his Danish ally. The Scots not only had an army in England, but also had a sharp civil war at home in 1644-45 as Covenanters under Argyll and Royalists under Montrose clashed violently. Ireland too was engaged in civil war and had soldiers active in Scotland as well as in Ireland. Despite this, Christian IV specifically requested 4,000 Scottish troops from Charles in November 1644, though these were not levied.[8] The records of the Scottish Privy Council show that a licence was issued to James Earl of Irvine to recruit 4,500 men for foreign service, but these were for the

---

[5] Lind, *Hæren og Magten*, 77-78.
[6] Thomas Riis' study does not include Norway and so he does not record these men.
[7] Lind, *Hæren og Magten*, 81.
[8] DRA, TKUA England, A II 15. Instructions to John Henderson from Christian IV to be related to Charles I, 28 November 1644.

service of France.[9] Irvine was the Marquis of Argyll's half brother and it could be speculated that the grant of this licence was an Argyll sponsored ploy to rid himself of his brother and dubious elements from Scotland. Fallon, however, attributes the grant of this licence to the influence of the French at the English Court.[10] The French were allied to the Swedes at this time and consequently on the opposing side to Denmark-Norway in the Torstensson War. It is uncertain if Charles encouraged this levy in the hope of relieving himself of some of his enemies in Scotland, albeit he was not really in a position to prevent it anyway, or if the levy was undertaken to help prosecute the continuing war against the Empire.[11]

The Stuarts had, as discussed above, directed troops from third countries to troubled zones before. On this occasion that option would have been limited largely to Scots in Dutch, Polish or Russian service, other recipient countries being allied to the Swedes. It is however as yet unclear if the officers who arrived in Denmark-Norway came directly from the British Isles or whether they were in fact directed into Danish-Norwegian service from third countries. It must be considered that some of them were Scots who chose to keep out of the conflict with their countrymen at home. A strong possibility is that a few of these individuals were also Royalist refugees heading to a 'safe' country during a lull in Covenanting-Royalist conflicts when Scotland became a dangerous place to be for the hardened anti-Covenanter. Certainly this can explain the arrival of the Marquis of Montrose and a number of his supporters. The advent of British officers in Christian IV's army must be considered in three main sections during the 1640s. There were obviously those who served in the army before the war started and simply remained in service during the conflict. A second grouping was composed of those men who arrived between 1643 and 1645 with the express intention of helping Christian IV against the Swedes. There was, however, a third group of officers between 1643-1649 who sought employment in Denmark to avoid persecution at home.[12]

[9]   *RPCS*, second series, VII, 247.
[10] Fallon, 'Scottish Soldiers', 42-43.
[11] These questions and circumstances notwithstanding, the severity of the Danish situation meant that Charles was unlikely not to contribute at least a token force to his uncle's cause regardless of whether he could afford to let them go or not. Charles owed Christian a favour for the guns and ammunition the Danish king had tried to send him in 1642. It is probable that Charles directed Scottish and English Royalists into Danish service primarily to help Christian IV, but perhaps also in the hope that his uncle might return the favour at a convenient opportunity. See also *KCFB*, V, 256-7. Christian IV to Korfitz Ulfeldt, 24 October 1642.
[12] *KCFB*, V, 501. Christian IV to Christen Thomesen Sehested. Christian noted that a Scot called King [possibly the Royalist General James King, but more probably his namesake, Colonel

Gunner Lind has established that the Torstensson War was largely conducted with the Danish-Norwegian peacetime army and that the recruitment of foreign regiments was low.[13] Riis states that during the course of this war there is evidence of only one Scottish regiment.[14] However, the army did have external support and because of this the officer corps grew. In fact, at the conclusion of the war there were nearly four times as many officers as there were at the start.[15] For the first time the Danish-Norwegian army contained a significant proportion of officers from Norway. At its height this amounted to some 26% of the total officers in service which in itself may be a reflection of the inability of the Danish crown to pay for officers from overseas.

Despite the short notice for recruitment of foreigners and the low numbers of foreign regiments, there was a large percentage of foreign officers in Christian's army – though not as high as during *Kejserkrig*. Days before the conflict, Donald Mackay, Lord Reay, had been asked in November 1643 to raise a regiment of foot for Danish service consisting of 1000 men.[16] The Scottish Estates felt he might use this levy to help the Royalists and they imprisoned him for the duration of the war. Christian IV personally wrote to the Scottish Parliament to ask for his release in May 1645.[17] Reay's imprisonment was unfortunate for Christian, but he was not the only foreign officer who failed to arrive in time to help the Danes. Lind attributes this situation to a lack of finances, as high ranking non-Danish officers demanded large salaries for their service. Through the course of the war, the officers received their pay on an irregular basis and were only guaranteed food and lodgings.[18] This may have prompted some officers to let their would-be comrades know that Danish service was not profitable as the war dragged on. However, it does not explain why there was not an influx at the start of the war, before mercenary officers could have known how tight the finances were going to be for Christian. In fact the absence of foreigners was simply due to the surprise nature of the Swedish attack. It was easier and quicker to move people from within Denmark or Norway to the war zones than trying to rely on officers and

James King who visited Denmark in 1640] who was known to him had arrived after having come 'badly' from all that he had commanded: 'Tii hand Er kommen Iide fraa alldt ded, hand haffuer hafft y commando'.

[13] Lind, *Hæren og Magten*, 197.
[14] Riis, *Should Auld Acquaintance*, 104.
[15] Lind says three times as many, but the figure using the statistics provided here is closer to four. See Lind, *Hæren og Magten*, 197.
[16] NAS, *Reay Papers*, GD 84 Section 2/197, Letter dated 5 November 1643.
[17] NAS, *Reay Papers*, GD 84 Section 2/199, Letter dated 30 May 1645.
[18] Lind, *Hæren og Magten*, 200.

soldiers from abroad. Because of this many men who had previously served in the Danish-Norwegian army were re-enlisted. Even people who had served before as common soldiers could now become officers and so the status of the military elite was being changed through force of circumstance.[19] The rise of private soldiers to officer status was not limited to Danish citizens and at least two Scottish common soldiers made this transition.

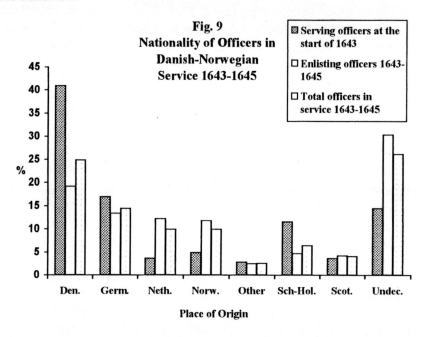

Fig. 9
Nationality of Officers in Danish-Norwegian Service 1643-1645

☒ Serving officers at the start of 1643

☐ Enlisting officers 1643-1645

☐ Total officers in service 1643-1645

Place of Origin

(Source: *SSNE* and *DDA 1573* databases)

At the outset of this war, 242 men served as officers in the Danish-Norwegian army. These men were joined in service by some 678 officers from various countries, giving the total number of officers who served as some 910 individuals, although not all would have been in service at the same time. Analysing the country of origin of the officers in service during this period reveals several things. It highlights that the combined subjects of Christian IV continued to form the largest group of officers in the army (Fig. 9). On the eve of the war the Danes formed 41% [99/242] of the officer corps, the Norwegians had 5% [12/242] while the subjects from the Duchies of Schleswig-Holstein provided just over 12% [28/242].

---

[19]   Lind, *Hæren og Magten*, 197.

Of the foreign officers, and not counting the 15% [35/242] of undecided origin, the only two significant foreign nations from a Danish perspective were Scotland and the United Provinces, given the amorphous nature of German recruitment. Both these countries had 4% [9/242] of the overall total.[20]

Assessing the group of officers who enlisted specifically for this conflict, from Fig. 9, we can see that the Danes themselves raised just under one in five of the enlisting officers with 19% [130/678] of the total. This figure was significantly bolstered by the Norwegians who provided a further 12% [80/678]. It can be seen from these numbers that there had been something of a role reversal between the domestic territories of Norway and the Duchies of Schleswig-Holstein compared with *Kejserkrig*. During the Torstensson War, 5% [32/678] of the officers were recruited in the Duchies, a significantly reduced statistic to previous wars. This can easily be explained by the fact that the Duchies were occupied by the Swedes and were not in a position to provide men through conscription as they had before. The Danes had to rely once more on a significant German recruitment of 13% [91/678] and a contribution from the United Provinces of 12% [83/678] to make up the deficit of officers. The only other nation of significance lending officers to the Danes was Scotland with 4% [29/678] while the total 'other' foreign officers including the French, Irish and English amounted to some 4% [27/678]. Following a developing pattern, the group described by Lind as the 'undecided origin' officer group contributed 30% [206/678] of the new intake, the majority of them probably being Danes, Germans and men from the Duchies.

Fig. 9 also clearly shows that the highest proportion of serving, as well as enlisting, officers of a known nationality were the Danes themselves with almost one in four of the contribution, 25% [229/910]. Again the German states form the largest group of foreign officers from a known location, 15% [133/910]. It should be noted however that in this war the largest single contributing foreign state was the United Provinces with 10% [92/910]. This percentage reveals that the Dutch had become more significant to the Danish-Norwegian army than the Scots as the war progressed. On the eve of the conflict, 4% [9/242] of the officers in Denmark-Norway had been Scots. They also contributed 4% [29/678] of

---

[20] J. Wahl, 'Et nyt bidrag till Bergenhus fæstnings historie', in *Bergens Historiske Forenings Skrifter*, no.12 (1906), 4. Wahl argues that there were 272 foreign officers alone recruited during this war who came largely from Germany and Scotland. This figure is greater than the total officers for the army estimated by Lind and the figure needs to be substantiated.

the new volunteers during the war which meant that throughout the course of the war a total of 4% [38/910] of the officers who served in the Danish army were Scots.

Fig. 10
Foreign Officers Enlisting into Danish-Norwegian Service
1643-1645

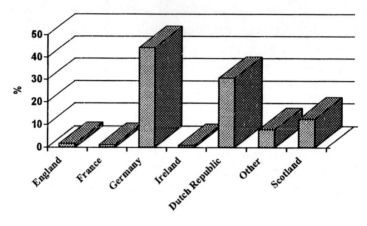

Place of Origin

(Source: *SSNE* and *DDA 1573* databases)

The foreign element of the Danish officer corps made up only a quarter of the total number of officers during the war, 25% [231/910]. Looking only at the foreign officers of known nationality, the Germans, with all the usual provisos, made up the greatest proportion at 45% [133/299]. The Dutch however had significantly increased their ratio, providing 31% [92/299] of the officers. By way of comparison, the Scots followed on behind with 13% [38/299]. The English and French contributed 1.5% [5/299] of the foreign officers each, while the Irish added a further 1% [3/299]. About 8% [24/299] of the foreign officers were of unknown origin. The Dutch were the largest single contributing foreign nation to this war. Bearing in mind that the United Provinces and the Scots held the same percentage at the outset of the war, this statistic is probably indicative of the disrupted domestic situation in Scotland.

Despite the turmoil at home, Scotland provided a significant number of officers to the conflict, ahead of England, France and Ireland. Reducing the enlistment down to the constituent nations of the three Stuart kingdoms it is clear that the Scots contributed the significant proportion of the 47 British Isles officers in the Danish-Norwegian army. Indeed, of the total Stuart kingdoms contribution, the Scots supplied some 81% [38/47] of the officers (Fig. 11). The English added 11% [5/47] of the British officers while the Irish contributed 9% [4/47].

Fig. 11
Scottish, English and Irish Officers [47 men] in the
Danish-Norwegian Army 1643-1645

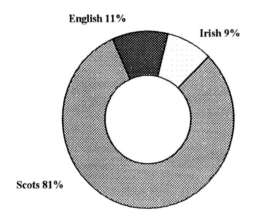

(Source: *SSNE* database)

The majority of the Scots enlisted in the years 1644 and 1645 (Fig. 12), the years of greatest conflict for the Danes, but also the time when Montrose and MacColla orchestrated their Royalist campaign in Scotland. Without further information on the officers than the scanty particulars relating to rank and date of enlistment, it is unsafe to draw conclusions as to the relationship between these two events. The possibility that at least some of these individuals were Royalist refugees cannot be dismissed, but nor can the possibility that they were simply mercenaries in search of work. However, Christian IV had been explicit in his request to Charles I, that if he could not have 4,000 Scottish troops for his campaign against the Swedish occupation of Denmark, then he would at least like Scottish officers to command his forces in Norway.[21]

---

[21] DRA, TKUA England, A II 15. Instructions to John Henderson from Christian IV to be related to Charles I, 28 November 1644.

Fig. 12
Enlistment of British Isles Officers into the Danish-
Norwegian Army
1641-1650

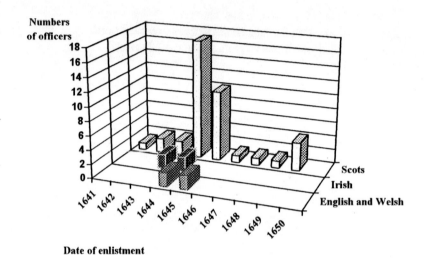

(Source: *SSNE* database)

There was also a continuous trickle of enlistments after the war, right up until 1649. That officers would be leaving the country to serve abroad at this time is indicative that they were indeed Montrosian sympathisers and unlikely to have been Covenanters save, perhaps, for some stragglers from the Scottish Engagement of 1648. Some, like Sir William Henderson, can clearly be identified as Stuart Royalists since they arrived, via The Hague, with testimonials from the Prince of Wales that describe their service during the wars in the three Stuart kingdoms.[22] Fig. 12 also shows us that there were lesser numbers of English, Welsh and Irish officers enlisting into the Danish-Norwegian army during the war with Sweden. Similar motivations for enlistment, that of being sent to help Christian IV and a lack of opportunity or desire to serve in their own countries, would probably apply to these individuals.

---

[22] *HMC, Pepys Manuscript*, 237-238. Prince of Wales to Frederick III, Korfitz Ulfeldt and Hannibal Sehested, all dated 24 November/4 December 1648.

Fig. 13
Rank of Scottish Officers at Enlistment and Departure from the Danish-Norwegian Army 1643-1645

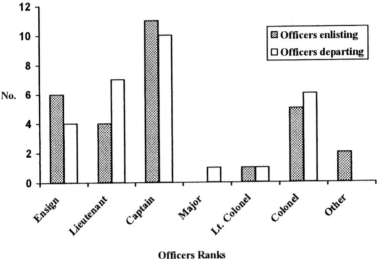

(Source: *SSNE* database)

Quality and Rank of the Scottish Officers

Of the 29 Scottish officers who volunteered during the war, six began as ensigns, seven as lieutenants and two were privates (Fig. 13). Of the more senior officers there were eleven captains, one lieutenant-colonel and five full colonels. As in the previous enlistment of the 1620s, the majority of the Scottish officers, some 62% [18/29], were captains or more senior ranks. By the time the officers came to depart Danish-Norwegian service, the privates had been promoted, Nicolaus Matheson made the rank of ensign and Alexander Stuart became a lieutenant. A non-commissioned officer, James Sinclair, also moved through the ranks to become a captain in the Norwegian army during the course of conflict.[23]

As there was only the one recorded Scottish company engaged in the war, the Scottish majors and colonels primarily held positions of command over Danish, Norwegian and German troops and garrisons. Throughout this period, John Cunningham continued to act as *lensman* of Finmark, protecting Norway's northern borders from the Swedes. Patrick

---

[23]   Nicolaus Matheson, *SSNE* no. 110; Alexander Stuart, *SSNE* no. 115; James Sinclair, *SSNE* no. 1532.

Dunbar, Count of Spannerup, served as commandant of Christianopel in eastern Blekinge, right on Sweden's south-eastern border.[24] Despite repeated assaults, Dunbar maintained control of his command for the duration of the campaign.[25] Colonel John Taylor assumed the position of colonel and chief of the Bergenhus infantry regiment in 1644. He played an important part in the Danish-Norwegian counter-attack against Sweden, distinguishing himself when he commanded the assault on the fortifications at Gothenburg in August 1645.[26] Another Scot, Colonel James Murray, arrived in Norway bearing a testimonial from Charles I in 1644. Charles noted that Murray had once been a traitor [Covenanter] but had since fought for him and had only recently been freed from the Tower of London. Charles asked that Murray receive expenses usual to his status and that he also be granted 'above the usual protection' which Christian would normally extend to one of Charles's subjects.[27] Murray took up the position of governor of Marstrand, the garrison town facing Gothenburg at the mouth of the river Göta, in May 1645, adding to the presence of Scottish soldiers in key positions along the Swedish frontiers. He later took over from Taylor as commander in chief of the Bergenhus regiment.[28] Once Murray took over control of Marstrand, the leadership of the regiment was transferred to the Scottish officers Colonel Lawrence Blair and Lt. Colonel Sir Thomas Gray.[29] Colonel Alexander Seaton, a

---

[24] During the attempted peace negotiations in 1644, Christian IV ordered his envoys to base themselves in Christianopel while their Swedish counterparts located themselves in Kalmar. The meetings themselves were to take place in Brømsebro. See *KCFB*, V, 513-514. Christian IV to Korfits Ulfeldt, 13 October 1644.

[25] Patrick Dunbar, *SSNE* no. 272, appears to have served in Mackay's regiment between 1626 and 1629. He chose to continue in Danish-Norwegian service rather than transfer with the regiment to Sweden. He married Karen Munk and was naturalised as a Danish nobleman on 4/5/1638. Riis, Thiset and Wittrup all note that and that he died around 1646. Hirsch and Lind both believe that he served on until the 1660's. The Danish Chancellery records certainly make mention of a widow of Patrick Dunbar in 1649. Nevertheless, in 1657 a Patrick Dunbar served as a major in Nadelwitz's infantry and this might be a relative. He is probably the same as 'oberstvagtmester' Dombach who is noted for being captured in 1658 in Elsinore who remained a prisoner of the Swedes for 18 months. He managed to ransom himself, became 'reduced' in 1661 and sought his dismissal from the army. See J. C. W. Hirsch and K. Hirsch eds, 'Fortegnelse over Dansk og Norske officerer med flere fra 1648 til 1814' (DRA manuscript, 12 vols., compiled 1888-1907), III, vol.2; Lind, *DDA 1573*; A. Thiset and P. L. Wittrup, *Nyt Dansk Adelslexicon* (Copenhagen, 1964), 70; *Kancelliets Brevbøger, 1650*, 200; Riis, *Should Auld Acquaintance*, II, 86.

[26] J. Wahl, *Det Gamle Bergenhusiske Regiments Historie 1628-1720* (Christiana, 1901), 10-14; *SSNE* no. 86.

[27] DRA, TKUA England A I. Charles I to Christian IV, 16 January 1644.

[28] James Murray, *SSNE* no. 113.

[29] Sir Thomas Gray, *SSNE* no.45, arrived in Norwegian service sometime after 1643 and is best remembered in Norway as being the officer who turned up drunk one night to the home of the Norwegian Viceroy, Hannibal Sehested, with a Lt. Colonel Cress. Sehested ordered the two men

veteran of Mackay's regiment in the 1620s, also saw service with Bergenhus regiment during the Torstensson War. Though appointed Colonel within the unit, Seaton performed most of his military duties in his capacity as admiral within the navy, as mentioned in chapter eight, directing the maritime operations against Gothenburg.[30]

Unlike the previous phase of officer enlistment in the 1620s, the Scots did not leave Danish-Norwegian service *en masse* when hostilities ended with Sweden in 1645. On this occasion many of the officers stayed on until the end of the decade. This adds to the case that they were Royalists in exile. The building of a Royalist invasion force in Denmark-Norway, which had been recruited from Scots in the service of several northern countries including Denmark-Norway, Sweden and the United Provinces, marks the end of this military period. This was part of Montrose's final attempt to defeat the Covenanters in Scotland. The rise and demise of this invasion force has been discussed in chapter six. The destruction of that force marries exactly with the depletion of Scottish officers from the Danish-Norwegian army. Certainly Sir Thomas Gray left with Montrose's expedition despite having been newly promoted to Lt. Colonel of the Trondheim Regiment in 1649.[31] One can only conclude from this evidence that the soldiers who arrived in Denmark-Norway and served with Murray were the Scottish officers requested by Christian IV and sent by Charles to his uncle and/or joined by remnants of the Royalist forces escaping after the Montrosian wars. They certainly formed a significant element in the group that officered the ill-fated expedition to Scotland in 1650. Once Sir Thomas Gray decided to leave Norway to take part in the

to return sober but they refused to leave. An encounter followed in which Gray assaulted Major Muhl, a German officer, as he left Sehested's house. A group of musketeers arrested Gray and Cress after Gray became involved in a brawl with Sehested himself. Sehested broke Gray's dagger during the incident and Gray was led away in irons. Muhl complained bitterly about the incident but Sehested seems to have treated the case extremely leniently. This episode is only related here to show that Gray must have been held in some esteem in his military capacity. He was not punished for his assault on Muhl or the Viceroy. After the war, unlike most foreign officers, he was kept in service and promoted to become the commander of the Lifeguard Company of the Bergenhus regiment, Sehested's bodyguard. He was also given a position overseeing improvements to Bergen's fortifications before assuming the position as military governor of Bergen after the departure of Henrich Thott. See Grant, *Scottish Soldiers of Fortune*, 126. Espelland, *Skottene i Hordaland og Rogaland*, 32-33; Wahl, *Det Gamle Bergenhusiske Regiments*, 8-20, Hannibal Sehested to Colonel Bjelke, c. August 1645; Wahl, 'Et nyt bidrag till Bergenhus fæstnings historie', 3-5. Thomas Gray to Henrich Thott, 10 August 1647; J. Wahl, 'Da Bergenhus blev en fæstning', in *Bergens Historiske Forening Skrifter*, no. 32 (1926), 9-11; C. S. Widerberg, *Norges Forste Militæringenior Isaac van Geelkerk og Hans Virke 1644-1656* (Christiana, 1924), 95.

[30] Wahl, *Det Gamle Bergenhusiske Regiments Historie 1628-1720*, 8-10.
[31] *Norske Rigs-Registranter*, IX, 270, Christian IV's promotion of Gray, 1 January 1649; Wahl, 'Et nyt bidrag till Bergenhus fæstnings historie', 5.

Montrosian expedition, he was apparently replaced as the governor of Bergen by Donald Mackay Lord Reay. Mackay, however, died soon after and perhaps did not even make it to the city.[32]

Though small in quantity, the Scots provided a significant body of experienced officers in Denmark and Norway between 1643-1645. The number of senior officers, especially colonels, garrison commanders and governors represents a disproportionate contribution to the senior ranks of the army. They were often given trusted positions of command in the strategic locations most exposed to Swedish attack, places such as Finmark, Marstrand and Christianopel. Throughout the war they formed a *corps d'élite* of respected professionals who served Christian IV particularly well. His son, Frederik III, later relied on a similar grouping from Britain and Ireland when he tried to rectify the territorial losses Denmark-Norway suffered at the end of the Torstensson War.

The Swedish Wars 1657-1660: A Third Scottish Military Wave

In preparing for the war with Sweden in 1657, Frederick III had taken great pains in building up his military forces. There had been an increase in common soldiers from around 20,000 in 1655 to perhaps as many as 50,000 by 1657. This was largely done by conscription and old units were subdivided to accommodate the increase of soldiers. Obviously more officers were required to command these new regiments, and that meant looking outwith Denmark-Norway for experienced men. Foreigners were given 14 of the 27 warrants issued for the raising of new units. However for a variety of reasons, 11 of these 14 men failed to meet their levy while two of them only levied officers which were later used to command conscripted troops. Of the three foreigners that did meet their levy, one had a contract that limited the intake of men to officers only. This meant that only two full regiments of foreign soldiers were raised during the war for integration into Frederik's army.[33]

Perhaps a factor behind the generally low participation and accomplishment in raising regiments can be found in the fact that the war lasted barely nine months, hardly enough time for the levying and transportation of troops from abroad to the war zone. Such was the success of the Swedish counter-offensive that 10 out of 45 of the Danish-Norwegian regiments were entirely destroyed and many more drastically reduced in number. The Danish army in Jutland and Holstein was

---

[32] H. Marryat, *One Year in Sweden including a visit to the Isle of Gotland* (London, 1862), 467.
[33] Lind, *Hæren og Magten*, 92.

completely defeated. The only successful parts of Frederik III's army were the Copenhagen garrison and the Norwegian regiments. These latter troops managed to conquer Jemtland without a fight and conducted a campaign in Sonderfield with only minor losses.[34] As part of the treaty of Roskilde in 1658, Frederick III had to give over 1,500 troops to the Swedes for service in Prussia. A Colonel Sinclair, probably James Sinclair who had served as a captain in the Trondheim infantry in 1649, led these men.[35]

At the opening of the 1658 war, the Danish-Norwegian army was concentrated in three large sections: the Norwegian army, the Copenhagen garrison and the Elbe garrisons that were stationed in a line of forts along the river. The Norwegian army continued its success, winning its campaign in Trondheim and Båhus, applying significant pressure to the Swedes for the duration of the war. Some Imperial, Brandenburger, Dutch and Polish forces reinforced the Danes. New regiments of indigenous soldiers also fought in the 1658-1660 war which were formed on the entrepreneur model. Lind notes that out of 19 colonels in the new army, 11 had served as officers in Denmark-Norway during at least one period before 1657, and seven had served in the 1657 war. Only eight of these men were born or naturalised Danish subjects, the rest were professional soldiers. The success of conscription coupled with the lack of finance meant that for the first time foreign regiments were hardly used in the Danish army. The presence of foreign officers was therefore largely a function of their either having been naturalised as Danish-Norwegian citizens before the war or having served in the Danish army on a previous occasion.[36] In any event, the Danish army was still heavily dependent on the foreign element within the officer corps.

The Danish-Norwegian army on the eve of war in 1657 had, as in previous wars, contained a variety of nationalities in its officer corps, some of whom had been brought in as part of the post-1655 preparations. At the outset of this war, 387 officers served in the Danish-Norwegian army. Some 1,454 officers from various countries joined these men, bringing their total number up to 1,841 individuals. The largest single component of this group came from Denmark herself, 37% [142/387] of the total (Fig. 14). Once again there were copious numbers of officers of 'undecided nationality', 23% [87/387]. The German states provided a

---

[34]   Lind, *Hæren og Magten*, 95.
[35]   Riis, *Should Auld Acquaintance*, II, 147; *SSNE* no. 1532.
[36]   Lind, *Hæren og Magten*, 105.

large contribution of the men of known nationality with 17% [64/387]. Norway and Schleswig-Holstein both had significant numbers, Norway adding 12% [45/387] and the Duchies 6% [21/387]. Again, the only other country with a statistically significant proportion of the officer corps were the Scots with 3% [11/387]. Apart from these soldiers, there was one French officer, one Dutch officer and 13 men of unknown foreign origin 3% [13/387].

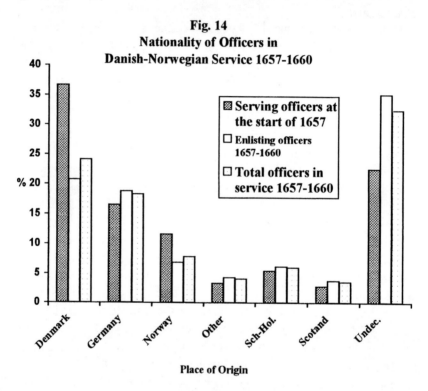

Fig. 14
Nationality of Officers in
Danish-Norwegian Service 1657-1660

(Source: *SSNE* and *DDA 1573* databases)

As Fig. 14 shows us, the numbers of enlisting officers of undecided origin rose significantly to 35% [510/1,454] during the course of the war. Of the identifiable nationalities, the majority of men were Danes, some 21% [302/1,454]. German officers formed 19% of the enlisting officers while the Duchies and Norway provided almost 200 officers between them. Norway gave 7% [100/1,454] while the Duchies added 6% [90/1,454]. Scotland contributed 4% of the new officers [55/1,454] while both France and the United Provinces bolstered the total with 1.5% [20/1,454] each.

For the first time in the seventeenth century, Ireland was also a notable contributor to the Danish officer corps with just under 1% [14/1,454] of the total.

In the final analysis of Fig 14, we find that of the total officer corps that served in the Swedish wars of 1657-1660, the highest percentage of officers are unfortunately, of undecided origin, 32% [597/1,841]. However, of the known nationalities the Danes are the most significant contributor providing one in four of the officers, 24% [444/1,841], throughout the course of the two short wars. The Germans added another 18% [338/1,841] while the Norwegians and Duchies constituted 8% [145/1,841] and 6% [111/1,841] respectively. For their part, the Scots added 4% of the officers [66/1,841] while the only two other nations contributing one percent or above were France and the United Provinces which both had 1% [21/1,841].

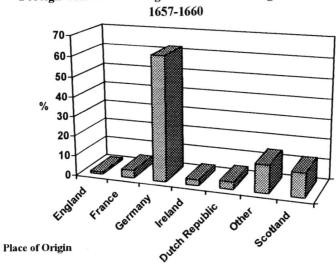

Fig. 15
Foreign Officers Enlisting into Danish-Norwegian Service
1657-1660

(Source: *SSNE* and *DDA 1573* databases)

The foreign element made up almost one third of all the officers in Danish-Norwegian service during this period. The specific analysis of the foreign officer corps shows that the Germans were overwhelmingly the most significant collective group within it (Fig. 15). The various German states provided 62% [338/544] of the foreign officers. The unitary Scottish state came second with 12% [66/544]. The next closest were the Dutch and the French, both with 4% [21/544] and the Irish with 3% [18/544]. The English registered just 1% [6/544] of the total foreign contribution.

Fig. 16
Scottish, English and Irish Officers [90 men] in the
Danish-Norwegian Army 1657-1659

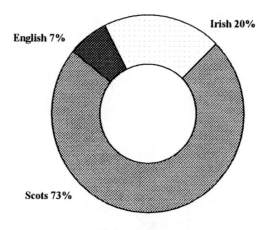

(Source: *SSNE* database)

Breaking this information down, it is possible to show the total percentage contribution of the 90 British Isles officers (Fig.16). The Scots are clearly the most significant, as before, with 73%, the Irish contributed 20% while the English and Welsh combined made up only 7%. As in the previous two wars, the Scots formed the majority proportion of officers from the British Isles in Danish-Norwegian service.

Surveying the two wars of 1657-1660, the Scots can be shown to have enlisted in the greater numbers during the first one, most officers arriving at the end of 1657. Again these Scots were joined by limited numbers of English, Irish and Welsh officers. Charles II probably directed some of these troops to Danish-Norwegian service to gain favour from Frederick III. Many Stuart-Royalist troops were already on the continent as part of the Royalist army based in Flanders.[37] When it became clear that there would be no imminent Royalist invasion of Britain, many Scots left for Danish-Norwegian service to await the appropriate opportunity to serve Charles II at a later date. The British and Irish officers joining the army of Denmark-Norway, therefore, often arrived from countries other than their native lands.

Fig. 17
Enlistment of British Isles Officers into the Danish-Norwegian Army 1655-1662

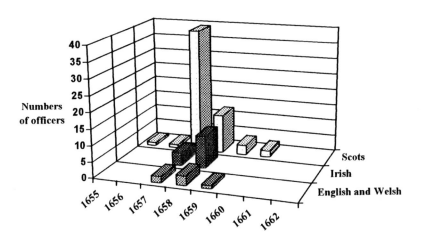

(Source: *SSNE* database)

A record of such officers entering Danish-Norwegian service as described above survives in the *Memoirs* of Sir James Turner. In October 1657, Frederik III sent Turner to be adjutant-general to General Hernia Lindanaw with other Scottish officers. While his fellow countrymen remained in Christianstad, Turner returned to Zealand on the orders of the General. When the castle of Kronborg fell to the Swedes, Frederik decided

---

[37] Turner, *Memoirs of his own Life and Times*, 122; *SSNE* no. 63.

to recruit six regiments of foreign mercenaries to bolster his beleaguered forces. Turner was to be given command of one of these regiments and he decided to raise half his force in Danzig and half in Amsterdam. He left Elsinore in December 1657 with half of his levy money and recruited a few officers, but not before Charles X of Sweden had crossed the Great and Little Belts across the ice, which had frozen over. The ensuing treaty of Roskilde forced the cancellation of the levy and so Turner neither raised his regiment nor received the second half of his levy money.[38]

Others took a more indirect route into Danish service than that of Turner. Some of these men were escaping from the English Protectorate's domination of Scotland and Ireland. Lord Cranston raised a regiment of Scots for Swedish service with authority from Oliver Cromwell, but 300 of them left as soon as they reached the continent. Some went to Denmark-Norway, specifically to Glückstadt, intending to serve Charles II in Scotland should he summon them, although they were probably absorbed into Danish regiments in the meantime.[39] The only other unit they might have tried to get into was Philip O'Sullivan's (Moore's) Irish-Scottish regiment.[40] If that was case, their service in Denmark was short lived as the regiment disbanded before it reached its strength, the officers believing they would be better employed in the service of Charles II elsewhere. Frederik III asked Oliver Cromwell for permission to levy troops in Scotland and England but to no avail. One historian, Wilbur Abbott, has attributed this lack of success to the numbers of Scots and English in the Swedish army, though this had never prevented enlistment into the Danish-Norwegian army before.[41]

Thomas Riis has noted that there was no specifically Scottish regiment in Danish-Norwegian service in the Danish-Swedish wars of the 1650s, and in this he is technically correct.[42] However, a Scottish regiment did operate as part of the relief forces sent by the Dutch to the Danes in 1659. Lieutenant-Colonel George Lauder commanded the regiment, part of the Scots-Dutch Brigade. While not serving in the Danish army directly, the Scots under Lauder deserve recognition for the part they played in the Danish-Swedish war, especially since their service ran contrary to the

[38]   Turner, *Memoirs*, 125-127. This led to a dispute between Turner and Frederik III in which Charles II intervened to try to secure Turner's money. See DRA, TKUA England A1, Charles II to Frederick III, 10 April 1659.

[39]   Firth, *Scotland and the Protectorate*, 353, footnote.

[40]   Hirsch and Hirsch, 'Fortegnelse over Dansk og Norske officerer'; Riis, *Should Auld Acquaintance*, II, 144-146.

[41]   Abbott, *The Writings and Speeches of Oliver Cromwell*, 676.

[42]   Riis, *Should Auld Acquaintance*, I, 105.

orders of the English Protectorate then controlling Scotland. Ironically, many of the 300 Scots who had left Cranston's army in 1655-1656 found their way into the Scots-Dutch Brigade and perhaps took part in the campaign against Cromwell's ally, the Swedes.[43]

Fig. 18
Rank of Scottish Officers at Enlistment and Departure
from the Danish-Norwegian Army 1657-1659

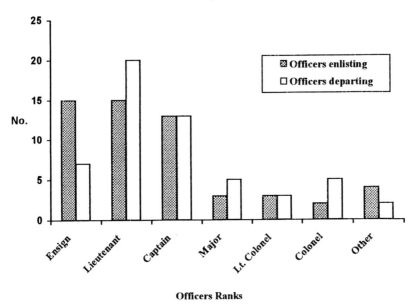

Officers Ranks

(Source: *SSNE* database)

Quality and Rank of British and Irish Officers

In contrast to the previous two wars, 55% [30/54] of the Scottish officers who enlisted during the 1650s were junior officers of the rank of ensign and lieutenant (Fig.18). The balance included 13 captains, while three majors also signed up for service. These included veterans of previous wars with Sweden including Major Gilbert Blair and Major John Forbes.[44] Three lieutenant-colonels, Arnold Cooper, Andrew Jackson and

---

[43] J. Ferguson, *Papers Illustrating the History of the Scots Brigade in the service of the United Netherlands, 1572-1697*, vol. I (Edinburgh, 1899), 326 and 467; Firth, *Scotland and the Protectorate*, 353, footnote. For Lauder see *SSNE*, no. 4981. As Lauder's men were part of the Dutch army, they do not form part of the statistical analysis of British Isles officers in Danish-Norwegian service.

[44] Gilbert Blair, *SSNE* no. 250 and John Forbes, *SSNE* no. 41.

James Turner accepted Danish-Norwegian service at this time.[45] Two full colonels, Magnus Alexander and the artillery colonel, William Patterson, joined them.[46] By the end of hostilities Thomas Fraser, an NCO had been promoted to lieutenant, although he was subsequently killed during the siege of Copenhagen.[47] Robert Hamilton made the greatest advance, entering service as a private soldier, finishing the war as a major and serving for several years thereafter.[48] During the two campaigns, the numbers of Scots holding the rank of major or above had risen from eight to fourteen, including the promotion of Colonel Sir John Henderson, the former Stuart diplomat, to the rank of major-general.

The lack of Scottish regiments meant that Scottish senior officers were distributed throughout the Danish, Norwegian and German regiments, and both Munchausen's and Both's contained Scottish officers. As a major-general, Henderson commanded his own regiment though it is unclear where his troops hailed from, only that they urged the general to surrender the garrison of Hindsgavl to the Swedes. Henderson was court-martialled for his part in the surrender though he was released due to diplomatic pressure, apparently from 'Britain'.[49] Another British officer, the Englishman Colonel Francis Edmonds, also gave up his garrison to the Swedes without a fight. He too avoided court-martial and served on as a commandant until 1662, after which he tried to re-enter Imperial service.[50] There were other British officers who had a considerably better reputation in Danish-Norwegian service at this time. The Scot, Captain Thomas Haliburton, acted in the capacity of commandant of the garrison at Steireburge despite only holding a middle rank.[51] Thomas Meldrum, another Scot, joined Danish service from that of Brandenburg, first as a dragoon captain and then in charge of the student regiment which took part in the defence of Copenhagen in 1658. Meldrum is worthy of note in that he was probably the longest serving Scot in the Danish-Norwegian army, cutting his teeth as a private soldier during *Kejserkrig* in the 1620s

---

[45] Arnold Cooper, *SSNE* no. 31; Andrew Jackson, *SSNE* no. 6.
[46] Magnus Alexander, *SSNE* no. 255 and William Patterson, *SSNE* no. 60.
[47] Thomas Fraser, *SSNE* no. 43.
[48] Robert Hamilton, *SSNE* no. 107.
[49] Riis, *Should Auld Acquaintance*, 2, 146. This statement raises the question of what is meant by 'Britain' here. If the diplomatic pressure did indeed come from Britain it tends to confirm the implied association between Henderson and the Cromwellian regime discussed in chapter six. However, it is equally possible that the diplomatic pressure came from the exiled Stuart Court for whom Henderson had also worked for many years.
[50] Riis, *Should Auld Acquaintance*, II, 145; *SSNE* no. 38.
[51] Thomas Haliburton, *SSNE* no. 289.

and retiring with the rank of general in the late 1680s after 60 years in the field.[52]

Gunner Lind rates the two most successful foreign officers as 'a former Imperial Field Marshall and a north German land owner', Edwin Dumsdorff and Ernst Albrecht von Eberstein.[53] However, several Scottish officers can also lay claim to a large degree of success during these wars for Denmark. Major John Forbes is accredited with preventing the Swedes from crossing the Elbe in 1659 and therefore lifting the siege of Copenhagen. He also gained distinction for himself during the siege of Halden in 1660.[54] However, Lieutenant-Colonel George Lauder of the Scots-Dutch Brigade distinguished himself as well as any other Dane or foreigner during the war. His regiment routed the Swedes on Fyn in 1659 and drove them off the island. Frederik III presented him with a gold chain and his portrait in diamonds in recognition of his role in that action, surely marking him out as a distinguished officer.[55]

The Danish-Swedish hostilities ended in 1660. Lieutenant-Colonel Lauder left with the rest of the Dutch forces at the conclusion of the war. Throughout the year, many other British and Irish soldiers were also released from Danish-Norwegian service. Their demobilisation coincided with Restoration of Charles II in the Stuart kingdoms. The end of the war and a desire of the men to return to their native countries may have facilitated the reduction in numbers of Britons and Irishmen. A few men remained in Frederick's service, suggesting that the exodus was not something rigorously enforced from the Danish side.

---

[52] There are references to a private Thomas Meldrum in Danish service during their period of the Thirty Years' War. However his military service can be traced more easily from 1657, when he is listed as being in Brandenburg's service. He became a dragoon captain in October 1657 in Skane and in 1658. Meldrum is listed as a captain amongst John Henderson's Scottish officers. Later he appears as a captain of the student's regiment during the siege of Copenhagen in 1658. In 1659 he was captain in Krag's infantry regiment and was still an infantry captain in 1663. Between 1670-6 he gained his promotion to lieutenant colonel of infantry. In 1676 he became commander and full colonel at the battle of Lund. In 1677, Meldrum was vice-commander of Landskrona castle, town, and finally as commandant at the castle. In 1684 Meldrum gained further promotion to brigadier. He died with the rank of general in 1693; *SSNE* no. 13.

[53] Lind, *Hæren og Magten*, 93.

[54] Espelland, *Skottene i Hordaland og Rogaland*, 33; Lind, *DDA 1573*; Riis, *Should Auld Acquaintance*, II, 130; This is probably Major John Forbes, known as Forbes 'den yngre' who had served in Mackay's regiment in the 1620s, the Bohus regiment in the 1640s and the Dal regiment in the 1650s-1660s. See *SSNE*, no. 41.

[55] Ferguson, *Papers Illustrating the History of the Scots Brigade*, 326 and 467; *SSNE*, no. 4981.

A comparative analysis of the Danish wars 1625-1660

The majority of works to date seem simply to conclude that there were numbers of Stuart subjects in Danish-Norwegian military service in the seventeenth century, especially in the 1620s. Most, if not all, fail to define the impact or significance of them in terms of the Scottish, English, Welsh and Irish contribution or, indeed, against men of other nationalities. The analysis given above shows that the Scots played a far greater role, in terms of military leadership, in Danish-Norwegian service than previously understood (Fig. 19). During the Danish period of the Thirty Years' War they contributed nine out of ten of all British Isles officers in Danish-Norwegian service. More importantly, they can be shown to have accounted for over one in five of the total of all officers who served in the Danish army during that war. It must be re-emphasised that the Scots provided more officers than any other single nation, more even than all the subjects of Christian IV combined.

Fig. 19

The comparative contribution of non-Danish officers during the 1625-29, 1643-1645 and 1657-1659 wars

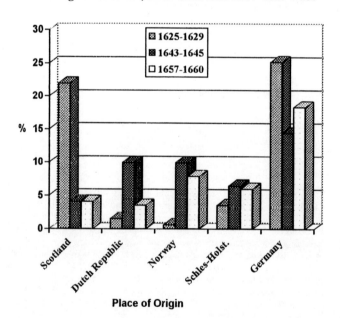

Place of Origin

(Source: *SSNE* and *DDA 1573* databases)

During the Torstensson War, the Scots still provided four out of five of the officers from the Stuart kingdoms (Fig.19). However the significance of this contribution within the Danish army was much less than in the previous conflict. Only about one in 20 officers in Denmark-Norway were Scots during this period. They were also numerically inferior to the Norwegian officers and those from the Duchies. There were also fewer Scottish officers than there were from the United Provinces. During the war with Sweden in the 1650s, the Scots regained their position ahead of the Dutch in terms of the significance of the officer contribution. They were however numerically inferior to the Germans, Norwegians and officers from the duchies of Schleswig-Holstein.

The importance of the officers from the various German states cannot be overlooked. Consistently in all three wars studied, the Germans provided between fourteen and twenty five percent of the total percent of serving officers (Fig.19). The Scottish contribution dropped from twenty one percent in the 1620s to less than four percent by the 1650s. However, given the composite nature of the German statistics, the best gauge of the Scottish contribution as a single contributing foreign state might be in relation to the number of officers from the United Provinces. A survey of the percentage contribution of the Norwegians and Schleswig-Holsteiners is also useful. Although not foreign in the eyes of the Danish kings, they continued to retain a unique identity under the Danish-Norwegian monarchy. These comparisons reveals that in each war the Scots contributed significantly to the Danish-Norwegian officer corps. In the first conflict they even challenged the total numbers of officers from the various German states combined. Their presence can be seen to be making up for a shortfall of officers from the Danish king's own subjects in Schleswig-Holstein and Norway. Certainly as the share of the officer corps increased from these regions in the subsequent wars, the Scottish percentage drops and levels off. There are, however other, more compelling reasons to be considered for the decline in Scottish participation in Danish conflicts.

The third Danish war took place in the reign of Frederick III. The close family relationship that had existed between the two royal families during the reign of King James, or even that of Charles I, was gone. Frederick was only a first cousin once removed from the reigning, but still exiled, Stuart monarch. In terms of any soldier wishing for, or being given an opportunity for promotion in the service of a close relative of the king, France was certainly now a more probable destination than Denmark-

Norway. The fact that the Stuart monarch was in exile during this period further inhibited the sort of promotion that had continued in the Jacobean period. The Danish Court did, however, receive exiled supporters of the Stuart kings, in some way making up for the lack of patronage opportunities that may have been available had the domestic situation allowed.

Throughout the course of these three conflicts, the percentage of Scots compared to the English and Irish always remained extremely high (Fig. 20). It did drop from just over 90% during *Kejserkrig* to just over 73% in the later Swedish Wars, from nine out of ten to three out of four. As the percentage of Scots declined, the numbers of Irish slightly increased. One possible reason for this is the secular nature of the later wars. With no religious reason *not* to join the Danish war against Sweden, opportunities for Irishmen must surely have increased. Given the prospect of a restoration of Charles II by military force, it is also unsurprising that some Irish exiles would wish to form a part of it.

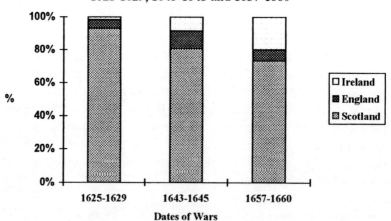

Fig. 20
Scottish, English and Irish Officers in the Danish-Norwegian Army
1625-1629, 1643-1645 and 1657-1660

(Source: *SSNE* database)

In terms of the percentage of officers going into Danish-Norwegian service, the Scots had significantly reduced their contribution from the first to the last war in simple numerical terms. Despite this, the 1657-

1660 wars saw a rise in the numbers of actual serving officers from all three kingdoms as compared to the Torstensson War and this is perhaps explained by the concept, discussed earlier, of an exiled Stuart army being assembled. Figs. 21 & 22 contrast the contribution of Scottish, English and Irish officers in terms of the physical percentages within the Danish-Norwegian army and the actual numerical contribution. The reason for such a contrast is to allow for the quite pronounced fluctuation in size of the officer corps of the army during the three time periods concerned. Some 1,380 officers served in the first war, 921 in the second and 1,841 in the third. Kept within the context of each specific war, this fluctuation does not distort the contributing percentages of officers from outwith Denmark-Norway. However, when trying to show the involvement of such officers in all three wars, a numerical evaluation is perhaps more appropriate than a percentage based one (Fig. 21).

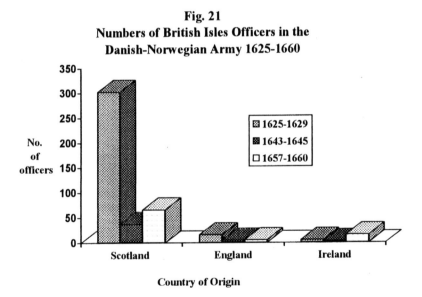

Fig. 21
Numbers of British Isles Officers in the
Danish-Norwegian Army 1625-1660

(Source: *SSNE* database)

Despite concerns that the percentage chart might distort the apparent contribution from each kingdom, the only significant conclusion to be drawn from these graphs is that the comparative analysis by percentage conceals a rise in the physical numbers of Scottish officers entering Danish service in the 1650s (Fig. 22). The comparative graph image between English and Irish individuals and their respective percentage contribution remains remarkably similar.

Fig. 22
% of Officers from the British Isles serving in the Danish-Norwegian Army 1625-1660

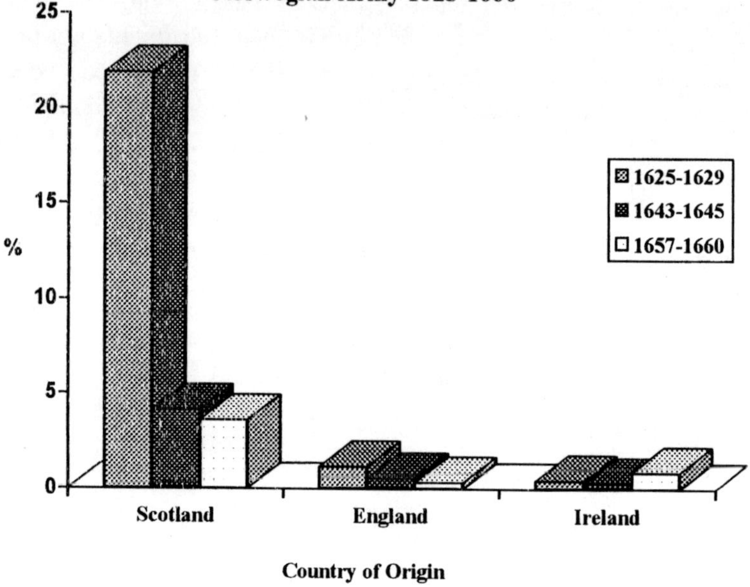

(Source: *SSNE* database)

An analysis of the ranks of those officers who enlisted specifically for the three wars, as opposed to those currently serving in the Danish-Norwegian, army shows that the likelihood of gaining an appointment as an officer of the rank of major or above was best during the 1643-1645 war. 27% of the Scottish officers who enlisted held this rank, as did several of those already serving. During the 1657-1660 war the chances of such an appointment were also good and 26% of the Scottish officers were within this group. This compares with the 1625-1629 war where just over one in ten of the Scottish officers counted in the most senior grouping. In terms of promotional opportunities rather than appointments, the third war provided the greatest scope for advancement. Between 1625-1629 only 2% [7/297] of the officers were promoted into the senior bracket. This rose in the Torstensson War to about 7% [2/29]. However in the Swedish wars in the 1650s, 11% [6/54], of the enlisting officers were promoted into the senior ranking group. Remarkably this shows us that for the Scots at least, the war Denmark performed worst in actually held the best prospect of promotion for the career soldier.

Considering all the Danish-Norwegian wars together, the comparative between Scottish officers and those from England, Wales and Ireland has yielded remarkable results. A critical analysis at officer level comparing Stuart subjects against Danes, Norwegians and their allies has established a number of facts. The Scots provided the most significant body of officers from the British Isles throughout the period studied. Even though the trend for Scottish participation was declining as a percentage of the whole British Isles contribution, it still represented nearly 75% of the total by 1660. Of the three Stuart kingdoms, Scotland was also the only country that could claim to represent a statistically significant percentage of the total officer corps of the Danish-Norwegian army in each of the conflicts studied. As a result they were frequently given commands of trust and positions of authority within Denmark-Norway. These rivalled the contribution of any other foreign nation and, as noted above, even the role played by the domestic nations of the Oldenburg state themselves.

CONCLUSION

This book began by addressing the problems posed by the Union of Crowns for the Stuart-Oldenburg alliance after 1603. The core issue was the construction of a British identity that would allow the House of Stuart greater opportunities for aggrandisement in Europe. There can be little doubt that Britain, in this sense, was a very Scottish project. David Stevenson has argued that 'the concept of 'Britain' [was] an unwelcome intrusion associated with the ambitions of the Stuarts and the Covenanters which had threatened England's identity'.[1] Yet a change occurred in the concept of 'Britain' throughout the Carolinian and Cromwellian periods, centred upon the sanctity most Englishmen held for the name of their country. Never-the-less, Ronald Hutton has argued that in order to understand the multiple Commonwealth of England, Scotland and Ireland properly, one requires a 'British not an English context [as] it was Cromwell's army that ensured that henceforth England would be clearly dominant over the other two realms'.[2] The name of Great Britain, a less cumbersome name for the 'Commonwealth of England, Scotland and Ireland', still retained currency among some of the Scottish population, but the very meaning of the name had changed. To the Scots, Great Britain had always meant something bigger than Scotland; an opportunity for partnership that would benefit Scotland and England. But there was a growing feeling in England in the post-Protectorate period that Great Britain and England could be viewed as one and the same thing. As Derek Hirst has noted that when most Englishmen spoke of 'Great Britain' they un-apologetically intended 'England', underscoring a desire for, or indeed a belief in, an English imperial hegemony.[3] The change from a Scottish-British to an Anglo-British focus for the House of Stuart altered not only domestic but also foreign politics.

From 1589-1625 Scotland, through the House of Stuart, enjoyed a high-profile role in the international developments of the time. The personal friendship of James VI & I and his brother-in-law, Christian IV, often provided a pivotal focus for Scottish, and after 1603 British, international relations. However, the Danish king lived to see both the rise and fall of significant Scottish influence in European politics. In aspiring

---

[1]   D. Stevenson, 'Cromwell, Scotland and Ireland' in J. Morrill (ed.), *Oliver Cromwell and the English Revolution* (London, 1990), p.180.

[2]   R. Hutton, *The British Republic, 1649-1660* (London, 1990), p.135.

[3]   D. Hirst, 'The English Republic and the meaning of Britain' in Bradshaw and Morrill, *The British Problem, c.1534-1707*, p.207.

to comprehend this diplomatic turnaround, particularly between the Stuart and Oldenburg states, several points have become clear. The royal marriage between Anna of Denmark and James VI of Scotland in 1589 undoubtedly marked a period of history that witnessed the flourishing of the relationship between the royal houses and the intellectual elites of the two states. In the post 1603 period, King James developed his existing Scottish *corps diplomatique* in Scandinavia and Poland to such a degree that Scotsmen maintained a 'British' diplomatic monopoly for almost thirty years. In a 'three kingdoms' context, this compounded the Scottish political domination of the internal 'British' agenda by allowing Scots frequent and direct access to the northern European potentates, albeit provided under the auspices of the new titular state of Great Britain and Ireland.

Upon the accession of Charles I in 1625, Britain and Denmark-Norway should have been drawn into an even closer confederacy. After all Charles, unlike his father, had a direct blood relationship to the Danish royal house. Yet Stuart diplomacy with the Oldenburg state suffered greater setbacks during Charles's reign than during that of King James. Among the multitude of reasons for these were the manipulative politics deployed by Christian IV and Charles I alike. As has been demonstrated throughout the chapters above, each monarch pressed policies that involved the deception of their kinsman. Tensions became particularly fraught in the post-Lübeck era as both kings sought to attach blame to the other for the failure of the Danish-Norwegian intervention in the *Reich*. The ensuing spate of claim and counter-claim led to a withdrawal of permanent residents and infrequent embassies that usually ended in failure. Yet, despite Thomas Roe's limited diplomatic success in the north, it was the Scots who were the most successful agents in ensuring that lines of communication remained open between Charles I and Christian IV. They simply retained a much greater wealth of experience in northern diplomacy. Even despite the military humiliation of Charles I during the Bishop's Wars, it continued to be Scottish diplomats who acted as the main conduit between the House of Stuart and Denmark-Norway during the 1640s most notably John Cochrane and John Henderson. Their integration into Christian IV's foreign service saw them undertake missions to the Stuart Court, the Scottish Estates and the English Parliament as well as to Poland and the Habsburg Empire.

The missions of Cochrane and Henderson in the 1640s were symptomatic of the willingness by Scotsmen to involve themselves in international affairs that transcended the confines imposed by national boundaries and traditional enmity for ones neighbours. Within the complex political and military spheres of early seventeenth century European politics, Great Britain played an important role due to the vision of King James in placing his geographically peripheral kingdoms at the intellectual centre of European politics. As king of Scotland or king of England he could not have done so. As king of Great Britain, European potentates had to take his views seriously especially given his confederal alliance with Denmark-Norway. James also needed support at home for his British project and, unsurprisingly, this came from his Scottish subjects allowing them greater exposure in continental politics as 'British' agents than they would have had as Scottish ones.

As one group of Scots involved themselves at the highest cerebral level, seeking a diplomatic solution to Europe's problems, the contribution of many others developed in a more militant form. This saw Scotland provide the bulk of the troops from the Stuart kingdoms during the Thirty Years' War and thereafter.[4] This rally to the House of Stuart found massive expression in the army of Denmark-Norway between 1625 and 1629 and even more so in Sweden after 1630. The military chapters above demonstrated that the Scots played a far greater role in Danish-Norwegian military and naval service than previously understood. An enormous disparity has also been highlighted regarding recruitment at both private soldier and officer level between subjects of the Stuart kingdoms. Additionally, Scottish officer enlistment has been shown to have been more important than that of any single state allied with Denmark-Norway during *Kejserkrigen*. That war established a pattern of officer recruitment which was to see the Scots dominate the British and Irish officer contingent in Danish-Norwegian service until 1660 – on land or at sea. Scottish involvement proved important not just in terms of the quantity of officers entering service. They frequently held commands and positions of authority within Denmark-Norway that rival the contribution of any other foreign nation providing numerous colonels, military governors, generals and admirals.

The Scots who had served on the continent returned in 1639 with a wealth of experience which they deployed within the three kingdoms. The reign of Charles I witnessed a perceptible rift opening up between the majority of the Scottish nation and the House of Stuart. Charles I sought to secure support against the Covenanters from his uncle in Denmark. The Scottish Estates also deployed ambassadors to Christian IV and they

---

[4]   See S. Murdoch ed, *Scotland and the Thirty Years' War, 1618-1648* (Leiden, 2001).

managed to secure Danish-Norwegian neutrality. Christian IV also sought to intervene diplomatically on behalf of the Covenanters and these missions went a long way towards the international legitimisation of the Covenanting movement. Undoubtedly Christian must have been persuaded to take this course of action due to the many high profile Scots within Danish-Norwegian society. But having won the Bishops' Wars, some Scots demanded more from Charles I than had been agreed at the Treaty of London in 1641. Several factions evolved in Scotland, and any discussion in terms of a politically coherent Scottish nation in the 1640s becomes progressively more difficult. From such a perspective, therefore, one cannot talk of a congruous relationship between the Scottish nation and the House of Stuart after these rifts had destroyed Scottish political unity. Instead, various groups of English, Scottish and Irish Royalists contested for the attentions of the king while the Covenanting movement lurched more radically towards a confederal British union with England through the Solemn League and Covenant.

As the Scots pressed ever harder to secure their pan-British agenda, events unfolded on the continent between English Parliamentarian commissioners and Christian IV which hinted at the start of the decline of Scotland as a major international player. The treaty between Christian IV and the English Parliament in 1645 signalled that, for the first time since the death of Elizabeth I, the English had moved ahead of the Scots in terms of diplomatic recognition at a Scandinavian Court. Thereafter, though for a multitude of reasons, the Scots became more distanced from their erstwhile English allies and the continued factionalisation of the country continued. This process ultimately led to the catastrophic Scottish Engagement undertaken against the English Parliamentarian army in 1648. That endeavour seriously undermined Scotland's status within Britain and on the continent. Scotland's downward political spiral continued after the battles of Dunbar and Worcester, following which she temporarily lost her status as an independent state. As Scotland plummeted into international insignificance during the Cromwellian era, the recognition of English power abroad became indisputable.

Denmark-Norway's position as a leading European power had also been undermined since the Treaty of Lübeck in 1629. Her situation had been further eroded after the Torstensson War in 1645 and finally collapsed after the Swedish wars in 1660. Throughout the 1650s and beyond, it was England and Sweden rather than Scotland and Denmark-Norway that dominated the agenda in the north. Peace and trade agreements between the English Protectorate and the United Provinces,

Sweden and Denmark-Norway in 1654 were indicative of the growing strength of Oliver Cromwell's foreign policy. By succumbing to Cromwellian diplomacy, Frederick III effectively sealed the lid on relations between the House of Stuart and the House of Oldenburg. Denmark-Norway, a state bound to the British kingdoms through the blood ties of their monarchs, had effectively declared herself for the enemies of the Stuarts. But Charles II now had closer dynastic and political links with France than Denmark-Norway, and any sense of a Stuart-Oldenburg dynasty in Great Britain had long since faded.

By the time of the Stuart Restoration in 1660, the original Scottish relationship with Denmark-Norway of 1589 had been reduced from a regal union between two equal nation states to one conducted by individual entrepreneurs and exiled military personnel. Even the officer corps of the army and navy had been drastically reduced through a combination of old age, decommissioning, and the casualties of war. The majority of the other individual Scots, Danes, and Norwegians responsible for cementing the former alliance between the two states were all but gone by 1660. The diplomats who had nurtured the diplomatic ties had either passed on or had been replaced by Englishmen. No new Scottish blood had found its way into the Danish nobility since Patrick Dunbar in 1638, and Scottish intellectual exchanges with Denmark-Norway had all but dried up. Moreover, by 1661, Scotland was subsumed within the new confederated alliance between Charles II and Frederik III. This compounded the diminishing Scottish influence in Denmark-Norway, as the Court of the House of Stuart now associated itself firmly with England and not Scotland. The three-way link which had once existed – 'Scotland--House of Stuart--Denmark-Norway' – had been broken at every joint. Within the reign of the first Stuart monarch born in England, the Scottish alliance with Denmark-Norway of 1589 had received the *coup de grâce*.

BIBLIOGRAPHY

In writing a book based on the relationship between the houses of Stuart and Oldenburg, a variety of sources have been consulted from numerous archives and libraries in Britain and Scandinavia. Obviously, scrutiny of the communications between the royal families has been essential. Several published volumes of royal letters have made the task of consulting these sources considerably easier, but the depth of correspondence reproduced in each varies considerably.[1] Undoubtedly the most valuable of these sets is the collection of Christian IV's letters edited by Bricka, Fridericia and Skovgaard.[2] Aspiring to be the definitive work, these eight volumes allow the reader to gain a reasonable perspective on the attitude and politics of the Danish king. They contain much political material, but also reproduce many personal letters to family and friends where Christian often reveals motives not contained within his diplomatic dispatches. The editors of the various collections relating to James VI/I, Charles I and Charles II have largely ignored Scandinavian correspondence in their collections. Instead, they focus on internal politics or Stuart relations with France or Spain, often giving the impression that these kings had little interest in their northern neighbours. The exception is the collection of James VI/I's letters to Christian IV which are housed in the *Rigsarkiv* in Copenhagen. These have been translated and edited by Ronald Meldrum and a bound typed manuscript can be consulted in the archive library.[3]

The *Rigsarkiv* in Copenhagen contains a wealth of invaluable material from the House of Stuart and their agents. This archive also has sections pertaining to Scottish Covenanting ambassadors, Scottish and English Royalist activists and English Parliamentary representatives operating between 1638-1660. Most valuable are the documents listed under 'England', although 'Skotland' and other bundles have revealed fascinating source material.

A similar store of information pertaining to Stuart-Oldenburg relations can be found in the Public Records Office in London. PRO SP/75 (Denmark), bundles 4-16, cover the years between 1600-1660. There are

[1]   G. V. P. Akrigg ed, *Letters of King James VI and I* (London, 1984); C Petrie ed., *The Letters, Speeches and Proclamations of King Charles I* (London, 1968); A Bryant ed., *The Letters, Speeches and Declarations of King Charles II* (New York, 1968).

[2]   C. F. Bricka and J. A. Fridericia, et al., eds, *Kong Christian den Fjerdes egenhændige Breve* (8 vols., Copenhagen, 1878-1947).

[3]   R. M. Meldrum ed, 'Translations and facsimiles of the original Latin letters of King James I of England (VI of Scotland), to his Royal Brother in Law, King Christian IV of Denmark. (compiled in 1977).

a few years which appear to be missing from this collection. During the last years of the 1630s, correspondence appears to dry up from the British agents based in Hamburg. In fact, these letters have simply been filed in PRO SP/81 (Germany) where many other items pertinent to Denmark-Norway can also be found. Another major gap appears between the years 1643-1660 where less than 30 items are included in the bundle, and most of these relate to the 1657-1660 period. Unfortunately in this instance the lack of material appears to represent a genuine dearth of documents.

Where there have been gaps in the archive, it has been necessary to rely on third party diplomatic papers. A very useful source for this is the *Riksarkiv* in Stockholm that contains thousands of bundles of correspondence from Scottish soldiers and diplomats. Often these men have strong links with Denmark-Norway. The diplomatic letters of James Spens is undoubtedly the most useful of this collection. Being the half-brother of the Stuart ambassador to Denmark-Norway, Robert Anstruther, his correspondence frequently dwells on Danish-Norwegian affairs. More importantly, Anstruther often included gems of information to his brother which any other Swedish partisan would never have gained access to. Spens' letters are by no means the only papers worthy of scrutiny in that Swedish archive.[4] The collections 'Scotica' and 'Anglica' are replete with information which has great bearing on this study.

In addition to manuscript sources, there are numerous published primary sources which should form the basis of any academic survey of the early modern period. The *Acts of the Privy Council of England*, *The Register of the Privy Council of Scotland*, the *Acts of the Parliament of Scotland* and the *Calendar of State Papers Domestic* were of fundamental importance. Another large source consulted was the *Calendar of State Papers, Venetian*. Although this collection contains nearly as much gossip as it does fact, the views expressed often give insight into events for which other sources have proved lacking. Treated with caution, the information to which the ambassadors relate may even be more useful and impartial than other royal correspondence since it has been shown that James VI/I, Charles I and Christian IV frequently tried to dupe each other. Indeed, not having the same axe to grind as the

---

[4]   This collection has been collated and typed up in manuscript form. However, the editor, Archibald Duncan, never got round to publishing the set. Some letters have only been summarised and some of the introduction is seriously flawed. However, in combination with the originals in Stockholm, Duncan's work is most useful. The manuscript can be found in Uppsala University Library. See A. Duncan ed, 'The Diplomatic Correspondence of Sir James Spence of Wormiston', (unpublished manuscript in Uppsala University Library - E379d).

monarchs, the information the Venetians provide has a value of its own, even if only as a starting point for a particular piece of research.

The military section of this thesis draws heavily on the variety of published lists of officers in Danish-Norwegian military service. Of greatest importance for the army are the works of Hirsch and Hirsch, Ovenstad, Riis and Lind.[5] In determining information relating to the navy an essential work is that of Topsøe and Marquard, while Riis again proved useful.[6] Much supplementary information was derived from the various regimental histories which have been scrupulously compiled in Denmark, Norway and Sweden. These mines of information proved quite elusive, tending only to be housed in libraries within the recruiting area in which the regiment was based. Nonetheless they frequently contain information pertaining to individuals overlooked in the larger collections.[7]

Of course the greatest wealth of information relating to British service in the Danish-Norwegian army comes from the writings of the soldiers themselves. In particular, the memoirs of Robert Monro and James Turner give fascinating accounts and insights into a variety of aspects of continental service.[8] Both these books can be found in Aberdeen University Library where, indeed, many of the works cited in this thesis can also be found. One can often forget that the richest resources in any study often lie closest to home.

[5] J. C. W. Hirsch and K. Hirsch, eds, 'Fortegnelse over Dansk og Norske officerer med flere fra 1648 til 1814, vol. 1-12, (unpublished manuscript compiled between 1888-1907); O. Ovenstad, *Militærbiografier: den norske hærs officerer* (Oslo, 1948); T. Riis, *Should Auld Acquaintance Be Forgot ... Scottish-Danish Relations c.1450-1707* (2 vols., Odense, 1988); G. Lind, *Danish Data Archive*, 1573.

[6] J. T. Topsøe, and E. Marquard, *Officerer i den danske-norske søetat 1616-1814 og den danske søetat 1814-1932* (2 vols., Copenhagen, 1935); Riis, *Should Auld Acquaintance*.

[7] See in particular J. O. Wahl, *Det Gamle Bergenhusiske Regiments Historie* (Oslo, 1901).

[8] R. Monro, *Monro his Expedition with a worthy Scots regiment - called Mac-Keye's regiment* (London, 1637); Sir James Turner, *Memoirs of his own life and times* (Edinburgh, 1829).

MANUSCRIPT SOURCES

Denmark

Copenhagen Rigsarkivet

T.K.U.A. General Part

91. Letter-book of treaties between Denmark and England (1640-91).
92. Treaties between Denmark and England (1432-1737).
93. Treaties and alliances between Denmark and England (1432-1667).

T.K.U.A. Special Part. SCOTLAND

4. 1572-1640 Documents concerning the political relations with Scotland.
6. 1536-1638 (1859) Various Documents.

T.K.U.A. Special Part. ENGLAND

A I 3. Correspondence between the Royal Houses 1613-89. Letters, partly with enclosures, from members of the Royal English House to members of the Royal Danish House and from Oliver and Richard Cromwell to King Frederik III.

A II 7. Documents concerning the Political Relations with England 1588-1644. Letters from various English (sic.) Government and court officials and others to King Christian IV, Prince Christian and both chancellors Christian Friis of Borreby and Kragerup, as well as to Dr. Jonas Charisius.

A II 8-24. 1401-1716 Documents concerning the political relations with England.

A III 38. 1432-1656 Documents concerning Trade and Shipping, Sundry Documents and Copies concerning in particular mutual complaints regarding arrested ships etc.

Hirsch, J. C. W. and K. Hirsch eds., 'Fortegnelse over Dansk og Norske officerer med flere fra 1648 til 1814, vol. 1-12 (unpublished manuscript compiled between 1888-1907).

Meldrum, R. M, ed., 'Translations and facsimiles of the original Latin letters of King James I of England (VI of Scotland), to his Royal Brother in Law, King Christian IV of Denmark. Edited and with an introduction by Ronald M. Meldrum' (compiled in 1977).

England

Public Records Office
State Papers 75 (Denmark) vols. 4-16
State Papers 81 (Germany) vols. 42-48
State Papers 88 (Poland) vols. 5-9
State Papers 95 (Sweden) vols. 2-5

Norway

Oslo Riksarkivet - Norske kancelliindlæg fra tiden før 1660 (Kat 1121/50): Registratur over norske kancelliindlæg fra tiden før 1660 i rigsarkivet i København. Parts I and II.

Scotland

Aberdeen University Library
Hartlib Papers CD rom (University of Aberdeen library)
British Library Thamason Tracts (microfilm)
TT 245 669 f.3 (1-64), no.62. *Copie of the Queen's letter from the Hague, 19 March 1641* (London, 1642).
TT 27 E.154 (3), Christian IV, *The King of Denmark's Resolution concerning, the King of Great Brittain* (London, 1642).
TT 22 E.124 (6). *A Declaration and Protestation of the Lords and Commons in Parliament to this Kingdome, and to the whole world* (23 October 1642).
TT 22 E.127 (25). *The Daily Proceedings of His Majesties Fleet on the Narrow Seas, from the 17 October to the 15 day of November* (London, 1642).
TT 27 E.150 (26), *The Earl of Warwickes victory over fifty Ships of the King of Denmarkes in the Narrow Seas* (15 June 1642 or 1643).
TT 19 E.105 (20). *A Coranto from beyond Sea: or True Intelligence from France, Spain, Germany, and Denmark, Amsterdam, 27 May* (London, 1643).
TT 12 E.68 (3), no. 36, p.7. *Certaine Informations from several parts of the Kingdome and from other places beyond the Seas* (23 September 1643).
TT 8 E.45 (7), *Christian IV and Queen Christiana, Two manefestos, or Declarations: The one by the King of Denmarke, the other by the Queene of Sweden, both concerning the present warres* (London, 1644).

TT I E.2 (29), *The true relation of the Queens departure from Falmouth into Brest* (22 July 1644).

TT E.465 (34), *Good News from Scotland* (27 September 1648).

TT E.552 (24) *A declaration to the English nation, from Don John de Austria the 8ᵗʰ. King of Germany, &c. Lewis 11ᵗʰ. King of France and Navarre. Philip the 5ᵗʰ. King of Spain & Aragon, &c. Christern the third King of Denmark, Zealand, &c. Lodowick Duke of Lorain, and Adolphina Queen of Sweden, in detestation of the present proceedings of the Parliament and Army, and of their intentions of coming over into England in behalf of King Charles II. Being translated out of the true copy.* (London, 1649).

TT 87 E.563 (4), 11 July 1649. *A declaration of the parliament of Scotland [...] AND the king of Denmark's sending forth a new Fleet to fall upon the English Ships* (London, 1649).

TT 87 E.564 (8). *A Great Victory obtained by Prince Charles his ships: upon the north Coast of England* (13 July 1649).

TT 89 E.584 (2), *A great Fight in Ireland [...] with a letter of news concerning Col King and Col Johnston and sixty sail of ships with soldiers going for Scotland* (Criplegate, 1649).

TT E.603 (4) *The great preparation made in Holland, for the King of Scots, going into Scotland. Also the D. of Buckingham, M. Hamilton, and the E. of Newcastle, to be sent embassadors into Germany, Sweden and Denmark; with the large promises of Col. Massey, and Ald. Bunce, to the forsaid King* (London, 1650).

TT E.603 (4) *The great preparation made in Holland* (1650).

Edinburgh University Library Special Collection-
Transactions of the Committee of Estates of Scotland from August 1640 to June 1641.

National Archives of Scotland
Register House Papers, 1632: RH 1/2/563
Hamilton Muniments. GD 406/1533, GD406/1/9638, GD406/1/10491.
Montrose Muniments. GD 220/6/ Misc.Acc. (Temp) box 1.
Newcastle Collection. Correspondence of Sir William Makdowall, GD 40/IV/72, GD 40/IV/81, GD40/IV/83.
Reay Papers. GD 84 2/194, /197, /199, /200, /201-231.

Dumfries House

Marquis of Bute's Archives, Loudoun and Rowallow Deeds, Bundle 1/1 and Bundle 2/2.

Huntingdon Library
Loudoun Scottish Collection, box 5, LO 8056-7, box 30, LO 10336.

Sweden

Stockholm Riksarkivet
Scotica vol. I.
Anglica vols. 3, 4, 5, 514, 517, 521, 522, 531, 532.
Axel Oxenstiernas bref växling E648, E657, E661, E703, E724.
'Svenske Sändebud till Udlandske Hof och deras Sändebud till Sverige' (unpublished manuscript compiled in 1841).

Stockholm Krigsarkivet
Krigsarkivet, 'Meritförteckningar. Svenska Sjöofficerare, vol. 2, 'Biografiska anteckningar om officerare vid örlogsflottan 1600-1699' (unpublished manuscript, compiled in 1971).

Göteborg Landsarkiv -Göteborgs Drätselkammare 1638, 1649, 1650 Genealogiska anteckningar om Göteborgs släkter, compiled by W.Berg. Förteckning över Göteborgs Tullarkiv (1933).

Uppsala University Library- Duncan, A, ed., 'The Diplomatic Correspondence of Sir James Spence of Wormiston' (unpublished manuscript - E379d).

PUBLISHED PRIMARY SOURCES

Abbotsford Club, *Letters and State Papers during the reign of King James the sixth chiefly from the manuscript collections of Sir James Balfour of Demlyn* (Edinburgh, 1837).
Abbott, W. C., *The Writings and Speeches of Oliver Cromwell* (4 vols., Harvard, 1938-1947).
Akrigg, G. P. V., ed., *Letters of King James VI and I* (London, 1984).
Airy, O., ed., *The Lauderdale Papers*, Camden new series, vol. 34 (London, 1884).
A. M., *A Relation of the Passages of our English Companies from time to time, since their first departure from England* (London, 1621).

Anstruther, Sir Robert, *The Oration or Substance of that which was delivered before his Majestie of Great Brittaine by the Emperours Ambassador, the high and excellent Lord, Count Schwarzenburg, at his day of Audience, being the seventh of Aprill in the Parliament Chamber. This is the True Copie of the Ambassadours speech, delivered by him in high Dutch; and repeated in English by Sir Robert Anstruther Knight, Gentleman of his Majesties Privie Chamber* (London, 1622).

Anon., *Articles concluded at Paris the XXIIIJ of February 1605 stylo Angliæ* (London, 1606).

Anon., *The Joyful Peace, concluded between the King of Denmarke and the King of Sweden, by the means of our most worthy Soveraigne, James, by the Grace of God, King of Great Britaine, France and Ireland* (London, 1613).

Anon., *Certaine Letters declaring in part the Passage of Affaires in the Palatinate from September of this present moneth of April* (Amsrterdam, 1621).

Benger, Miss, *Memoirs of Elizabeth Stuart, Queen of Bohemia, Daughter of King James the First* (2 vols., London, 1885).

Berencreutz, N, *Don Antonia Pimentels Depescher från drottning Christinas hov 1652-1656 jämte svarsskrivelser och spanska statsrådsprotokoll*, Historiska Handlignar, del 37, no. 1 (Stockholm, 1961).

Brereton, H., *Newes of the present Miseries of Rushia: Occassioned By the late Warres in that Countrrey [...] together with the memorable occurrences of our owne National forces, English, and Scottes, under the Pay of the now King of Swethland* (London, 1614).

Bricka, C. F. and J. A. Frederica et al., eds., *Kong Christian den Fjerdes egenhændige Breve* (8 vols., Copenhagen, 1878-1947).

Brucc, J., ed., *Charles I in 1646, letters of King Charles the first to Queen Henrietta Maria*. Camden no.63 (London, 1856).

Bryant, Sir A., ed., *The Letters, Speeches and Declarations of King Charles II* (New York, 1968).

Burnet, G., *The memoires of the lives and actions of James and William Dukes of Hamilton and Castleherald, &c.: in which an account is given of the rise and progress of the civil wars of Scotland* (London, 1677).

Calendars of State Papers, Domestic Series, First Series, 1547-1625 (13 vols., London, 1856-1992).

Calendars of State Papers, Domestic Series, Second Series, 1625-1649 (23 vols., London, 1858-1897).

Calendars of State Papers, Domestic Series, Third Series, 1649-1660 (13 vols., London, 1875-1886).

Calendars of State Papers and Manuscripts relating to English affairs, existing in the archives and collections of Venice and in other libraries of Northern Italy (38 vols., London, 1864-1947).

Calendars of the State Papers Relating to Scotland (13 vols., Edinburgh, 1898-1969).

The Camden Society, *The Hamilton Papers* (London, 1980).

Chamberlaine, E., *Angliae Notitia: or The Present State of England. The First Part together with divers reflections upon the ancient state thereof* (1669).

Chambers, R., *Domestic Annals of Scotland* (3 vols., Edinburgh, 1858-61).

Coate, M., ed., *The letter-book of John Viscount Mordaunt 1658-1660*. Camden third series, vol. 69 (London, 1945).

Cope, E. S. and W. H. Coates, eds., *Proceedings of the Short Parliament*. Camden fourth series, vol. 19 (London, 1977).

Couthrope, E. J., ed., *The Journal of Thomas Cuningham of Campvere 1640-1654 with his thrissels-banner and explication thereof* (Edinburgh, 1928).

Dahlgren, E. W., ed., *Louis de Geers brev och Affärshandlingar 1614-1652*, Historiska Handlingar, tjugonde delen (Stockholm, 1934).

Elder, J., 'A proposal for Uniting Scotland with England, addressed to Henry VIII', in *Bannatyne Miscellany, I* (Edinburgh, 1827).

Engberg, J., *Kilder til Danske historie i Engelske arkiver* (Copenhagen, 1968).

Erslev, K., ed., *Aktstykker og Oplysninger till Rigsraadets og Stændermødernes Historie i Kristian IV's tid* (3 vols., Copenhagen, 1888).

Ferguson, J., ed., *Papers illustrating the history of The Scots Brigade in the service of the United Netherlands 1572-1782* (3 vols. Edinburgh, 1899).

Ferrar, N., and N. Culpepper, eds., *Seventeenth Century Political and Financial Papers*. Camden Miscellany, Camden fifth series, vol. 7 (London, 1996).

Firth, C. H., ed., *Scotland and the Commonwealth, letters and papers relating to the military government of Scotland from August 1651 to December 1653* (Edinburgh, 1895).

Firth, C. H., ed., *Scotland and the Protectorate, letters and papers relating to the military government of Scotland from January 1654 to June 1653* (Edinburgh, 1899).

Firth, C. H., and R. S. Rait, eds., *Acts and Ordinances of the Interregnum 1642-1660*. vol.2 (London, 1911).

Fotheringham, J. G., ed., *Correspondence of Jean de Montereul and the brothers De Bellievre, French Ambassadors in England and Scotland, 1645-48* (2 vols., 1898-1899).

Fryxell, A., *Handlingar rörande sverges historia ur utrikes arkiver* (Stockholm, 1836).

Fyfe, J. G., *Scottish Diaries and Memoirs 1550-1746* (Stirling, 1928).

Gardiner, S. R., ed., *Hamilton Papers:being selections from original letters in the possession of his grace the Duke of Hamilton and Brandon relating to the years 1638-1650*. Camden new series, vol. 27 (London, 1880).

Gardiner, S. R., ed., *Letters and papers illustrating the relations between Charles the second and Scotland in 1650* (Edinburgh, 1894).

Gardiner, S. R., ed., *The Constitutional Documents of the Puritan Revolution 1625-1660* (Oxford, 1899).

Gibson Craig, J. T., ed., *Papers relative to the marriage of King James the Sixth of Scotland with the Princess Anna of Denmark, AD. MDLXXXIX. And the form and manner of Her Majesty's coronation at Holyrood House, AD., MDXC* (Edinburgh, 1828).

Goodrick, Rev. A.T.S, ed., *The Relation of Sydnam Poyntz 1624-1636*. Camden third series, vol. XIV (London, 1908).

Gordon, P., *A Short Abridgement of Britane's Distemper from the Yeare of God M.DC.XXXIX to M.DC.XLIX* (Aberdeen, 1844).

Guthry, H., *Memoirs of Henry Guthry wherein the Conspiracies and Rebellion against Charles I of blessed memory to the time of the murther of that monarch* (London, 1702).

Hamilton, J., 'Tidings of the progress of the war in Germany', reproduced in *Ullans*, no.5, (1997).

Hansen, C. R., ed., *Akstykker og Oplysninger til Rigsradets og Stænderødernes Historie i Frederik III's tid, 1648-1650* (Copenhagen, 1959).

Hasso, A. G., and E. Kroman, *Danish Departmet of Foreign Affairs until 1770*. Translated by Mogens Møller (Copenhagen, 1973).

Hedar, S., ed., *Kammarkollegiets Protokoll, med bilagor*; handlingar rörande sveriges historia, fjarden serien (3 vols., Stockholm, 1934-1941).

Hervey, M. F. S., ed., *The Life, Correspondence and Collections of Thomas Howard, Earl of Arundel "Father of Vertu in England"* (Cambridge, 1921).

Historical Manuscripts Commission, *Sixth Report* (London, 1877).

Historical Manuscripts Commission, *Eleventh Report Appendix, part vi, The manuscripts of the Duke of Hamilton*, K.T. (London, 1887).

Hyde, Edward, Earl of Clarendon, *The History of the Great Rebellion*, (7 vols., Oxford University Press, 1849)

Hyde, Edward, Earl of Clarendon, *The History of the Great Rebellion*, ed., Roger Lockyer (Oxford, 1967).

James VI and I, *By the King, Although we have made it knowen by publike edict, that our entrance into these our kingdomes of England and Ireland, we stood, as we still doe, in good amity and friendship with all the Princes of Christendom* (London, 1603).

James VI and I, *By the King, Whereas the King's majestie hath always bene ready to imbrace and cherish such a perfect amitie betweene him and the King of Spaine...* (London, 1605)

Jansson, M., P. Buskovitch and N. Rogozhin, eds., *England and the North: The Russian Embassy of 1613-1614* (Philadelphia, 1994).

Kancelliets Brevbøger-Vedrørende Danmarks Indre Forhold i uddrag (13 vols., Copenhagen, 1925-1969).

Kellie, T., *Pallas Armata or Militarie Instructions for the Learned* (Edinburgh, 1627).

Konung Gustaf den förstes Registratur, Handlingar Rörande Sveriges Historia, första serien (29 vols., Stockholm, 1861-1916).

Kleberg, J., *Krigskollegii Historia Biografiska Anteckningar, 1630-1865* (Stockholm, 1930).

Kleberg, J., *Amiralitetskollegium Marinförvaltingen Biografiska Anteckningar, 1634-1934* (Stockholm, 1934).

Kleberg, J., *Kammarkollegium 1634-1718* (Norrköping, 1957).

Konovalov, S., ed., 'Anglo-Russian Relations, 1617-1618', in *Oxford Slavonic Papers*, I (1950).

Konovalov, S., ed., Two Documents concerning Anglo-Russian Relations in the Early Seventeenth Century', in *Oxford Slavonic Papers*, II (1951).

Konovalov, S., ed., 'Anglo-Russian Relations, 1620-1624', in *Oxford Slavonic Papers*, IV (1953).

Konovalov, S., ed., 'Thomas Chamberlayne's Description of Russia, 1631', in *Oxford Slavonic Papers*, V (1954).

Konovalov, S., ed., 'Seven Russian Royal Letters (1613-1623)', in *Oxford Slavonic Papers*, VII (1957).

Konovalov, S., ed., 'Twenty Russian Royal Letters (1626-1634)', in *Oxford Slavonic Papers*, VIII (1958).

Konovalov, S., ed., 'England and Russia: Three Embassies 1662-65', in *Oxford Slavonic Papers*, 10 (1962).

Kullberg, N. A., et. al., eds., *Svenska Riksrådets Protokoll, 1621-1658* (vols. 1-18, Stockholm, 1878-1959).

Laing, D., ed., *A Diary of the Public Correspondence of Sir Thomas Hope of Craighall, Bart., 1633-1645* (Edinburgh, 1843).

Laing, D., ed., *The letters and journals of Robert Baillie, principal of the university of Glasgow* (3 vols., London, 1844).

Laing, D., ed., *Correspondence of Sir Robert Kerr First Earl of Lothian and his son William, Third Earl of Lothian* (2 vols., Edinburgh, 1875).

Lang, C. C. A., and O. G. Lundh, et al., eds., *Norske Rigs-Registranter Tildeels i Uddrag* (12 vols., Oslo, 1861-1891).

Larkin, J. F., ed., *Stuart Royal Proclamations, vol. II. Royal Proclamations of King Charles I* (Oxford, 1983).

Laursen, L., and C. S. Christiansen, eds., *Danmark-Norges Traktater 1523-1750, med dertil hørende aktstykker* (11 vols., Copenhagen, 1907-1949).

Lithgow, W., *The Totall Discourse of the Rare Adventures and Painefull Peregrinations of long Nineteene Yeares Travayles from Scotland to the most famous Kingdomes in Europe, Asia and Affrica* (Glasgow, 1906).

Loomie, A. J., ed., *Ceremonies of Charles I, The Note Book of John Finet* (New York, 1987).

Major, J., *Historia Majoris Britanniae tam Angliae quam Scotiae* (Paris, 1521).

Mackenzie, A. M., ed., *Oran Iain Luim* (Edinburgh, 1964),

McMaster, J. H., and M. Woods, eds., *Historical Manuscripts Commission Supplementary report on the Manuscripts of His Grace the Duke of Hamilton* (London, 1932).

MacMhuirich, N., 'The Black Book of Clanranald' in J. Kennedy and A. Macbain eds., *Reliquae Celticae*, vol. II (Inverness, 1894).

MacPhail, J. R. N., ed., *Highland Papers* (Edinburgh, 1914).

Mahr, H., ed., *Oberst Robert Monro. Kriegserlebnisse eines schottischen Söldnerführers in Deutschland 1626 - 1633* (Neustadt an der Aisch: 1995).

Manley, R., *The history of the late warres in Denmark comprising all the transactions, both military and civil; during the differences betwixt the two Northern Crowns. In the years 1657, 1658, 1659, 1660* (London, 1670).

Mansfeld, P., Count of Mansfeld, *More News From the Palatinate* (London, 1622).

Marquard, E., ed., *Kancelliets Brevbøger, 1637-1639* (Copenhagen, 1949).

Marquard, E., ed., *Prins Christian (V)'s Breve. I bind: Kancellibreve i Uddrag, 1626-1642* (Copenhagen, 1952).

Marquard, E., and J. O. Bro-Jorgensen, eds., *Prins Christian (V)'s Breve. II bind: Kancellibreve i Uddrag, 1643-1647 med et tillæg af prinsens egenhændige breve 1627-1647* (Copenhagen, 1956).

Meikle, H. W., ed., *Correspondence of the Scots Commissioners in London 1644-1646* (Edinburgh, 1917).

Meulenbroek, B. L., ed., *Briefwisseling van Hugo Grotius*, vol. XI (The Hague, 1981).

The Miscellany of The Spalding Club, vol. 1 (Aberdeen, 1841).

The Miscellany of The Spalding Club, vol. 2 (Aberdeen, 1842).

Monro, R., *Monro His Expedition with a worthy Scots regiment - called Mac-Keyes regiment - levied in August 1626 by Sir Donald Mackeye Lord Rhees, Colonell for His Majesties sevice of Danmark, and reduced after the battaile of Nerling to one company in September 1634, at Wormes in the Paltz. Discharged in Severall duties and observations of service first under the magnanimous King of Denmark, during his warres against the Emperour; Afterward, under the invincible King of Sweden, during His Majesties life time; and since, under the Directour Generall, the Rex-Chancellor Oxensterne and his generals* (London, 1637).

Morland-Simpson, H. F., ed., 'Civil War Papers 1643-1650', in *Miscellany of the Scottish Historical Society*, vol. 1 (Edinburgh, 1893).

Napier, M., *Memoirs of the Marquis of Montrose* (2. vols., Edinburgh, 1856).

Naval Records Society, 'The Jacobean commissions of enquiry 1608 and 1618' in *Publications of the Navy Records Society*, vol. 116 (1971).

Nicoll, J., 'A diary of Public Transactions and other occurences, chiefly in Scotland, from January 1650 to June 1667' in A. Peterkin, ed., *Records of the Kirk of Scotland, containing the Acts and proceedings of the General Assemblies from the year 1638 downwards* (Edinburgh, 1843).

Nya Handlingar rörande Skandinaviens historia, 17, Handlingar rörande Skandinaviens historia part 29 (Stockholm, 1845).

Obolenski, M. A., and Posselt, M. C., eds., *Tagbuch der Generalen Patrick Gordon* (Moscow, 1849-52).

Ó Baoill, C., ed., *Gair nan Clarsach: The Harper's Cry, An anthology of 17th Century Gaelic Poetry*. Translated by Meg Bateman (Edinburgh, 1994).

Ossolinski, G., *A Trve Copy of the Latine oration of the Excellent Lord George Ossolinski, Count Palatine of Tenizyn, and Sendomyria, Chamberlain to the Kings Majestie of Poland, and Suethland, and Embassadour to the Kings most Excellent Majesty. As it was pronounced to his Majestie at white-hall by the said Embassadour, on Sunday the 11 of March 1620* (London, 1621)

Ó Tuama, S., ed., *An Duanaire, 1600-1900; Poems of the Dispossessed* (Mountrath, 1981).

Park, T., ed., *The Harliean Miscellany: A collection of scarce, curious, and entertaining Pamphlets and Tracts, as well in manuscript as in print. Selected from the library of Edward Harley, second Earl of Oxford. Interspersed with historical, political and critical annotations by the late William Oldy's esq. and some additional notes by Thomas Park, F.S.A.* (London, 1811).

Patterson, F. A., et al., eds., *The Works of John Milton: State Papers* (Columbia, 1937).

Patton, H., ed., *Historical Manuscripts Commission Supplementary Report on the manuscripts of the Earl of Mar and Kellie* (London, 1930).

Paul, G. M., ed., *Diary of Sir Archibald Johnston of Wariston, 1632-1639* (Edinburgh, 1911).

Peacham, H., *A Most True relation of the Affaires of Cleve and Gulick* (London, 1615).

Peterkin, A., ed., *Records of the Kirk of Scotland, containing the Acts and proceedings of the General Assemblies from the year 1638 downwards* (Edinburgh, 1843).

Petrie, C., *The Letters, Speeches and Proclamations of King Charles I* (London, 1968).

Polisensky, J. V., et al., eds., *Documenta Bohemica Bellum Tricennale Illustrantia*, vols.3-7 (Prague, 1976-1981).

Powell, J. R., and Timmings, E. K., ed., *Navy Records Society; Documents relating to the Civil War, 1642-1648* (London, 1963).

Prothero, G. W., ed., *Select Statues and Other Constitutional Documents Illustrative of the Reigns of Elizabeth and James I* (Oxford, 1946).

H. R., *The most Royall and Hounarable entertainment of the famous and renowned King, Christian the Fourth, King of Denmarke & C. who with a fleet of gallant ships, arrived on Thursday the 16. Day of July 1606 in Tylbery Hope neere Gravesend* (Hall Gate, 1606).

Reynor, W. F., *The Declaration and Protestation of the Parliament of Scotland to their declared King: Touching their late agreement, the settling of the Presbytery Government with the resolution of the Emperor of German, the Queen of Sweden, and the King of Denmark.[...] Also, the proceedings of the Scottish Ministers, to their respective congregations, concerning their King, and the advance of the English Army* (London, 1650).

Rikskansleren Axel Oxenstiernas Skrifter och Brefvexling (15 vols., Stockholm, 1888-1977).

Rise Hansen, C., ed., *Aktstykker og Oplysninger til Rigsrådets og Stændermødernes Historie i Frederik III's tid* (2 vols., Copenhagen, 1974 -1975).

Rogers, C., ed., *The Earl of Stirling's Register of Royal Letters, relative to the affairs of Scotland and Nova Scotia from 1615 to 1635* (2 vols., Edinburgh, 1885).

Row, J., ed., *The History of the Kirk of Scotland from the year 1558 to August 1637* (Edinburgh, 1842).

Rydberg, O. S., ed., *Sverges Traktater med Främmande Magter*, vol. 5:I, 1572-1609 (Stockholm, 1903).

Sandvik, H., and H. Winge, eds., *Tingbok for Finmark 1620-1633* (Oslo, 1987).

Scotland, Great Seal, *The Register of the Great Seal of Scotland, AD. 1634-1651* (Edinburgh, 1897).

Scotland, Parliament, *The Acts of the Parliaments of Scotland* (12 vols., London, 1814-1875).

Scotland, Parliament, *A Declaration of the Convention of Estates in Scotland, concering their armie: with their reasons for continuance thereof until march next; and in what manners the officers and soldiers shall be paid. Dated at Edinburgh October 15, 1647.*

Together with an exhortation of the General Assembly of the Kirk of Scotland, unto the Scots merchants and other their country-people scattered in Poland, Swedland, Denmark and Hungry (Edinburgh, 1647).

Scotland, Privy Council, *Registers of the Privy Council of Scotland*, First Series, 1545 -1625 (14 vols., Edinburgh, 1877-1898).

Scotland, Privy Council, *Registers of the Privy Council of Scotland*, second series, 1625-1660 (8 vols., Edinburgh, 1899-1908).

Searle, A., ed., *Barrington Family Letters*. Camden fourth series, vol. 28 (London, 1983).

Sellers, M., ed., *The Acts and Ordinances of the Eastland Company* (London, 1906).

Spalding, J., *Memorialls of the trubles in Scotland and in England ad 1624-ad 1645* (Aberdeen, 1828-1829).

Spalding, R., ed., *The Dairy of Bulstrode Whitelocke 1605-1675* (Oxford, 1990).

Spottiswoode, J., *The History of the Church of Scotland* (London, 1655, 1972 reprint)

Statholderskabets Extra Protokol af Supplicationer og Resolutoner (2 vols., Oslo, 1896-1903).

Stuart, J., ed., *The Miscellany of the Spalding Club*. vol. 5 (Aberdeen, 1852).

Styffe, C. G., ed., *Konung Gustaf II Adolfs Skrifter* (Stockholm, 1861).

Sveriges Traktater med Främmande Magter, jemte andra dit hörande handlingar (15 vols., Stockholm, 1877-1934).

Sweden National Archives, *Sweden and the World: Documents from the Swedish National Archives* (Stockholm, 1960).

Tandrup, L., ed., *Svensk agent ved Sundet; Toldkommissær og agent i Helsingør. Anders Svenssons depecher till Gustav II Adolf og Axel Oxenstierna 1621-1625* (Aarhus, 1971).

Tanner, J. R., *Constitutional Documents of the reign of James I, 1603-1625* (Cambridge, 1930).

Taylor, J., *Taylor his travels: From the city of London in England, to the city of Prague in Bohemia* (London, 1620).

Taylor, L. B., ed., *Aberdeen Council Letters 1552-1681* (6 vols., Oxford, 1942-1961).

Thomson, E., ed., *The Chamberlain Letters: A selection of the letters of John Chamberlain concerning life in England from 1597-1626* (Toronto, 1966).

Thurloe, J., *A collection of State Papers* (7 vols., London, 1742).

Turnbull, G. H., *Hartlib, Dury and Comenius: Gleanings from Hartlib's Papers* (London, 1947).

Turner, Sir James, *Memoirs of his own life and times* (Edinburgh, 1829).

Warner, G. F., ed., *The Nicholas Papers: Correspondence of Sir Edward Nicholas secretary of State*. Camden third series (4 vols., London, 1892-1920).

Whitelocke, B., *Memorials of the English Affairs from the beginning of the reign of Charles the First to the happy restoration of king Charles the second* (4 vols., Oxford, 1853).

Wishart, Rev. G., *The memoirs of James Marquis of Montrose 1639-1650*, translated and edited by Rev. A. Murdoch and H. F. Morland-Simpson (London, 1893).

UNPUBLISHED DISSERTATIONS:

Armstrong, R. M., 'Protestant Ireland and the English Parliament 1641-1647' (unpublished PhD thesis, Trinity College Dublin, 1995).

Bellamy, M., 'Danish naval Administration and Shipbuilding in the Reign of Christian IV, 1596-1648' (unpublished Ph.D. thesis, University of Glasgow, 1997).

Fallon, J. A., 'Scottish Mercenaries in the Service of Denmark and Sweden 1626-1632' (unpublished Ph.D. thesis, University of Glasgow, 1972).

Grosjean A., 'Scots and the Swedish State: Diplomacy, Military Service and Ennoblement 1611-1660' (unpublished Ph.D. thesis, University of Aberdeen, 1998).

Herd, G. P., 'General Patrick Gordon of Auchleuchries - A Scot in Seventeenth Century Russian Service' (unpublished Ph.D. thesis, University of Aberdeen, 1994).

MacNiven, D., 'Merchant and trader in early seventeenth century Aberdeen' (unpublished M.Litt. thesis, University of Aberdeen, 1977).

Smuts, R. M., 'The culture of Absolutism at the Court of Charles 1' (unpublished Ph.D. thesis, Princeton University, 1976).

REFERENCE WORKS:

Almqvist, J. A., et al., eds., *Svenskt Biografiskt Lexicon* (vol.1- , Stockholm, 1918-).

Bang, N., ed., *Tabeller over Skibsfart og Varetransport gennem Øresund 1497-1660,* vol. I (Copenhagen, 1906).

Bang, N., and K. Korst eds., *Tabeller over Skibsfart og Varetransport gennem Øresund 1497-1660,* vol. II:II (Copenhagen, 1933).

Bell, G. M., *A Handlist of British Diplomatic Representatives 1509-1688* (London, 1990).

Birket-Smith, S., ed., *Kjøbenhavns Universitets Matrikel* (2 vols., Copenhagen, 1890-1894).

Bohman, N. et al., eds., *Svenska Män och Kvinnor Biografisk Uppslagsbok* (8 vols., Stockholm, 1942-1955)

Bricka, C. F., *Dansk Biografisk Leksikon* (27 vols., Copenhagen, 1933-1944, 2nd edition).

Bricka, C. F., et al., eds., *Dansk Biografisk Leksikon* (16 vols., 1979-1984, 3rd edition).

Bull, E., Krogvig, A., et al., eds., *Norske Biografisk Leksikon* (19 vols., Oslo, 1923-1983).

Cockayne, G. E., *The Complete Peerage of England, Scotland, Ireland, Great Britain and the United Kingdom* (12 vols., London, 1910-1959).

Cockle, M. J. D., *A bibliography of English Military Books up to 1642 and of contemporary foreign works* (London, 1900).

Dahl, F., *A bibliography of English corantos and periodical newsbooks 1620-1642* (London, 1952).

Elgenstierna, G., *Den Introducerade Svenska Adelns Ättartavlor, med tillägg och rättelser* (9 vols., Stockholm, 1925-36).

Hofberg, H., *Svenskt Biografiskt Handlexikon alfabetiskt ordnande lefnadsteckningar af sveriges namnkunniga män och kvinnor från reformationen till nuvarande tid* (2 vols., Stockholm, 1906).

Kroman, E., *Privatarkiver Før 1660 i Rigsarkivet* (Copenhagen, 1940).

Leslie, Sir Stephen and Sir Sydney Lee, eds., *Dictionary of National Biography* (66 vols., London 1885-1901; reprinted with corrections in 22 vols., London 1908-1909).

Lodge, J., *The Peerage of Ireland; or a geneologocal history of the present nobility of that Kingdom* ed., M. Archdall (7 vols. 1789 edition).

Marquard, E., *Danske Gesandter og Gesandtskabs Personale indtil 1914* (Copenhagen, 1952).

Meijer, B., *Svenskt-Historiskt Handlexicon* (Stockholm, 1882).

Paul, Sir James Balfour and R. Douglas, *The Scots Peerage* (9 vols., Edinburgh, 1904-1914).

Rosborn, S., and F. Schimanski, *När Hände Vad i Nordens Historia* (Lund, 1995).

Tapsell, A., *A guide to the materials for Swedish historical research in Great Britain*, Meddelanden från Kungliga Krigsarkivet, V (Stockholm, 1958).

Thiset, A., and P. L. Wittrup, eds., *Nyt Dansk Adelslexikon: fortegnelse over dansk adel i fortid og nutid* (Copenhagen, 1904).

Topsøe J. T., and E. Marquard, *Officerer i den danske-norske søetat 1616-1814 og den danske søetat 1814-1932* (2 vols., Copenhagen, 1935)

PRINTED SECONDARY SOURCES:

Ahnlund, N., *Axel Oxenstierna intill Gustav Adolf's död* (Stockholm, 1940).

Almqvist, H., *Sverige och Ryssland 1595-1611* (Uppsala, 1907).

Almqvist, H., *Göteborgs historia grundläggningen och de första hundra åren* (2 vols., Göteborg, 1629-1635).

Anderson, A., *The Civil Wars, 1640-49* (Wiltshire, 1995).

Anderson, P. D., *Black Patie: the life and times of Patrick Stewart, Earl of Orkney, Lord of Shetland* (Edinburgh, 1992).

Anderson, R. C., 'English Officers in Sweden' in *Mariner's Mirror*, XII (1926).

Anon., *An Historical Account of the British Regiments Employed since the Reign of Queen Elizabeth and King James I in the Formation and Defence of the Dutch Republic* (London, 1794).

Asch, R. G., ed., *Three Nations - a common history? England, Scotland, Ireland and British History, c.1600-1920* (Bochum, 1993).

Ashton, R., *Charles I and Oliver Cromwell* (London & New York, 1987).

Attman, A., *The Russian and Polish Markets in International Trade 1500-1650*, Meddelanden från Ekonomisk-historiska institutionen vid Göteborgs universitet, vol. 26 (Göteborg, 1973).

Attman, A., *The Struggle for Baltic Markets: Powers in Conflict 1559-1618*, Kungl. Vetenskaps och Vitterhets-Samhället Acta Humaniora, vol. 14 (Göteborg, 1979).

Attman, A., *Swedish Aspirations and the Russian Market during the seventeenth century*. Kungl. Vetenskaps och Vitterhets-Samhället Acta Humaniora, vol. 24 (Göteborg, 1985).

Aylmer, G. E., *The King's Servants: the civil service of Charles I, 1625-1642* (London, 1974).

Aylmer, G. E., *1603-1689 The Struggle for the Constitution England in the Seventeenth Century* (London, 1963).

Åberg, A., 'Scottish Soldiers in the Swedish Armies in the Sixteenth and Seventeenth Centuries' in G. G. Simpson, ed., *Scotland and Scandinavia 800-1800* (Edinburgh, 1990).

Barker, T., ed., *Army, Aristocracy, Monarchy: Essays on War, Society and Government in Austria, 1618-1780* (New York, 1982).

Barnhill, J. W., and P. Dukes, 'North-east Scots in Muscovy in the seventeenth century', in *Northern Scotland*, vol.7 (1972).

Barroll, L., 'The Court of the First Stuart Queen' in L. L. Peck, ed., *The Mental World of the Jacobean Court* (Camridge, 1991).

Behre, G., 'Gothenburg in Stuart War Strategy 1649-1760' in G. G. Simpson, ed., *Scotland and Scandinavia 800-1800* (Edinburgh, 1990).

Belfrage, N., *Kungl. Västgöta Regemente Personhistoria, 1540-1723* (Stockholm, 1947).

Beller, E. A., 'The Mission of Sir Thomas Roe to the Conference at Hamburg, 1638-1640', in *The English Historical Review*, XLI (1926).

Beller, E. A., 'The Military Expedition of Sir Charles Morgan to Germany, 1627-1629', in *The English Historical Review*, XLIII (1928).

Beller, E. A., 'Recent Studies on the Thirty Years' War', in *Journal of Modern History*, vol.3, no.1 (March 1931).

Beller, E. A., *Propaganda in Germany during the Thirty Years' War* (Princeton, 1940).

Beller, E. A., 'The Thirty Years' War' in J. P. Cooper, ed., *The New Cambridge History, vol. IV. The Decline of Spain and the Thirty Years' War 1609-1648/59* (Cambridge, 1970).

Bence-Jones, M., *The Cavaliers* (London, 1976).

Berg, J., and B. Lagercrantz, *Scots in Sweden* (Stockholm, 1962).

Bieganska, A., 'James Murray a Scot in the making of the Polish navy', in *Scottish Slavonic Review*, no.3 (Autumn 1984).

Bieganska, A., 'Scottish merchants and traders in seventeenth and eighteenth century Warsaw', in *Scottish Slavonic Review*, no.5 (Autumn 1985).

Bieganska, A., 'Scottish Immigrants in Poland", in *Scottish Slavonic Review*, no.19 (Autumn 1991).

Blom, O., 'Smaa Bidrag til Artilleriets Historie under Kristian d. 4de; I. Robert Scott og Læderkanonerne', in *Historisk Tidskrift*, VII, III (1900-1902).

Bonney, R., 'The English and French Civil Wars', *History*, vol. 65, no. 215 (October 1980).

Bradshaw, B., and J. Morrill, eds., *The British Problem, c.1534-1707; State Formation in the Atlantic Archipelago* (London, 1996).

Bradshaw, B., and P. Roberts, eds., *British Conciousness and Identity: The Making of Britain 1533-1707* (Cambridge, 1998).

Brady, T. A., H. A. Oberman and J. D. Tracy eds., *Handbook of European History 1400-1600, late Middle Ages, Renaissance, and Reformation, vol. I: Structures and Assertions* (New York and Köln, 1994).

Brinckmann, H., *Balladen med Svenskerne: Danmarks forhold til Sverige fra 1550 til 1720* (Alokke, 1990).

Brooks, H. F., 'English Verse Satire, 1640-1660, Prolegomena', *The Seventeenth Century*, vol. III, no. 1 (1988).

Brown, K., *Bloodfeud in Scotland 1573-1625* (Edinburgh, 1986).

Brown, K., 'Courtiers and Cavaliers: Service, Anglicisation and loyalty among the royalist nobility' in J. Morrill, ed., *The Scottish National Covenant in its British Context 1638-1651* (Edinburgh, 1990).

Brown, K., *Kingdom or Province? Scotland and the Regal Union 1603-1715* (London, 1992).

Brown, K., 'British History: A Sceptical Comment' in R G Asch, ed., *Three Nations-a common history? England, Scotland, Ireland and British History c. 1600-1920* (Bochum, 1993).

Brown, M. J., *Itinerant ambassador: the life of Sir Thomas Roe* (Lexington, 1970).

Bryce, J., *The Holy Roman Empire* (London, 1864).

Burton, J. H., *The Scot Abroad* (2 vols., Edinburgh, 1864).

Butchart, C. B. R., 'Sir Alexander Hamilton general of artillery', in *Aberdeen University Review*, vol. xlii, 4, no.140 (Autumn 1968).

Canny, N., 'The Attempted Anglicisation of Ireland in the Seventeenth Century: An Exemplar of British History', in R. G. Asch, ed., *Three*

Nations - a common history? England, Scotland, Ireland and British History, c.1600-1920 (Bochum, 1993).

Cant, R., 'The Embassy of the Earl of Leicester to Denmark in 1632', in *The English Historical Review*, LIV (1939).

Capp, B., 'Naval Operations' in J. Kenyon and J. Ohlmeyer eds., *The Civil Wars. A Military History of Scotland and Ireland, 1638-1660* (Oxford, 1998).

Carlson, W., *Gustav Adolf och Stralsund 1682-juli 1630* (Uppsala, 1912).

Carlton, C., *Charles I, the personal monarch* (London, 1983).

Carlton, C., *Going to the wars: the experience of the British civil wars 1638-1651* (London, 1994).

Casada, J. A., 'The Scottish representatives in Richard Cromwell's Parliament', *Scottish Historical Review*, vol. li, 2, no. 152 (October 1972).

Chapman, P., *History of Gustavus Adolphus and the Thirty Years' War up to the King's death* (London, 1856).

Christensen, T. L., 'Scots in Denmark in the sixteenth century', in *Scottish Historical Review*, vol. xlix, 2, no.148, October 1970.

Christensen, T. L., 'The Earl of Rothes in Denmark' in I. B. Cowan and D. Shaw, eds., *The Renaissance and Reformation in Scotland. Essay's in Honour of Gordon Donaldson* (Edinurgh, 1983).

Clark, P., 'Thomas Scott and the Growth of Urban Opposition to the Early Stuart Regime', in *The Historical Journal*, vol. 21, no. 1 (1978).

Coleman, D. C., 'The 'Gentry' Controversy and the Aristocracy in Crisis, 1558-1641', in *History*, vol. li, no. 172 (June 1966).

Cooper, J. P, 'The Fall of the Stuart Monarchy' in J.P. Cooper, ed., *The New Cambridge Modern History*, vol. IV (Cambridge, 1970).

Cowan, E., *Montrose, For Covenant and King* (Edinburgh, 1995).

Cowan, I. B., and D. Shaw, eds., *The Renaissance and Reformation in Scotland. Essay's in Honour of Gordon Donaldson* (Edinburgh, 1983).

Coward, B., *Early Stuart England 1605-1640* (London, 1980).

Coward, B., *The Stuart Age: A History of England 1603-1714* (London, 1980).

Cust, R., 'News and Politics in Early Seventeenth Century England', in *Past &Present a journal of historical studies*, no. 112 (August, 1986).

Dahlgren, S., 'Estates and Classes' in M. Roberts, ed., *Sweden's Age of Greatness 1632-1718* (London, 1973).

Davidson, J., and A. Gray, *The Scottish Staple at Veere: A Study in the Economic History of Scotland* (London, 1909).

Davies, G,. *The Restoration of Charles II, 1658-1660* (Oxford, 1955).

Davies, G., *The Early Stuarts, 1603-1660* (Oxford, 1959).

Dewald, J., *The European Nobility 1400-1800* (London, 1996).

Ditchburn, D., 'A note on Scandinavian trade with Scotland in the later middle ages' in G. G. Simpson, ed., *The Scottish Soldier Abroad, 1247-1967* (Edinburgh, 1992).

Donagan, B., 'Codes and Conduct in the English Civil War', in *Past and Present*, no. 118 (1988).

Donner, O., *A brief sketch of the Scottish families in Finland and Sweden* (Helsingfors, 1884).

Donaldson, G., *The Memoirs of Sir James Melville of Halhill* (London, 1969).

Donaldson, G., *A Northern Commonwealth: Scotland and Norway* (Edinburgh, 1990).

Douglas, A., *Robert Douglas en krigaregestalt från vår storhetstid* (Stockholm, 1957).

Dow, F. D., *Cromwellian Scotland* (Edinburgh, 1979).

Dukes, P., 'Scottish Soldiers in Muscovy' in *The Caledonian Phalanx*, comp. National Library of Scotland (Edinburgh, 1979).

Dukes, P., 'The Leslie family in the Swedish period (1630-5) of the Thirty Years' War', in *European Studies Review*, vol. 12 (1982).

Dukes, P., *A history of Europe 1648-1948: the Arrival, the Rise, the Fall* (London, 1985).

Dukes, P., 'The First Scottish Soldiers Abroad' in G. G. Simpson, ed., *The Scottish Soldier Abroad 1247-1967* (Edinburgh, 1992).

Dukes, P., *The Making of Russian Absolutism 1613-1801* (London, 1990).

Eastham, J. K., ed., *Economic Essays in Commemoration of the Dundee School of Economics 1931-1955* (Dundee, 1955).

Edwards, P., 'Logistics and Supply' in J. Kenyon and J. Ohlmeyer, eds., *The Civil Wars: a military history of England, Scotland and Ireland 1638-1660* (Oxford, 1998).

Ekman, E., 'Three decades of research on Gustav Adolf', *Journal of Modern History*, vol. 38, no. 3 (1966).

Elliot, J. H., 'The Year of the Three Ambassadors' in H. Lloyd-Jones, V. Pearl and B. Worden, eds., *History & Imagination: Essays in Honour of H. R. Trevor-Roper* (London, 1981).

Elliot, J. H., 'Spain and the War', in G. Parker, ed., *The Thirty Years' War* (London, 1997).

Espelland, A., *Skottene: Hordaland og Rogaland fra aar 1500-1800* (Norhemsund, 1921).

Fabritius, A., *Danmarks Riges Adel* (Copenhagen, 1946).

Fedorowicz, J. K., *England's Baltic trade in the early seventeenth century: A study in Anglo-Polish commercial diplomacy* (Cambridge, 1980).

Fedosov, D., *The Caledonian Connection: Scotland-Russia ties, Middle Ages to early Twentieth Century. A Concise Biographical List* (Aberdeen, 1996).

Fischer, T. A., *The Scots in Germany, being a contribution towards the history of the Scot abroad* (Edinburgh, 1902).

Fischer, T. A., *The Scots in Eastern and Western Prussia* (Edinburgh, 1903).

Fischer, T. A., *The Scots in Sweden* (Edinburgh, 1907).

Fissel, M. C., *The Bishop's Wars: Charles I's campaigns against Scotland 1638-1640* (Cambridge, 1994).

Fladby, R., *Hvordan Nord-Norge ble styrt: Nord Norske administrasjons historie fra 1530-åra til 1660* (Tromsø, 1978).

Forbes-Leith, W., *The Scots Men-at-Arms and Life Guards in France, 1458-1830* (2 vols., Edinburgh, 1882).

Fraser, Sir W., *Memorials of the Earl of Haddington* (2 vols., Edinburgh, 1889).

Fraser, Sir W, *The Melvilles, Earls of Melville, and the Leslies, Earls of Leven* (3 vols., Edinburgh, 1890).

Fridericia, J. A., *Danmarks ydre politiske historie i tider fra freden i Lybeck till freden i Prag 1629-1635* (Copenhagen, 1972 reprint).

Fridericia, J. A., *Danmarks ydre politiske historie i tider fra freden i Prag till freden i Brömsebro, 1635-1645* (Copenhagen, 1972 reprint).

Fridericia, J. A., *Adelsvældens Sidste Dage. Danmarks historie fra Christian IV's død til enevældens indførelse 1648-160* (Copenhagen, 1972 reprint).

Fryde, E. B, et al., eds., *Handlist of British Chronology* (London, 1986).

Fröding, H., *Berättelser ur Göteborgs Äldsta Historia* (Göteborg, 1908).

Furgol, E., *A regimental history of the covenanting armies 1639-1651* (Edinburgh, 1990).

Furgol, E., 'Scotland turned Sweden: the Scottish Covenanters and the military revolution' in J. Morrill, ed., *The National Covenant in its British Context 1638-51* (Edinburgh, 1990).

Furgol, E., 'The civil wars in Scotland' in J. Kenyon and J. Ohlmeyer, eds., *The Civil wars: a military history of England, Scotland and Ireland 1638-1660* (Oxford, 1998).

Gade, J. A., *Christian IV, King of Denmark and Norway: A Picture of the Seventeenth Century* (Boston and New York, 1928).

Galloway, B., *The Union of England and Scotland* (Edinburgh, 1986).

Gardiner, S. R., *History of the Great Civil War 1641-49* (4 vols., London, 1893).

Gardiner, S. R., *History of the Commonwealth and Protectorate* (4 vols., Gloucestershire, 1988 reprint).

Generalstaben, *Sveriges Krig 1611-1632* (6 vols., Stockholm, 1936-1939).

Gordon, J., *History of Scots Affairs from 1637-1641* (3 vols., Aberdeen, 1841).

Gouhier, P., 'Mercenaires Irlandais au service de la France (1635-1664)', in *Irish Sword*, vol. 7 (1965-1966).

Grage, E., 'Scottish Merchants in Gothenburg, 1621-1850' in T. C. Smout, ed., *Scotland and Europe 1200-1850* (Edinburgh, 1986).

Grant, J., *The Scottish Soldiers of Fortune- their adventures and achievements in the armies of Europe* (Edinburgh and London, 1890).

Grant, J., *Memories and Adventures of Sir John Hepburn* (Edinburgh and London, 1851).

Greengrass, M., M. Leslie and T. Raylor, eds., *Samuel Hartlib and Universal Reformation: Studies in Intellectual Communication* (Cambridge, 1994).

Gregg, P., *King Charles I* (London, 1981).

Grimble, I., *Chief of Mackay* (London, 1965).

Grimble, I., 'The Royal Payment of Mackay's Regiment', in *Scottish Gaelic Studies*, vol. 8-9 (Aberdeen, 1955-62).

Grosjean, A., 'The Alternative Band; Scotlan's ties wi Sweiden, 1550-1599', in *Cairn*, no.1 (March 1997).

Grosjean, A., 'Scottish-Scandinavian Seventeenth Century Naval Links; A case study for the SSNE database', in *Northern Studies*, no. 32 (1997).

Gustafsson, H., 'Conglomerates or unitary States? Integration processes in early modern Denmark-Norway and Sweden', *Wiener Beitrage zur Geshichte der Neuzeit*, vol. 21 (Vienna, 1994).

Göransson, G., *Gustav II Adolf och hans folk* (Stockholm, 1994).

Hamel, J., *England and Russia* (London, 1854).

Hay, G., *History of Arbroath to the present time with notices of the civil and ecclesiastical affairs of the neighbouring district* (Arbroath, 1899).

Hibbard, C., *Charles 1 and the Popish Plot* (Chapel Hill, 1983).

Higham, F. M. G., *Charles I* (London, 1932).

Hill, D. J., *A History of Diplomacy in the International Development of Europe*, vol. II (London, 1906).

Hirst, D., 'The Politics of Literature in the English Republic', in *The Seventeenth Century*, V, no. 2 (1990).

Hollings, J. F., *The Life of Gustavus Adolphus* (London, 1838).

Holm, N. F., ed., *Det Svenska Svärdet: tolv avgörande händelser i Sveriges historia* (Helsingfors, 1948).

Houston, S. J., *James 1* (Harlow, 1973).

Howatt, G. M. D., *Stuart and Cromwellian Foreign Policy* (London, 1974).

Hutton, R., *The British Republic 1649-1660* (London, 1990).

Israel, J. I., *The Dutch Republic; Its Rise, Greatness, and Fall 1477-1806* (Oxford, 1995).

Jespersen, J. V., 'Absolute monarchy in Denmark, change and continuity', in *Scandinavian Journal of History*, vol. 12 (1987).

Jespersen, L., 'The Machstaadt in seventeenth century Denmark', in *Scandinavian Journal of History*, vol. 10, no. 4 (1985).

Johnson, A., *The Swedes on the Delaware 1638-1664* (Philadelphia, 1927).

Jones, J. R., *Charles II Royal Politician* (London, 1987).

Jordan, J., 'Wild Geese in the North, Denmark and Norway', in *An Cosantóir*, xiv, no. 2 (1954).

Jordan, J., 'Wild Geese in the North, Sweden', in *An Cosantóir*, xiv, no. 3 (1954).

Jordan, J., 'Wild Geese in the North, Russia', in *An Cosantóir*, xiv, no. 4 (1954).

Kamen, H., *European Society 1500-1700* (London, 1984).

Kamen, H., *The Iron Century Social Change in Europe 1550-1660* (London, 1971).

Kan, A., *Sverige och Ryssland ett 1200-årigt förhållande* (Stockholm, 1996).

Kennedy, P., *The Rise and Fall of the Great Powers - Economic Change and Military Conflict from 1500 - 2000* (London, 1988).

Kent, H. S. K., 'The Scandinavian community in 17th and 18th century London', in *The Norseman*, XII (1954).

Kenyon, J. and J. Ohlmeyer, eds., *The civil wars: a military history of England, Scotland and Ireland 1638-1660* (Oxford, 1998).

Kirby, D., *Northern Europe in the Early Modern Period: the Baltic World 1492-1772* (London & New York, 1990).

Konovalov, S., 'Two documents concerning Anglo Russian relations in the early seventeenth century', in *Oxford Slavonic Papers*, vol. 2 (1951).

Konovalov, S., 'Thomas Chamberlyne's description of Russia in 1631', in *Oxford Slavonic Papers*, vol. 9 (1954).

Kunzle, D., *History of the comic strip vol. 1: the Early Comic Strip: Narrative Strips and Picture Stories in the European Broadsheet from c.1450 to 1825* (Los Angeles and London, 1973).

Lamont, W. M., *Godly Rule: Politics and Religion 1603-60* (London, 1969).

Landberg, G., *Den Svenska utrikes politikens historia*, part.1, vol. 3 (Stockholm, 1952).

Lauridsen, J. T., 'Skibsbyggeri for den Danske Krone i Neustadt i 1640'rne' in *Særtryk af Handels - og Søfartsmuseets Årbog* (1982).

Lauridsen, J. T., *Marselis Konsortiet* (Århus, 1987).

Lee, M. jr., 'James VI's government of Scotland after 1603', in *The Scottish Historical Review*, vol. lv, 1, no.159 (April 1976).

Lee, M. jr., *The Road to Revolution: Scotland under Charles I, 1625-37* (Illinois, 1985).

Lee, S., *The Thirty Years' War* (London & New York, 1991).

Leowenson, R. J., 'The leathergun of Gustavus Adolphus of Sweden in the Rotunda collection at Woolwich' in *17th Century War, Weaponry and Politics*, IAMAX, X (Stockholm, 1984).

Lillehammer, A., 'The Scottish Norwegian Timber Trade in the Stavanger Area in the Sixteenth and the Seventeenth Centuries' in T. C. Smout, ed., *Scotland and Europe 1200-1850* (Edinburgh, 1986).

Limm, P., *The Thirty Years' War* (London & New York, 1987).

Lind, G., *Hæren og Magten i Denmark 1614-1662* (Odense, 1994).

Lisk, J., *The Struggle for Supremacy in the Baltic* (London, 1967).

Lockhart, P. D., 'Denmark and the Empire; A Reassessment of Danish Foreign Policy under King Christian IV', *Scandinavian Studies*, vol. 64, no. 3 (1992).

Lockhart, P. D., *Denmark and the Thirty Years' War, 1614-1648; King Christian IV and the decline of the Oldenburg State* (Selinsgrove, 1996).

Loeber, R., 'The military revolution in seventeenth century Ireland' in J. Ohlmeyer, ed., *Ireland from Independence to Occupation 1641-1660* (Cambridge, 1995).

Lynch, M., 'Response: old games and new', in *Scottish Historical Review*, vol. lxxiii, 1, no. 195 (1994).

Lynch, M., *Scotland a New History* (London, 1991).

Lythe, S. G. E., 'Scottish trade with the Baltic', in J. K. Eastham, ed., *Economic Essays in Commemoration of the Dundee School of Economics 1931-1955* (Dundee, 1955).

Långström, E., *Göteborgs stads borgerlängd 1621-1864* (Gothenburg, 1926).

Macinnes, A. I., 'The First Scottish Tories?', in *The Scottish Historical Review*, vol. LXVII, I, no. 138: (April 1988).

Macinnes, A. I., 'The Scottish Constitution, 1638-1651: the rise and fall of oligarchic centralism' in J. Morrill, ed., *The Scottish National Covenant in its British Context, 1638-1651* (Edinburgh, 1990).

Macinnes, A. I., *Charles 1 and the making of the Covenanting movement 1625-1641* (Edinburgh, 1991).

Macinnes, A. I., 'Covenanting, Revolution and Municipal Enterprise' in J. Wormald ed., *Scotland Revisited* (London, 1991).

Macinnes, A. I., *Clanship, Commerce and the House of Stuart, 1603-1788* (Edinburgh, 1996).

Macinnes, A. I., 'The Court and Anglo-Scottish union 1603-1707' in S. J. Connolly, ed., *Kingdoms United?* (Dublin, 1998).

MacKay, A., *The Book of Mackay* (Edinburgh, 1906).

MacKay, J., *An Old Scots Brigade* (Edinburgh and London, 1885).

MacKay, J., 'Mackay's Regiment', in *Transactions of the Gaelic Society of Inverness*, VIII (1878-1879).

Mackay, R., *The house and clan of Mackay* (Edinburgh, 1829).

Maclean, F., *A Concise History of Scotland* (London, 1970).

Maclean, J. N. M., 'Montrose's preparations for the invasion of Scotland, and Royalist missions to Sweden, 1649-1651', in R.

Hatton and M. Anderson, eds., *Studies in Diplomatic History* (London, 1970).

Madan, F. F., *A new bibliography of the Eikon Basilike of King Charles the First* (London, 1950).

Malcolm, J. L., 'A King in search of soldiers: Charles 1 in 1642', in *The Historical Journal*, vol. 2, no. 2 (1978).

Mandelbrote, S., 'John Dury and the practise of Irenicism' in N. Aston, ed., *Religious Change in Europe 1650-1914 essays for John McManners* (Oxford, 1997).

Marryat, H., *One Year in Sweden including a visit to the Isle of Gotland* (2 vols., London, 1862)

Marschall, T. H., *The History of Perth from the earliest period to the present time* (Perth, 1849).

Mason, R. A., ed., *Scots and Britons: Scottish political thought and the union of 1603* (Cambridge, 1994).

Mason, R. A., *Kingship and the Commonweal: Political thought in Renaissance and Restoration Scotland* (East Lothian, 1998).

Masson, G., *Queen Christina* (London, 1968).

Mathew, D., *Scotland under Charles I* (London, 1955).

Mayfield, N. H., *Puritans and Regicide* (London, 1837).

McCusker, J. J., *Money and Exchange in Europe and America, 1600-1775* (London, 1978).

Meikle, M. M., 'The invisible divide: the greater lairds and the nobility of Jacobean Scotland', in *Scottish Historical Review*, vol. lxxi, 1, 2; nos. 191/2 (1992).

Michell, T., *A History of the Scottish Expedition to Norway in 1612* (London, 1886).

Milton, A., 'The Unchanged peacemaker'?, John Dury and the politics of irenicism in England, 1628-1643' in M. Greengrass, M. Leslie and T. Raylor, eds., *Samuel Hartlib and Universal Reformation: Studies in Intellectual Communication* (Cambridge, 1994).

Mitchell, J., *The Life of Wallenstein Duke of Friedland* (London, 1837).

Mitchison, R., *Lordship to Patronage: Scotland 1603-1745* (Edinburgh, 1990).

Morland-Simpson, H. F., ed., 'Civil War Papers 1643-1650' in *Miscellany of the Scottish Historical Society*, vol. 1 (Edinburgh, 1893).

Morrill, J., ed., *Oliver Cromwell and the English revolution* (London, 1990).

Morrill, J., ed., *The Scottish National Covenant in its British Context 1638-51* (Edinburgh, 1990).

Morrill, J., 'The Britishness of the English Revolution 1640-1660' in R. G. Asch, ed., *Three Nations - a common history? England, Scotland, Ireland and British History c.1600-1920* (Bochum, 1993).

Morrill, J., 'The British Problem, c.1534-1707' in B. Bradshaw and J. Morrill, eds., *The British Problem, c.1534-1707. State formation in the Atlantic Archipeligo* (Hampshire, 1996).

Mousnier, R., 'The Exponents and Critics of Absolutism' in J.P. Cooper, ed., *The New Cambridge Modern History*, vol.IV (Cambridge, 1970).

Mowat, R. B., 'The Mission of Sir Thomas Roe to Vienna, 1641-1642', *The English Historical Review*, vol. XXV (1910).

Mowat, S., *The Port of Leith: its history and its people* (Edinburgh, 1993).

Muddiman, J. G., *The King's Journalist 1659-1689: Studies of the reign of Charles II* (New York, 1971).

Munck, T., 'Keeping up Appearances: Patronage of the Arts, City Prestige, and Princely Power in Northern Germany and Denmark', in *German History*, vol. 6 (1988).

Munck, T., *Seventeenth Century Europe: State, Conflict and the Social Order in Europe, 1598-1700* (London, 1990).

Munthe, L. W., *Kongliga Fortifikations Historia* (Stockholm, 1902).

Murdoch, S., 'Robert Anstruther, A Stuart Diplomat in Norlan Europe', in *Cairn*, no. 1 (March 1997).

Murdoch, S., 'Soldier, Sailor, Jacobite Spy; Russo-Jacobite relations 1688-1750', *Slavonica*, no. 3, vol. 1 (Spring, 1997).

Murdoch, S., 'The Database in Early Modern Scottish History: Scandinavia and Northern Europe, 1580-1707', in *Northern Studies*, vol. 32 (1997).

Murdoch, S., 'The House of Stuart and The Scottish Professional Soldier 1613-1640: A Conflict of Nationality and Identities', in B. Taithe and T. Thornton eds., *War: Identities In Conflict 1300-2000* (Gloucestershire, 1998).

Murdoch, S., 'The Search for Northern Allies. Stuart and Cromwellian Propaganda and Propagandists in Scandinavia, 1649-1660' in Taithe, B. and T. Thornton, eds., *Propaganda, 1300-2000* (Gloucestershire, 1999).

Murray-Lyon, D., *The History of Freemasonry in Scotland* (Edinburgh, 1873),

Nicolaysen, N., *Bergens Borgerbog 1550-1751* (Oslo, 1878).

Nielsen, Y., *Norges Historie Anden Del Tidsrummet, 1588-1660* (4 vols., Oslo, 1911).

Norrman, D., *Gustav Adolfs Politik mot Ryssland och Polen Under Tyska Kriget, 1630-1632* (Uppsala, 1943).

Oakley, S. P., *Scandinavian History 1520-1970* (London, 1984).

Ó Buachalla, B., 'Na Stíubhartaigh agus an t-aos léinn', in *Proceedings of the Royal Irish Academy*, 83, no. 4 (1983).

Ó Buachalla, B., 'James Our True King: The ideology of Irish Royalism in the Seventeenth Century', in D.G. Boyce, et al., eds., *Political thought in Ireland since the Seventeenth century* (London, 1993).

Ó Buachalla, B., *Aisling Ghéar; Na Stíubhartaigh agus an t-aos léinn* (Dublin, 1996).

O Callaghan, J. C., *History of the Irish Brigades in the service of France* (Shannon, 1969).

Ó Siochrú, M., *Confederate Ireland 1642-1649* (Dublin, 1999)

Ogg, D., *Europe in the 17th Century* (New York, 1962).

Ohlmeyer, J. H., 'The Dunkirk of Ireland: Wexford privateers during the 1640's', in *Journal of the Wexford Historical Society*, no.12 (1988-9).

Ohlmeyer, J. H., 'Irish Privateers during the Civil War, 1642-1650', *Mariner's Mirror*, vol. 76, no. 2 (May 1990).

Ohlmeyer, J. H., *Civil War and Restoration in the Three Stuart Kingdoms: The Career of Ranald Macdonnell, Marquis of Antrim, 1609-1683* (Cambridge, 1993).

Ohlmeyer, J. H., *Ireland from Independence to Occupation* (Cambridge, 1995).

Ohlmeyer, J. H., 'Seventeenth-Century Ireland and the New British and Atlantic Histories', in *American Historical Review* (1999).

Ovenstad, O., *Militærbiografier: den norske hærs officerer* (Oslo, 1948).

Parker, G., *Europe in Crisis 1598-1648* (Cornell, 1979).

Parker, G., and L. M. Smith, eds., *The General Crisis of the Seventeenth Century* (London, 1985).

Parker, G., *The Military Revolution: military innovation and the rise of the West, 1500-1800* (Cambridge, 1988).

Parker, G., *The Dutch Revolt* (London, 1990).

Parker, G., 'The 'Military Revolution 1560-1660' - A Myth?' in C. J. Rogers, ed., *The Military Revolution Debate* (Oxford, 1995).

Parker, G., ed., *The Thirty Years' War* (London, 1997).

Parker, W. R., *Milton, A Biography* (Oxford, 1968).

Peacey, J. T., 'Order and Disorder in Europe: Parliamentary Agents and Royalist Thugs 1649-1650', in *The Historical Journal*, vol. 40, no. 4 (1997).

Penn, C. D., *The navy under the early Stuarts and its influence on English History* (London, 1970).

Petersen, E. L., 'Defence, war and finance: Christian IV and the council of the realm 1596-1629', in *Scandinavian Journal of History*, vol.7 (1982).

Petersen, E. L., 'The Danish Intermezzo' in G. Parker, ed., *The Thirty Years' War* (London, 1997).

Pinckney, P. J., 'The Scottish representation in the Cromwellian parliament of 1656', in *The Scottish Historical Review*, vol. xlvi, 2, no. 142 (October, 1967).

Platonov, S. F., *The Time of Troubles* (Kansas, 1971).

Polisensky, J. V., *Anglie a Bílá hora* (Prague, 1649).

Polisensky, J. V., 'Denmark-Norway and the Bohemian Cause in the early part of the Thirty Years' War' in *Festgabe für L. L. Hammerich aus Anlass seines Siebzigsten Geburtstag* (Copenhagen, 1962).

Polisensky, J. V., 'The Thirty Years' War and the crises and revolutions of seventeenth century Europe', in *Past and Present*, vol. 38, (1968).

Polisensky, J. V., *The Thirty Years' War*, Translated by Robert Evans (London, 1971).

Polisensky, J. V., *Tragic Triangle* (Prague, 1991).

Porshnev, B. F., *Muscovy and Sweden in the Thirty Years' War, 1630-1635*, Translated by Brian Pearce and edited by Paul Dukes (Cambridge, 1995).

Potter, L., *Secret Rites and Writing: Royalist Literature 1641-1660* (Cambridge, 1989).

Probst, N. M., *Den Danske Flådes Historie, 1588-1660; Christian 4.s Flåde* (Copenhagen, 1996).

Raab, T. K., *The Thirty Years's War - Problems of Motive Extent and Effect* (Boston, 1964).

Reddaway, W. F., 'The Scandinavian North 1559-1660' in A. W. Ward, G. W. Prothero and S. Leathes, eds., *The Cambridge Modern History, The Thirty Years' War*, vol. IV (Cambridge, 1906).

Richards, J., 'His Nowe Majestie and the English Monarchy: The Kingship of Charles I before 1640', in *Past and Present*, no. 113 (1986).

Riis, T., *Should Auld Acquaintance Be Forgot ... Scottish-Danish Relations c.1450-1707* (2 vols., Odense, 1988).

Risdall-Smith, G., and M.. Toynbee, *Leaders of the Civil Wars 1642-1648* (Kineton, 1977).

Ritchie, W. K., *Scotland in the time of the Covenanters* (London, 1975).

Roberts, M., 'The Military Revolution 1560-1660' in C. J. Rogers, ed., *The Military Revolution debate* (Oxford, 1995).

Roberts, M., ed., *Sweden's Age of Greatness 1632-1718* (London, 1973).

Roberts, M., 'Sweden and the Baltic 1611-54' in J. P. Cooper, ed., *The New Cambridge Modern History*, vol. IV (Cambridge, 1970).

Roberts, M., *Gustavus Adolphus: A history of Sweden 1611-1632* (2 vols., London, 1953-1958).

Roberts, M., 'Gustavus Adolphus and the art of War', in *Historical Studies*, vol. 1 (1958).

Roberts, M., 'The political objectives of Gustavus Adolphus in Germany 1632', in *Transactions of the Royal Historical Society*, 5th Series, vol. 7 (London, 1957).

Rogers, C. J., ed., *The Military Revolution Debate* (Oxford, 1995).

Rogers, H. C. R., *Battles and Generals of the Civil Wars, 1642-51* (London, 1968).

Rooseboom, M. P., *The Scottish Staple in the Netherlands an account of the trade relations between Scotland and the Low Countries from 1292 till 1676, with a calendar of illustrative documents* (The Hague, 1910).

Rosén, J., 'Scandinavia and the Baltic' in F. L. Carsten ed., *The New Cambridge Modern History*, vol. 5 (Cambridge, 1961).

Roy, I., 'England turned Germany? The aftermath of the civil war in its European context', in *Transactions of the Royal Historical Society*, 5th Series, vol. 28 (London, 1978).

Royle, T., *The Macmillan Companion to Scottish Literature* (London, 1983).

Rubin, Z., *Collection Latomus vol.173: Civil-War Propaganda and Historiography* (Bruxelles, 1980).

Russell, C., ed., *The Origins of the English Civil War* (London, 1973).

Russell, C., 'The Foreign Policy Debate in the House of Commons in 1621', in *The Historical Journal*, vol. 20, no. 2 (1977).

Russell, C., *The Crisis of Parliaments, English History 1504-1660* (Oxford, 1982).

Russell, C., 'The British Problem and the English Civil War', in *History*, vol. 72, no. 236 (October, 1987).

Russell, C., 'Composite monarchies in early modern Europe: the British and Irish example' in A. Grant and K. J. Stringer, eds., *Uniting the Kingdom? The making of British history* (London, 1995).

Russell, C., *The Fall of the British Monarchies 1637-1642* (Oxford, 1995).

Rye, W. B., *England as seen by Foreigners* (London, 1865).

Sandstedt, F., ed., *17th Century War, Weaponry and Armies, Report of the Xth International Congress of International Army and Military Museums* (Stockholm, 1987).

Sawday, J., 'Re-writing a Revolution; History, Symbol and Text in the Restoration', in *The Seventeenth Century*, VII, no. 2 (1992).

Schokkenbroek, J. C. A., ed., *Plying between Mars and Mercury: Political, economic and cultural links between the Netherlands and Sweden during the Golden Age* (The Hague, 1994).

Scott, E., *The King in Exile, the wanderings of Charles II from June 1646 to July 1654* (London, 1905).

Scott, H. M., ed., *The European nobilities in the seventeenth and eighteenth centuries* (2.vols., London, 1995).

Sehested, T., *Cantsler Christen Thomesen Sehested* (Copenhagen, 1894).

Seliga, S., and L. Koczy, *Scotland and Poland: a chapter of forgotten history* (Glasgow, 1969).

Sharpe, K., *The Personal Rule of Charles I* (New Haven and London, 1992).

Skerpan, E., *The Rhetoric of Politics in the English Revolution 1642-1660* (University of Missouri Press, 1992).

Smith, G. R., and M. Toynbee, *Leaders of the Civil Wars 1642-1648* (Kineton, 1977).

Smith, N., *Literature and Revolution in England 1640-1660* (Yale, 1994).

Smout, T. C., ed., *Scotland and the Sea* (Edinburgh, 1992).

Spalding, R., ed., *Contemporaries of Bulstrode Whitelocke 1605-1675, biographies illustrated by letters and other documents, an appendix to The Diary of Bulstrode Whitelocke* (Oxford, 1990).

Stade, A., *Carl X Gustaf och Danmark, källkritik och krigshistoria* (Kristianstad, 1965).

Steckzén, B., *Karl Gustaf Wrangels Fälttåg 1646-1647* (Stockholm, 1920).

Steinberg, S. H., *The "Thirty Years' War" and the Conflict for European Hegemony 1600-1660* (London, 1966).

Stephen, Rev. W., *History of Inverkeithing and Rosyth* (Aberdeen, 1921).

Steuart, A. F., 'Scottish Officers in Sweden' in *The Scottish Historical Review*, vol. 1 (Glasgow, 1904).

Steuart, A. F., *Scottish Influences in Russian History, from the end of the 16th to the beginning of the 19th century* (Glasgow, 1913).

Stueart, A. F., ed., *Papers relating to the Scots in Poland, 1576-1793* (Edinburgh, 1915).

Stevenson, D., 'The financing of the cause of the Covenants, 1638-51' in *The Scottish Historical Review*, vol. li, 2, no. 152 (October 1972).

Stevenson, D., *The Scottish Revolution 1637-1644* (Newton Abbot, 1973).

Stevenson, D., 'The King's Scottish revenues and the Covenanters, 1625-1651', in *The Historical Journal*, vol. xvii, no. 1 (1974).

Stevenson, D., *Revolution and Counter Revolution in Scotland, 1644-51* (London, 1977).

Stevenson, D., *Scottish Covenanters and Irish Confederates* (Belfast, 1981).

Stevenson, D., ed., *The Government of Scotland under the Covenanters 1637-1651*. Scottish History Society 4th series, vol. 18 (Edinburgh 1982).

Stevenson, D., *The Covenanters: The National Covenant and Scotland* (Edinburgh, 1988).

Stevenson, D., 'Cromwell, Scotland and Ireland' in J. Morrill, ed., *Oliver Cromwell and the English Revolution* (London, 1990).

Stevenson, D., *Highland Warrior: Alasdair MacColla and the Civil Wars* (Edinburgh, 1994).

Stevenson, D., *Scotland's last Royal Wedding: The marriage of James VI and Anne of Denmark* (Edinburgh, 1997).

Stewart, A. M., ed., *Scots in the Baltic* (Aberdeen, 1977).

Stradling, R. A., *The Spanish Monarchy and Irish Mercenaries, the Wild Geese in Spain, 1618-68* (Dublin, 1994).

Supphellen, S., *Trondeims Historie 977-1997* (2 vols., Trondeim, 1997).

Sutherland, N. M., 'The origins of the Thirty Years War and the structure of European Politics', in *The English Historical Review*, vol. cvii (1992).

Taithe, B., and T. Thornton, eds., *War: Identities in conflict 1300-2000* (Gloucestershire, 1998).

Taithe, B., and T. Thornton, eds., *Propaganda: 1300-2000* (Gloucestershire, 1999).

Tayler, A. and H., eds., *The House of Forbes* (Bruceton Mills, 1987).

Tennfjord, F., *Stamhuset Rosendal* (Oslo, 1944).

Terry, C. S., *Life and Campaigns of Alexander Leslie, first Earl of Leven* (London ,1899).

Tham, W., *Axel Oxenstierna hans ungdom och verksamhet intill år 1612* (Stockholm, 1935).

Thirsk, J., 'Younger Sons in the Seventeeth Century', in *History*, vol. liv, no. 182 (October 1969).

Thomas, P. W., 'Two Cultures? Court and Country under Charles I' in C. Russel ed., *The Origins of the English Civil War* (London, 1973).

Tocher, J. F, ed., *The Book of Buchan*, Jubilee Volume (Aberdeen, 1943).

Toynbee, M., and G. Risdall-Smith, *Leaders of the Civil Wars 1642-1648* (Kineton, 1977).

Tønnesen, A., 'Skotterne og englænderne' in *Helsingørs udenlandske borgere og indbyggere ca.1550-1600* (Ringe, 1985).

Underdown, D., *Royalist Conspiracy in England 1649-1660* (New Haven, 1960).

Vaage, E., *Kvinnherad* (Bergen, 1972).

Venning, T., *Cromwellian Foreign Policy* (London, 1995).

Wahl, J. O., *Det Gamle Bergenhusiske Regiments Historie* (Oslo, 1901).

Wahl, J. O., 'Et nyt bidrag til Bergenhus fæstnings historie', in *Bergens Historiske Forenings Skrifter*, no. 12 (1906).

Wahl, J. O., 'Da Bergenhus blev en fæstning', in *Bergens Historiske Forenings Skrifter*, no. 32 (1926).

Ward, A. W., G. W. Prothero and S. Leathers, eds., *The Cambridge Modern History IV; The Thirty Years' War* (Cambridge, 1906).

Watson, F., *Wallenstein: Soldier under Saturn* (London, 1938).

Wedgewood, C. V., *The King's Peace, 1637-1641* (New York, 1991 reprint).

Wendt, E, *Amiralitetskollegiets Historia, I, 1634-1695* (Stockholm, 1950).

White, B., 'King Christian IV in England' in *National Review* LXII (1939).

Widerberg, C. S., *Norges Første Militæringeniør Isaac van Geelkerck og hans virke 1644-1656* (Oslo, 1924).

Wiesener, A. M., 'Axel Movat og hans Slegt', in *Bergens Historiske Forening Skrifter*, no. 36 (1930).

Wijn, J. W., 'Military Forces and Warfare 1611-54' in J. P. Cooper, ed., *The New Cambridge Modern History*, vol. IV (Cambridge, 1970).

Wilding, M., *Dragons Teeth, literature in the English Revolution* (Oxford, 1987).

Willan, T. S., *The Early History of the Muscovy Company 1553-1603* (Manchester, 1968).

Williams, E. C., *Anne of Denmark Wife of James VI of Scotland: James I of England* (London, 1970).

Williamson, A. H., *Scotch National Consciousness in the age of James VI: the apocalypse, the union and the shaping of Scotland's public culture* (Edinburgh, 1979).

Wolter, H. C., *Adel og Embede: Embedsfordeling og karriermobilititet hos den Dansk-Norsk Adel 1588-1660* (Copenhagen, 1982).

Worden, B., 'Providence and Politics in Cromwellian England', in *Past and Present*, no. 109 (1985).

Wormald, J., *Court, Kirk and Community: Scotland 1470-1625* (Edinburgh, 1981).

Wormald, J., 'James VI and I: Two Kings or One?', in *History*, vol. 68, no. 223 (June 1983).

Wormald, J., *Scotland Revisited* (London, 1991).

Wormald, J., 'The High Road from Scotland: One king, two kingdoms' in A. Grant and K. J. Stringer, eds., *Uniting the Kingdom? The making of British history* (London, 1995).

Wormald, J., 'James VI, James I and the Identity of Britain', in B. Bradshaw and J. Morrill, eds., *The British Problem, c.1534-1707; State Formation in the Atlantic Archipelago* (London, 1996).

Yates, F. A., *The Rosicrucian Enlightenment* (New York, 1996).

Young, J. R., *The Scottish Parliament 1639-1661* (Edinburgh, 1996).

Young, J. R., ed., *Celtic Dimensions of the British Civil Wars* (Edinburgh, 1997).

DATABASE SOURCES

Lind, G., *Danish Data Archive, 1573* (1995 version).

Lind, G., *Danish Data Archive, 1574* (1995 version).

Murdoch, S., and A. Grosjean, *Scotland Scandinavia and Northern Europe 1580-1707* (Aberdeen, 1998). Revised and published to the Internet at <www.abdn.ac.uk/history/datasets/ssne>.

Index

Abercrombie, Barbara, maid of Queen Anna, 3

Aberdeen, 99, 122

Adventure, Stuart warship, 198

Ahlefeldt, Frederik, 184

Alexander, Colonel Magnus, 246

Alexander, William, 1st earl of Stirling, tutor of Charles I, 5

Almond, Lord, *see* Livingstone, James.

Altafjord, 191, 193

Älvsborg, 190

Americas, colonies in, 13

Amsterdam, 106, 154, 244

'Angels of England', 39

Anna, queen of James VI and I, 3-4, 25. and James VI;

> court of, 3-4; dowry of, 23; Danish attendants of, 3; influence of on Charles I, 6, 7; marriage difficulties of, 25, 43; opposed to marriage of Princess Elizabeth to Elector Palatine, 10; receives secularised estates of Dunfermline Abbey, 23; Scots attendants of, 3-4; servants of, 43

Anstruther, Captain John, defects from Covenanters, 154

Anstruther, Sir Robert, 9, 10, 32, 38, 39, 40, 41, 52, 63, 69, 70, 71, 74, 75, 77, 81, 82, 85, 86, 87, 111-112, 135; attends Diet of Frankfurt, 83, 89; attends Diet of Ratisbon, 75; attends meeting at Segeberg, 52-53; based in Hamburg, 71, 73, 84; career of, 39-41 *passim*; dual British-Danish ambassador, 38-39, 59, 61, 81, 141; to John George of Saxony, 61; holds talks with Oxenstierna, 80-81, 88; identifies with unitary British state, 18; marries daughter of Sir Robert Swift, 18; negotiates between Charles I and Gustav II Adolf, 64; negotiates Danish finance for Frederick V, 48; negotiates peace of Knäred between Denmark-Norway and Sweden, 40, 43; negotiations with Lübeck, 41; role in Danish-Swedish diplomacy, 41, 58; relationship with Sir James Spens, 39, 40, 41, 59, 88; seeks to arrange full military alliance between Denmark-Norway and Great Britain, 52; suspected of supporting Frederick V's cause, 49; suspicious of Danish motives in Treaty of Lübeck, 70, 71

Antelope, English Republican ship, 176

Archangel, 102, 197; Russian trade through, 30, 197

Argyll, Earl of, 118, 119, 163, 227; attempts to gain control of Committee of Estates, 139; dominates Scottish politics, 140; enmity of towards 2nd Duke of Hamilton and Montrose, 139, 149; executed, 186; negotiates with Charles II, 149, 150, 159; supporters of, seize arms in Leith, 140

Arken, Royal Danish vessel, 132, 133, 136, 137, 143

Armagh, synod of, 210

Aros, Lord, *see* MacDonald, Angus, of Glengarry.

Arrat, Captain Alexander, 103, 199, 201

Arundel, Earl of, 84

Ascham, Antony, murdered in Madrid by English Royalists, 147

Aston, Friar, 88, 89

Augsburg, Peace of, 44

Auld Alliance, 22, 92

Austria, 46, 181

> Archdukes of, *see* Ferdinand II; promises aid to Charles II, 171; promises aid to Frederik III against Swedes, 181

Averie, Joseph, 18, 19, 75, 80, 81, 88, 119, 132, 133, 134, 135, 142; attempts to defuse Danish trade embargo on Britain, 133; missions by to Copenhagen, 84, 88, 112, 113, 119

Ayscue, Sir George, 182

Baden-Durlach, Margrave of, Protestant commander, 55; defeated by Count Tilly at Wimpfen, 55

Baillie, Robert, merchant, 35

Baillie, Robert, Principal of Glasgow University, 19

Balfour, David, 194, 195

Balfour, William, 67

Ball, Captain, 175, 176

Baltic Sea, 1, 24, 27, 92; *Dominium Maris Baltici*, 41, 193; British trade in, 8-9; strategic significance of, 70; Swedish control of, 81; Swedish tolls in, 77; war in, 217

Barker, William, 135

Batten, Captain, 123

Bavaria, duchy of, 44; dukes of, *see* Maximillian

Bedow, Hugo, 194

Bellamy, Martin, 196

Bellarmine, 210

Bellenden, Sir William, 158

Below, William, Danish resident at Stuart court, 87

Bergen, 35, 103, 104, 134, 138, 155, 157, 185; governor of, *see* Gray, Sir Thomas; Mackay, Donald; Scottish trading community in, 30, 134

Bergen-op-Zoom, 56

Bergenhus regiment, 236, 237, 238